SYMBOLIC COMPUTATION

Artificial Intelligence

Springer Series
SYMBOLIC COMPUTATION - *Artificial Intelligence*

N. J. Nilsson: Principles of Artificial Intelligence. XV, 476 pages, 139 figs., 1982

J. H. Siekmann, G. Wrightson (Eds.): Automation of Reasoning 1. Classical Papers on Computational Logic 1957-1966. XXII, 525 pages, 1983

J. H. Siekmann, G. Wrightson (Eds.): Automation of Reasoning 2. Classical Papers on Computational Logic 1967-1970. XXII, 638 pages, 1983

L. Bolc (Ed.): The Design of Interpreters, Compilers, and Editors for Augmented Transition Networks. XI, 214 pages, 72 figs., 1983

R. S. Michalski, J. G. Carbonell, T. M. Mitchell (Eds.): Machine Learning. An Artificial Intelligence Approach. XI, 572 pages, 1984

L. Bolc (Ed.): Natural Language Communication with Pictorial Information Systems. VII, 327 pages, 67 figs., 1984

J. W. Lloyd: Foundations of Logic Programming. X, 124 pages, 1984

A. Bundy (Ed.): Catalogue of Artificial Intelligence Tools. XXV, 150 pages, 1984. Second, revised edition, IV, 168 pages, 1986

M. M. Botvinnik: Computers in Chess. Solving Inexact Search Problems. With contributions by A. I. Reznitsky, B. M. Stilman, M. A. Tsfasman, A. D. Yudin. Translated from the Russian by A. A. Brown. XIV, 158 pages, 48 figs., 1984

C. Blume, W. Jakob: Programming Languages for Industrial Robots. XIII, 376 pages, 145 figs., 1986

L. Bolc (Ed.): Natural Language Parsing Systems. XVIII, 367 pages, 151 figs., 1987

L. Bolc (Ed.): Computational Models of Learning. IX, 208 pages, 34 figs., 1987

Natural Language Parsing Systems

Edited by Leonard Bolc

With Contributions by
J. G. Carbonell K. W. Church W. Dilger T. W. Finin
P. J. Hayes W. A. Martin J. G. Neal R. S. Patil
J. Pitrat A. Sågvall Hein S. C. Shapiro
S. L. Small M. Stone Palmer M. Thiel

With 151 Figures

Springer-Verlag
Berlin Heidelberg New York
London Paris Tokyo

Volume Editor

Leonard Bolc
Institute of Informatics, Warsaw University,
PKiN, pok. 850, PL-00-901 Warsaw, Poland

ISBN-13:978-3-642-83032-7 e-ISBN-13:978-3-642-83030-3
DOI: 10.1007/978-3-642-83030-3

Library of Congress Cataloging-in-Publication Data
Natural language parsing systems. (Symbolic computation. Artificial intelligence) Includes bibliographies and index. 1. Parsing (Computer grammar) I. Bolc, Leonard, 1934- .
II. Carbonell, Jaime G. (Jaime Guillermo) III. Series. P98.N34 1987 415 87-12856

Softcover reprint of the hardcover 1st edition 1987

2145/3140-543210

Preface

Up to now there has been no scientific publication on natural language research that presents a broad and complex description of the current problems of parsing in the context of Artificial Intelligence. However, there are many interesting results from this domain appearing mainly in numerous articles published in professional journals. In view of this situation, the objective of this book is to enable scientists from different countries to present the results of their research on natural language parsing in the form of more detailed papers than would be possible in professional journals. This book thus provides a collection of studies written by well-known scientists whose earlier publications have greatly contributed to the development of research on natural language parsing.

Jaime G. Carbonell and Philip J. Hayes present in their paper "Robust Parsing Using Multiple Construction-Specific Strategies" two small experimental parsers, implemented to illustrate the advantages of a multi-strategy approach to parsers, with strategies selected according to the type of construction being parsed at any given time. This presentation is followed by the description of a parsing algorithm, integrating some of the best features of the two smaller parsers, including case-frame instantiation and partial pattern-matching strategies.

Timothy W. Finin and Martha Stone Palmer discuss in the paper "Parsing with Logical Variables" one of the most powerful techniques for an ATN grammar, that is, the use of logical variables and unification, which is also one of the main sources of the strength of the Definite Clause Grammar formalism. In studying this technique, the authors have come to some interesting conclusions which are presented in their paper.

Jeannette G. Neal and Stuart C. Shapiro report in the paper "Knowledge-Based Parsing" on their Natural Language Understanding system, implemented in the form of a general rule-based inference system which reasons according to the rules of its knowledge base, and which uses its knowledge base for both linguistic and other knowledge. The authors discuss the ability of their NLU system to use a language as its own metalanguage. This ability is used to extend the language understood by the system.

Jacques Pitrat discusses in the paper "Using Declarative Knowledge for Understanding Natural Language" different programs using declarative knowledge to both understand and generate natural language. The author divides these programs into three sets and includes his own program in the third class. He describes different kinds of knowledge used by the system and the interpreter that uses the knowledge to understand a text; the interpreter is chosen from very different interpreters which it is possible to develop for the same knowledge.

Manfred Thiel presents in his paper "Weighted Parsing" part of the theoretical basis of a parser, putting stress on weights (scores) and the function of weighting embedded in the control structure and in linguistic data like rules, grammars, or dictionaries. The author describes a weighted parser, developed as part of the MT-system Susy and associated projects.

Steven L. Small discusses in the paper "A Distributed Word-Based Approach to Parsing" the problem of the natural language comprehension process. A formal theory of Word Expert Parsing is presented, in which natural language understanding is approached as a non-uniform distributed process of interacting words. A computer model is constructed to provide evidence to support this theory.

Anna Sågvall Hein presents in the paper "Parsing by Means of Uppsala Chart Processor (UCP)" the Uppsala Chart Processor. This is a linguistic processor of the General Syntactic Processor family, which acts as a parser for a language, after being provided with its language description. In addition to syntactic analysis, it also supports phonological and morphological analysis.

William A. Martin, Kenneth W. Church and Ramesh S. Patil report in their paper "Preliminary Analysis of a Breadth-First Parsing Algorithm: Theoretical and Experimental Results" on their experiences in adapting Earley's context-free parsing algorithm and its variations to the parsing of a difficult and wide-ranging corpus of sentences. The sentences were taken from an experiment carried out by Malhotra, in which businessmen users were fooled into thinking that they were interacting with a computer.

Werner Dilger discusses in his paper "Syntax Directed Translation in the Natural Language Information System PLIDIS" the natural language translation component of the information system PLIDIS as a tree directed grammar, where translation is done by such a grammar as a derivation, directed by the parse tree or even, under some conditions, by the parsing process. Tree directed grammars are shown to have less computational capacity than transformational grammars.

We hope this collection of papers, written by internationally-known scientists, as well as that previously published in the "Symbolic Computation" series*, will contribute to the better understanding of present problems of natural language parsing and to greater interest in this field of science.

We would also like our book to inspire scientists engaged in research on natural language parsing to write in the near future an extensive work presenting a complex overview of the present state of research in this field.

Warsaw, June 1987 Leonard Bolc

* Bolc L. (Ed.): The Design of Interpreters, Compilers, and Editors for Augmented Transition Networks. In series: Symbolic Computation - Artificial Intelligence. Berlin Heidelberg New York Tokyo, Springer 1983

Contents

List of Contributors

Jaime G. Carbonell
Carnegie-Mellon University, Pittsburgh, PA 15213, USA

Kenneth W. Church
AT & T Bell Laboratories, 600 Mountain Avenue,
Murray Hill, NJ 07974-2070, USA

Werner Dilger
Fraunhofer-Gesellschaft, IITB, Sebastian-Kneipp-Straße 12/14,
D-7500 Karlsruhe 1, FR Germany

Timothy W. Finin
Computer and Information Science, University of Pennsylvania, Philadelphia, PA, USA

Philip J. Hayes
Carnegie-Mellon University, Pittsburgh, PA 15213, USA

William A. Martin
Massachusetts Institute of Technology, Laboratory for Computer Science,
Cambridge, MA 02139, USA

Jeannette G. Neal
Department of Computer Science, State University of New York at Buffalo,
Buffalo, NY 14260, USA

Ramesh S. Patil
Massachusetts Institute of Technology, Laboratory for Computer Science,
Cambridge, MA 02139, USA

Jacques Pitrat
Groupe de Recherche Claude-François Picard du CNRS associé à l'Institut de Programmation de l'Université Pierre et Marie Curie, 4, place Jussieu, F-75230 Paris Cédex 05, France

Anna Sågvall Hein
Department of Computational Linguistics, Språkdata, S-41298 Göteborg,
Sweden

Stuart C. Shapiro
Department of Computer Science, State University of New York at Buffalo, Buffalo, NY 14260, USA

Steven L. Small
Decision Systems Laboratory, University of Pittsburgh, 1360 Scaife Hall, Pittsburgh, PA 15261, USA

Martha Stone Palmer
Logic Based Systems, SDC, A Burroughs Company, Paoli, PA, USA

Manfred Thiel
Fasanenstraße 24, D-8560 Lauf, FR Germany

Robust Parsing Using Multiple Construction-Specific Strategies*

J. G. Carbonell and P. J. Hayes

Abstract. Robust natural language interpretation requires strong semantic domain models, "fail-soft" recovery heuristics, flexible control structures, and focused user interaction when automatic correction proves unfeasible. Although single-strategy parsers have met with some success, a multi-strategy approach, with strategies selected dynamically according to the type of construction being parsed at any given time, is shown to provide a higher degree of flexibility, redundancy, and ability to bring task-specific domain knowledge (in addition to general linguistic knowledge) to bear on both grammatical and ungrammatical input. This construction-specific, multi-strategy approach can also help provide tightly focused interaction with the user in cases of semantic or structural ambiguity by allowing such ambiguities to be represented without duplication of unambiguous material. The approach also aids in task-specific language development by allowing direct interpretation of languages defined in terms natural to the task domain, and with the definition of data base interfaces by facilitating a unified treatment of update and access requests. Two small experimental parsers that were implemented to illustrate these advantages are presented, followed by the description of a parsing algorithm that integrates several of the best features of the two smaller parsers, including case-frame instantiation and partial pattern-matching strategies. The algorithm can deal with conjunctions, fragmentary input, and ungrammatical structures, as well as less exotic, grammatically correct input.

1 Introduction

When people use language spontaneously, they seldom respect grammatical niceties. Instead of producing sequences of complete, grammatically well-formed sentences, they typically omit or repeat words, break off in mid-utterance, interject spurious phrases, elliptic sentences, or otherwise use abbreviatory devices or incorrect grammar. People experience little difficulty comprehending ungrammati-

* This research was sponsored in part by the Defense Advanced Research Projects Agency (DOD), ARPA Order No. 3597, monitored by the Air Force Avionics Laboratory under contract F33615-78-C-1551, and in part by the Air Force Office of Scientific Research under Contract F49620-79-C-0143. The views and conclusions contained in this document are those of the authors and should not be interpreted as representing the official policies, either expressed or implied, of DARPA, the Air Force Office of Scientific Research, or the US government.

cal utterances, but most natural language computer systems are unable to process errorful input in any form. Such inflexibility in parsing is a serious impediment to the use of natural language in interactive computer systems. Accordingly, we [15] and other researchers, including Weischedel and Black [29], and Kwasny and Sondheimer [22], have attempted to produce flexible parsers, i.e., parsers that can accept ungrammatical input, correcting the errors when possible, and generating several alternative interpretations for later selection by the user if necessary.

While different in many ways, all prior approaches to flexible parsing have operated by applying a single parsing process to a uniformly represented grammar. Because of the linguistic performance problems involved, including the need to extract semantic relations in the parsing process, no uniform procedure can be as simple and elegant as the methods incorporated in a pure linguistic competence model, such as Parsifal [23]. Indeed, flexible parsing based on a uniform grammar may involve several strategies applied in a predetermined order when the input deviates from the grammar, but the choice of strategy is never sensitive to the specific type of construction being parsed. In the light of experience with FlexP [15], our first flexible parser for limited-domain task-oriented languages, we came to the conclusion that such uniformity is unnecessary, inefficient, and inferior in functionality to an approach capable of selecting among several parsing strategies, always applying the one most appropriate to the particular type of construction being parsed at the time. A parser using this construction-specific approach might, for instance, use linear pattern-matching to parse idiomatic phrases or specialized noun phrases such as names, dates, or addresses (see also [12]), but switch to a special case-oriented parsing strategy to deal with case constructions, such as noun phrases with trailing prepositional phrases, or imperative phrases. The underlying principle is simple: *The appropriate knowledge must be brought to bear at the right time - and it must not interfere at other times.*

The advantages we claim for a multi-strategy construction-specific approach to parsing include:

- greater accuracy and coverage in the flexible parsing of ungrammatical input
- greater efficiency in parsing grammatical input
- an ability to represent ambiguity without duplicating unambiguous parts, making it easier to indicate the exact source and nature of the ambiguity to the user, and thus facilitating interactive correction
- improved task-specific language development by allowing language definitions, natural in terms of the underlying domain, to be used directly as a grammar without prior compilation into a uniform formalism
- easier construction of restricted domain interfaces to data bases that allow update as well as access

In addition to explaining the theoretical advantages of a construction-specific approach, this paper describes two small experimental parsers that we have constructed to validate the advantages we claim, and presents the design of a larger scale multi-strategy parsing algorithm designed along the same construction-specific lines. In the new design, our objective is not to develop a totally general and complete parser applicable to all of English, but rather to develop a flexible and robust task-oriented parser, applicable to a wide range of tasks, where domain knowledge and specialized constructions can be exploited and integrated with more general syntax and semantics. The initial application domain for the parser is an interface to various computer subsystems (or tools). This interface and, therefore, the parser should be adaptable to new domains by substituting domain-specific data bases (called “tool descriptions”) that govern the behaviour of the interface, including the invocation of parsing strategies, dictionaries, and concepts, rather than requiring any domain adaptations to the interface system itself.

2 Construction-Specific Flexible Parsing

Our original flexible parser, which we call FlexP, is intended to parse input that corresponds to a fixed grammar, and also to deal with input that deviates from that grammar by erring along certain classes of common ungrammaticalities. In order to realize this dual objective, the parser is based on the combination of two uniform parsing strategies: bottom-up parsing and pattern-matching. The choice of a bottom-up rather than a top-down strategy was derived from our need to recognize isolated sentence fragments and to detect restarts and continuations after interjections. However, since completely bottom-up strategies lead to the consideration of an unnecessarily large number of potentially spurious alternatives in correct input, a top-down strategy was applied. Technically speaking, this made the parser left-corner rather than bottom-up.

We chose to use a grammar of linear patterns rather than, say, a transition network for three reasons.

1. Pattern-matching meshes well with bottom-up parsing by allowing lookup of a pattern from the presence in the input of any of its constituents.
2. Pattern-matching facilitates recognition of utterances with omissions and substitutions when patterns are recognized on the basis of partial matches.
3. Pattern-matching is necessary for the recognition of idiomatic phrases. More details of the justifications for these choices can be found in [15].

2.1 Problems with a Rigid Uniform Grammar

FlexP has been tested extensively in conjunction with a gracefully interacting interface to an electronic mail system [1]. “Gracefully interacting” means that the interface appears friendly, supportive, and robust to its user. In particular, graceful interaction requires the system to tolerate minor input errors and typos, so a flexible parser is an important component of such an interface. Whereas FlexP performed this task adequately, the experience turned up some problems related to the major theme of this paper. These problems are all derived from the incompatibility between the uniform nature of the grammar representation and the kinds of flexible parsing strategies required to deal with the inherently non-uniform nature of some language constructions. In particular:

- Different elements in the pattern of a single grammar rule can serve radically different functions and/or exhibit different ease of recognition. Hence, an efficient parsing strategy should react to their apparent absence, for instance, in quite different ways.

2.2 *The Need for Case Constructions*

- The representation of a single unified construction at the language level may require several linear patterns at the grammar level, making it impossible to treat that construction with the integrity required for adequate flexible parsing.

The second problem is directly related to the use of a pattern-matching grammar, but the first would arise with any uniformly represented grammar applied by a uniform parsing strategy.

For our application, these problems manifested themselves most markedly by the presence of case constructions in the input language. Thus, our examples and solution methods will be in terms of integrating case-frame instantiation with other parsing strategies. Consider, for example, the following noun phrase with a typical postnominal case frame:

"the messages from Smith about ADA pragmas dated later than Saturday".

The phrase has three cases marked by "from", "about", and "dated later than". This type of phrase is actually used in FlexP's current grammar, and the basic pattern used to recognize descriptions of messages is:

⟨?determiner *MessageAdj MessageHead *MessageCase⟩

which says that a message description is an optional (?) determiner, followed by an arbitrary number (*) of message adjectives followed by a message head word (i.e., a word meaning "message"), followed by an arbitrary number of message cases. In the example, "the" is the determiner, there are no message adjectives, "messages" is the message head word, and there are three message cases: "from Smith", "about ADA pragmas", and "dated later than". Because each case has more than one component, each must be recognized by a separate pattern:

⟨% from Person⟩
⟨% about Subject⟩
⟨% since Date⟩

Here % means anything in the same word class; "dated later than", for instance, is equivalent to "since" for this purpose.

These patterns for message descriptions illustrate the two problems mentioned above: the elements of the case patterns have radically different functions - the first elements are case markers and the second elements are the actual subconcepts for the case. Also, a single construction at the language level is spread over several patterns in the grammar. What consequences does this have for the parsing process? Because the parser has no information about the relationship between the cases and the top-level pattern, several powerful, but specialized, strategies for dealing with (regular or irregular) case constructions cannot be employed. For instance, since case indicators are typically much more restricted in range of expression, and therefore much easier to recognize than their corresponding subconcepts, a plausible strategy for a parser that "knows" about case constructions is to scan input bottom-up for the case indicators, and then parse the associated subconcepts top-down. This strategy is particularly valuable if one of the subconcepts is malformed or of uncertain form, such as the subject case in our example. Neither "ADA" nor "pragmas" is likely to be in the vocabulary of our system, so the only way the end of the subject field can be detected is by the presence of the case indicator "from" which follows it. However, the present parser cannot distinguish case indicators from case fillers - both are just elements in a pattern with exactly the same computational status, and hence it cannot use this strategy.

3 The Representation of Ambiguity and Focused Interaction

If a flexible parser being used as part of an interactive system cannot correct ungrammatical input with reasonable certainty, then the user must be involved in the resolution of the difficulty or the confirmation of the parser's correction. The approach taken by Weischedel and Black [29] in such situations is to inform the user about the nature of the difficulty, in the expectation that he will be able to use this information to produce a more acceptable input next time. But, this approach provides only negative feedback, forcing the user to rethink and retype without guarantee of success. A related technique, adopted by the COOP system [20], is to paraphrase back to the user the one or more parses that the system has produced from the user's input, and to allow the user to confirm the parse or select one of the ambiguous alternatives. This approach still means a certain amount of work for the user. He must check the paraphrase to see if the system has interpreted what he said correctly and without omission, and in the case of ambiguity, he must compare the several paraphrases to see which most closely corresponds to what he meant, a non-trivial task if the input is lengthy and the differences small.

Experience with FlexP suggests that the way requests for clarification in such situations are phrased makes a big difference in the ease and accuracy with which the user can correct his errors, and that the user is helped most by a request focusing as tightly as possible on the exact source and nature of the difficulty. Accordingly, we have adopted the following simple principle for our new flexible parser: *when the parser cannot uniquely resolve a problem in its input, it should ask the user for a correction in as direct and focused a manner as possible.* Moreover, the request for clarification should not prejudice the processing of the rest of the input, either before or after the problem occurs. In other words, if the system cannot parse one segment of the input, it should be able to bypass it, parse the remainder, and then ask the user to restate that and only that segment of the input. Similarly, if a small part of the input is missing or garbled and there are a limited number of possibilities for what ought to be there, the parser should be able to indicate the list of possibilities together with the context from which the information is missing rather than making the user compare several complete paraphrases of the input that differ only slightly.

3.1 Focused Error Recovery

In the remainder of this section, we show how a construction-specific approach to parsing can contribute to focused interaction in cases of error. We restrict our attention to situations in which a flexible parser can correct an input error or ungrammaticality, but only to within a constrained set of alternatives. We show why it is difficult for a flexible parser based on uniform methods to produce a focused ambiguity resolution request for the user to distinguish between such a set of corrections, and how a construction-specific parser can produce one much more easily. Realizing the advantages afforded by the construction-specific approach requires that special representations be devised for all the structural ambiguities that each construction type can give rise to. We illustrate these arguments with examples involving case constructions. The example ambiguity representations for case constructions are similar to those employed by the experimental parser described in Sect. 6 and were designed for use with the parsing algorithm described in Sect. 8.

The following input is typical for an electronic mail system interface [1] with which FlexP was extensively used:

the messages from Fred Smith that arrived after Jon 5

The fact that this is not a complete sentence in FlexP's grammar causes no problem. The only real difficulty comes from "Jon", which should presumably be either "Jun" or "Jan", FlexP's spelling corrector can generate both alternatives, so the output contains two complete parses which are passed onto the next stage of the mail system interface. The first of these parses looks like:

```
[DescriptionOf: Message
 Sender: [DescriptionOf: Person
          FirstName: fred
          Surname: smith
         ]
 AfterDate: [DescriptionOf: Date
             Month: january
             DayOfMonth: 5
            ]
]
```

The second alternative is identical with the one above except that "june" appears in the month slot. This schematized property list style of representation should be interpreted in the obvious way. Since FlexP operates by bottom-up pattern-matching of a semantic grammar of rewrite rules, it can parse directly into this form of representation, which is the form required by the next phase of the interface.

3.2 Representing Case-Filler Ambiguity

If the next stage has access to other contextual information that allows it to conclude which one of these parses was intended, then it can proceed to fulfill the user's request. Otherwise it has little choice but to ask a question involving paraphrases of each of the ambiguous interpretations, such as:

> Do you mean:
> 1. the messages from Fred Smith that arrived after January 5
> 2. the messages from Fred Smith that arrived after June 5

Because it is not focused on the source of the error, this question gives the user very little help in seeing where the problem with his input actually lies. Furthermore, the system's representation of the ambiguity as several complete parses gives it very little help in understanding a response of "June" from the user, a very natural and likely one under the circumstances. In essence, the parser has thrown away the information on the specific source of the ambiguity that it once had, and would again need to deal adequately with that response from the user. The recovery of this lost information would require a complicated (if done in a general manner) comparison between the two complete parses.

One straightforward solution to the problem ist to augment the output language with a special ambiguity representation. The output from our example might look like:

```
[DescriptionOf: Message
 Sender: [DescriptionOf: Person
          FirstName: fred
          Surname: smith
         ]
  AfterDate: [DescriptionOf: Date
                 Month: [DescriptionOf: AmbiguitySet
                          Choices: (january june)
                         ]
                 DayOfMonth: 5
                ]
]
```

This representation is exactly like the one above except that the Month slot is filled by an AmbiguitySet record. This record allows the ambiguity between january and june to be confined to the month slot where it belongs rather than expanding to an ambiguity of the entire input as in the first approach we discussed. By expressing the ambiguity set as a disjunction, it would be straightforward to generate from this representation a much more focused request for clarification such as:

> Do you mean the messages from Fred Smith that arrived after *January* or *June* 5?

A reply of "June" would also be much easier to deal with, since the focused interaction process can generate an expectation for an element of the AmbiguitySet.

3.3 Representing Structural Ambiguity

Our approach thus far only works if the ambiguity corresponds to an entire slot filler. Suppose, for example, that instead of mistyping the month, the user omitted or so completely garbled the preposition "from" that the parser effectively saw:

the messages Fred Smith that arrived after Jan 5

In the grammar used by FlexP for this particular application, the connection between Fred Smith and the message could have been expressed only by "from", "to", or "copied to" (or synonyms thereof). To represent the ambiguity, FlexP generates three complete parses isomorphic to the first output example above, except that Sender is replaced by Recipient and CC in the second and third parses respectively. Again, this form of representation does not allow the system to ask a focused question about the source of the ambiguity or interpret naturally elliptical replies to a request for a distinction among the three alternatives. The previous solution is not applicable because the ambiguity lies in the structure of the parser output rather than at one of its terminal nodes. Using a case notation, it is not permissible to put an "AmbiguitySet" in place of one of the deep case markers[1]. To localize such ambiguities and avoid duplicate representation of unambiguous parts of the input, it is necessary to employ a representation like the one designed for use by the new flexible parsing algorithm described in Section 8:

```
[DescriptionOf: Message
 AmbiguousSlots: (
                   [PossibleSlots: (Sender Recipient CC)
                    SlotFiller: [DescriptionOf: Person
                                 FirstName: fred
                                 Surname: smith
                                ]
                   ]
 AfterDate: [DescriptionOf: Date
             Month: january
             DayOfMonth: 5
            ]
]
```

This exemple parser output is similar to the two given previously, but instead of having a Sender slot, it has an AmbiguousSlots slot. The filler of this slot is a list of records, each of which specifies a SlotFiller and a list of PossibleSlots. The SlotFiller is a structure that would normally be the filler of a slot in the top-level description (of a message in this case), but the parser has been unable to determine exactly which higher-level slot it should fit into; the possibilities are given in

[1] Nor is this problem merely an artifact of case notation; it would arise in exactly the same way for a standard syntactic parse of a sentence such as the well known "I saw the Grand Canyon flying to New York." The difficulty arises because the ambiguity is structural, and structural ambiguities can occur no matter what form of structure is chosen.

PossibleSlots. With this representation, it is now straightforward to construct a directed question such as:

> Do you mean the messages *from, to,* or *copied to* Fred Smith that arrived after January 5?

Such questions can be generated by outputting and highlighting AmbiguousSlot records as the disjunction of the normal case markers for each of the PossibleSlots followed by the normal translation of the SlotFiller. The main point here, however, does not concern the question generation mechanism, nor the exact details of the formalism for representing ambiguity, it is, rather, that a radical revision of the initial formalism was necessary in order to represent structural ambiguities without duplication of non-ambiguous material.

The adoption of such representations for ambiguity has profound implications for the parsing strategies employed by any parser that tries to produce them. For each type of construction that such a parser can encounter, and here we mean construction types at the level of case constructions, conjoined lists, or linear fixed-order patterns, the parser must "know" about all the structural ambiguities that the construction can give rise to, and must be prepared to detect and encode appropriately such ambiguities when they arise. Construction-specific parsing techniques fit this requirement perfectly. Each construction-specific parsing strategy can encode detailed information about the types of structural ambiguity possible with that construction and incorporate the specific information necessary to detect and represent these ambiguities.

We must reiterate, however, that when possible we advocate the use of domain semantics to resolve selectional and structural ambiguities. Only when semantic disambiguation proves unequal to the task, a not uncommon situation with ill-formed input, do we suggest interaction with the user; but when this interaction occurs it must be as tightly focused as possible on the source of the ambiguity so that both the cognitive and the mechanical (typing) demands on the user are kept to a minimum.

4 Limited-Domain Language Definition

Another advantage of a construction-specific approach to parsing is related to the definition of limited-domain task-oriented languages. As we will show in this section, the uniform grammar representation required by a uniform parsing strategy makes it difficult to define task-oriented languages in terms natural for the task domain. An alternative is to define the language in a formalism well suited to the domain and then compile this formalism into rules in the uniform grammar representation that the parser actually requires. However, this considerably inhibits the process of language development because it requires an often time-consuming phase of compilation into the uniform grammar after each change to the language definition. On the other hand, as we shall see, a construction-specific approach allows a grammar representation well suited to the domain to be interpreted directly without any compilation phase.

4.1 Compiling Descriptions into Linear Patterns

Since our initial flexible parser, FlexP, applied its uniform parsing strategy to a uniform grammar of pattern-matching rewrite rules, it was not possible to cover constructions like the one used in the examples above in a single grammar rule. A postnominal case frame such as the one that covers the message descriptions used as examples above must be spread over several rewrite rules. Recall that the patterns actually used in PlexP look like:

⟨?determiner *MessageAdj MessageHead *MessageCase⟩
⟨% from Person⟩
⟨% since Date⟩
⟨% to Person⟩

The point here is not the details of the pattern notation, but the fact that this is a very unnatural way of representing a postnominal construction. Not only does it cause problems in the process of flexible parsing, as explained in Section 2, but it is also quite inconvenient to create in the first place. Essentially, one has to know the specific trick of creating intermediate (and from the language point of view, superfluous) categories like *MessageCase* in the example above, and then one must write patterns to recognize these categories independent of their structuring context. Since we designed FlexP as a tool for use in natural language interfaces, we considered it unreasonable to expect the designer of a task-oriented language to have the specialized knowledge to create such obscure rules. Accordingly, we designed a language definition formalism that enabled a grammar to be specified in terms much more natural to the system being interfaced to. The above construction for the description of a message, for instance, could be defined as a single unified construction without specifying any artificial intermediate constituents, as follows:

```
  [
StructureType: Object
ObjectName: Message
Schema: [
        Sender: [FillerType: &Person]
        Recipient: [FillerType: &Person Number: OneOrMore]
        Date: [FillerType: &Date]
        After: [FillerType: &Date UseRestriction: DescriptionOnly]
        ]
Syntax: [
        SynType: NounPhrase
        Head: (message note ⟨?piece ?of mail⟩ letter)
        Case: (
              ⟨%from ↑Sender⟩
              ⟨% to ↑Recipient⟩
              ⟨% dated ↑Date⟩
              ⟨% since ↑After⟩
              )
        ]
  ]
```

In addition to the syntax of a message description, this piece of formalism also describes the internal structure of a message, and is intended for use with a larger interface system [1] of which FlexP is a part. The larger system provides an interface to a functional subsystem or tool, and is tool-independent in the sense that it is driven by a declarative data base in which the objects and operations of the tool currently being interfaced to are defined in the formalism shown. The example is, in fact, an abbreviated version of the definition of a message from the declarative tool description for an electronic mail system tool with which the interface was actually used.

In the example, the Syntax slot defines the input syntax for a message; it is used to generate rules for FlexP, which are in turn used to parse input descriptions of messages from a user. FlexP's grammar for parsing input for the mail system tool is the union of all the rules compiled in this way from the Syntax fields of all the objects and operations in the tool description. The Syntax field of the example says that the syntax for a message is that of a noun phrase, i.e., any of the given head nouns (angle brackets indicate patterns of words), followed by any of the given postnominal Cases, preceded by any adjectives - none are given here - which can in turn be preceded by a determiner. The up-arrows in the Case patterns refer back to slots of a message, as specified in the Schema slot of the example - the information in the Schema slot is also used by other parts of the interface. The actual grammar rules needed by FlexP are generated by first filling in a pre-stored skeleton pattern for NounPhrase, automatically generating the following (by now familiar) pattern:

⟨?determiner *MessageAdj MessageHead *MessageCase⟩

and then generating patterns for each of the Cases, substituting the appropriate Fillier Types for the slot names that appear in the patterns used to define the Cases, thus generating the subpatterns:

⟨% from Person⟩
⟨% to Person⟩
⟨% dated Date⟩
⟨% since Date⟩

The slot names are not discarded but used in the results of the subrules to ensure that the objects which match the substituted FillerTypes end up in the correct slot of the record produced by the top-level message rule. This compilation procedure must be performed in its entirety before any input can be parsed.

While this approach to language definition was successful in freeing the language designer from having to know details of the parser that were essentially irrelevant to him, it also made the process of language development very much slower. Every time the designer wished to make the smallest change to the grammar, it was necessary to go through the time-consuming compilation procedure. Since the development of a task-specific language typically involves many small changes, each requiring interactive testing, this has proved a significant impediment to the utility of FlexP.

4.2 *Direct Interpretation of Case Descriptions*

The construction-specific approach offers a method of circumventing this problem. Since the parsing strategies and ambiguity representations are specific to particular constructions, it is possible to represent each type of construction differently - there is no need to translate the language into a uniformly represented grammar. In addition, the constructions are exactly those for which there will be specific parsing strategies and grammar representations. It therefore becomes possible to dispense with the compilation step required for FlexP, and instead interpret the language definition directly. This drastically cuts the time needed to make changes to the grammar, and so makes the language definition system much more useful and productive. For example, the Syntax slot of the previous example formalism might become:

```
Syntax: [
          SynType: NounPhrase
          Head: (message note ⟨?piece ?of mail⟩ letter)
          Cases: (
                  [Marker: %from Slot: Sender]
                  [Marker: %to Slot: Recipient]
                  [Marker: %dated Slot: Date]
                  [Marker: %since Slot: After]
                  )
          ]
```

This grammar representation, equally convenient from a user's point of view, should be directly interpretable by a parser specific to the NounPhrase case type of construction. All the information needed by such a parser, including a list of all the case markers, and the type of object that fills each case slot, is directly accessible from this representation eliminating the need for an intermediate, cumbersome compilation phase.

5 Parsing Data Base Queries and Updates

A further advantage of multiple construction-specific parsing techniques and grammar representations arises in the case of interfaces for accessing and updating data bases. Most current data base interfaces that use natural language are concerned purely with data base access rather than update, though see Kaplan [21] for some discussion of the problems involved in the latter activity. The typical approach of such interfaces has been to translate a user's natural language questions about the contents of a data base into a formal query language which is then interpreted by a program specific to the particular data base to produce the required answer. The answer is then expressed to the user in some more or less natural format. The translation into the formal query language can be done directly from the input, as is the case in LADDER [27], or indirectly via a syntax tree of the input as in LUNAR [30].

5.1 The Non-Uniformity Problem

Although one could argue that this arrangement is fine for pure data base access, it is less than optimal if a mixture of access and update is desired. The problem is that the structure of the query languages employed does not mirror the structure of the data base being queried. This means that an access request and an update request of essentially similar form will result in radically different parses. Hence, constituents which are identical at the language level must be parsed in radically different ways depending on whether they are part of an access or an update request.

To make this point concrete, consider the following two requests that might be presented to a college registrar data base interface.

> *Who is the instructor of Economics 247?*
> *Change the instructor of Economics 247 to be Solway.*

Translating the first input into a typical[2] formal query language might look something like:

```
(FOR (X in COURSES)
     (and (=(DEPT X) Economics)
          (=(NUMBER X) 247))
     (LIST (INSTRUC X)))
```

A corresponding translation for the update request[3] on the other hand might be:

```
(FOR (X in COURSES)
     (and (=(DEPT X) Economics)
          (=(NUMBER X) 247))
     (CHANGE-INSTRUC X Solway))
```

While the representation of "Economics 247" is the same in both cases, the treatment of "instructor" is quite different. In the access example, it is encoded into the access function, INSTRUC, and in the update example, it turns into the update function, CHANGE-INSTRUC. The reason for such radically different treatment is a desire to make the query language independent of the structure of the data. For example the relations between courses of their departments, numbers, and instructors could be contained in one file, or in three separate files. By making no assumption about the structure of the data, and just using neutral functions like

---

[2] These examples are actually patterned after, though not identical to, the language employed by Woods in the LUNAR system [30], which is one of the more easily human-readable of the query languages that have been used. Most DB query languages adopt a similar, if more cryptic, formalism. For instance, CODASYL [11] queries are stated in a linearized form whose content resembles that of our example above. Kaplan [20], however, first translates queries into a intermediate formalism, satisfying some but not all the features of the representation we propose in the following pages, before generating the cryptic CODASYL query form.

[3] We do not consider here "non-obvious" interpretations for update requests like those discussed by Kaplan [21].

INSTRUC and CHANG-INSTRUC which assume that there is a relation between course and instructor, but nothing about the way it is represented, the query language avoids dependencies of this sort.

5.2 Unifying Update and Query Representations

However, adopting a query language of this type has unfortunate consequences for a parser that must recognize both access and update requests. Clearly, it would be desirable for such a parser to use the same grammar rules to recognize "the instructor of Economics 247" in both examples above, but the target representation makes this quite inconvenient at best. Because "instructor" must be translated in two quite different ways, it is most natural to control the parsing of the phrase from a higher level, so there would probably be rules[4] that recognized complete phrases like:

⟨tell-me⟩ ⟨instructor⟩ of ⟨course⟩
⟨change⟩ ⟨instructor⟩ of ⟨course⟩ to ⟨person⟩

and turned them into internal representations like the ones above. In order to be able to recognize patterns like "⟨instructor⟩ of ⟨course⟩" or better still "⟨slot⟩ of ⟨structure⟩" without regard to whether they were part of an access or update request, one would have to represent output from the parser something like:

```
[RequestType: Access
 SlotSpec:
   [Slot: instructor
    Structure:
      [Type: COURSE Dept: Economics Number: 247]
   ]
]
[RequestType: Update
 SlotSpec:
   [Slot: instructor
    Structure:
      [Type: COURSE Dept: Economics Number: 247]
   ]
 UpdateValue: Solway
]
```

Here the representation of "the instructor of Economics 247" is the same for both the access and update requests, and hence can be recognized and constructed by a common constituent in the grammar. The fact that one is a query and the other an update is determined only once at a higher level and factored into the Request Type slot in the representation.

This form of representation has the advantages we have described for parsing. A potential objection, however, is that the representation presumes too much

[4] The exact form of the grammar representation, network or pattern, is not important here, but only the idea that phrases of this type would be recognized as a whole.

about the structure of the data base. We do not believe that this objection is valid because the assumptions made are only about the logical structure of the data base from the user's point of view, rather than its detailed organization into files. Any relational data base would certainly fit into the slot and filler, property list, style of representation we have used, and other forms of logical organization could also be accommodated. In addition, the work in LADDER [27] shows how an abstract intermediate representation is very useful when several data bases of different detailed structures are involved, and the above style of representation should serve splendidly for that purpose.

5.3 Benefits of the Construction-Specific Approach

So far, nothing we have said in this section makes the construction-specific approach to parsing preferable to the uniform approach, with respect to data base interactions. There would be nothing to stop a uniform parser producing the kind of representation we are advocating for update and access requests just as well as a construction-specific one could. The primary advantage of construction-specific parsing involves the creation of a common and useful sublanguage for query and update tasks. Since the particular constructions used in a construction-specific approach can be those "natural" for the task domain, the input language can be defined in a way that is tied closely to the slot and filler structure of the objects of the data base. To be more precise, the input syntax for the description of a given kind of data base object can be expressed in terms of the fillers for slots of that object type embedded in whatever kind of construction is natural for describing such an object. As an example of the kind of language definition we have in mind, consider the following three complementary syntax definitions for descriptions of a course:

```
[SyntaxType: NounWithCases
Head: (course section class)
PostCases: [Instructor:
               (((?taught) (?given) by))
            Department: ((?held in))
            Number: (numbered)
               ...
           ]
]
[SyntaxType: PossessiveCases
 NamedCases:
      [Instructor:
         (instructor teacher (faculty member))
       Department: (department)
       ...
      ]
]
[SyntaxType: SlotPattern
 Pattern: (Department Number)
]
```

Without going into great detail, the first syntax definition above says that a construction type of NOUNWITHCASES may be used to describe a COURSE, This means that it may be described by a head noun (a list of alternatives is given), optionally preceded by a determiner (part of the construction definition), followed by a sequence of descriptive cases. These cases are defined as a property list indicated by POSTCASES. The indicators (IINSTRUCTOR, DEPARTMENT, etc.) are slot names of the object type, and the values are a list of possible case markers for that case (both single words and linear patterns of words). For instance, "taught by" can signal the presence of an instructor description. The fact is that INSTRUCTOR is a slot of COURSE, and the syntax for fillers of that slot are recorded elsewhere. The second syntax definition gives a listing of the slots of COURSE, and the words used to describe them.

From this information, a phrase like "the instructor of ⟨course⟩" can be parsed. Finally, an alternative syntax for COURSE of (⟨department⟩ ⟨number⟩) is given. We have already developed a similar kind of language definition formalism for command interface applications [1]. We intend to extend this work to interfaces that access and update data bases. For instance, the noun-phrase head and the case markers can be represented by more complex patterns that may include non-terminals from a semnatic grammar.

6 The CASPAR Parser

In this section we turn from the general advantages of the construction-specific approach to examination of CASPAR, a small parser we constructed as an illustration of the power of the construction-specific approach in dealing with ungrammatical input. It also turned out to provide a very efficient way of recognizing grammatical input in the class of domain-specific languages for which it was designed.

CASPAR was designed to provide a natural language command interface to an interactive computer system. Since an imperative is a natural way to issue commands, CASPAR was designed to recognize simple imperative verb phrases, i.e., imperative verbs followed by a sequence of noun phrases possibly marked by prepositions. Examples for an interface to a data base keeping track of registration for college courses include:

cancel math 247
enroll Jim Campbell in English 324
transfer student 5518 from Physics 101 to comp sci 111

The imperative verbs identify the system commands and the noun phrases provide their arguments. Such constructions are classic examples of case constructions; the verb or command is the central concept, and the noun phrases or arguments are its cases. Considered as surface cases, the command arguments are either marked by a preposition, or unmarked and identified by position, such as the position of direct object in the examples above.

6.1 The Two CASPAR Strategies

In line with the construction-specific approach we are advocating, CASPAR was given two quite distinct parsing strategies:

- A strategy to identify the appropriate case frame and activate its case markers and filler-patterns to deal with the rest of the input utterance.
- A strategy to recognize individual constituent case fillers and markers, including the verb, noun phrases in the role of case fillers, and prepositions in the role of case markers.

The first of these strategies is dominant in the sense that it decides where in the input the second, more detailed, recognizer should be applied and what it should try to recognize when it is applied. The second strategy is a simple linear pattern-matcher. This is just what is needed for verbs, prepositions, and simple object descriptions such as those in the examples above, but it is inadequate for more complicated kinds of object descriptions, and in particular, for object descriptions that are themselves case constructions as in:

cancel the classes taught by Solway on Tuesday

This deficiency is what relegates CASPAR to the realm of toy systems. However, the extended design of a multi-strategy parser discussed in a later section and its implementation in DYPAR-II [8] can deal with nested case constructions.

6.2 Error-Tolerant Parsing

Although CASPAR is just an experimental system, the flexibility and robustness obtained by providing separate parsing strategies for the two different construction types it recognizes (case and fixed-order linear patterns) is quite striking. The types of grammatical deviation that can be dealt with include:

- Unexpected and unrecognizable (to the system) interjections as in:
  ↑S↑Q↑S[5] *enroll student 2476 in I think CS 348.*
- missing case markers:
  enroll Jim Campbell Economics 247.
- out of order cases:
  In Economics 247 Jim Campbell enroll.
- ambiguous cases:
  transfer Jim Campbell Economics 247 English 332.

Combinations of these ungrammaticalities can also be dealt with.

CASPAR achieves this degree of robustness by exploiting certain specialized characteristics of case constructions; most importantly, it takes advantage of the differences between case markers and case fillers. Case markers are typically drawn

[5] The reason for including these particular extraneous characters will be easily guessed by users of certain computer systems.

from a small set of words or phrases, and it is thus much easier to recognize them (or correct their spelling) than case fillers, which have much more variety. This ease of recognition of case markers makes it practical for CASPAR to scan the entire input for them, and thus to locate and parse the case fillers that follow; interjections and out of order cases are recognized in this way. CASPAR also keeps track of which cases have been filled, and thus cuts down on the number of filler types that it has to try when a segment of input must be parsed without the guidance of case markers, for instance, if some case markers have been omitted. Neither of these heuristics are available to the more uniform parsing procedures of Weischedel and Black [29], or Kwasny and Sondheimer [22], or our own FlexP parser [15], simply because there is no convenient way for these parsers to represent or make use of the information that case markers are much easier to recognize than case fillers or that most cases can be filled only once. Exactly, how these heuristics operate, along with other details of how CASPAR is tailored to case constructions, can be seen from the following description of CASPAR's parsing algorithm.

6.3 The CASPAR Algorithm

CASPAR has two parsing strategies: a case-oriented strategy and a linear pattern-matching strategy. The case-oriented strategy controls the operation of the pattern-matching strategy, which in turn actually recognizes words from the input. The linear pattern-matcher may be operated in anchored mode, where it tries to match one of a number of linear patterns starting at a fixed word in the input, or in scanning mode, where it tries to match the patterns it is given at successive points in the input string until one of the patterns matches, or it reaches the end of the string. The case-oriented parsing strategy operates in the following way.

1. Starting from the left of the input string, apply the linear pattern-matcher in scanning mode using all the patterns which correspond to commands. If this succeeds, the command corresponding to the pattern that matched becomes the current command, and the remainder of the input string is parsed relative to its domain-specific case frame. If it fails, CASPAR cannot parse the input.
2. If the current command has an unmarked direct object case, apply the linear matcher in anchored mode at the next[6] word using the set of patterns appropriate to the type of object that should fill the case. If this succeeds, record the filler thus obtained as the filler for the case.
3. Starting from the next word, apply the pattern-matcher in scanning mode using the patterns corresponding to the surface markers of the marked cases that have not yet been filled. If this fails, terminate.
4. If the last step succeeds, CASPAR selects a marked case - the one from which the successful pattern came. Apply the matcher in anchored mode at the next word using the set of patterns appropriate to the type of object that should fill

[6] The word after the last one the pattern-matcher matched the last time it was applied.

the case selected. If this succeeds record the filler thus obtained as the filler for the case.

5. Go to step 3.

Unless the input turns out to be completely unparsable, this algorithm will produce a command and a (possibly incomplete) set of arguments. It is also insensitive to spurious input immediately preceding a case marker. However, it is not able to deal with any of the other ungrammaticalities mentioned above. Dealing with them involves going back over any parts of the input that have been skipped by using the pattern-matcher in scanning mode. If, after the above algorithm has terminated, there are any such skipped substrings, and there are also arguments to the command that have not been filled, the pattern-matcher ist applied in scanning mode to each of the skipped substrings using the patterns corresponding to the filler types of the unfilled arguments. This will pick up any arguments which were misplaced, or had garbled or missing case markers. If one of the arguments matched in this way could fill more than one slot, the special ambiguity representations discussed earlier come into play to enable focused user interaction.

The grammar description that CASPAR uses is tied very closely to the structure of the domain. For each possible command to the underlying system, the grammar definition contains a list of the linear patterns which can be used to detect the command itself, plus a list of cases corresponding to arguments of the command. For each argument the definition gives the type of domain object that should fill that argument, plus the linear patterns used as surface case markers to signal the argument (or an indication that the argument is an unmarked case such as the direct object). The grammar definition also gives the linear patterns needed to recognize each type of domain object. See Sec. 4 for a discussion of how a construction-specific approach to parsing fits well with a grammar definition that is tied closely to domain structure, and Sec. 5 for an example of a grammar definition in a similar style. This form of grammar definition fits naturally into a description of the underlying interactive system as a whole. Such a description can be used to control other aspects of a cooperative and graceful user interface - see [1] for more details of other work we have done in that area.

Though simplistic in many ways, CASPAR demonstrates the power of a construction-specific approach to parsing, both in the range of grammatical deviations it can handle, and in the efficiency it displays in straightforward parsing of grammatical input. This efficiency is derived from the limited number of patterns that the pattern-matcher has to deal with at any one time. On its first application, the matcher only deals with command patterns; on subsequent applications, it alternates between the patterns for the markers of the unfilled cases of the current command, and the patterns for a specific object type signaled by the relevant case being instantiated. Except in post-processing of skipped input, only case marker and command patterns are employed when the pattern-matcher is in its less efficient scanning mode. The more difficult to recognize object descriptions are processed in the more efficient anchored mode. This efficiency is sound evidence that such a construction-specific approach is a good way to bring the powerful semantic restrictions available in limited domains to bear on the parsing of both grammatical and ungrammatical input.

7 The DYPAR Parser

As a related investigation of the practical feasibility of dynamic strategy selection by a domain-oriented parser, we also developed the DYPAR[7] system. DYPAR has a Kernel control module to select the appropriate parsing strategy as a function of the expected input structure, plus three parsing strategies to select amongst, each with its own grammatical and/or semantic knowledge encodings, and global data structures to share information. The control structure, strategies, and linguistic knowledge representations are augmented with domain-specific semantic knowledge bases. Thus, the same kernel parser may be applied to different domains if a detailed, domain-specific, semantic knowledge base is provided.

7.1 The Objectives of the DYPAR Approach

Whereas the central focus of CASPAR was to exploit domain semantics and construction-specific case frames for processing some types of malformed input, DYPAR was built to explore issues for user interaction and multi-strategy synthesis in the context of a working parser. More explicity, our objectives for developing DYPAR were threefold:

- to Test the feasibility of a multi-strategy approach
- to investigate a simple data base task requiring interaction and feedback between the system and the user
- to eventually integrate the best features of CASPAR and DYPAR into a robust, construction-specific, multi-strategy parser.

In encoding domain semantics, we found that some information can be expressed more naturally and parsiminiously in one form (e.g., linear patterns), while other information is best expressed in other forms (e.g., equivalence transformations or semantic grammar productions). To illustrate this point, we attempted to encode all the knowledge in DYPAR as a pure semantic grammar. This task has more than tripled the size of the task-specific knowledge base, and we have not yet finished (nor do we intend to finish) the conversion. The primary reason for the increase in size is that much of the information must be stated with a high degree of redudancy and often in an awkward, roundabout manner when it is coerced into a uniform, context free representation. Therefore, the primary lesson one can draw from the DYPAR effort is that multi-strategy parsing is tractable in practice and moreover can perform the work of single-strategy approaches with much greater economy of programmer effort[8].

---

[7] DYnamic PARsing is still in its infant stages, requiring frequent changes in its software.

[8] It was not our intention in building DYPAR that it outperform existing parsers in terms of theoretical coverage, but rather that it replicate known performance in a more natural, parsimonious, easier-to-extend manner. However, our next step - integrating DYPAR and CASPAR - strives for both improved coverage and much more robust reliable performance in well-defined domains.

7.2 Parsing Strategies in DYPAR

DYPAR combines three parsing strategies:

- *A context free semantic grammar component* grouping domain information into hierarchical semantic categories useful in classifying individual words and phrases in the input language, similar to the LIFER [18] and SOPHIE [3] semantic grammar mechanisms.
- *A partial pattern-match component* represented as pattern-action rules. The patterns may contain individual words, semantic categories (from the semantic grammar), wild cards, optional constituents, register assignment, and register reference. This method enables the semantic grammar non-terminal categories to be applied in a much more effective context sensitive manner than in a pure context free grammar recognizer.
- *Equivalence transformations* map domain-dependent and domain-independent constructs into canonical form, thus reducing the number of patterns and semantic grammar rules to a fraction of what would otherwise be needed. If a phrase structure can be expressed in several different ways, while retaining the same meaning, it is clearly beneficial to first map it into canonical form, rather than being forced to include all possible variants in every context where that constituent could occur.

Below we give an example of each type of linguistic information used in DYPAR. In order to understand these examples, a few notational conventions must be introduced. ⟨*BRACKETS*⟩ denote a non-terminal semantic grammar symbol. A word starting with an exclamation mark (e.g., *REGISTER*) denotes the name of a register. A vertical bar (|) denotes disjunction in a pattern. A # in a pattern matches a single word. An asterisk (*) matches an arbitrary sequence of words. The construction *(REGISTER pattern)* assigns whatever matches the pattern to the register specified. A question mark (?) before a constituent in a pattern indicates that constituent is optional.

One application of DYPAR, as we see in the dialogue below, is as a natural language front end to a semantic network data base update and query system. Therefore, its domain knowledge consists of language constructs relevant to this task. First, consider a fragment of its semantic grammar:

⟨INFO-REQ⟩→(⟨WHAT-Q⟩ | ⟨INFO-REQ1⟩)
⟨INFO-REQ1⟩ → (?⟨POLITE⟩ ⟨INFO-REQ2⟩ ?⟨WHAT-Q⟩)
⟨INFO-REQ2⟩ → (TELL ⟨me-US⟩ ?ABOUT | GIVE ⟨me-US⟩ | PRINT | TYPE)

This fragment, together with the rewrite rules for the other non-terminals above (e.g., ⟨WHAT-Q⟩, whose rewrite is a set of common factual WH-query forms) recognizes the initial segment of information-request queries such as: "What is ...", "Tell me what is ...", "Tell me about ...", "Would you give me ...", etc.

Now, consider a pattern-match rule:

```
(?⟨det⟩ (!val ≠) ⟨be-pres⟩ ? ⟨DET⟩ (! PROP ≠) OF
        ?⟨DET⟩ (!NAM ≠) ?⟨dpunct⟩)
⇒
(LTM-STORE !NAM !VAL !PROP)
```

This rule recognizes sentences such as: "Felix is a friend of Fido", or „Reagan is president of the USA", and passes the information to the data base manager for consistency checking and storage. In order to pass the information gathered in the pattern-match process, the registers are assigned appropriate values. For instance, in the second example, !NAM is assigned "USA", !PROP is assigned "president", and !VAL is assigned „Reagan".

The equivalence transformations also use the pattern-matcher. For instance, consider the following simple (but useful) transformation:

```
((!S1 *) (!W1 ⟨NOMINAL⟩) ⟨POSS⟩ (!W2 ⟨ATTRIBUTE⟩)
 (!S2 *) ?(!P ⟨PUNCT⟩))
::⟩
(NCONC !S1 !W2 (LIST 'OF) !W1 !S2 !P)
```

This transformation maps possessive constructions into attribute-value constructions, which we chose as canonical. For instance "Tell me about the VAX-785's performance." is mapped into "Tell me about the performance of the VAX-785." The latter construction is recognized by a pattern-action rule. Since possessive constructions can occur in many contexts, the single transformation above saves us from duplicating pattern-match rules for each different context where an attribute-value construction can occur.

7.3 A Sample DYPAR Dialogue

The control structure of DYPAR is an applicative condition-action cycle, which halts upon no rules being triggered (in which case a partial pattern-match strategy is attempted), or upon one of the pattern-action rules firing and passing its information to the data base manager. Let us see a dialogue fragment with DYPAR. For simplicity, we start out with an empty data base. Items in italics below were typed in by the user. Everything else was output by the system. Items in UPPER CASE are paraphrases of internal semantic network relations output by a rudimentary English generator. When DYPAR does not recognize concepts in the input, it prompts the user for additional information required by the integrity-checker in the data base manager. Items in SMALLCAPS signal text synthesized by the template-based English generater. The remainder of the text consists of fixed-format messages output by the back-end system.

**(parser)*

You can build and query a simple semantic network
by stating information and questions in English.

+Fido is a grey dog.

Storing assertion in semantic net: FIDO IS A DOG.
Inference: DOG IS A GENERIC CONCEPT.

What is grey?
+grey is a color.

Storing assertion in semantic net: GREY IS A COLOR.

Is it correct to say that THE COLOR OF FIDO IS GREY? (Y, N): *Yes.*
Adding new assertion: THE COLOR OF FIDO IS GREY.

+Meat is the favorite-food of dogs.

Storing assertion in semantic net: THE FAVORITE-FOOD OF A DOG IS MEAT.

+Felix's cousin is Fido.

Transforming (FELIX'S COUSIN IS FIDO PERIOD)
Into::⟩ (THE COUSIN OF FELIX IS FIDO PERIOD)

Transforming (THE COUSIN OF FELIX IS FIDO PERIOD)
Into::⟩ (FIDO IS THE COUSIN OF FELIX PERIOD)

Adding new assertion: FIDO IS THE COUSIN OF FELIX.

+Cousin is a symmetric relation.

I already knew that: COUSIN WAS A RELATION.

Adding new assertion: THE RELATION OF COUSIN IS SYMMETRIC.
Inference: Adding new assertion: THE INVERSE OF COUSIN IS COUSIN.
Inference: Adding new assertion: FELIX IS THE COUSIN OF FIDO.

+Would you tell me everything you know about Fido?
FIDO IS A DOG.
THE COLOR OF FIDO IS GREY.
THE FAVORITE-FOOD OF FIDO IS MEAT. (by inheritance)
THE COUSIN OF FIDO IS FELIX (by symmetric inference)

As we see in the above example, robust communication with the user requires not only a flexible domain-oriented parser, but also an interactive query capability and a natural language generator. However, the latter two processes are conceptually simpler, and not the topic of this paper. (But see the XCALIBUR documentation [8, 9] for a discussion of these issues and the upgraded DYPAR-II system).

8 Combining the Strengths of CASPAR and DYPAR

CASPAR illustrates the power of case-frame parsers when they can exploit very strong domain-specific semantic constraints. DYPAR illustrates the harmonious integration of three parsing strategies. However, these parsers are only first steps in exploiting the multi-strategy approach to developing real-world, robust, natural language interfaces. In terms of sophistication, DYPAR straddles the boundary between an advanced toy and a rudimentary real-application system. One direction of continued development would be to enhance its pattern-matcher, build additional general transformations, and augment its language interface to serve as a medium in which to express extensions to the grammar by a domain expert (not necessarily a natural-language expert). A first step in the direction of automating and simplifying user extensibility has been taken in the Nano-KLAUS system [13].

Our research is focused in a direction different from, but complementary to, the one taken in Nano-KLAUS. Since the performance obtained by integrating several parsing strategies has, for both CASPAR and DYPAR, proven more effective than the application of any single strategy, we continue to explore this principle by including additional parsing strategies in future parsers. As a step along this road, we have designed a flexible control structure [6] that integrates case-instantiation with other parsing strategies discussed in this paper, together with additional construction-specific strategies. As in CASPAR, the case-oriented strategy is the dominant one. We expect this new design to provide a quantum jump in the range of applicability of our task-oriented parsers. Moreover, techniques such as expectation-driven disambiguation [2, 7, 26], developed in non-applied natural language work, can now be brought to bear in real-world applications. The reason why case-frame parsers have not been developed in task-oriented domains is that, while they capture general principles admirably and can bring detailed semantic knowledge to bear, they are not well suited to recognizing specific idioms, compound nouns, and the like. However, the addition of partial pattern-matching (ideally suited to detecting idiomatic expressions) integrated with case-frame instantiation and other parsing methods should provide a high degree of generality without sacrificing robustness.

8.1 A Multi-Strategy Algorithm

Our new parser is designed primarily for task domains where the prevalent forms of user input are commands and queries, both expressed in imperative or pseudo-imperative constructs. Since in imperative constructs the initial word (or phrase) establishes the case frame for the entire utterance, we chose the case-frame parsing strategy as primary. In order to recognize an imperative command, and to instantiate each case, other parsing strategies are invoked. Since the parser knows what can fill a particular case, it can choose the parsing strategy best suited for linguistic constructions expressing that type of information. Moreover, it can pass any global constraints from the case frame or from other instantiated cases to the subsidiary parsers - thus reducing potential ambiguity, speeding the parse, and enhancing robustness.

The multi-strategy parsing algorithm we have designed is as follows. Input is assumed to be in the imperative form:

1. *Apply string PATTERN-MATCH procedure to the initial segment of the input using only the patterns previously indexed as corresponding to command words/phrases in imperative constructions.* Patterns contain both optional constituents

and non-terminal symbols that expand according to a semantic grammar (e.g., "copy" and "do a file transfer" are synonyms for the same command in a file management system).

2. *Access the CASE-FRAME associated with the command just recognized, and push it onto the context stack.* In the above example, the case frame is indexed under the token ⟨COPY⟩, which was output by the pattern-matcher. The case frame consists of a list of pairs ([case-marker]) [case-filler-information], . . .)
3. *Match the focused segment of the input with the case markers using the same PATTERN-MATCH procedure mentioned above.* If no match occurs, assume the input corresponds to the unmarked case (or the first unmarked case, if the verb is ditransitive), and proceed to the next step.
4. *Apply the parsing strategy indicated by the type of construct expected as a case filler. Pass any available case constraints to the substrategy. A partial list of parsing strategies indicated by expected fillers is:*
   - *Subimperative* - Case-frame parser, starting with the command-identification pattern-match above.
   - *Structured-object* (e.g., a concept with subattributes) - Case-frame parser, starting with the pattern-matcher invoked on the list of patterns corresponding to the names (or compound names) of the semantically permissible structured objects, followed by case-frame parsing of any present subattributes.
   - *Simple Object* - Apply the pattern-matcher, using only the patterns indexed as relevant in the case-filler-information field.
   - *Special Object* - Apply the parsing strategy applicable to that type of special object (e.g., proper names, dates, quoted strings, stylized technical jargon, etc . . .).
   - *Set* - Apply a simple strategy that recognized an enumeration of elements (as a conjoined list) for extensive descriptions, or an indirect strategy that analyzes intensive descriptions and calls the structured object, relative clause, or other strategy depending upon the form of the description.
   - *None of the above* (Errorful input or parser deficiency) - Apply the graceful recovery techniques discussed below.
5. *If an embedded case frame is activated when parsing a case filler, push it onto the context stack.*
6. *When a case filler is instantiated, remove the ⟨case-marker⟩, ⟨case-filler-information⟩ pair from the list of active cases in the appropriate case frame, proceed to the next case marker, and repeat the process above until the input terminates.*
7. *If all the cases in a case frame have been instantiated, pop to context stack until that case frame is no longer in it.* (Completed frames typically reside at the top of the stack, requiring a single pop.)
8. *If there is more than one case frame on the stack when trying to parse additional input, apply the following procedure:*
   - If the input only matches a case marker in one frame, proceed to instantiate the corresponding case filler as outlined above. Also, if the matched case marker is not on the most embedded case frame (i.e., not at the top of the context stack), pop the stack until the frame whose case marker was matched appears at the top of the stack.

- If no case markers are matched, attempt to parse unmarked cases, starting with the most deeply embedded case-frame (the top of the context stack) and proceeding outwards (i.e., downwards through the context stack). If an unmarked case is matched, pop the context stack until the corresponding case frame is at the top. Then, instantiate the case filler, remove the case from the active case-frame, and proceed to parse additional input. If more than one unmarked case matches the input, choose the most embedded one (i.e., the most recent context) and save the state of the parse on the global history stack. (This suggests an ambiguity that cannot be resolved with the information at hand.)
- If the input matches more than one case marker in the context stack, try to parse the case filler via the parsing strategy indexed in each filler-information slot corresponding to a matched case marker. If more than one case filler parses (this is a somewhat rare situation, indicating underconstrained case frames or truly ambiguous input) save the state in the global history stack and pursue the parse assuming the most deeply embedded constituent. [Our case-frame attachment heuristic favors the most local attachment permitted by semantic case constraints.]

9. *If a conjunction or disjunction occurs in the input, cycle through the context stack trying to parse the right-hand side of the conjunction as filling the same case as the left hand side. If no such parse is feasible, interpret the conjunction as top-level, e.g., as two instances of the same imperative, or two different imperatives. If more than one parse results, interact with the user to disambiguate.* To illustrate this simple process, consider:

   "Transfer the programs written by Smith and Jones to ..."
   "Transfer the programs written in Fortran and the census data files to ..."
   "Transfer the programs written in Fortran and delete ..."

   The scope of the first conjunction is the "author" subattribute of program, whereas the scope of the second conjunction is the unmarked "object" case of the transfer action. Domain knowledge in the case-filler information of the "object" case in the "transfer" imperative inhibits "Jones" from matching a potential object for electronic file transfer. Similarly "Census data files" are inhibited from matching the "author" subattribute of a program. Thus conjunctions in the two syntactically comparable examples are scoped differently by our semantic-scoping rule relying on domain-specific case information. "Delete" matches no active case filler, and hence it is parsed as the initial segment of a second conjoined utterance. Since "delete" is a known imperative, this parse succeeds.

10. *If the parser fails to parse additional input, pop the global history stack and pursue an alternative parse. If the stack is empty, invoke the graceful recovery heuristics.* Here the DELTA-MIN method [5] can be applied to improve upon depth-first unwinding of the stack in the backtracking process.

11. *If the end of the input is reached, and the global history stack is not empty, pursue the alternative parses. If any survive to the end of the input (this should not be the case unless true ambiguity exists), interact with the user to select the appropriate parse in a focused manner as discussed in an earlier section.*

The need for embedded case structures and ambiguity resolution based on domain-dependent semantic expectations of the case fillers is illustrated by the following pair of sentences:

"Edit the programs in Fortran"
"Edit the programs in Teco"

"Fortran" fills the language attribute of "program", but cannot fill either the location or instrument case of Edit (both of which can be signaled by "in"). In the second sentence, however, "Teco" fills the instrument case of the verb "edit" and none of the attributes of "program". This disambiguation is significant because in the first example the user specified *which* programs (s)he wants to edit, whereas in the second example (s)he specified *how* (s)he wants to edit them.

8.2 Flexible Error-Recovery Mechanisms

The algorithm presented is sufficient to parse grammatical input. In addition, since it operates in a manner specifically tailored to case constructions, it is easy to add modifications dealing with deviant input. Currently, the algorithm includes the following steps that deal with ungrammaticalities:

12. *If step 4 fails, i.e., a filler of appropriate type cannot be parsed at that position in the input, then repeat step 3 at successive points in the input until it produces a match, and continue the regular algorithm from there. Save the contiguous segments not matched on a SKIPPED list.* This step takes advantage of the fact that case markers are often much easier to recognize than case fillers to realign the parser if it gets out of step with the input (because of unexpected interjections, or other spurious or missing words).
13. *If words are on SKIPPED at the end of the parse, and cases remain unfilled in the case frames that were on the context stack at the time the words were skipped, then try to parse each of the case fillers against successive positions of the skipped sequences. This step picks up cases for which the marker was incorrect or garbled.*
14. *If words are still on SKIPPED attempt the same matches, but relax the pattern-matching procedures involved.*
15. *If this still does not account for all the input, interact with the user by asking questions focused on the uninterpreted part of the input.* The focused interaction technique discussed earlier is used to resolve semantic ambiguities in the input.
16. *If user interaction proves impractical, apply the project-and-integrate method [4] to narrow down the meanings of unknown words by exploiting syntactic, semantic, and contextual cues.*

These flexible parsing steps rely on the construction-specific aspects of the basic algorithm, and would not be easy to emulate in either a syntactic ATN parser or one based on a pure semantic grammar.

8.3 Advantages of the Multi-Strategy Approach

A major advantage of our mixed-strategy approach is that the top-level case structure, in essence, partitions the semantic world into categories according to the semantic constraints on the active case fillers. The power of the approach derives from these top-down case-frame expectations significantly constraining bottom-up pattern-matching. Thus, when a pattern-matcher is invoked to parse the recipient case of a file-transfer case frame, it need only consider patterns (and semantic-grammar constructs) that correspond to logical locations inside a computer. This form of expectation-driven parsing in restricted domains adds a two-fold effect to its robustness:

- Many spurious parses are never generated (because patterns yielding potentially spurious matches are never tried in inappropriate contexts).
- Additional knowledge (such as additional patterns, grammar rules, etc.) can be added without a corresponding linear increase in parse time since the case frames focus only upon the relevant subset of patterns and rules. Thus, the efficiency of the system may actually increase with the addition of more domain knowledge (in effect enabling the case frames to restrict context further). This behavior makes it possible to build the parser incrementally without the ever-present fear that a new extension may cause the entire parser to fail due to an unexpected application of that extension in the wrong context.

It is worth while noting that the algorithm described above does not mention interaction with morphological decomposition or spelling correction. Lexical processing is particularly important for robust parsing; indeed, based on our limited experience, lexical-level errors are a significant source of deviant input. The recognition and handling of lexical-deviation phenomena, such as unrecognized abbreviations and misspellings, must be integraged with the more usual morphological analysis. Some of these topics are discussed independently in [15]. However, integrating resilient morphological analysis with the algorithm we have outlined is a problem we consider very important and urgent if we are to construct a practical flexible parser.

In general, graceful interaction with the user is an important goal for any natural language front end whose users may be unfamiliar with computers (more details on our broader efforts towards this goal are given in [16, 14, 10]). People invariably produce ungrammatical utterances, leave out words, add interjections, and use terms outside the vocabulary of any system. It is essential that a real-world system "fail soft" in such circumstances, and interact with the user to enable graceful recovery. We saw simple examples of this in DYPAR, and more mechanisms are discussed in [15]. The expectation-setting provided by a case system incorporating domain knowledge may prove a more powerful tool to minimize failure than mechanisms based on relaxing grammatical rules or pattern-matching requirements.

Consider, for instance, a file management system where a user may type

Transfer the flies in my directory to the accounts directory.

It is fairly clear to us humans that the user meant to type "files", even if we know perfectly well that "flies" is a legitimate word in our vocabulary[9]. A case-frame system knows that the object case of the transfer command (as applied to the file management domain) requires a logical data entity, which "flies" is not. Observing this violated semantic requirement, it can proceed to see whether by spelling correction, morphological decomposition, or detecting potential omissions it can map "flies" into a known filler of that case. Here, spelling correction works (given a very restricted pool of candidate words satisfying the semantic requirements), and the system can proceed to inform the user of its correction (allowing the user to override if need be).

8.4 A Review of Principal Parsing Strategies

To conclude this section, we list the more important parsing strategies that we envisage might be used in an expanded version of the above algorithm. Most of these strategies exploit the constrained task-oriented nature of the input language:

- *Case-Frame Instantiation* is necessary to parse general imperative constructs and noun phrases with postnominal modifiers. This method has been applied before with some success to linguistic or conceptual cases [26] in more general parsing tasks. However, it becomes much more powerful and robust if domain-dependent constraints among the cases can be exploited. For instance, in a file management system, the command "Transfer UPDATE.FOR to the accounts directory" can be easily parsed if the information in the unmarked case of *transfer* ("update.for" in our example) is parsed by a file-name expert, and the destination case (flagged by "to") is parsed not as a physical location, but a logical entity inside a machine. The latter constraint enables one to interpret "directory" not as a phone book or bureaucratic agency, but as a reasonable destination for a file in a computer.
- *Semantic Grammars* [17, 19, 3] prove useful when there are ways of hierarchically clustering domain concepts into functionally useful categories for user interaction. Semantic grammars, like case systems, can bring domain knowledge to bear in disambiguating word meanings. However, the central problem of semantic grammars is non-transferability to other domains, stemming from the specificity of the semantic categorization hierarchy built into the grammar rules. This problem is somewhat ameliorated if this technique is applied only to parsing selected individual phrases [28], rather than being responsible for the entire parse. Individual constituents, such as those recognizing
- the initial segment of factual queries, apply in many domains, whereas a constituent recognizing an entire clause about file transfer is totally domain specific. Of course, this restriction calls for a different parsing strategy at the clause and sentence level, as we have advocated in this paper.

[9] No presently-implemented spelling correction scheme is ever applied to "correctly" spelled words.

- *(Partial) Pattern-Matching* on strings, using non-terminal semantic grammar constituents in the patterns, proves to be an interesting generalization of semantic grammars. This method is particularly useful when the patterns and semantic grammar non-terminal nodes interleave in a hierarchical fashion.
- *Transformations to Canonical Form* prove useful both for domain-dependent and domain-independent constructs. For instance, the following rule transforms possessives into "of" phrases, which we chose as canonical:

  [⟨ATTRIBUTE⟩ in possessive form, ⟨VALUE⟩ legitimate for attr.]
  [⟨VALUE⟩ "OF" ⟨ATTRIBUTE⟩ in simple form]

  Hence, the parser need only consider "of" constructions ["file's destination" = > "destination of file"). These transforms simplify the pattern-matcher and semantic grammar application process, especially when transformed constructions occur in many different contexts. A simple form of string transformation was present in PARRY [25].
- *Target-specific methods* may be invoked to parse portions of sentences not easily handled by the more general methods. For instance, if a case-grammar determines that the case just signaled is a proper name, a special name-expert strategy may be called. This expert knows that names can contain unknown words (e.g., Mr. Joe Gallen D'Aguila is obviously a name with D'Aguila as the surname) but subject to ordering constraints and morphological preferences. When unknown words are encountered in other positions in a sentence, the parser may try morphological decomposition, spelling correction, querying the user, or more complex processes to induce the probable meaning of unknown words, such as the project-and-integrate technique described in [4]. Clearly these unknown-word strategies ought to be suppressed in parsing person names.

Finally, to reiterate the central them of our investigations: *Integration of multiple construction-specific parsing strategies is a powerful organizing principle for robust, task-oriented natural language interfaces.*

9 Conclusion

This paper has proposed an approach to parsing limited-domain task-oriented languages based on dynamic selection among a number of different parsing strategies, one for each type of construction covered by the language. This approach was shown to have a number of advantages over more traditional uniform parsing strategies, including:

- Grammatical input can be parsed efficiently by the strategy most appropriate to each type of expected construction, bringing exactly the appropriate domain knowledge to bear.
- Ungrammatical input can be analyzed by first isolating the troublesome portions of the input, and subsequently applying our "fail-soft" recovery heuristics (exploiting constraints from other, better-understood constituents in the input), or engaging in focused interaction with the user.

- Semantic and structural ambiguities can be represented straightforwardly without duplication of unambiguous material, facilitating the construction of focused queries to the user concerning the ambiguity. Moreover, focused interaction facilitates interpretation of elliptical user replies to clarification queries.
- The task-oriented language development process can be simplified and made more efficient since the interface designer can define the language in terms natural to the task domain. In addition, the construction-specific approach enables the resulting language definition to be interpreted directly without time-consuming compilation into a uniform grammar formalism, thus allowing interactive incremental testing when new constructs are added to the grammar and tool description data base.
- Limited-domain interfaces to data bases that provide both access and update facilities can interact with the data base in a unified way, since the constructions used can be tied closely to the logical structure of objects represented by the data base, and need not be coerced into a rigidly uniform artificial grammar.

As a concrete illustration of some of these advantages, we also described two experimental parsers developed along construction-specific lines, and a more comprehensive parsing algorithm that attempts to combine the advantages of these two parsers and should form the basis of a more comprehensive restricted-domain parsing system. A variant of this algorithm has recently been implemented in DYPAR-II [8, 9], an interactive front end to the XSEL expert system [24]. We are currently working on integrating morphological analysis and fail-soft recovery mechanisms.

References

1. Ball, J.E. and Hayes, P.J.: Representation of Task-Independent Knowledge in a Gracefully Interacting User Interface. Proc reedings of the 1st Annual Meeting of the American Association for Artificial Intelligence, Stanford University, August 1980, pp. 116-120
2. Birnbaum, L. and Selfridge, M.: Conceptual Analysis in Natural Language. In: Schank, R. and Riesbeck, C. (eds.): Inside Computer Understanding. New Jersey: Erlbaum 1980, pp. 318-353
3. Burton, R.R.: Semantic Grammar. An Engineering Technique for Constructing Natural Language Understanding Systems. Technical Report 3453. Bolt, Beranek, and Newman, Inc., Cambridge, Mass., 1975
4. Carbonell, J.G.: Towards a Self-Extending Parser. Proceedings of the 17th Meeting of the Association for Computational Linguistics, 1979, pp. 3-7
5. Carbonell, J.G.: Δ-MIN: A Search-Control Method for Information-Gathering Problems. Proceedings of the First AAAI Conference, August 1980
6. Carbonell, J.G. and Hayes, P.J.: Dynamic Strategy Selection in Flexible Parsing. Proceedings of the 19th Annual Meeting of the Association for Computational Linguistics, Stanford University, June 1981, pp. 143-147
7. Carbonell, J.G.: POLITICS: An Experiment in Subjective Understanding and Integrated Reasoning. In: Schank, R.C. and Riesbeck, C.K. (eds.): Inside Computer Understanding: Five Programs Plus Miniatures. New Jersey: Erlbaum, 1981
8. Carbonell, J.G., Boggs, W.M., Mauldin, M.L., and Anick, P.G.: The XCALIBUR Project, A Natural Language Interface to Expert Systems. Proceedings of the Eighth International Joint Conference on Artificial Intelligence, 1983
9. Carbonell, J.G., Boggs, W.M., Mauldin, M.L., and Anick, P.G.: XCALIBUR Progress Report No. 1: First Steps Towards an Integrated Natural Language Interface. Technical Report. Carnegie-Mellon University, Computer Science Department, Karlsruhe, 1983

10. Carbonell, J.G.: Robust Man-Machine Communication, User Modelling and Natural Language Interface Design. In: Andriole, (ed.): Applications in Artificial Intelligence. Petrocelli Books Inc. 1983
11. ACM Publications: Data Base Task Group of CODASYL Programming Language Committee Report, NY, 1971
12. Gershman, A.V.: Knowledge-Based Parsing. Ph. D. Dissertation. Yale University, April 1979, Computer Science Department Report No. 156
13. Haas, N. and Hendrix G.G.: Learning by Being Told: Acquiring Knowledge for Information Management. In: Michalski, R.S., Carbonell, J.G., and Mitchell, T.M. (eds.): Machine Learning, An Artificial Intelligence Approach. Palo Alto: Tioga Press 1983
14. Hayes, P.J., Ball, J.E., and Reddy, R.: Breaking the Man-Machine Communication Barrier. Computer **14** (3), March 1981
15. Hayes, P.J. and Mouradian, G.V.: Flexible Parsing. Proceedings of the 18th Annual Meeting of the Association for Computational Linguistics, Philadelphia, June 1980, pp. 97-103
16. Hayes, P.J. and Reddy, R.: An Anatomy of Graceful Interaction in Man-Machine Communication. Technical Report. Computer Science Department, Carnegie-Mellon University, 1979
17. Hendrix, G.G., Sacerdoti, E.D., and Slocum, J.: Developing a Natural Language Interface to Complex Data. Technical report. Artificial Intelligence Center, SRI International, 1976
18. Hendrix, G.G.: Human Engineering for Applied Natural Language Processing. Proceedings of the Fifth International Joint Conference on Artificial Intelligence, 1977, pp. 183-191
19. Hendrix, G.G.: The LIFER Manual: A Guide to Building Practical Natural Language Interfaces. Technical Report, Technical Note 138. SRI International, 1977
20. Kaplan, S.J.: Cooperative Responses from a Portable Natural Language Data Base Query System. Ph. D. Dissertation. Department of Computer and Information Science, University of Pennsylvania, Philadelphia, 1979
21. Kaplan, S.J.: Interpreting Natural Language Data Base Updates. Submitted for the 19th Annual Meeting of the Association for Computational Linguistics, Stanford University, June 1981
22. Kwasny, S.C. and Sondheimer, N.K.: Ungrammatically and Extra-Grammaticality in Natural Language Understanding Systems. Proceedings of the 17th Annual Meeting of the Association for Computational Linguistics, La Jolla, CA, August 1979, pp. 19-23
23. Marcus, M.P.: A Theory of Syntactic Recognition for Natural Language. Cambridge: MIT Press 1980
24. McDermott, J.: XSEL: A Computer Salesperson's Assistant. In: Hayes, J., Michie, D., and Pao, Y.-H. (eds.): Machine Intelligence 10. Chichester, UK: Ellis Horwood 1982, pp. 325-337
25. Parkison, R.C. Colby, K.M. and Faught, W.S.: Conversational Language Comprehension Using Integrated Pattern-Matching and Parsing. Artificial Intelligence **9**, 111-134 (1977)
26. Riesbeck, C. and Schank, R.C.: Comprehension by Computer: Expectation-Based Analysis of Sentences in Context. Technical Report 78. Computer Science Department, Yale University 1976
27. Sacerdoti, E.D.: Language Access to Distributed Data with Error Recovery. Proceedings of the Fifth International Joint Conference on Artificial Intelligence, 1977, pp. 196-202
28. Waltz, D.L. and Goodman, A.B.: Writing a Natural Language Data Base System. Proceedings of the Fifth International Joint Conference on Artificial Intelligence, 1977, pp. 144-150
29. Weischedel, R.M. and Black, J.: Responding to Potentially Unparseable Sentences. American Journal of Computational Linguistics **6**, 97: 109 (1980)
30. Woods, W.A., Kaplan, R.M., and Nash-Webber, B.: The Lunar Sciences Language System: Final Report. Technical Report 2378. Bolt, Beranek, and Newman, Inc., Cambridge, Mass., 1972

Parsing with Logical Variables

T. W. Finin and M. Stone Palmer

1 Introduction

Logic based programming systems have enjoyed increasing popularity in applied AI work in the last few years. One of the contributions that the logic programming paradigm has made to computational linguistics is the *Definite Clause Grammar* (DCG). An excellent introduction to this formalism can be found in [9] in which the authors present the formalism and make a detailed comparison to Augmented Transition Networks (ATN) as a means of both specifying a language and parsing sentences in that language.

We feel that the major strengths offered by the DCG formalism arise from its use of *logical variables* with *unification* as the fundamental operation on them. These techniques can be abstracted from the theorem proving paradigm and adapted to other parsing systems (see [8] and [2]). We have implemented an experimental ATN system which treats ATN registers as logic variables and provides a unification operation over them.

The DCG formalism provides a powerful parsing mechanism based on a context free grammar. The grammar rule

$$S \rightarrow NP\ VP$$

can be seen as the universally quantified logical statement,

$$\forall x\ \forall y\ \forall z:\ NP(x) \wedge VP(y) \wedge Concatenate(x,y,z) \rightarrow S(z).$$

in which the variables x, y, and z range over strings of words, NP and VP are predicates which are true just in the case their arguments are a string of words representing a noun phrase and verb phrase, respectively, and Concatenate(x,y,z) is true if word strings x and y can be concatenated to form word string z. Prolog, a programming language based on predicate calculus, allows logical statements to be input as Horn clauses in the following (reversed) form:

```
s(Z) :- np(X), vp(Y), concatenate(X,Y,Z).
```

The resolution theorem prover that "interprets" the Prolog clauses would take the negation of s as the goal and try and produce the null clause. Thus the preceding clause can be interpreted procedurally as, "To establish goal s, try and establish subgoals np, vp, and concatenate." DCGs provide syntactic sugar on top of Prolog so that the arrow can be reversed and the concatenate predicate can be dispensed with. The words in the input string are examined sequentially each time a

"[Word]" predicate is executed which implicitly tests for concatenation (see Fig. 1). DCGs allow grammar rules to be expressed very cleanly, while still allowing ATN-type augmentation through the addition of arbitrary tests on the contents of the variables.

Pereira and Warren [9] argue that the DCG formalism is well suited for specifying a formal description of a language and also for use with a parser. In particular, they assert that it is a significant advance over an ATN approach on both philosophical and practical grounds. Their chief claims are that:

1. DCGs provide a common formalism for theoretical work in computational linguistics and for writing efficient natural language processors.
2. The rule-based nature of a DCG results in systems of greater clarity and modularity.
3. DCGs provide greater freedom in the range of structures that can be built in the course of analyzing a constituent. In particular, the DCG formalism makes it easy to create structures that do not follow the structure implied by the rules of a constituent and to create a structure for a constituent that depends on items not yet encountered in the sentence.

The first two points have been discussed in the past whenever the ATN formalism is compared with a rule-based grammar (see [10], [7], [3], or [1]). The outcome of such discussions varies. It is safe to say that how one feels about these points depends quite heavily on stylistic considerations and past experience in using the two formalisms.

We find the third point to be well founded, however. It is clear that the DCG differs most from previous rule based parsing systems in its inclusion of *logical variables*. The use of logical variables results in greater flexibility in building structures to represent constituents that do not follow the inherent structure determined by the rules themselves. It also allows one to create structures which refer to items that have not yet been discovered in the course of analyzing the sentence.

We have built an experimental ATN system which can treat ATN registers as logical variables and, we feel, capture these important strengths offered by the DCG formalism in the otherwise standard ATN formalism.

The next section of this paper gives a more detailed description of DCGs and presents a simple grammar. In the third section we show an ATN grammar which is "equivalent" to the DCG grammar and discuss the source of its awkwardness. The fourth section then presents an ATN formalism extended to include viewing ATN registers as logical variables which are subject to the standard unification operation. The final section draws a parallel between DCGs and *lexical functional grammars* (LFGs) and suggests that logical variables might be fruitfully introduced into other parsing algorithms and systems.

2 Definite Clause Grammars

Figure 1 shows a simple DCG grammar adapted from [9]. Figure 2 gives a sentence in the language recognized by this grammar together with the associated surface syntactic structure and the semantic structure built by the grammar.

```
/* let & be an infix operator signifying ∧ */
:- op(1000,xfy,'&').

s(Sentence) --> np(X, Verbform, Sentence), vp(X, Verbform).

np(X, Verbform, Sentence) --> det(X, Nounpred, Verbform, Sentence),
                              n(X, Noun),
                              relclause(X, Noun, Nounpred).

np(X, Sentence, Sentence) --> name(X).

relclause(X, Noun, (Noun & Relverb)) --> [that], vp(X, Relverb).
relclause(X, Noun, Noun) --> [].

det(X,Nounpred,Verbform,forAll(X,(Nounpred -> Verbform))) --> [every].
det(X,Nounpred,Verbform,forSome(X, (Nounpred & Verbform))) --> [a].

vp(X, Verbform) --> transv(X, Y, Partverb), np(Y, Partverb, Verbform).

vp(X, Verbform) --> intransv(X, Verbform).

n(X, man(X)) --> [man].
n(X, woman(X)) --> [woman].
n(X, dog(X)) --> [dog].

name(john) --> [john].
name(mary) --> [mary].
name(fido) --> [fido].

transv(X, Y, loves(X,Y)) --> [loves].
transv(X, Y, breathes(X,Y)) --> [breathes].

intransv(X, loves(X)) --> [loves].
intransv(X, lives( X)) --> [lives].
intransv(X, breathes(X)) --> [breathes].
```

Fig. 1. A simple definite clause grammar

Sentence

```
"john loves every woman who breathes"
```

Syntactic Structure

```
(S (NP (NAME john))
   (VP (TRANSV loves)
       (NP (DET every)
           (NOUN woman)
           (REL (VP (INTRANSV breathes))))))
```

Semantic Representation

```
forAll($X_1$, (woman($X_1$) & breathes($X_1$)) → loves(john,$X_1$))
```

Fig. 2. A sentence, structure, and representation

2.1 The DCG Notation

For readers who may be unfamiliar with this notation for DCGs, we will briefly summarize it here. Each rule in a DCG is of the form:

nt→body.

where *nt* is a non-terminal symbol and *body* is a sequence of one or more terms separated by commas. This specifies a rule in a context free grammar in which the left hand side corresponds to *nt* and the right hand side corresponds to *body*. Note the following important extensions to the standard notation for context free grammars:

- Terminal symbols (i.e., words) in the right hand side of a rule must be enclosed in square brackets, as in the following rule:

  s→[please], vp.

- Non-terminals can be compound terms rather than simple atomic symbols and can include variables. The variables are treated as logical variables (i.e., they may only take on a single value) with a scope equal to the rule in which they appear. We will follow the standard Edinburgh Prolog convention and consider any symbol beginning with a capital letter to be a variable. For example:

  s(s(Np. VP))→nounPhrase (Np), verbPhrase (Vp).

- Procedural tests may be included in the right hand side of a rule by enclosing them in braces. These tests are executed when the terms to their left have been satisfied and cause the rule to fail if they do not succeed. For example, the following rule

  noun(W)→[W]. {rootform(W,Root), category (Root, noun)}.

  might be used to recognize a word as a noun given a data base consisting of the *rootform* relation which links words to their root forms (e.g., rootform(dogs, dog)) and the *category* relation which links root forms to their syntactic categories (e.g., category (dog, noun)).

2.2 Interpreting DCG Rules as Definite Clauses

In order to use a DCG rule it is first transformed into a definite clause. In the previous section we briefly outlined how the *concatenate* predicate could be used to ensure that the constituents on the right hand side of a rule span contiguous portions of the input. A somewhat more efficient technique is to augment the predicates for non-terminals with additional arguments which enforce the contiguity constraint. Non-terminals corresponding to predicates of arity n and are translated into predicates of arity $n+2$. The two extra arguments are appended to the end of the argument list and represent the words in the input *just before* and *just after* the constituent corresponding to the non-terminal. For example, the following two rules:

s(s(Np, Vp))→nounPhrase(Np), verbPhrase(Vp).
noun (Word)→[Word], {rootform(Word, Root), category (Root, noun)}.

become these two definite clauses:

s(s(Np, Vp), X_0, X_1):- nounPhrase (Np, X_0, X_2). verbPhrase (Vp, X_2, X_1).
noun (Word, [Word|X_0], X_0):- rootform (Word, Root), category (Root, noun).

where X_0, X_1, and X_2 are the system generated names of variables.

In order to find a parse corresponding to a DCG non-terminal *nt* of arity *n* it is merely necessary to satisfy the new goal *nt'* formed by appending two extra arguments to *nt:* the list of words to be parsed and the empty list. For example, to find a sentence corresponding to the non-terminal *s(X)* given the words *"the dog chased the cat"* we attempt to prove the goal *S(X, [the, dog, chased, the, cat], []).* If we use a conventional Prolog interpreter to satisfy the top level goal, then the grammar rules will be applied in a top-down, left to right manner. Alternatives will be explored via backtracking.

2.3 An Example in More Detail

Let us turn our attention to how the grammar in Figure 1 discovers a parse for the example sentence in Figure 2. The way in which unification produces the appropriate bindings for this example is actually quite subtle, and requires a detailed analysis. In this grammar, the first determiner encountered in the sentence selects a quantification form for the entire sentence. In the example sentence *"John loves every woman who breathes"* the determiner *every* selects

forAll (X, Nounpred→Verbform)

for the overall sentence form. Had the example been *"John loves a woman who breathes",* the determiner *a* would choose

forSome (X, Nounpred & Verbform)

for the overall sentence form.

Parsing the rest of the sentence will produce predicate representations that will be slotted into the appropriate places in the sentence pattern. The sentence, *"Every woman breathes,"* would produce *"women (X_1)"* for the variable *Nounpred* and *"breathes (X_1)"* for the variable *Verbform,* resulting in a sentence representation of

forall (X_1, woman (X_1)→ breathes (X_1)).

This is explained in more detail below, using the example, "John loves every woman who breathes." This discussion is illustrated by the diagram in Figure 3. In trying to prove the *s(Senctence)* goal, the only applicable rule is:

s (Sentence)→np(X, Verbform, Sentence), vp (X, Verbform).

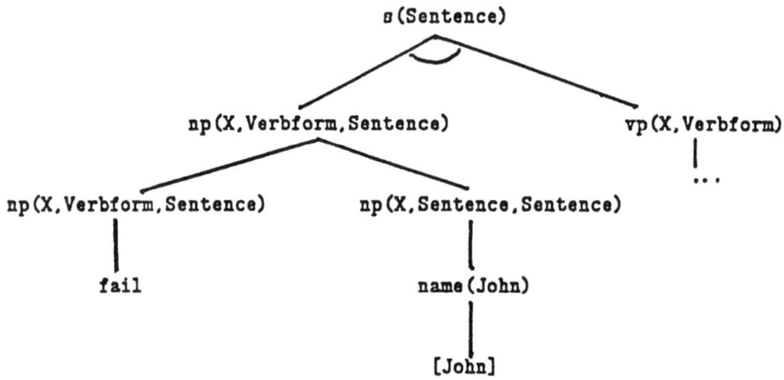

Fig. 3. Finding the subject noun phrase

This rule causes *np(X, Verbform, Sentence)* to be set up as the first subgoal. There are two *np* clauses that match this subgoal:

np(X, Verbform, Sentence)→ det(X, Nounpred, Verbform, Sentence).
n(X, Noun),
relclause (X, Noun, Nounpred).
np(X, Sentence)→ name (X).

the first of which eventually fails since "John" is not preceded by a determiner. The second one succeeds, binding *X* to *John,* and identifying the original *Verbform* variable with the original *Sentence* variable. The assumption is that the logical form produced for the verb will be the logical form for the entire sentence.

The second major subgoal in attempting to instantiate a sentence is *vp(X, Verbform),* where *X* is now bound to *John.* Once again there are two possible clauses:

vp(X, Verbform)→transv(X, Y, Partverb), np(Y, Partverb, Verbform).
vp(X, Verbform)→intransv(X, Verbform).

only one of which will succeed, as Figure 4 shows.

Two new subgoals are set up, *transv(John, Y, Partverb)* and *np(Y, Partverb, Verbform).* The first one succeeds since "loves" is a transitive verb, and results in Partverb being bound to **loves(John, Y),** where *Y* is still unbound. The binding for *Y* is expected to be produced by the successful evaluation of the next subgoal, *np(Y, Partverb, Verbform).* Figure 4 shows the status of the parse at this point.

The variable *Partverb* is also passed as a parameter, so that it can be included in the *Verbform* structure. This time the first *np* clause is applicable, and the presence of the determiner "every" results in the *Verbform* variable, now renamed as *Sentence,* being bound to **forAll(Y, Nounpred→loves (John, Y)).** This is the complete *Verbform* structure, which for this sentence is also the *Sentence* structure (Figure 5). It does, however, still have some unbound variables, namely *Y* and *Nounpred,* which will be filled in as the rest of the noun phrase is processed. The binding for Nounpred will be supplied during the evaluation of the other two subgoals

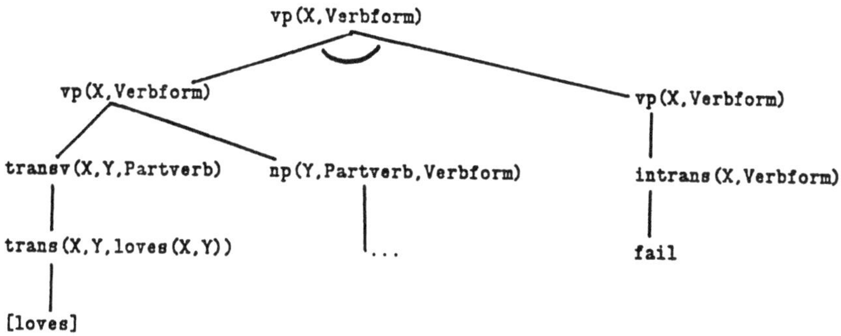

Fig. 4. Finding the verb phrase

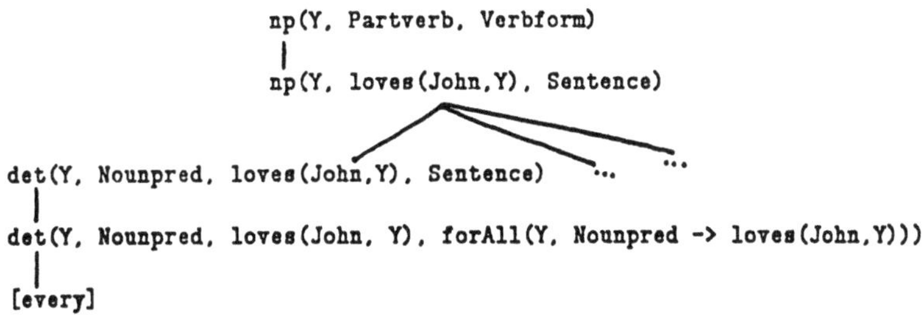

Fig. 5. Determining the sentence form

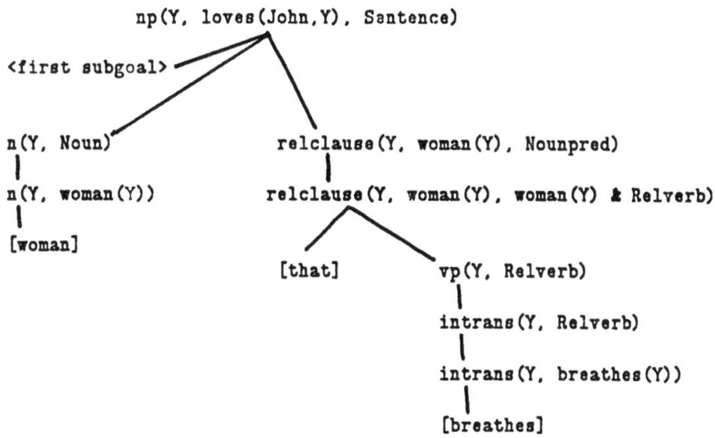

Fig. 6. Finding the relative clause

associated with *np, noun* and *relclause*. The evaluation of the noun goal produces **women(Y)** which is passed to *relclause* as something to be included in *Nounpred*. The final binding for *Nounpred* is **woman(Y) & breathes(Y)** (Figure 6). The variable Y stays unbound, since it is universally quantified.

The result of this processing is that the *relclause* goal is satisfied, with Nounpred bound to:

woman (Y) & breathes (Y)

which caused the *np* goal be completed with *Sentence* bound to:

forAll (Y, woman (Y) & breaths (Y)→loves (John, Y))

which satisfies the *vp* goal with *Verbform* bound to:

forAll (Y, woman (Y) & breaths (Y)→loves (John, Y))

and yields a satisfied s goal with the ultimate binding for *Sentence* of:

forAll (Y, woman (Y) & breaths (Y)→loves (John, Y))

In following the application of this grammar it becomes clear that very strong predictions are made about which parts of the parse will be supplying particular types of information. Determiners provide the quantifiers for the propositional structure of the sentence. The first noun phrase and the noun phrase following the verb are the two participants in the predicate implied by the verb. Obviously the rules given here are part of a toy grammar, but the power of the logical variables can only be made use of through the encoding of these strong linguistic assumptions. DCGs provide a mechanism well qualified for expressing such assumptions and then executing them. The same type of assumptions can be found in LFGs as discussed in the conclusion.

3 Comparing DC and ATN Grammars

Figure 7 shows an ATN grammar which is the "equivalent" of the DCG grammar given in Figure 1. The format used to specify the grammar is the one described in [4] and [5]. There are only two minor ways in which this particular formalism differs from the standard ATN formalism described in [11] or [1]. First, the dollar sign character (i. e., $) followed by the name of a register stands for the contents of that register. Second, the function DEFATN defines a set of arcs, each of which is represented by a list whose first element is the name of the state and whose remaining elements are the arcs emanating from the state.

In addition, this example uses a very simple lexical manager in which a word has (1) a set of syntactic categories to which is belongs (2) an optional set of features, and (3) an optional root form for the word. These attributes are associated with a word using the function LEX, which supplies appropriate default values for unspecified arguments. Thus the expression

(LEX dogs n (animate (number plural)) dog)

could be used to indicate that the word dogs belongs to the syntactic category *n* (for noun), has the two features *animate* and *number plural,* and has the word *dog* as its root word.

One immediate difference between the DCG and ATN formalism has to do with communication between different levels of processing. In the DCG formalism, the application of each rule involves a different level of processing. The arguments to the predicates representing a non-terminal serve as communication channels between the levels. As is standard in logic programming languages, each of these variables can be used either for input or output or both.

The standard ATN model adopts a more functional approach. A PUSH arc invokes a sub-computation which takes no arguments and, if successful, returns a single value. One can achieve the effect of passing parameters to a sub-computation by giving a register an initial value via a SENDR action. There are two methods by which one can achieve the effect of returning more than one value from a sub-computation. The first is for the sub-computation to POP with a value which is a list of the items to be passed back to the higher level. Actions on the invoking PUSH arc would then be responsible for decomposing the list into its constituent items. The second method is to use the LIFTR action to directly set registers in the higher level computation. The grammar in Figure 7 makes use of SENDR and LIFTR to pass parameters into and out of ATN computations and thus mimic the actions of the DCG example.

Consider what must happen when looking for a noun phrase. The representation for an NP will be a *predicate* if the noun phrase is indefinite (i.e., "a man" becomes (man X))[1] or a *constant* if the noun phrase is a name (i.e., "John" becomes John). In this simple language, a NP is dominated by a either a sentence (if it is the subject) or by a verb phrase (if it is the object). In either case, the NP determines, or must agree with, the overall structure used to represent the dominating constituent. If the NP is definite[2], then it exerts no additional constraint on the representation of its dominator. If the NP is indefinite it will eventually result in a quantified expression for the dominating sentence or verb phrase. In this case we need to tell the dominating computation what the *predicate, quantifier, connective,* and *variable* name must be. In this ATN grammar, this is done by having the NP network **return** a value to represent the NP predicate and **lift** values for the *quantifier, connective,* and *variable names.*

Similarly, when we are looking for a verb phrase, we must know what token (i.e., variable name or constant) represents the subject (if the verb phrase is dominated by an S) or the head noun (if the verb phrase acts as a relative clause). This is done by sending the **subjvar** register in the sub-computation the appropriate value via the SENDR function. The techniques used to handle quantification and build an overall sentence structure in this ATN grammar are similar to those used in the BBN Lunar Grammar [12].

This heavy use of SENDR and LIFTR to communicate between levels in the grammar violates many accepted programming maxims and results in an ATN

---

[1] Note that we are switching to a lispy syntax for representing the meanings.

[2] Which in this toy grammar reduces to it being a name.

```
(defatn

 (s (push np t (setr subj *) (to s/subj)))

 (s/subj (push vp t (setr vp *) (sendr subjvar $var) (to s/end)))

 (s/end (pop (list $quant $var (list $connect $subj $vp)) $subj)
        (pop $vp (null $subj)))

 (np (wrd a t (liftr quant 'ForSome) (liftr connect 'And)(to np/det))
     (wrd every t (liftr quant 'ForAll)  (liftr connect '→) (to np/det))
     (cat name t (setr var *) (to np/np)))

 (np/det (cat n t (setr var (gensym)) (setr n (list * $var)) (to np/n)))

 (np/n (wrd (who that which) t (to np/n/who))
       (jump np/np t))

 (np/np (pop $n t (liftr var)))

 (np/n/who
  (push vp t (sendr subjvar $var) (setr n (list 'And $n *)) (to np/np)))

 (vp (cat v t (setr v *) (to vp/v)))

 (vp/v (push np (getf trans $v) (setr obj *) (setr objvar $var) (to vp/vp))
       (pop '(list $v $subjvar) (getf intrans $v)))

 (vp/vp (pop (list $quant $objvar (list $connect
                                         $obj
                                         (list $v $subjvar $objvar)))
              $obj)
        (pop (list $v $subjvar $objvar) (null $obj))))

; The Lexicon
; (lex <word> <category> <features> <rootform>)

(lex man n)
(lex woman n)
(lex loves v (intrans trans))
(lex breathes v (intrans trans))
(lex lives v (intrans))
(lex John name)
  ... etc ...
```

Fig. 7. An equivalent ATN grammar

grammar which is cumbersome and difficult to understand. In the next section we investigate treating ATN registers as logic variables and providing a unification operation on them.

4 Replacing ATN Registers with ATN Variables

Although the previous ATN grammar does the job, it is clearly awkward. We can achieve much of the elegance of the DCG example by treating the ATN registers as **logical variables** and including a unification operation on them. We will call such registers *ATN variables.*

Since our ATN variables must not be tampered with between unifications, assignment operations such as SETR, LIFTR, and SENDR are precluded. Thus the only operations on ATN Registers are **access** and **unify.** It is possible to provide operations similar to the standard SENDR and LIFTR by defining unification operations which do the unification in another environment, but we have not explored these possibilities.

The scheduler component of the ATN parser has been modified to be sensitive to the success or failure of attempted unifications. If a unification operation on an arc fails, the are is blocked and may not be taken.

Figure 8 shows a grammar in the extended ATN formalism. A symbol preceded by a "$" represents an ATN Variable and "*" will again stand for the current constituent. Thus in the state S in the grammar:

(S (PUSH NP (UNIFY '($SUBJVAR $VP $S) *) (TO S/SUBJ)))

the parser pushes to the state NP to parse a noun phrase. If one is found, it will pop back with a value which will then be unified with the expression ($SUBJVAR $VP $S). If this unification is successful, the parser will advance to state S/SUBJ. If it fails, the arc is blocked causing the parser to backtrack into the NP network. Figure 9 shows the results of applying this ATN grammar to a number of simple sentences.

Although our grammar succeeds in paralleling the behavior of the DCG, there are some open questions involving the use of unification in parsing natural languages. An examination of this ATN grammar shows that we are really using unification as a method of passing parameters. The full power of unification is not needed in this example since the grammar does not try to find "most-general unifiers" for complicated sets of terms. Most of the time it is simply using unification to bind a variable to the contents of another variable. The most sophisticated use involves binding a variable in a term to another copy of that term which also has a variable to be bound as in the "a man loves a woman" example in Figure 9. But even this binding is a simple one-way application of standard unification. It is not clear whether this is due to the simple nature of the grammars involved or whether it is an inherent property of the directedness of natural language parsing.

A situation where full unification might be rquired would arise when one is looking for a constituent matching some partial description. For example, suppose we were working with a syntactic grammar and wanted to look for a singular noun phrase. We might do this with the following PUSH arc:

```
(defatn

 (s (push np (unify '($subjvar $vp $s) *) (to s/subj)))

 (s/subj (push vp t (unify '$vp *) (to s/s)))

 (s/s (pop $s t))

 (np (wrd a t (unify '$np '(ForSome $var (And $pred $hole))) (to np/det))
     (wrd every t (unify '$np '(ForAll $var (→ $pred $hole))) (to np/det))
     (cat name t (unify '$np '$hole) (unify '$var *) (to np/np)))

 (np/det (cat n t (unify '$var (gensym)) (unify '$pred '(* $var)) (to np/n)))

 (np/n (wrd (who that which) t (to np/n/who))
       (jump np/np t))

 (np/np (pop (list $var '$hole $np) t ))

 (np/n/who
  (push vp t (unify '$subjvar '$var) (unify '$pred '(And $pred *)) (to np/np)))

 (vp (cat v (getf trans *) (unify '$v '(* $subjvar $objvar)) (to vp/vtrans))
     (cat v (getf intrans *) (unify '$v '(* $subjvar)) (to vp/vp)))

 (vp/vtrans (push np t (unify '($objvar $v $vp) *) (to vp/vp)))

 (vp/vp (pop $vp t))
```

Fig. 8. An equivalent ATN grammar with ATN variables

```
(PUSH NP T (UNIFY * '(NP (DET $DET) (NUMBER SINGULAR) (ADJ
$ADJS) . . .))
. . .)
```

If we follow the usual schedule of interpreting ATN grammars the unification will not occur until the NP network has found a noun phrase and popped back with a value. This would require a fully symmetric unification operation since there are variables being bound to values in both arguments. It is also highly inefficient since we may know immediately that the noun phrase in the input is not singular. What we would like is to be able to do the unification just after the push is done, which would more closely parallel a Prolog-based DCG parse. Then an attempt to "unify" the number register with anything other than singular would fail immediately.

This could be done automatically if we constrain a network to have only one state which does a pop and place some additional constraints on the forms that can be used as values to be popped. Although we have not explored this idea at any length, it appears to lead to some interesting possibilities.

```
"John loves every woman who breathes"

    (ForAll X1 (→ (And (woman X1) (breathes X1)) (loves John X1)))


"John loves a woman"

    (ForSome X1 (And (woman X1) (loves John X1)))


"a man loves a woman"

    (ForSome X1
            (And (man X1)
                 (ForSome X2 (And (woman X2) (loves X1 X2)))))


"every man who lives loves"

    (ForAll X1 (→ (And (man X1) (lives X1)) (loves X1)))


"every man who loves mary loves a woman who loves John"

    (ForAll X1
            (→ (And (man X1) (loves X1 mary))
               (ForSome X2 (And (And (woman X2) (loves X2 John))
                                     (loves X1 X2)))))


"every man who loves a woman who loves every dog loves every dog"

    (ForAll X1
      (→ (And (man X1)
              (ForSome X2
                (And (And (woman X2)
                          (ForAll X3 (→ (dog X3) (loves X2 X3))))
                     (loves X1 X2))))
         (ForAll X4 (→ (dog X4) (loves X1 X4)))))
```

Fig. 9. Example parses with the ATN grammar

5 Conclusions

The particular DCG example we have used in this paper illustrates the similarity between the use of logical variables in DCGs and the evaluation of equations in *lexical functional grammars* (LFGs). The passing of logical variables in the DCG from the *det* clause to the *np* clause to the *vp* clause corresponds to equating the variables from different parts of the syntactic structure being built by an LFG. LFGs also produce functional representations of the sentence at the same time as a syntactic parse is being built, another important similarity. However, they do not build the quanification into the functional structure in the way illustrated by the DCG example. This is done later by the semantic component. Also, in the current implementation of LFG, the functional structure is actually built after the syntactic parsing is completed, but a new implementation designed to build the structures in parallel is in progress.

The DCG example is really a toy example based on Montague grammars. DCGs are a powerful tool for encoding grammar rules that support a particular theory. DCGs do not represent a linguistic theory in themselves, whereas LFGs do. The purpose of this comparison is to simplify the explanation of equating variables in LFGs, and to indicate the suitability of DCGs for implementing this type of approach.

LFGs have two components: 1) grammar rules with associated equations for building up a functional description of the sentence and 2) the lexical rules. The lexical rules consist of rules for the individual lexical entries of words as well as redundancy rules that take advantage of cross-word generalizations such as active-passive forms of verbs. The grammar rules are context free rules that generate several possible syntactic structures, many of which are not grammatical. The resolution of the equations associated with the grammar rules is intended to eventually exclude the ungrammatical structures. The equations contain variables that must be filled in by information supplied by the lexical entries. There are arrows associated with the equations as well as with the lexical entries to guide the instantiation of the variables. The LFG grammar rule in Figure 10 is the standard one for doubly transitive verbs:

GRAMMAR RULE:

```
VP --> Verb (        NP              (        NP       ))
        ↑ ↓  ((↑ Object1)=↓        ((↑ Object2)=↓))
```

LEXICAL ENTRY:

```
handed VERB (↑ Tense) = Past
  (↑ Predicate) = 'Hand<(↑ Subject),(↑ Object1),(↑ Object2)>
```

Fig. 10. An LFG rule

VP→Verb NP NP

and the equation associated with it indicates which components the NPs will instantiate in the function structure, namely the $Object_1$ and $Object_2$.

The arrow notation has a somewhat involved explanation. LFGs first generate a tree from the context free grammar rules, filling in the leaf nodes with the appropriate lexical items. Every node on the tree is then assigned a variable. The arrows give directions for the instantiation of the variables. Sometimes instantiations are passed upwards in the tree, and sometimes downwards. Tense, for instance is passed up to the parent of VERB node. Not surprisingly, $Object_1$ will eventually get instantiated with the value of the NP corresponding to the direct object of the sentence, and $Object_2$ will eventually be given the value of the indirect object. $Object_1$ and $Object_2$ are the arguments to the verb predicate, and in the final functional description, the verb predicate itself will be assigned a unique identifier, say *f3*, and the $Object_1$ of that predicate will be assigned another unique identifier, *f4*. The use of an equation such as $(\uparrow Object_1) = \downarrow$ can now be demonstrated, since $(f3\ Object_1) = f4$ represents just that information, namely, that the $Object_1$ of *f3* is *f4*. The upward arrow indicated that *f3* was the node immediately above in the tree, and the downward arrow indicated that *f4* is associated with the node the equation is associated with.

The point to be made here is simply that the logical variables in DCGs can be used to accomplish the same end as the arrow notation. The example of a DCG parse showed how logical variables could be passed values from other parts of the parse. The DCG also used context free grammar rules to parse a clause while building up a functional structure at the same time. The main difference is that unification offers an advantage in providing a capability for instantiating variables while in the middle of the parse, instead of waiting until the parse is finished to "resolve the equations." The arrows in the original equation, $(\uparrow Object_1) = \downarrow$, can be replaced by logical variables such as *F3* and *F4*. These variables would have to be explicitly bound to the variables assigned to the nodes in the tree. Then, when the node variables are assigned unique identifiers, those same identifiers would automatically instantiate the variables in the equations. An extra pass to "resolve" the equations would no longer be necessary.

We have found the use of logical variables and unification to be a powerful technique in parsing natural language. It is one of the main sources of the strengths of the Definite Clause Grammar formalism. In attempting to capture this technique for an ATN grammar we have come to several interesting conclusions. First, the strength of the DCG comes as much from the skillful encoding of linguistic assumptions about the eventual outcome of the parse as from the powerful tools it relies on. Second, the notion of logical variables (with unification) can be adapted to parsing systems outside of the theorem proving paradigm. We have successfully adapted these techniques to an ATN type parser and are beginning to embed them in an existing parallel bottom-up parser [6]. The similarities between a DCG and the LFG formalism have been sketched out and we have sugested that DCGs might be a good vehicle for implementing an LFG system. Third, the full power of unification may not be necessary to successfully use logical variables in natural language parsers.

References

1. Bates, M.: Theory and Practice of Augmented Transition Network Grammars. In: Bolc, L. (ed.): Natural Language Communication with Computers. Berlin-Heidelberg-New York: Springer 1978
2. Bossie, S.: A Tactical Component for Text Generation: Sentence Generation Using a Functional Grammar. Technical report MS-CIS-1982-26. Computer and Information Science, University of Pennsylvania, 1982
3. Codd, E.F., Arnold, R.S., Cadiou, J-M., Chang, C.L., and Roussopoulos, N.: RENDEZVOUS Version 1: An Experimental English-Language Query Formulation System for Casual Users of Relational Data Bases. Report RJ2144. IBM Research Laboratory, San Jose, January, 1978
4. Finin, T.: An Interpreter and Compiler for Augmented Transition Networks. Technical report T-48. Coordinated Science Laboratory, University of Illinois, 1977
5. Finin, T.: Parsing with ATN Grammars. In: Bolc, L. (ed.): Data Base Question Answering Systems. Berlin-Heidelberg-New York: Springer 1982
6. Finin, T. and Webber, B.: BUP - A Bottom Up Parser. Technical Report MS-CS-83-12. Department of Computer and Information Science, University of Pennsylvania, 1983
7. Heidorn, G.: Augmented Phrase Structure Grammar. TINLAP-1, Theoretical Issues in Natural Language Processing, August, 1975
8. Kay, M.: Functional Grammar. Proceedings of the Fifth Annual Meeting of the Berkeley Linguistic Society, Berkeley Linguistic Society, Berkeley, CA, 1979
9. Pereira, F. and Warren, D.: Definite Clause Grammars for Language Analysis - A Survey of the Formalism and a Comparison with Augmented Transition Networks. Artificial Intelligence 13, 231-289 (1980)
10. Pratt, V.: LINGOL, A Progress Report. Proceedings of the 4th International Joint Conference on Artificial Intelligence, IJCAI, 4 (1975)
11. Woods, W.: Transition Network Grammars for Natural Language Analysis. Communications of the ACM 13 (10), 591-606 (1970)
12. Woods, W.A., Kaplan, R.M., and Webber, B.L.: The Lunar Sciences Natural Language Information System: Final Report. Report 2378. Bolt, Beranek, and Newman, Inc., Cambridge, Mass., 1972

Knowledge-Based Parsing

J. G. Neal and S. C. Shapiro

Abstract. An extremely significant feature of any natural language (NL) is that it is its own metalanguage. One can use an NL to talk about the NL itself. One can use an NL to tutor a non-native speaker, or other poor language user, in the use of the same NL. We have been exploring methods of knowledge representation and NL understanding (NLU) which would allow an artificial intelligence (AI) system to play the role of poor language user in this setting. The AI system would have to understand NL utterances about how the NL is used, and improve its NLU abilities according to this instruction. It would be an NLU system for which the domain being discussed in NL is the NL itself.

Our NLU system is implemented in the form of a general rule-based inference system which reasons according to the rules of its knowledge base. These rules comprise the system's knowledge of language understanding in the same way that the rules of any rule-based system comprise that system's knowledge of its domain of application. Our system uses the same knowledge base for both linguistic and other knowledge since we feel that there is no clear boundary line separating syntactic, semantic, and world knowledge.

We are exploring the possibility of an NLU system's becoming more facile in its use of some language by being told how that language is used. We wish this explanation to be given in an increasingly sophisticated subset of the language being taught. Clearly, the system must start with some language facility, but we are interested in seeing how small and theory-independent we can make the initial, "kernel" language. This article reports the current state of our work.

1 Introduction

1.1 Overview

An extremely significant feature of any natural language (NL) is that it is its own metalanguage. One can use an NL to talk about the NL itself. One can use an NL to tutor a non-native speaker, or other poor language user, in the use of the same NL. We have been exploring methods of knowledge representation (KR) and NL understanding (NLU) which would allow an artificial intelligence (AI) system to play the role of poor language user in this setting. The AI system would have to understand NL utterances about how the NL is used, and improve its NLU abilities according to this instruction. It would be an NLU system for which the domain being discussed in NL is the NL itself.

It is essential to our approach to have the system's parsing and linguistic knowledge be an integral part of its domain knowledge. Acknowledging that what is meant by "meaning" is controversial (Quine, 1948), we take the meaning or significance of a word or phrase to include linguistic knowledge about the word or phrase. For example, we feel that how a word like "dog" is used in language is a part of its "meaning", along with other properties such as the fact that "dog" denotes a special kind of animal with typical characteristics. The implementation of our system is based upon the above stated view and therefore the rules and assertions comprising the system's knowledge of language understanding, including syntax, is integrated into the system's knowledge base along with its other task domain knowledge.

We are exploring the possibility of an NLU system's becoming more facile in its use of some language by being taught how that language is used. The teacher might be a conversation partner who happens to use some phrase the system is not yet familiar with, or a language theorist who wants to find out if she can explain her theory completely and clearly enough for the system to use language according to it. We wish this explanation to be given in an increasingly sophisticated subset of the language being taught. That is, why not test and make use of the system's language capability by using it to continue the system's "education"? Clearly, the system must start with some language facility, but we are interested in seeing how small and theory-independent we can make the initial, "kernel" language.

In this chapter, we will discuss our knowledge representation techniques, the system's kernel language (KL), and parsing strategy. We will demonstrate how our system can be instructed in the use of some language defined by the teacher and how the system's acquired language can itself be used as its own metalanguage. The kernel language only incorporates primitive relations such as one token being a predecessor of another in a string, membership in a lexical or string category, and constituency. As an example of using the system's language as its own metalanguage to enhance its language capability, we will demonstrate, starting with only the KL, how the system can be instructed with regard to the number (i. e., singular or plural) of some words and then be informed that "If the head-noun of a noun-phrase X has number Y, then X has number Y". This newly acquired knowledge can then be applied by the system to infer that since "glasses" is plural, so is "the old man's glasses" when it reads this phrase in a sentence such as "The old man's glasses were filled with water".

Our system is able to understand when strings are *mentioned* in input utterances as well as when they are *used* to communicate with the system. This capability is demonstrated frequently in this chapter, but particularly in Sect. 4 with the classic sentence from Tarski (1944): "'Snow is white' is true if and only if snow is white".

The use of inference and world knowledge is essential for a system to parse sentences such as "John saw the bird without binoculars" and "John saw the bird without tailfeathers" from Schubert and Pelletier (1982) or "John saw the man on the hill with a telescope". Our research is based upon the concept of having parsing performed by a general reasoning system which has the capability of applying world knowledge inferences during parsing, since the "parser" is not a separate isolated component with special sublanguage, representations, or knowledge base.

1.2 Fundamental Assumptions

Our system incorporates the *use-mention distinction* (Quine, 1951) for language. Our representations reflect the fact that the meaning of a token or surface string is distinct from the token or string itself. Our system's knowledge base maintains a representation for a token or surface string that is distinct from the representation of the interpretation of the input token or string. This distinction is the same as between a numeral and a number in mathematics. To refer to a word or string rather than its meaning, the user must use the usual English convention of prefacing the word by a single-quote mark or enclosing the string in quotation marks. (See Sections 2.2.1 and 2.4.2 for more information.)

A second principle upon which our work is based is that each occurrence of a given surface string in the input stream is assumed to have a different interpretation, unless the teacher has entered rules into the system to dictate otherwise. For example, if a name such as "John" has been entered into the lexicon and is used twice, either in successive utterances or within the same utterance, then the system interprets each occurrence of the name as referring to a different entity unless the teacher has instructed the system otherwise. Since an NLU system must be capable of handling ambiguities, and, in a situation in which no explicit rules are known to the system to guide it in determining whether a word or phrase is ambiguous, it must have a default procedure to follow, we have chosen to implement the above principle. Although our approach would seem to overly complicate the network, it is a reasonable default principle since there is some evidence that merging of nodes is easier than splitting nodes (Maida and Shapiro, 1982).

A third principle which is fundamental to our theory is that all possible parses and interpretations of a surface string are to be determined according to the language definition used by the system. We feel that multiple interpretations, when justified by the language definition, are warrented since agile human minds frequently perceive alternative interpretations and, in fact, a great deal of humor is dependent upon this.

Our system does not currently do morphological analysis. One of the areas in which we plan to do future research is knowledge-based morphological analysis. We plan to develop a system component that would perform morphological analysis and function as a preprocessor or coprocessor with the system discussed in this article.

1.3 Declarative Knowledge Representation in an Integrated Knowledge Base

Our approach is to represent knowledge in declarative form, to the greatest extent possible, in the semantic network formalism. This applies to all knowledge including linguistic knowledge and the rules which are applied by the inference machine to guide the system's reasoning, the parsing process being one manifestation of the system's reasoning according to the rules of its network knowledge base. It is our intent that the system's knowledge, including its linguistic knowledge, be available to the teacher in the same way that domain knowledge is in other AI systems.

Furthermore, the declarative form is a more suitable form for linguistic knowledge in theoretical studies of language. A language definition or description is inherently declarative, and as Pereira and Warren have pointed out: "The theorists have concentrated on describing *what* natural language is, in a clear and elegant way. In this context, details of *how* natural language is actually recognized or generated need not be relevant, and indeed should probably not be allowed to obscure the language definition" (1980, p. 269, italics in the original). In this regard, a declarative representation is preferable to a formalism such as an ATN, in that the ATN is a description of a *process* for recognizing a language.

Our system uses an integrated knowledge base for both linguistic and other knowledge as advocated by Pollack and Waltz (1982) and by Dahl (1981). As indicated in Section 1.1, we take the meaning of a word or phrase to include linguistic knowledge about the word or phrase and its use. Furthermore, we feel that there is no clear boundary line separating syntactic, semantic, and world knowledge. For example, it is not clear to what extent the classification of words into lexical categories depends on meaning, function, or form. Should certain words be classified as mass nouns because they fit certain distributional frames or have a certain form (e.g., I used {sand, the sand, a bag of sand, *a sand, *two sands.}) or are the frames and forms simply a reflection of the property we think of as characterizing the substances named by mass nouns, namely that the substance is not naturally physically bounded and that when two amounts of the substance are "put together" they become one amount? Perhaps certain aspects of syntax cannot or should not be separated from semantics. Furthermore, the terms "semantic knowledge" and "world knowledge" seem only to be used to informally express a measure of the sophistication or complexity of knowledge.

1.4 System Overview

Our Natural Language System is being developed and implemented using the SNePS semantic network processing system (Shapiro, 1979a; Shapiro and the SNePS Group, 1981). The terminology and representations for some of the basic categories, objects, and relations of this work evolved from a preliminary study reported in Shapiro and Neal (1982). Figure 1 illustrates an overview of the system.

The semantic network formalism has been used by many researchers for knowledge representation (Quillian, 1968, 1969; Rumelhart and Norman, 1973; Simmons, 1973; Woods, 1975; P. Hayes 1977; Schubert, 1976; Hendrix, 1978, 1979; Schubert et al., 1979; Brachman, 1979). In contrast to other semantic network implementations, the SNePS system provides a uniform declarative representation for both rules and assertions in the network (Shapiro, 1971, 1979b). Furthermore, our system comprises an effort to utilize a common representation for problem-solving and language-comprehension information as advocated by Charniak

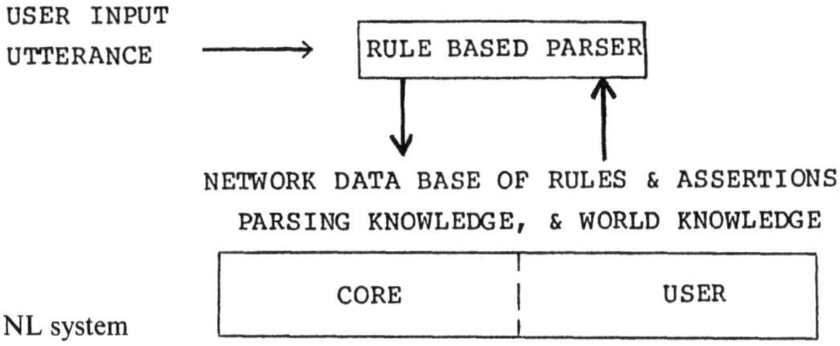

Fig. 1. Overview of the NL system

(1981). Our system is similar to the Prolog-based (Roussel, 1975) systems of Warren and Pereira (1982), Dahl (1979, 1981), and McCord (1982) in that it is implemented in a logic-based system in which processing is a form of inference. The SNePS inference package (Shapiro et al., 1982), however, is not based on the resolution principle (Robinson, 1965) as is Prolog, but on a multi-processing approach (Kaplan, 1973; McKay and Shapiro, 1980) incorporating a producer-consumer model. SNePS also provides a facility for "procedural attachment" in rules to handle processing knowledge for which the declarative network representation is unnatural.

The PSI-KLONE system (Bobrow and Webber, 1980) uses linguistic knowledge represented in a KL-ONE network (Brachman, 1978a, 1978b, 1979) to function as semantic interpreter for parsed surface strings. The PSI-KLONE interpreter, however, functions in cooperation with an ATN parser in the RUS framework (Bobrow, 1978). In contrast, we are implementing an integrated system for syntactic and semantic processing which uses a uniform representation for syntactic and semantic knowledge.

The rule-based parser of Figure 1 is essentially the SNePS inference package which reasons according to the rules of the knowledge base.

The knowledge base consists of CORE knowledge and USER knowledge. The CORE knowledge is provided by the designers of the system and defines a kernel language initially acceptable to the system. USER knowledge results from the processing of user input utterances.

The function of our NL parser is twofold:

1. derivation of zero or more annotated parse trees for the input surface string;
2. construction of a network representation for the interpretation of the input utterance from the annotated parse tree and from other relevant knowledge from the network data base.

The above two functions are not handled by separate processors, but, instead, are both accomplished by the SNePS inference package as a result of the application of CORE and USER rules. The processes of accomplishing the two functions are interrelated and can cooperate. The interpretation of a surface string will depend on how it is syntactically parsed and, conversely, the syntactic parse of a surface string can depend on the meanings of related, constitutent, or neighboring strings.

The two processes are not carried out in a purely sequential fashion for a given input utterance, since interpretations can be constructed for parsed constituent strings before the parsing of the entire utterance is complete.

1.5 Knowledge Representation Techniques

A SNePS semantic network is a directed graph with labeled arcs in which nodes represent concepts and the arcs represent nonconceptual binary relations between concepts. It is generally agreed that the nodes of a semantic network represent intensional concepts (Woods, 1975; Brachman, 1977; Maida and Shapiro, 1982). A "concept" is something in our domain of interest about which we may want to store information and which may be the subject of "thought" and inference. Since each concept is represented by a node, the relations represented by the arcs of our system are not conceptual, but structural (Shapiro, 1979a).

The primary type of arc in a SNePS network is the *descending* arc and if there is a path of descending arcs from node N to node M, N is said to *dominate* M. Two important types of nodes are *molecular* and *atomic* nodes. Molecular nodes are nodes that dominate other nodes. Atomic nodes are simply not molecular. Atomic nodes can be *constant* (representing a unique semantic concept) or *variable*. Variable nodes are used in SNePS as variables are used in normal predicate logic notations. Network nodes can also be categorized as in the table in Figure 2.

A propositional molecular node N together with the arcs incident from the node and the nodes $M_1, \ldots, M_k$ immediately dominated by N correspond to a case frame (Fillmore, 1968; Bruce, 1975) where the arc names correspond to the slot names, and the nodes $M_1, \ldots, M_k$ represent the slot fillers. Undominated molecular nodes in a SNePS network represent propositions believed by the system. Concepts such as the following are propositional and are represented by molecular nodes: Lexeme L is a member of category C; S1 is a constituent string of S2; lexeme L has number N (i.e. singular or plural). Simple examples of propositional nodes are M1 and M2 of Figure 3.

Node M1 represents the proposition that B1 represents the concept expressed by the word "NOUN" and M2 represents the proposition that the lexeme "SNOW" is in the category called "NOUN".

The syntactic objects represented in our network knowledge base include morphemes, surface strings, and nodes of annotated parse trees. Individual morphemes are represented as nodes whose identifiers or print names are the morphemes themselves. The representation of a surface string utilized in this study consists of a network version of the list structure used by Pereira and Warren (1980). This representation is also similar to Kay's charts (1973) in that whenever alternative analyses are made for a given substring of a sentence, the sentence structure is enhanced by multiple structures representing these alternative analyses. Retention of the alternatives avoids the reanalyses of previously processed substrings which occurs in a backtracking system. Our basic representation of a surface string is illustrated in Figure 4.

Nodes identified by the atoms B0, SNOW, IS, and WHITE are atomic nodes and represent objects: the empty string, and tokens "SNOW", "IS", and

Node Category	Type of Concept
Non-dominated (asserted) molecular node	Asserted proposition which is "believed" by the System
Dominated molecular node	Proposition or structured object which is a participant in a proposition
Atomic node	Object

Fig. 2. Table of node categories

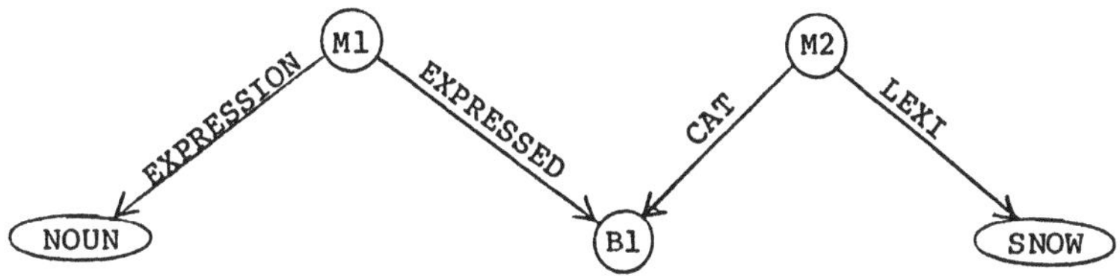

Fig. 3. M1 and M2 are simple examples of propositional nodes

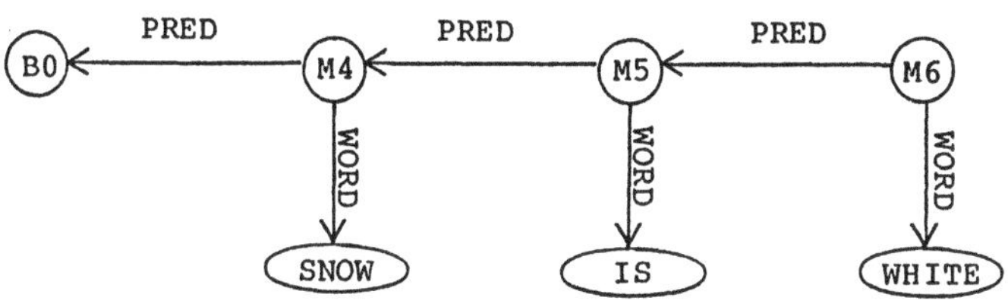

Fig. 4. Basic network representation of a surface string

"WHITE", respectively. Node M4 is molecular and represents the initial string "SNOW". M5 is also molecular and represents the initial string "SNOW IS", and similarly for node M6. A node such as M6 that represents an object would typically be dominated in our system by some node representing a proposition about it.

As each word of an input string is read by the system, the network representation of the string is extended and relevant rules stored in the SNePS network are triggered.

Interpretations of surface strings are also represented as nodes of our network knowledge base. The kernel language of the system enables the user to define case frame structures and to define rules to guide the system in interpreting input utterances.

1.6 Core Knowledge and the Kernel Language

Our approach is to provide the teacher (user) with a kernel language in which she can begin to "explain" the syntax and semantics of some natural or invented language to the system. The present version of our kernel language includes:

a) predefined terms such as L-CAT, the set of the names of lexical classes, and S-CAT, the set of the names of string classes; S-CAT contains the important category names ANT-CLAUSE, CQ-CLAUSE, and RULE-STMT, which are used to bootstrap into a more sophisticated rule input capability;
b) predefined objects such as (i) initial strings and (ii) bounded strings with beginning and ending token;
c) predefined relations such as (i) lexeme L is a member of category C; (ii) bounded string B is a member of category C and this structure is represented by S; (iii) structure S expresses concept C; (iv) structure S1 is a constituent of structure S2;
d) predefined functions such as (i) a test to determine whether two network nodes are identical, (ii) a test to determine whether two bounded surface strings match, and (iii) a test to determine whether one bounded string precedes another bounded string.

The KL provides the teacher with a basic language of rewrite rules for the purpose of defining *syntactic* lexical insertions, context free phrase structure rules, and context sensitive rules as well as *semantic* mappings from string categories to case frame structures and mappings from string categories to case frame participant or component slots.

1.7 Metalanguage Conventions and Symbols

In this chapter, we use the notational convention that words written in upper case letters denote words of KL and we use the metasymbols:

⟨⟩ denote a non-terminal; if the angle brackets enclose the name of a category of the core or a user-defined category, then such usage denotes a variable whose domain is the category named within the enclosing brackets.
() for grouping.
* Kleene star: when used as a superscript on an item, denotes zero or more of the items in a finite sequence.
\+ when used as a superscript on an item, denotes one or more of the items in a finite sequence.
... ellipsis.

2 Core Knowledge and Representations

2.1 Uniform Representation and Intensional Constructs

We use the semantic network formalism to represent both syntactic and semantic knowledge in the form of assertions and rules to be applied in inference formation. We include linguistic knowledge in the network knowledge base and use the network formalism as a uniform "language" with which to represent all types of knowledge. Thus we model surface strings and syntactic properties and categories as intensions (Woods, 1975; Brachman, 1977; Maida and Shapiro, 1982), concepts, or objects of thought.

2.2 Predefined Categories, Objects, Relations, Functions

2.2.1 Predefined Categories

We are investigating the capability of an NLU system becoming more adept in the use of some language by being instructed in the use of the language. The system must start with some language facility, but we are striving to make the core knowledge base as small and theory-independent as possible.

Included among the core primitives are certain predefined categories. Since we are designing a language *capability* that is as theory-independent as possible and not a robust parser for a predetermined language such as English, some of these categories are initially empty, while others have very few members. All the categories are to be utilized by the teacher, either directly or indirectly, and the membership of the categories expanded by the teacher as the definition of her target language takes shape.

The most basic of these categories are L-CAT, S-CAT, and VARIABLE. L-CAT consists of the names of lexical classes or classes of terms. L-CAT initially contains the predefined terms L-CAT, S-CAT, VARIABLE, PUNCTUATION, and FUNCTION-NAMES. Names that the teacher would add to L-CAT might include, for example, NOUN, VERB, and PREPOSITION.

The purpose of VARIABLE is to contain all the identifiers that the teacher will use as variables in her processing rules when stated as input to the system. The VARIABLE category is initially empty.

The category PUNCTUATION initially contains the punctuation marks period, single-quote, and double-quote.

The class FUNCTION-NAMES contains the names of the functions that the teacher has available to be used in a form of procedural attachment to the declarative rules of the network knowledge base. FUNCTION-NAMES initially contains the names of the tests discussed in Section 2.2.4: IDENTITY-TEST, STRING-MATCH-TEST, and PRECEDES-TEST.

S-CAT is defined to be the set of all the names of string categories. S-CAT initially contains the names of the predefined string categories UTTERANCE, P-RULE, CASE-FRAME-DEFINITION, CASE-SLOT-DEFINITION, LITERAL, LITERAL-STRING, UNIQUE-MEANING-CAT, VAR-APPOSITION-PHR,

MAIN-APPOS-PHR, VAR-NAME, ANT-CLAUSE, CQ-CLAUSE, and RULE-STMT. The string categories P-RULE, CASE-FRAME-DEFINITION, CASE-SLOT-DEFINITION, LITERAL, LITERAL-STRING, and VAR-NAME each have predefined syntax. For the remaining string categories except UTTERANCE, the definition of the syntax is left to the teacher, VAR-APPOSITION-PHR and RULE-STMT having restrictions discussed later in this article. The class UTTERANCE contains all input surface strings.

The predefined string category P-RULE includes all strings that qualify as production or syntactic rewrite rules as discussed in Section 2.5.2. These rewrite rules are part of the kernel language understood by the system.

The kernel language includes semantic rewrite rules to enable the teacher to define case frames and associations between case frames and particular string categories for use in the interpretation of input utterances. CASE-FRAME-DEFINITION and CASE-SLOT-DEFINITION are string categories that contain the two types of semantic rewrite rules. The capability associated with the CASE-FRAME-DEFINITION and CASE-SLOT-DEFINITION classes is discussed in Section 2.5.3.

LITERAL is the category of strings consisting of a single-quote mark followed by a lexeme. LITERAL-STRING is the category of strings that consist of a pair of double-quote marks enclosing a surface string.

VAR-APPOSITION-PHR, MAIN-APPOS-PHR, and VAR-NAME are string categories that enable a variable to be used as an appositive so as to establish the variable as the identifier for the MAIN-APPOS-PHRase which it is adjacent to. For example, after input of appropriate user-defined rules to the system, the string "a noun-phrase X" (from the sentence "If the head-noun of a noun-phrase X has number Y then X has number Y") could be parsed as a VAR-APPOSITION-PHR with "a noun-phrase" as the MAIN-APPOS-PHR and "X" the VAR-NAME so that in parsing the stated rule, X is remembered by the system as an identifier for the unknown noun-phrase refered to in the phrase and is thus capable of being referred to again later as in the given rule example. Since no referencing mechanisms are built into our system to enable the teacher to refer to previously mentioned concepts, the above string categories assist the teacher in establishing rules to determine the referencing process according to her own theory. The use of this capability is illustrated by example in Section 3.

As the teacher proceeds to instruct the system in her language definition, she will need to enter rules that cannot be expressed in the language of rewrite rules. Such rules would include rules concerning the semantics of utterances. Therefore, the core primitives include three initially empty string categories, RULE-STMT, ANT-CLAUSE, and CQ-CLAUSE to enable the teacher to define the syntax of general conditional rules. These categories are discussed in subsequent sections.

UNIQUE-MEANING-CAT is defined to be the class of all the strings that have a unique meaning. That is, if a string is in UNIQUE-MEANING-CAT, it must express the same intension each time it is encountered in an input utterance. As stated in Section 1.2, a premise of our theory and NL system is that each time a given word or string is "read" by the system, it has a new or different meaning unless this meaning is determined by rules and/or assertions input by the teacher.

2.2.2 Predefined Objects

The predefined objects essential to our theory and implementation are the concepts of the Initial String and the Bounded String. These objects and their network representations are described below.

a) Initial string S consists of the word or symbol W concatenated to the initial string Q. Q may be the null string represented by node B0.

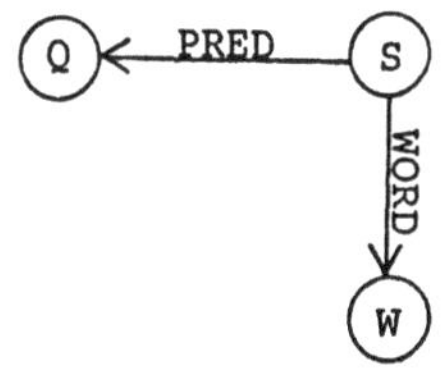

b) Bounded string B represents the surface string beginning with the last word of initial string S1 and ending with the last word of initial string S2 where S1 precedes S2.

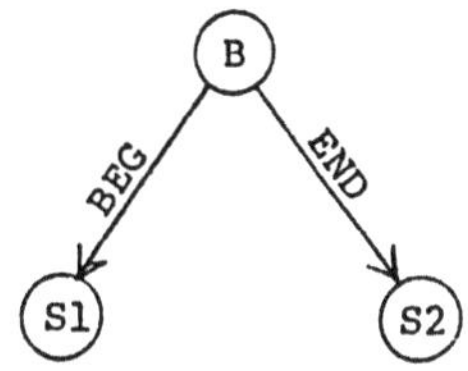

2.2.3 Predefined Relations

It is necessary for the NL system to have a set of predefined relations for knowledge representation. The current set of these relations and their corresponding semantic network structures are listed below.

a) Lexeme L is a member of category C; e.g., node M21 of Figure 5 represents the concept that ‘STUDENT is a NOUN.

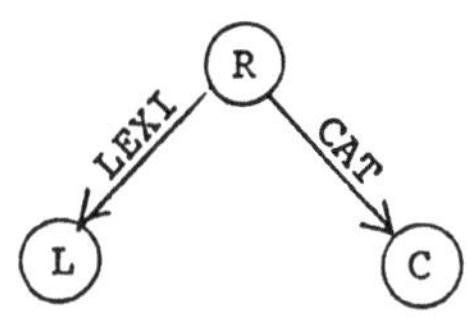

b) The bounded string B is in category C and this structure or parse of the string B is represented by node S (analogous to a node of an annotated parse tree); e.g., node M43 of Figure 5 represents the concept that the structure represented by B21 represents a parsing of the bounded string represented by M42 as an INDEF-NOUN-PHRASE.

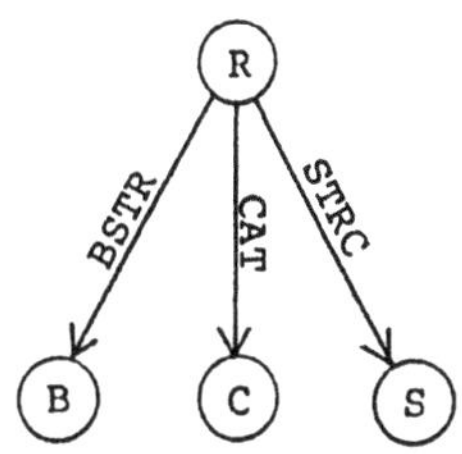

c) Structure or parsed string S expresses concept C; e.g., node M20 of Figure 5 represents the concept that the string “NOUN” expresses the category of nouns represented by node B10.

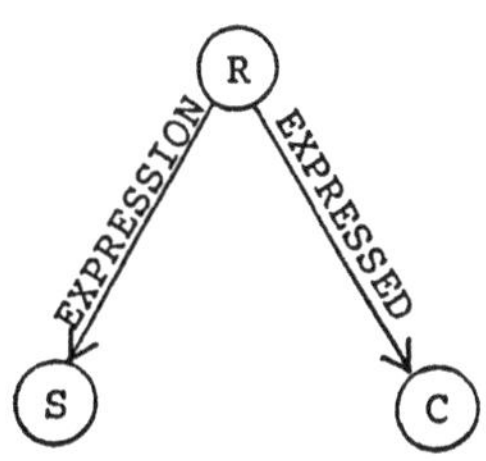

d) The structure S1 is a constituent of structure S2; e.g., node M44 of Figure 5 represents the concept that the literal 'STUDENT is a constituent of the structure represented by node B21.

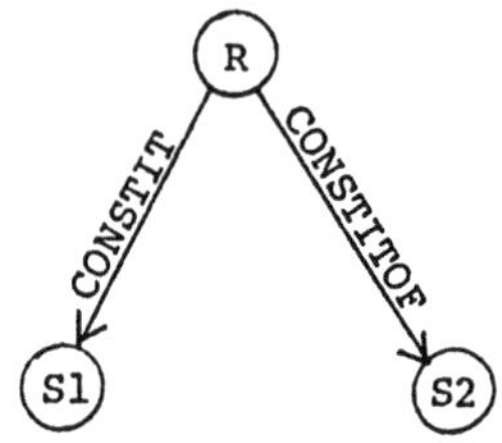

e) The rule structures of SNePS (Shapiro, 1979a).

Figure 5 shows a surface string enhanced by additional structure that would result from the system's reading and parsing the input string "A STUDENT" after some syntactic rules had been input by the teacher (e.g., 'A is an INDEF-DET, 'STUDENT is a NOUN, a string consisting of an INDEF-DET followed by a NOUN is an NOUN-PHRASE).

2.2.4 Predefined Functions

The following functions are essential for the NL system and could not be efficently implemented in the declarative SNePS language.

a) *Identity test* takes two network nodes as arguments, and returns true if the two nodes are identical and returns false otherweise.
b) *String-match test* takes two bounded strings in network representation as arguments, and returns true if the sequence of words or symbols in the two strings are identical, and returns false otherwise.
c) *Precedes test* takes two bounded strings in network representation as arguments, and returns true if the first string precedes the second string in the input stream, and returns false otherweise.

2.3 The Reading Function

The system's reading function "reads" one token (lexeme or punctuation mark) at a time from the input stream. For each input token, the structure of Figure 6 is added to the network, where node S represents the previously added initial string, C represents the lexical category of the token, I represents the newly established initial string, and B represents the newly added bounded string.

If the token belongs to any lexical categories, this membership would already be represented in the network in the form of relation (a) of Section 2.2.3 (how such relations are established in explained in Section 2.4). The lexical categories to which the input token belongs are found in the network by the reading function and, for each such category C, a node such as M of Figure 6 is added. If no such categories exist, then only the initial string and the bounded string are added.

Forward inference may be triggered by the addition of the network of Figure 6 for each token, depending on what rules are already in the system. For example, in

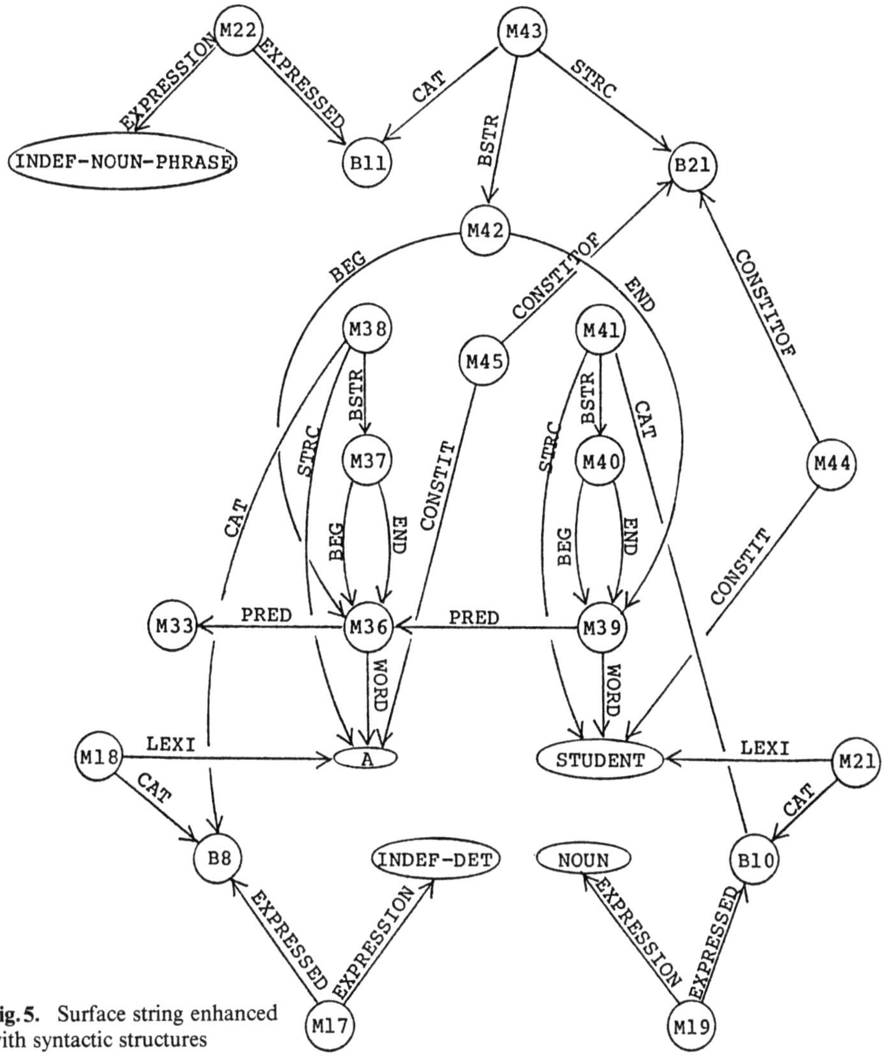

Fig. 5. Surface string enhanced with syntactic structures

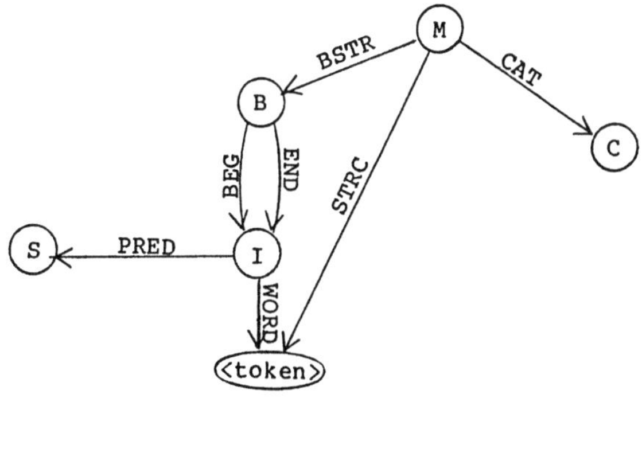

Fig. 6. The structure added to the network for each input token

Figure 5, nodes M38 und M41 are added by the reading function and nodes M42, M43, M44, and M45 are built only if there is a rule in the system that asserts that an INDEF-DET followed by a NOUN is an INDEF-NOUN-PHRASE.

2.4 The Representational Mapping

2.4.1 Introduction

Not all strings of a language form meaningful "chunks". For example, the substring "a large" from the sentence "A large aggressive dog frightened the girl" is not a conceptually coherent constituent of the sentence. Many researchers, e.g., Fodor and Garrett (1967), Bever (1970, 1973), and Levelt (1970, 1974), have investigated the relationship between surface constituents and the conceptually coherent components of an utterance. There seems to be good evidence for surface constituents being the coherent units for comprehension of discourse. How sentential constituents or discourse constituents (moving up to a higher level in the organization of text) are utilized in the comprehension process is an active field of research (Brown and Yule, 1983).

We let R designate the representational mapping (Allen, 1978) from surface strings to their interpretations. The domain of R contains the categories of strings that form conceptually coherent units, possibly depending on linguistic or other contexts. The domain of R initially contains predefined categories L-CAT, S-CAT, VARIABLE, LITERAL, LITERAL-STRING, VAR-APPOSITION-PHR, RULE-STMT, P-RULE, CASE-FRAME-DEFINITION, and CASE-SLOT-DEFINITION. They are discussed in the following sections.

We provide the teacher of the system with the facility for determining what the conceptually coherent constituents will be, in addition to the core, and for instructing the system in their use.

2.4.2 Base Cases

The categories L-CAT, S-CAT, VARIABLE, LITERAL, and LITERAL-STRING are the base cases for the representational mapping. The most basic subclass of the domain of R is L-CAT, the class of identifiers for the lexical categories of the system, including both system identifiers and user-defined identifiers. The class L-CAT contains the predefined identifiers L-CAT, S-CAT, and VARIABLE. The representational mapping applied to any identifier in L-CAT maps to a constant base node. In Figure 6, the interpretations of the identifiers L-CAT and S-CAT are represented by nodes B1 and B2 respectively. Similarly, if the system is informed that 'NOUN is an L-CAT, then its interpretation is represented by a base node (B4 of Fig. 7). The information that 'GOOSE is a NOUN and that 'NOUN-PHRASE is in S-CAT is also represented in Figure 7.

A member of VARIABLE maps to a corresponding network variable node. Since the interpretation of a user variable must be local to the rule in which it is used, the representational mapping applied to the class VARIABLE is handled in a special manner as explained in Section 3.

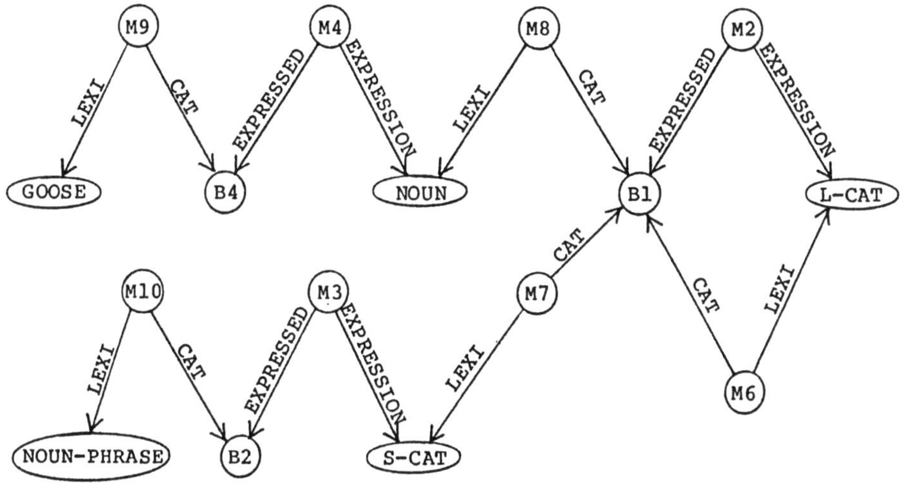

Fig. 7. Representation of some basic lexical knowledge

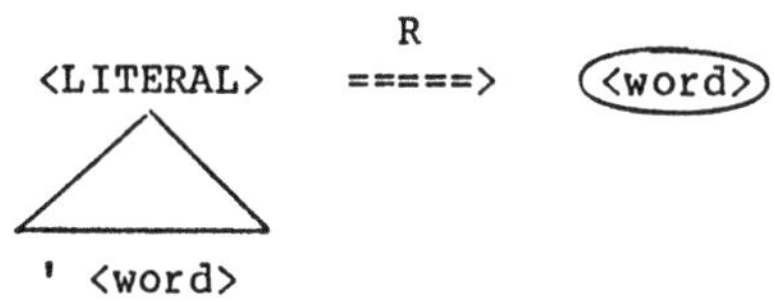

Fig. 8. The representational mapping applied to a LITERAL

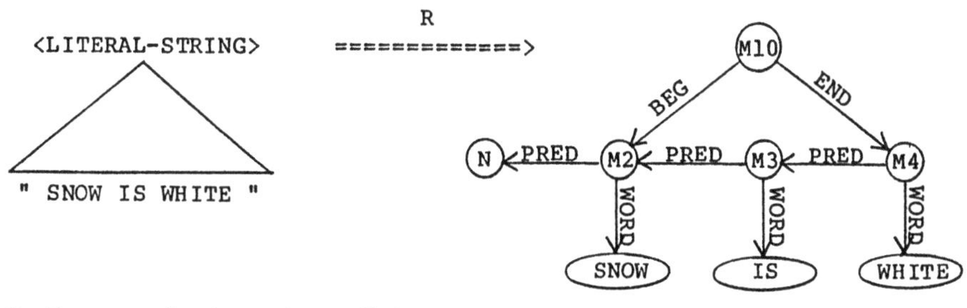

Fig. 9. Representational mapping applied to a LITERAL-STRING

The representational mapping applied to a LITERAL (defined in Section 2.2.1 as the single-quote mark followed by a word) maps to the node whose identifier is the word itself, as illustrated in Figure 8.

The representational mapping applied to a LITERAL-STRING (a string enclosed by double-quote marks) maps to the bounded string representing the string enclosed by the quote marks. Figure 9 illustrates the representational mapping applied to the literal string “SNOW IS WHITE”.

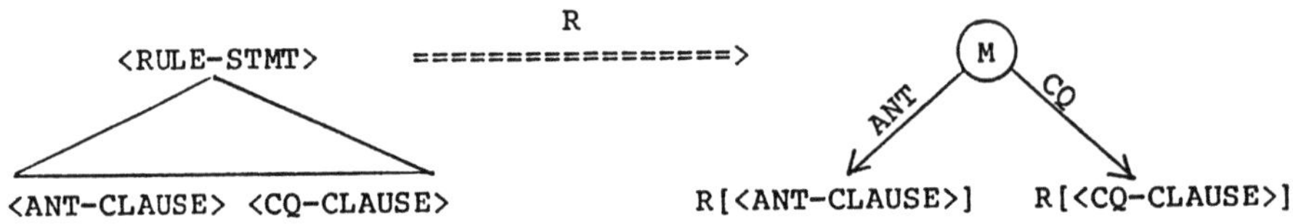

Fig. 10. Representational mapping applied to a RULE-STMT

2.4.3 Propositions and Structured Objects

Some string categories contained in the domain of R are mapped to non-atomic network (case frame) structures representing propositions or structured objects by the representational mapping. The system has just two predefined string categories, namely P-RULE and RULE-STMT, whose members' interpretations are represented as non-atomic structures by the representational mapping. P-RULEs have a predetermined syntax and are translated into SNePS network rules using the predefined structures. RULE-STMT is defined as the class of strings that are interpreted by the system as general rules. This class is initially empty and the syntax is to be determined by the teacher. A RULE-STMT must have an ANT-CLAUSE and a CQ-CLAUSE as constituents. The structure resulting from the application of the representational mapping R to a RULE-STMT is illustrated in Figure 10.

The ANT-CLAUSE category is defined as the class of strings that can be used in antecedent position in rules input by the teacher. Similarly, the CQ-CLAUSE category is defined as the class of strings that can be used in consequent position in rules input by the teacher. Both of these classes are initially empty and the syntax of RULE-STMTs, ANT-CLAUSEs, and CQ-CLAUSEs is to be determined by the teacher. An example is discussed in Section 3.

The teacher can add new string categories, whose interpretations are to be represented by non-atomic network structures, to the domain of R and specify the semantics of these string categories by using the semantic rewrite rule capability discussed in Sect. 2.5.3.

2.4.4 Participants in Propositions or Relations; Components of Structured Objects

In the previous section, the category of natural language phrases that assert relations between concepts or objects was discussed briefly. This type of phrase maps to the top node of a molecular representational structure.

Many phrases of natural language refer to individual concepts or objects that are participants in relations or propositions or that are components of structured objects. This type of phrase would map to a slot of one or more network case frame structures. The system has no predefined string categories which map to "participant" slots. The syntax for creating new categories of this type and their associated semantics is discussed in Section 2.5.3.

2.5 Kernel Language

2.5.1 Predefined Terms

As previously indicated, we are attempting to provide a facility with which a person can define a target language and yet keep the core as small and unbiased as possible. It is essential to provide the person (teacher) with a kernel language with which to start building up her language definition. The kernel language (KL) of our system consists of predefined terms, syntactic rewrite rules, and semantic rewrite rules. The predefined terms of the system are the names of the categores discussed in Section 2.2.1.

2.5.2 Syntactic Rewrite Rules

The kernel language includes linguistic rewrite rules to enable the teacher to instruct the system in the basic syntax of her target language.

a) Lexical Entry: The KL includes syntactic production rules of the form ⟨L-CAT⟩ → ⟨LITERAL⟩ where ⟨L-CAT⟩ represents the name of a lexical category that has already been defined. A LITERAL was defined in Section 2.2.1 as consisting of the single-quote followed by a word (the single-quote is part of the KL and indicates that the following word is mentioned rather than used). This form of production rule is the means of entering lexical items such as

L-CAT → ’NOUN
L-CAT → ’PROPER-NOUN
L-CAT → ’DEF-DET
L-CAT → ’INDEF-DET
L-CAT → ’VERB
L-CAT → ’BE-VERB
L-CAT → ’ADVERB
L-CAT → ’ADJECTIVE
NOUN → ’GOOSE
NOUN → ’GEESE
PROPER-NOUN → ’GRADY
PROPER-NOUN → ’GLADYS
DEF-DET → ’THE
INDEF-DET → ’A
VERB → ’HAS
BE-VERB → ’IS

ADVERB → ’THEN

L-CAT → ’PREPOSITION
L-CAT → ’CONJ
L-CAT → ’PROPERTY
S-CAT → ’HEAD-NOUN
S-CAT → ’STRING
VARIABLE → ’X
VARIABLE → ’Y

ADJECTIVE → ’WHITE
ADJECTIVE → ’SINGULAR
ADJECTIVE → ’PLURAL
PREPOSITION → ’OF
CONJ → ’IF
PROPERTY → ’COLOR
PROPERTY → ’NUMBER
UNIQUE-MEANING-CAT → ’ADJECTIVE
UNIQUE-MEANING-CAT → ’PROPERTY

b) Context Free Rules: The KL includes rules of the form

$$\langle \text{S-CAT} \rangle \rightarrow \langle s \rangle_1 \ldots \langle s \rangle_k,\ k > 0,$$

where $\langle \text{S-CAT} \rangle$ represents the name of a string category and for each i, $\langle s \rangle_i$ is either a LITERAL, the name of a lexical category previously entered as a member of L-CAT as in (a) above, or the name of a string category.

Examples: PROPERTY-CLAUSE → SUBJECT PREDICATE
SUBJECT → NOUN-PHRASE
NOUN-PHRASE → LITERAL
NOUN-PHRASE → VARIABLE
NOUN-PHRASE → PROPER-NOUN
PREDICATE → RELATION-PREDICATE
PREDICATE → BE-PREDICATE
RELATION-PREDICATE → RELATION PREDICATE-ADJ
BE-PREDICATE → BE-VERB PROPERTY-INDICATOR
RELATION → 'HAS PROPERTY-INDICATOR
PROPERTY-INDICATOR → PROPERTY-CLASS-INDICATOR
PROPERTY-INDICATOR → PROPERTY
PROPERTY-CLASS-INDICATOR → PREDICATE-ADJ
RULE-STMT → 'IF ANT-CLAUSE 'THEN CQ-CLAUSE

c) Context Sensitive Rules: The KL includes syntactic production rules of the form

$$\langle ls \rangle_1 \ldots \langle ls \rangle_n \rightarrow \langle rs \rangle_1 \ldots \langle rs \rangle_n,\ n > 0,$$

where each element $\langle ls \rangle_i$ or $\langle rs \rangle_i$ is either a LITERAL, the name of a lexical category, or the name of a string category; both sides of the rule must have the same number of elements and for each element $\langle ls \rangle_i$ of the left side,

1) if $\langle ls \rangle_i$ is a LITERAL or lexical category, then the corresponding element $\langle rs \rangle_i$ of the right side must be the same as $\langle ls \rangle_i$;
2) if $\langle ls \rangle_i$ is the name of a string category, then the corresponding element $\langle rs \rangle_i$ of the right side can be either a LITERAL, lexical category name, or string category name.

This facility allows the user to enter context sensitive rules, such as:

RELATION PREDICATE-ADJ → RELATION ADJECTIVE
RELATION PREDICATE-ADJ → RELATION VARIABLE
BE-VERB PREDICATE-ADJ → BE-VERB ADJECTIVE
'IF ANT-CLAUSE → 'IF PROPERTY-CLAUSE
'THEN CQ-CLAUSE → 'THEN PROPERTY-CLAUSE

The first rule asserts that in the context of a RELATION, an ADJECTIVE is recognized as a PREDICATE-ADJ, the second asserts that in the context of a RELATION, a VARIABLE is parsed as a PREDICATE-ADJ, and the third asserts that in the context of a BE-VERB, an ADJECTIVE is parsed as a PREDICATE-ADJ. Similarly, the fourth and fifth rules state that following the word "IF" or "THEN", a PROPERTY-CLAUSE is parsed as an ANT-CLAUSE or CQ-CLAUSE, respectively.

2.5.3 Semantic Rewrite Rules

a) Case Frame Definitions: The KL includes language to enable the teacher to define case frames and instruct the system in their use by using the syntax of a CASE-FRAME-DEFINITION:

⟨string-cat⟩ : : ⟨slot-name⟩$_1$ ⟨constit-name⟩$_1$ . . .
⟨slot-name⟩$_n$ ⟨constit-name⟩$_n$

where $n > 0$. Such a CASE-FRAME-DEFINITION is used by the system as follows: A string that is identified as being in category ⟨string-cat⟩ is mapped into a case frame such that for each slot identified by ⟨slot-name⟩$_i$, the slot-filler is the interpretation of the constituent string identified by ⟨constit-name⟩$_i$. The constituent strings need not be immediate constituents of the string in category ⟨string-cat⟩. The same ⟨constit-name⟩ can be used to specify the filler for more than one slot. For example, suppose the teacher wants to define a language in which an utterance such as "JOHN BOUGHT A HOUSE", involving the act of purchase, is interpreted to mean that the person bought the object for himself unless otherwise stated. To handle the semantics of such a clause, the teacher might want to define a case frame with AGENT and BENEFICIARY slots which are both filled by the interpretation of the same constituent of the clause. Our CASE-FRAME-DEFINITION facility provides for this eventuality.

If a string is parsed as a ⟨string-cat⟩ but is missing a constituent specified by the semantic rewrite rule, then a default representation of the slot-filler corresponding to the missing constituent is established in the form of an atomic node about which the system knows nothing, other than its being a participant in the case frame. In the context of a RULE-STMT the atomic node will be a variable node (see Section 1.3), otherwise a constant node. For example, to represent the interpretation of a sentence such as "THE HOUSE WAS PURCHASED YESTERDAY" the teacher might want to use the same case frame mentioned in the preceding paragraph. Since an AGENT and BENEFICIARY are implicitly part of the act of purchase, but not explicitly mentioned in the sentence, it is reasonable for the unmentioned participants to be represented in the interpretation of the sentence. The above default representation for the interpretation of a missing constituent provides the teacher with a facility for instructing the system how to interpret such a sentence.

An alternative syntax for the CASE-FRAME-DEFINITION is

⟨string-cat⟩: :⟨constit-name⟩.

The right side of the : : symbol is a degenerate case frame and the definition is interpreted as meaning that the semantics of the string of category ⟨string-cat⟩ is the same as that of the constituent string of category ⟨constit-name⟩. For example,

```
PROPERTY-CLAUSE: : PROPERTY OF SUBJECT
                   PROPERTY      PROPERTY-INDICATOR
                   VALUE         PREDICATE-ADJ
ANT-CLAUSE     : : PROPERTY-CLAUSE
CQ-CLAUSE      : : PROPERTY-CLAUSE
```

SUBJECT :: NOUN-PHRASE
NOUN-PHRASE :: LITERAL
NOUN-PHRASE :: VARIABLE
NOUN-PHRASE :: PROPER-NOUN
PROPERTY-INDICATOR :: PROPERTY-CLASS-INDICATOR
PROPERTY-INDICATOR :: PROPERTY
PREDICATE-ADJ :: ADJECTIVE
PREDICATE-ADJ :: VARIABLE

define the semantics of a PROPERTY-CLAUSE to be a case frame with three slots, such that the PROPERTYOF slot is filled by the interpretation of the SUBJECT of the PROPERTY-CLAUSE, the PROPERTY slot is filled by the interpretation of the PROPERTY-INDICATOR constituent of the PROPERTY-CLAUSE, and the VALUE slot is filled by the interpretation of the PREDICATE-ADJ constituent. The second and third definitions above indicate that the interpretation of an ANT-CLAUSE is the same as the interpretation of its PROPERTY-CLAUSE constituent and that the interpretation of a CQ-CLAUSE is the same as the interpretation of its PROPERTY-CLAUSE constituent, respectively. The next rule defines the interpretation of a SUBJECT to be the same as the interpretation of its NOUN-PHRASE constituent. The next three rules define the interpretation of a NOUN-PHRASE to be the interpretation of either its LITERAL constituent, its VARIABLE constituent, or its PROPER-NOUN constituent, whichever it has. The remaining rules are similarly understood by the system.

The representational mapping R builds a network structure such as that dominated by node M of Figure 11 as the interpretation of a PROPERTY-CLAUSE.

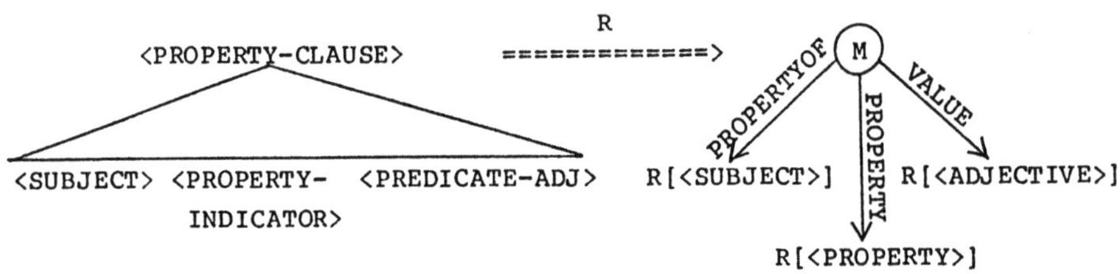

Fig. 11. Representational mapping applied to a PROPERTY-CLAUSE

b) Case Frame Slot-Filler Definitions: In order to provide a capability for defining the semantics of a phrase whose interpretation is a slot-filler in a case frame, the following type of semantic rewrite rule is included. The syntax of the CASE-SLOT-DEFINITION is

$$\langle\text{phr-name}\rangle >> ([\langle\text{slot-name}\rangle_1 \langle\text{string-name}\rangle_1 \ldots \langle\text{slot-name}\rangle_n \langle\text{string-name}\rangle_n])^+$$

where the square brackets are part of the object language and the + and the parentheses are metasymbols. The ⟨phr-name⟩ is the name selected by the teacher for the category of strings whose semantics are defined by the expression to the right of the symbol > >. The object language symbol + must be used in place of at least one ⟨string-name⟩, designating the position of the interpretation of the string ⟨phr-name⟩ in the case frame.

Each set of brackets encloses a case frame definition as described in the previous section. That is, each slot named ⟨slot-name⟩$_i$ is filled by the interpretation of a string in category ⟨string-name⟩$_i$, if a string of category ⟨string-name⟩$_i$ is present as a (not necessarily immediate) constituent of the string of category ⟨phr-name⟩. The + symbol marks the slot whose filler is the interpretation of the ⟨phr-name⟩ string. The system represents the interpretation of the ⟨phr-name⟩ string (1) as a variable atomic node if the semantic rule is used in the context of a RULE-STMT and (2) as a constant atomic node, otherwise. If a slot-filler constituent is specified in a semantic rewrite rule, but is missing from the surface string to which the rule is being applied, a default representation of the slot-filler corresponding to the missing constituent is established in the form of an atomic node about which the system knows nothing, other than its being a participant in the case frame (as in the previous section for a CASE-FRAME-DEFINITION).

Consider the following example CASE-SLOT-DEFINITION:

PROPERTY-CLASS-INDICATOR > > [MEMBER ADJECTIVE PROPERTY-CLASS +]

According to this rule, a PROPERTY-CLASS-INDICATOR should have an ADJECTIVE constituent and the interpretation of a string of the PROPERTY-CLASS-INDICATOR category would be represented by an atomic node which fills the PROPERTY-CLASS slot of a case frame whose MEMBER slot is filled by the interpretation of the ADJECTIVE constituent. The mapping from a surface string to the network representation of its interpretation is illustrated in Figure 12.

In order to prepare for the example discussed in Sect. 3, the following rule is input:

INDEF-S-PHRASE > > [BSTR STRING CAT S-CAT STRC+]

According to this rule, the interpretation of a string parsed by the system as an INDEF-S-PHRASE would be represented by an atomic node filling the STRC slot of a case frame whose CAT slot is filled by the interpretation of the S-CAT constituent of the INDEF-S-PHRASE and whose BSTR slot is filled by the STRING constituent. This is illustrated in Figure 13.

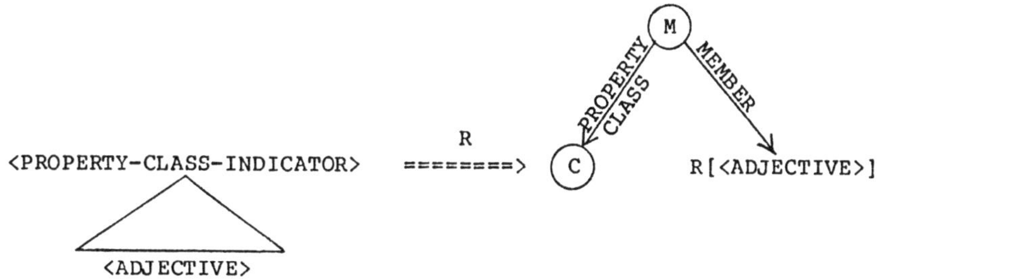

Fig. 12. Representational mapping applied to a PROPERTY-CLASS-INDICATOR

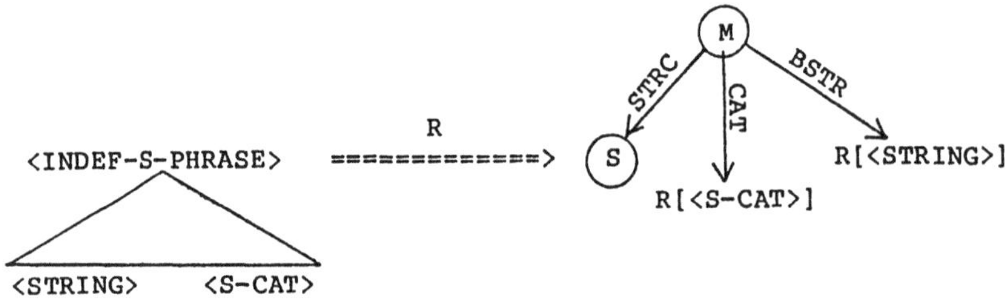

Fig. 13. Representational mapping applied to an INDEF-S-PHRASE

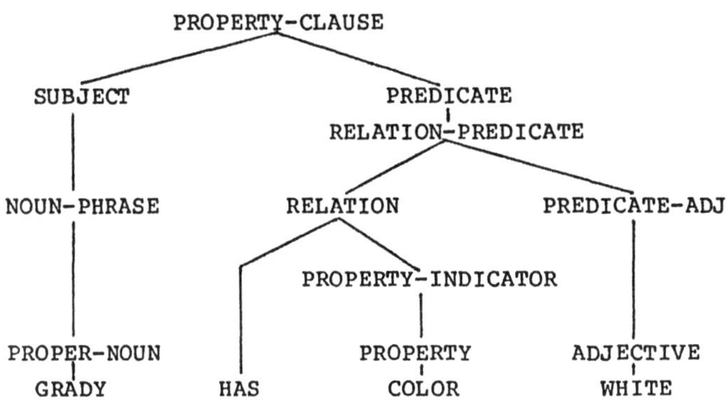

Fig. 14. Parse tree for sample input utterance

2.6 *Use in Language Processing*

To illustrate the system's use of the language definition developed via the rewrite rules of the preceding sections, we show some sentences of this language which refer to the language itself compared with some that refer to a non-linguistic domain. Thinking affectionately of her pet geese, the teacher informs the system that "GRADY HAS COLOR WHITE". The system recognizes and builds the parse tree of Figure 14 for the utterance. We show the more conventional form of the parse tree, rather than the equivalent network parse tree that the system actually builds in order to simplify the figure.

In the preceding sections, the teacher has entered rewrite rules into the system to define the semantics for certain string classes (e.g., PROPERTY-CLAUSE, PROPERTY-INDICATOR), thereby identifying the conceptually coherent constituents for the language definition. The system applies these semantic rewrite rules and builds the structure of Figure 15 as the interpretation of the utterance. The assertion that the parsed input utterance expresses the concept represented by node M75 is also established in the network.

Similarly, the system can process the input utterance "'GOOSE HAS NUMBER SINGULAR". The resulting parse tree is shown in Figure 16.

The representation of the interpretation of the utterance is shown in Figure 17.

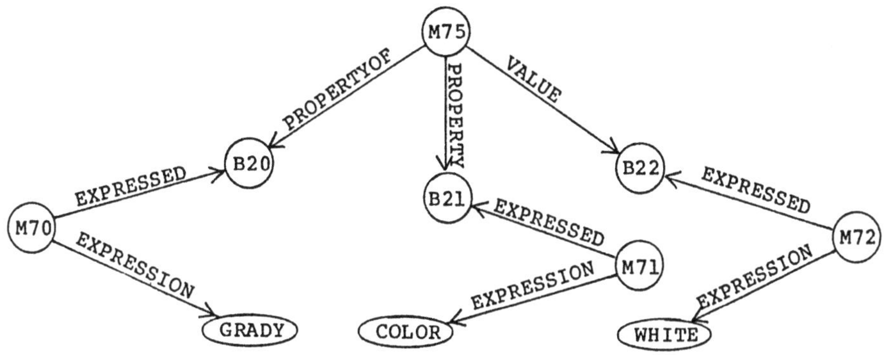

Fig. 15. Representation of the interpretation of input utterance

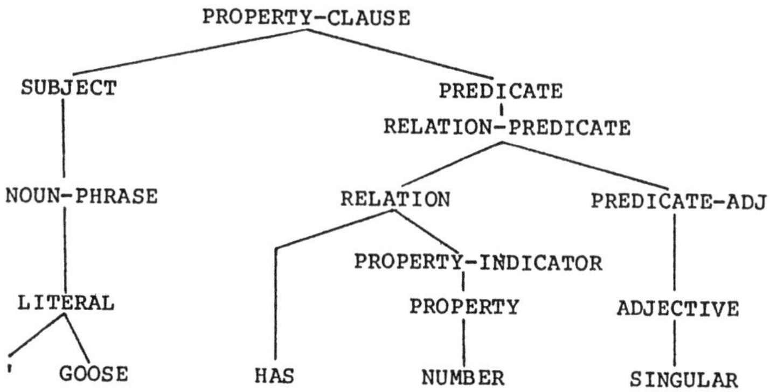

Fig. 16. Parse tree for utterance concerning language

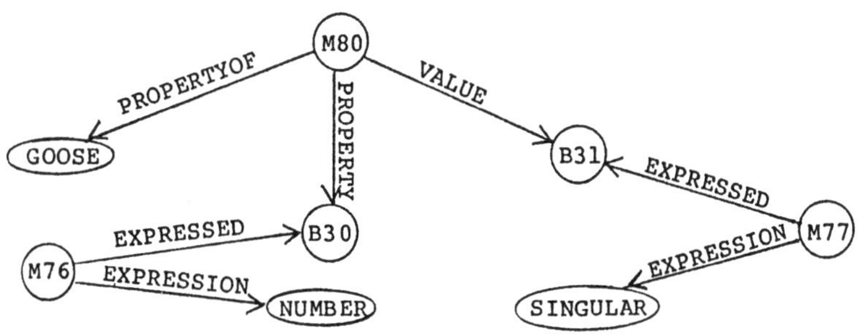

Fig. 17. Representation of interpretation of utterance

As stated in Section 1.5, the NL system distinguishes between a word or phrase and its interpretation. The interpretation of a LITERAL is the word following the quote mark (the word 'GOOSE, in this case). Thus node M80 represents the proposition that singular number is a property of the word 'GOOSE and not of the concept expressed by the word 'GOOSE. On the other hand, the interpretation of the word 'GRADY is represented by node B20 of Figure 15, and it is this entity that has color white. Comparing these two examples illustrates the knowledge representations we have established as well as the capability for handling strings and their interpretations as domain knowledge, which is fundamental to our theory and system.

At this stage, the teacher can simplify the language to use with the system for expressing properties. She does this by inputting the following rewrite rules so that property class entries can be made.

PROPERTY-CLASS-ENTRY → ADJECTIVE 'IS 'A PROPERTY
PROPERTY-CLASS-ENTRY : : MEMBER ADJECTIVE
PROPERTY-CLASS PROPERTY

Since the system has previously been informed that 'WHITE is an ADJECTIVE and 'COLOR is a PROPERTY, the utterance "WHITE IS A COLOR" would be recognized by the system as a PROPERTY-CLASS-ENTRY. Also since, in Section 2.5.3, for the purposes of this example, the teacher entered 'ADJECTIVE and 'PROPERTY into UNIQUE-MEANING-CAT, the surface strings that are in the categories ADJECTIVE and PROPERTY are each treated as having a unique interpretation. Thus different instances of the same string such as 'WHITE are treated by the system as having the same interpretation and it uses just one network structure to represent this interpretation. Therefore, using the above semantic rewrite rule, the system builds the structure of node M85 of Figure 18 to represent the interpretation of the utterance, finding the nodes B21 and B22 of Figure 15 to represent the interpretation of 'COLOR and 'WHITE, respectively.

Similarly, the system can be informed that "PLURAL IS A NUMBER" and it builds a structure similar to that of Figure 18 to represent the assertion that the concept expressed by 'PLURAL is a member of the property-class NUMBER.

If the utterance "GLADYS IS WHITE" is now input to the system, the utterance is also recognized as a PROPERTY-CLAUSE as shown in Figure 19.

The semantic rewrite rules of the previous section are used by the system to build the structure dominated by node M90 as the representation of the interpretation of the utterance.

According to the semantic rule for a PROPERTY-CLAUSE, the PROPERTY slot in the case frame is filled by the interpretation of the PROPERTY-INDICATOR constituent of the utterance. Referring to the parse tree of Figure 19, the PROPERTY-INDICATOR consists of the PROPERTY-CLASS-INDICATOR. The semantic rule

PROPERTY-INDICATOR: : PROPERTY-CLASS-INDICATOR

of the previous section instructs the system to use the interpretation of the PROPERTY-CLASS-INDICATOR as the interpretation of the PROPERTY-INDICATOR. The rule for interpreting a PROPERTY-CLASS-INDICATOR is the CASE-SLOT-DEFINITION presented in the previous section:

PROPERTY-CLASS-INDICATOR > > [MEMBER ADJECTIVE PROPERTY-CLASS +]

This rule instructs the system to interpret the PROPERTY-CLASS-INDICATOR as the PROPERTY-CLASS slot-filler of the frame whose MEMBER SLOT is

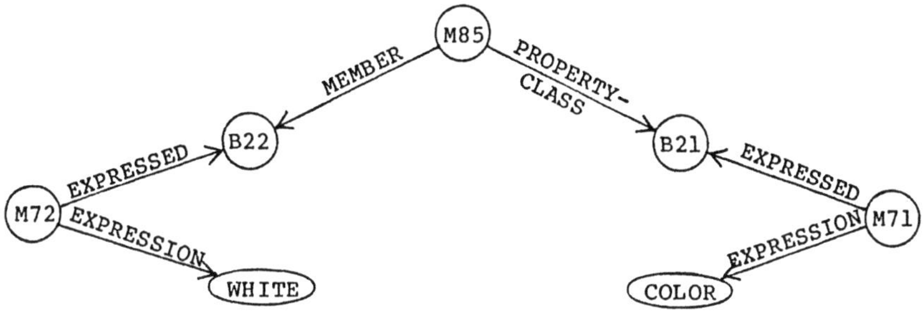

Fig. 18. Representation of interpretation of utterance

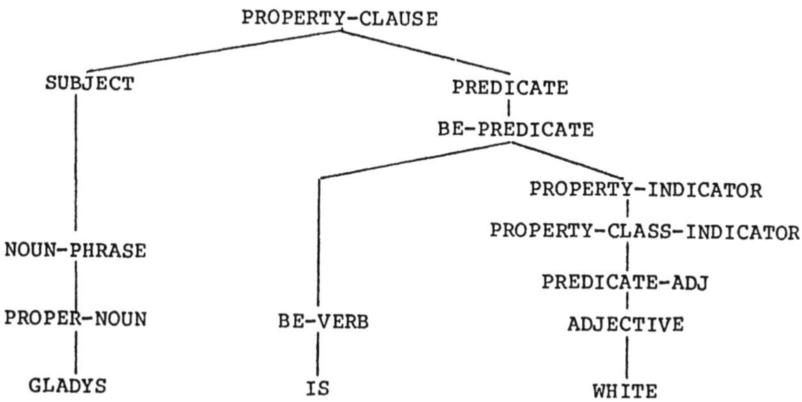

Fig. 19. Parse tree for input utterance

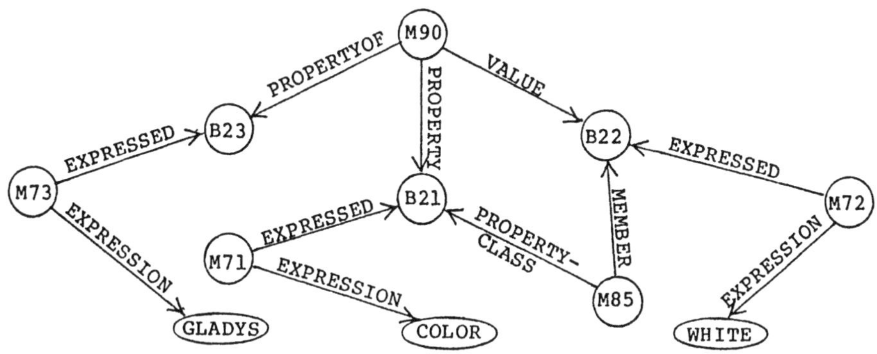

Fig. 20. Representation of interpretation of utterance

filled by WHITE. Node B22 of Figures 15 and 18 is found as the representation of the interpretation of 'WHITE, since the members of the class ADJECTIVE have been defined by the teacher as having "unique semantics". Thus, the system uses node B22 to use as the MEMBER slot-filler for the case frame associated with a PROPERTY-CLASS-INDICATOR. Then B21 of Figure 15 is found and used as the PROPERTY-CLASS slot-filler as shown in Figure 20, since it represents the

PROPERTY-CLASS that has WHITE as a MEMBER. Node B21 is also the representation of the interpretation of the PROPERTY-CLASS-INDICATOR string. In general, a CASE-SLOT-DEFINITION maps a surface string to a participant in a relation or proposition.

In a manner similar to the parsing and interpretation of the utterance "GLADYS IS WHITE", the system also understands the utterance "'GEESE IS PLURAL". The system's language definition is again used as a metalanguage to expand upon the same language itself.

3 Increasing the System's Language Capability Through Its Language Capability

3.1 Motivation

Since we treat linguistic knowledge as domain knowledge, the system teacher (user) can add to the knowledge base and instruct the system as to how to process or understand ever more sophisticated language.

Just as a person is continually influenced by interaction with his environment, the data base of our system is modified by each input. The knowledge base is incrementally enhanced to form a more sophisticated system.

Since we represent language processing knowledge in the same knowledge base and in the same formalism as other domain knowledge, it is possible to make the system's language processing knowledge the subject of its language processing and this is a fundamental aspect of our approach. Thus by instructing the system in the domain of linguistics as we would expect to be able to do with another domain in an interactive NLU system, we can increase the system's language capability through its language capability. A user can communicate with our system in just one language via one processor without switching "modes" or interacting with supportive processors in special purpose languages.

The rewrite rules of the KL are certainly not sufficient for expressing all the rules a teacher would need to define a language of her choice. Therefore, one of the most important capabilities that the system needs is to understand a more general form of rule statement. A teacher should be able to bootstrap into a more powerful rule statement language from the KL. In the next sections, we present an example from such a bootstrap process.

3.2 Defining More-General Rule Forms

The teacher first extends the system's language definition so that it can begin to understand general "IF-THEN" rules. As stated in Section 2.2.1, RULE-STMT is a predefined category. The syntax of a RULE-STMT is not predefined, but for the interpretation process, each RULE-STMT must have an ANT-CLAUSE and a CQ-CLAUSE constituent. The ANT-CLAUSE constituent is interpreted as the antecedent of the rule and the CQ-CLAUSE constituent as the consequent of the rule. Thus the rewrite rule

RULE-STMT → 'IF ANT-CLAUSE 'THEN CQ-CLAUSE

defines a syntax for the RULE-STMT. The syntax and semantics of ANT-CLAUSE and CQ-CLAUSE must also be defined. This was done is Section 2.5 (see Appendix).

The additional rules that the teacher chooses to input to the system to increase its capability of understanding linguistic-domain language for this example are listed below. In order to make use of the system's ability to use a VARIABLE as an appositive to another phrase and remember the association of the VARIABLE to the prase, the teacher inputs:

DEF-S-PHRASE → DEF-DET S-CAT
INDEF-S-PHRASE → INDEF-DET S-CAT
MAIN-APPOS-PHR VAR-NAME → INDEF-S-PHRASE VARIABLE
VAR-APPOSITION-PHR → MAIN-APPOS-PHR VAR-NAME

To explain to the system how to parse and interpret language which describes one phrase being a constituent of another, the teacher inputs:

SUP-STRING-REF → VAR-APPOSITION-PHR
CONSTIT-REF → DEF-S-PHRASE
CONSTIT-PHRASE → CONSTIT-REF 'OF SUP-STRING-REF
NOUN-PHRASE → CONSTIT-PHRASE
CONSTIT-PHRASE >> [CONSTIT + CONSTITOF SUP-STRING-REF]
[BSTR STRING CAT DEF-S-PHRASE STRC +]
SUP-STRING-REF :: VAR-APPOSITION-PHR
MAIN-APPOS-PHR :: INDEF-S-PHRASE
NOUN-PHRASE :: CONSTIT-PHRASE
DEF-S-PHRASE :: S-CAT

These rules will be used in the next sections.

3.3 Parsing Strategy

The parsing strategy applied by our NL system is a combined bottom-up, top-down strategy. As each word of an input string is read by the system, the network representation of the string is extended as discussed in Section 2.3 and relevant rules stored in the SNePS network are triggered. All applicable rules are started in parallel in the form of processes created by our MULTI-processing package (McKay and Shapiro, 1980). These processes are suspended if not all their antecedents are satisfied and are resumed if more antecedents are satisfied as the reading of the string proceeds. As parsing proceeds, the annotated parse (tree(s) for an input utterance is (are) represented in the system's network knowledge base. Our system builds and retains network structures corresponding to alternative analyses of a given input string. Retention of the alternatives avoids the reanalysis of previously processed surface strings that occurs in a backtracking system.

Processing is controlled by the SNePS Inference Package (Shapiro et al., 1982), which employs bi-directional inference. This is a form of inference resulting from interaction between forward and backward inference and loosely corresponds to bi-directional search through a space of inference rules. This technique focuses attention towards the active parsing processes and prunes the search through the space of inference rules by ignoring rules which have not been activated. This cuts down the fan out of pure forward or backward chaining. New rules are activated only if no active rules are applicable.

Consider the sample input utterance "IF THE HEAD-NOUN OF A NOUN-PHRASE X HAS NUMBER Y THEN X HAS NUMBER Y". When the first word is read by the system, it is recognized as matching the word 'IF in the rules

RULE-STMT → 'IF ANT-CLAUSE 'THEN CQ-CLAUSE
'IF ANT-CLAUSE → 'IF PROPERTY-CLAUSE

and parsing begins in a bottom-up manner. Both rules are triggered in parallel by the SNePS MULTI package. When originally input, each of the above rules was interpreted by the system and stored in the form of a network rule which we paraphrase as follows (NOTE: In all the paraphrased rules of this section, V_1 and V_2 are universally quantified variables):

(1) If a word of an input string is the word 'IF, then
(2) if V_1 f-llows the word 'IF and V_1 is an ANT-CLAUSE, then
(3) if the word 'THEN follows V_1, then
(4) if V_2 follows the word 'THEN and V_2 is a CQ-CLAUSE,
then the string consisting of 'IF followed by V_1
followed by 'THEN followed by V_2 is a RULE-STMT.
(5) If a word of an input string is the word 'IF, then
(6) if V_1 follows the word 'IF and V_1 is a PROPERTY-CLAUSE,
then V_1 is an ANT-CLAUSE.

(The numbers in parentheses are rule numbers, not line numbers. Thus, for example, nested rule (3) begins with "if the word 'THEN" and continues to the period at the end of the sentence.)

Since the antecedent of rule (1) above is satisfied, the system questions whether a string immediately following the word 'IF is an ANT-CLAUSE. When a SNePS rule is triggered, a process is created forming the active version of the rule for the purpose of such activities as data collection and variable binding. Some of these processes act as demons, waiting for instances of their antecedents so that instances of their consequents can be deduced. This is the case for the nested rule (2). Since no string follows the word 'IF yet, the process for rule (2) is suspended.

These active processes, with their communication links, form the equivalent of a hypothesized parse tree with associated expectations. The inference system ignores unactivated rules as long as there are applicable active rule processes awaiting data, essentially parsing in a top-down manner in this situation. The hypothesized parse tree corresponding to the process of rule (2) is illustrated in Figure 21. The parsing strategy of our system is similar to "left-corner bottom-up parsing" (Burge, 1975) in that construction of a parse tree begins at the bottom left corner, processing of a surface string proceeds in a left-to-right manner, and whenever an initial segment of a string has been parsed, the system attempts to establish a goal analysis of the string or substring thereof. In the following figures, the bro-

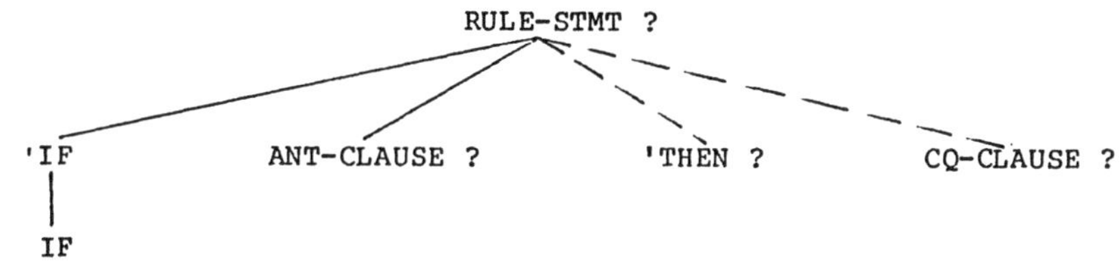

Fig. 21. Hypothesized parse tree

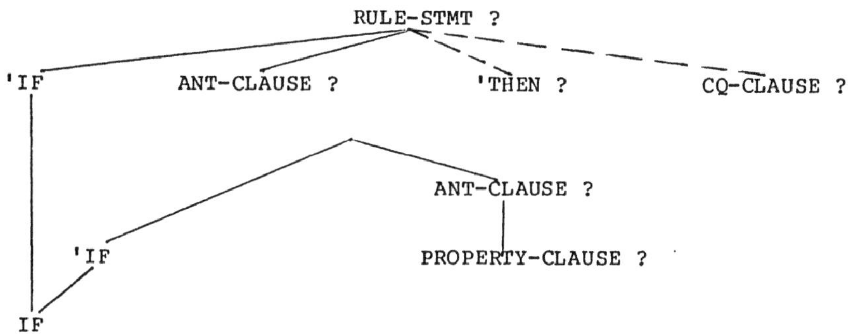

Fig. 22. Hypothesized parse tree

ken lines indicate goals or expectations represented by antecedents of nested rules for which active demons have not yet been created. The question-marks indicate expectations which have not yet been satisfied.

The antecedent of rule (5) is also satisfied. This is a context sensitive rule which constrains the parsing process. According to this rule, a PROPERTY-CLAUSE is parsed as an ANT-CLAUSE in the context of the word 'IF. A process is created forming the active version of rule (6) and this process awaits a PROPERTY-CLAUSE following the word 'IF. Figure 22 reflects the current state of the system in terms of its active processes, implicit expectations, and the tokens that it has consumed.

When the word 'THE is read by the system, the rule

DEF-S-PHRASE $\rightarrow$ DEF-DET S-CAT

is triggered as parsing continues in a bottom-up manner. This rule is paraphrased as:

(7) If V_1 is a DEF-DET, then
(8) if V_2 follows V_1 and V_2 is an S-CAT,
then the string consisting of V_1 followed by V_2 is a
DEF-S-PHRASE.

The antecedent of rule (7) is satisfied and a process is created for nested rule (8) to await an S-CAT following the DEF-DET. The active processes form another hypothesized parse tree shown in Figure 23.

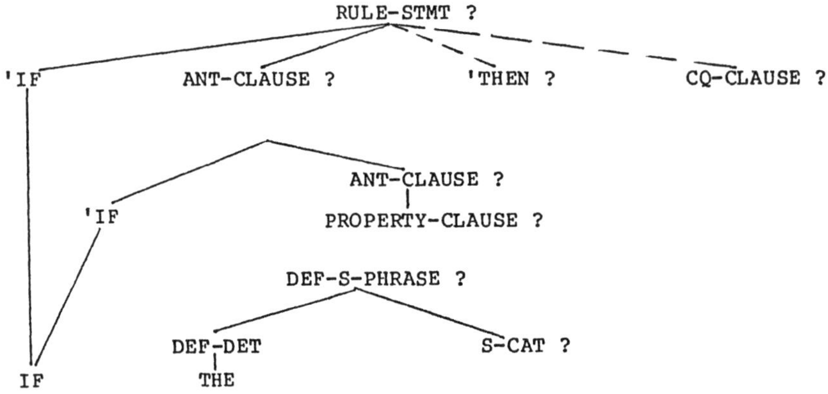

Fig. 23. Hypothesized parse tree

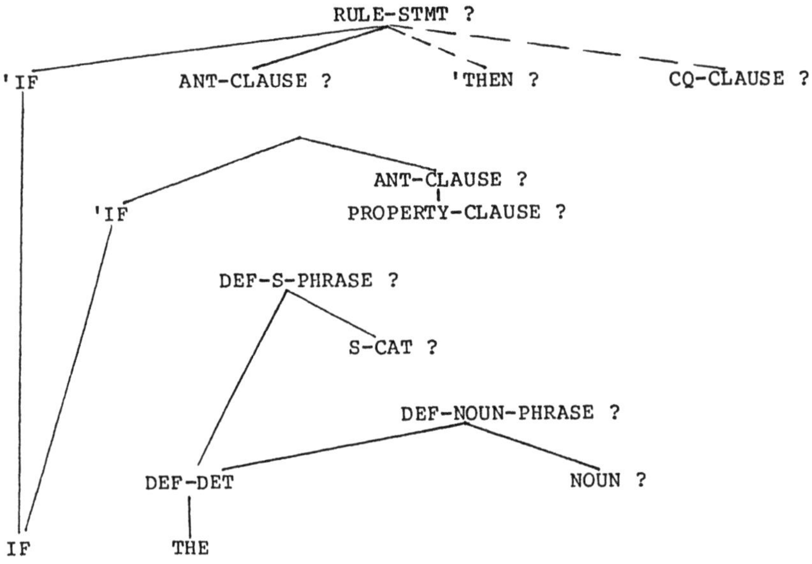

Fig. 24. Hypothesized parse trees

Suppose another rule such as DEF-NOUN-PHRASE → DEF-DET NOUN had been entered by the teacher and is present in the network knowledge base. This rule is paraphrased as:

(9) If V_1 is a DEF-DET, then
(10) if V_2 follows V_1 and V_2 is a NOUN, then the string consisting of V_1 followed by V_2 is a DEF-NOUN-PHRASE.

This latter rule is also triggered by the system's reading of the word 'THE and the processes created for rules (9) and (10) form another set of hypothesized parse trees as illustrated in Figure 24.

The parse trees of Figure 24 dominated by DEF-S-PHRASE? and DEF-NOUN-PHRASE? represent alternative possibilities for the parse of the string beginning with the word 'THE. A process such as the process for rule (10) waiting for a NOUN may remain suspended indefinitely if the expected data is not forthcoming.

When the next word 'HEAD-NOUN is read, the system recognizes it as an S-CAT and the process corresponding to rule (8) is resumed since it is waiting for an S-CAT following the word 'THE. Thus the string "THE HEAD-NOUN" is recognized as a DEF-S-PHRASE by application of the teacher's rules. This DEF-S-PHRASE then triggers the network version of the following rule and the DEF-S-PHRASE is then recognized as a CONSTIT-REF:

CONSTIT-REF → DEF-S-PHRASE

Recognition of a CONSTIT-REF triggers the rule

CONSTIT-PHRASE → CONSTIT-REF 'OF SUP-STRING-REF

whose network representation can be paraphrased as

(11) If V_1 is a CONSTIT-REF, then
(12) if the word 'OF follows V_1, then
(13) if V_2 follows the word 'OF and V_2 is a SUP-STRING-REF, then the string consisting of V_1 followed by the word 'OF followed by V_2 is a CONSTIT-PHRASE.

Activation of rule (11) is analogous to bottom-up processing again. A process is established for rule (12) to await the word 'OF in the input stream.

When the next word 'OF is read by the system, the demon corresponding to rule (12) is activated and since the antecedent of rule (12) is satisfied, a process is established for rule (13) to expect a SUP-STRING-REF following the word 'OF. No other rules are activated by the reading of the word 'OF since an active process was waiting for this word in the input stream.

The system parses the next string "A NOUN-PHRASE" as an INDEF-S-PHRASE by application of the rule

INDEF-S-PHRASE → INDEF-DET S-CAT

This triggers the rule

MAIN-APPOS-PHR VAR-NAME → INDEF-S-PHRASE VARIABLE

which is paraphrased as

(14) If V_1 is an INDEF-S-PHRASE, then
(15) if V_2 follows V_1 and V_2 is a VARIABLE,
(16) then V_1 is a MAIN-APPOS-PHR and V_2 is a VAR-NAME.

Since the antecedent of rule (14) is satisfied, a process is set up for rule (15). When the next word 'X is read, it is recognized as a VARIABLE and since the active process for rule (15) is waiting for a VARIABLE, no unactivated rules are applied. An example of such an unactivated rule is

NOUN-PHRASE → VARIABLE

which we previously input to the system. Thus an alternative parse is blocked by the expectation of a VARIABLE by the process for rule (15). By application of the rules

VAR-APPOSITION-PHR → MAIN-APPOS-PHR VAR-NAME
SUP-STRING-REF → VAR-APPOSITION-PHR

the expected SUP-STRING-REF of rule (13) is satisfied and the string "THE HEAD-NOUN OF A NOUN-PHRASE X" is parsed as a CONSTIT-PHRASE. By application of the rule

NOUN-PHRASE → CONSTIT-PHRASE

the string is also recognized as a NOUN-PHRASE. Notice that the term NOUN-PHRASE is *mentioned* in the input string and *used* in the application of the above rule.

At this point in the parsing process the hypothesized parse trees are illustrated in Figure 25.

As parsing proceeds using the rules introduced in this and preceding sections of this chapter, the resulting parse of the entire input statement is shown in Figure 26. The string category identifiers in the tree that are underlined are the categories that are included in the domain of the representational mapping. These are the categories for which the teacher has defined a rule to determine the interpretation of any member of the category (i.e., the underlining identifies the string categories defined by the teacher as the conceptually coherent constituents of the utterance).

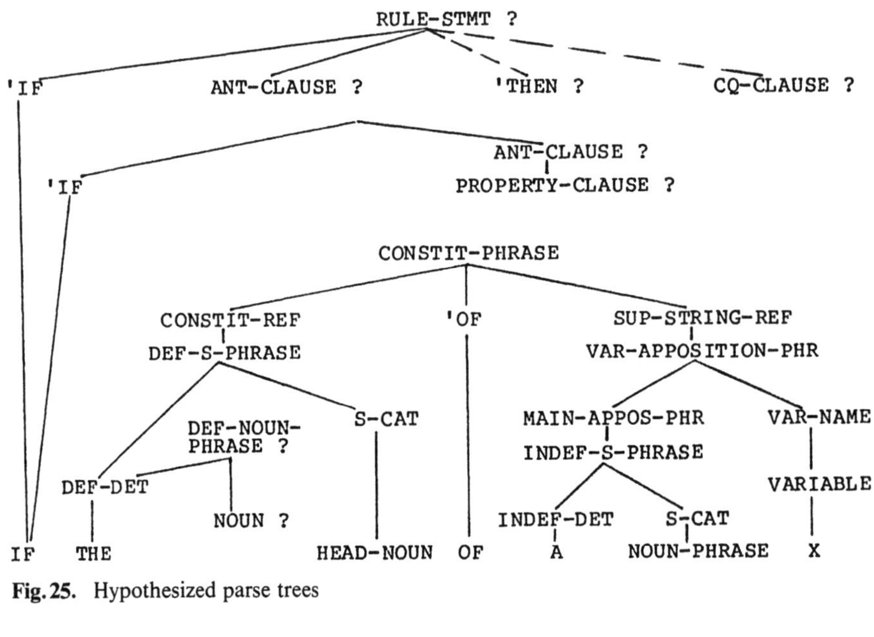

Fig. 25. Hypothesized parse trees

In this section on parsing, we have illustrated the following characteristics of our system's strategy:

(1) the parallel processing of applicable rules;
(2) constraint of the parsing process by the use of context sensitive rules;
(3) constraint of the parsing process by the SNePS Inference Package focusing on active rule processes - the manifestation being the blocking of multiple parses by previously established expectations;
(4) suspension and resumption of rule processes during the parsing process.

The retention of alternative analyses of a string, which avoids the reanalysis of certain strings in the case of a backtracking system, was not illustrated by the example of this section, but is a characteristic of our system.

Also of importance in this section is the fact that the system is again using its acquired language definition as a metalanguage to understand another instruction from the teacher concerning the language itself.

3.4 Interpretation of the Input Rule Statement

During the interpretation process, a VARIABLE of the user's language is translated into a variable node of the semantic network. The scope of a user VARIABLE is the utterance in which it occurs. The association of a user VARIABLE to its interpretation is maintained on a list only during translation of the utterance in which the VARIABLE occurs.

The interpretation of a user VARIABLE is as follows: If a VARIABLE is used as the VAR-NAME of a VAR-APPOSITION-PHR, discussed briefly in Section 2.2.1, then the system uses the interpretation of the MAIN-APPOS-PHR as the interpretation of the VARIABLE, and stores this association on the variable association list. Otherwise, the system checks the variable association list for a corresponding interpretation already established. Otherwise, a new variable node is created as the interpretation of the user VARIABLE, the new pair once again being added to the variable association list.

As shown in Figure 25, the phrase "A NOUN-PHRASE X" was recognized by the system as a VAR-APPOSITION-PHR, with "A NOUN-PHRASE" recognized as the MAIN-APPOS-PHR and 'X as the VAR-NAME. Thus the interpretation of the phrase "A NOUN-PHRASE" is remembered by the system as the interpretation of 'X. The string "A NOUN-PHRASE" has been recognized as an INDEF-S-PHRASE and thus the semantic rule

INDEF-S-PHRASE > > [BSTR STRING S-CAT STRC +]

of Section 2.5.3 applies. As discussed in Section 2.5.3, if a constituent is mentioned in a semantic rule but is missing from the surface string to which the rule applies, then the system represents the interpretation of the constituent as an atomic node. Furthermore, this atomic node is a variable node in the context of a RULE-STMT. Since the slot-filler constituent of category STRING is not present in our example INDEF-S-PHRASE, an atomic variable node (V2 of Fig. 26) is built to represent

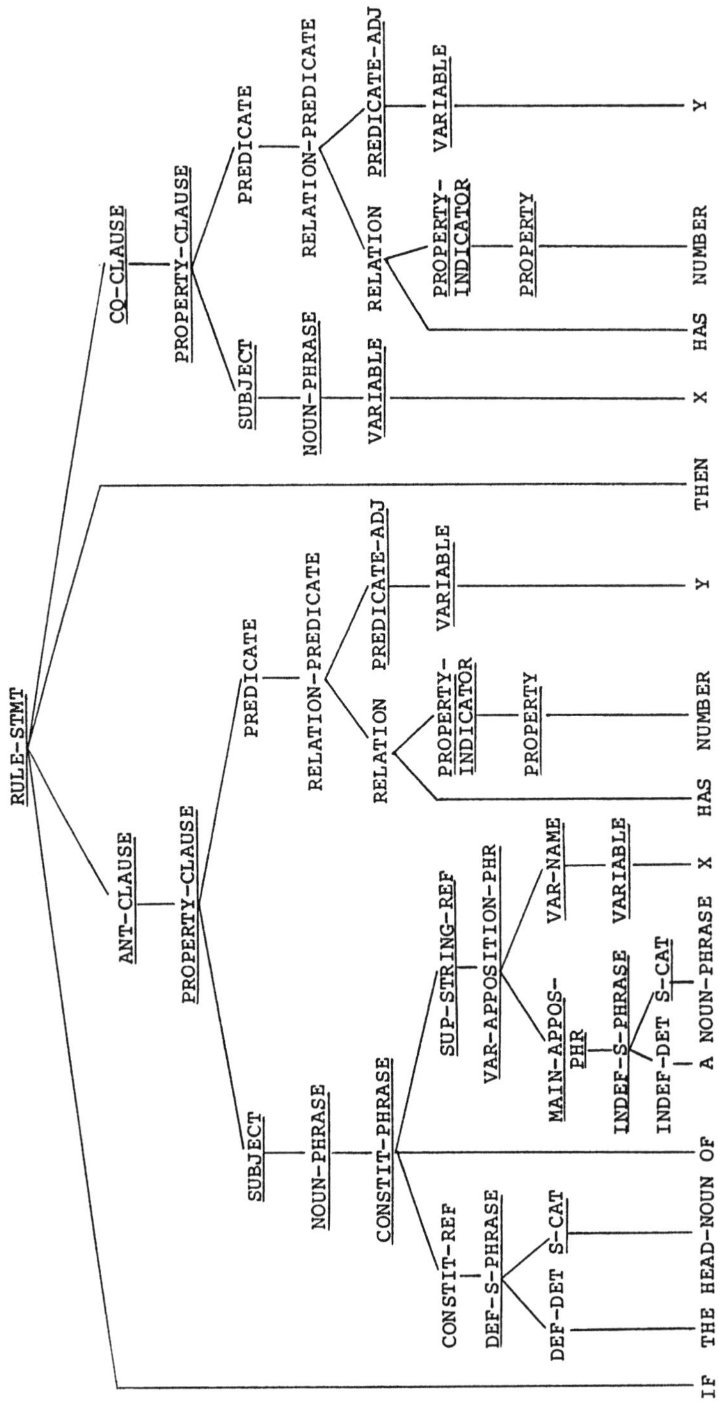

Fig. 26. Parse tree for the input rule statement

the interpretation of the missing STRING constituent. The representation of the interpretation of the S-CAT constituent "NOUN-PHRASE" is node B25, representing the category of NOUN-PHRASEs. The STRC slot-filler becomes the interpretation of the INDEF-S-PHRASE. This slot-filler is also represented by an atomic variable node (V1 of Fig. 26) as explained in Sect. 2.5.3. The + symbol in the rewrite rule marks the participant of the proposition represented by the case frame whose representation is also the representation of the interpretation of the INDEF-S-PHRASE. Thus the interpretation of the INDEF-S-PHRASE "A NOUN-PHRASE" is node V1 of Figure 26. That is, the INDEF-S-PHRASE is interpreted as a variable node to be instantiated by a structure representing an analyzed surface string which has an associated bounded-string (see Sect. 2.2.3) and category NOUN-PHRASE. V1 is also the interpretation of user VARIABLE 'X due to the string "A NOUN-PHRASE X" being a VAR-APPOSITION-PHR and the association of V1 and 'X is stored on the variable association list.

The input string "THE HEAD-NOUN OF A NOUN-PHRASE X" was parsed as a CONSTIT-PHRASE (refer to Fig. 26). The rule for interpreting a CONSTIT-PHRASE was given in Section 3.3 as

CONSTIT-PHRASE > > [CONSTIT + CONSTITOF SUP-STRING-REF]
[BSTR STRING CAT DEF-S-PHRASE STRC +]

This rule stipulates that the interpretation of a CONSTIT-PHRASE is a participant in two case frames as defined in the two sets of brackets and the + symbol marks the slot-filler that is the interpretation of the CONSTIT-PHRASE. Again an atomic variable node is built to represent this slot-filler which also represents the CONSTIT-PHRASE. The SUP-STRING-REF ist the constituent "A NOUN-PHRASE X" (refer to Fig. 26), whose interpretation is represented by node V1 of Figure 27. The structure representing the case frame defined in the second set of brackets is built in a manner similar to that used in building the structure of Figure 27 and described above.

The interpretation of the example CONSTIT-PHRASE "THE HEAD-NOUN OF A NOUN-PHRASE X" is represented by node V3 of Figure 28. The node V1 of Figure 28 ist the same node as V1 of Figure 27.

Assembling the interpretations of the constituents of our RULE-STMT from Figures 27 and 28 and completing the interpretation of the RULE-STMT as the system does using the semantic rewrite rules of this article, node M86 of Figure 29 represents the interpretation of the RULE-STMT. All of the variable nodes V1, V2,

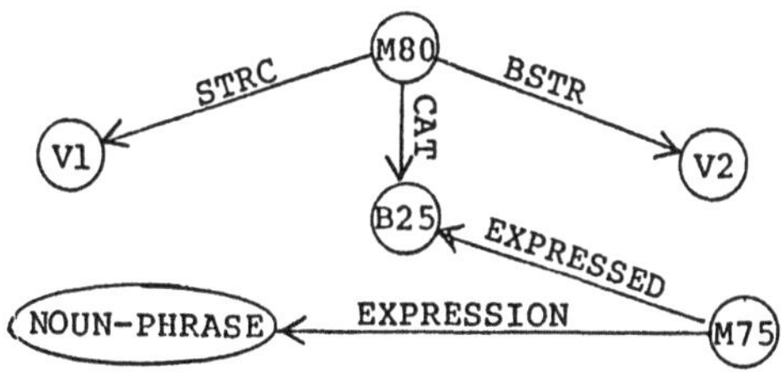

Fig. 27. Node V1 represents the interpretation of "A NOUN-PHRASE"

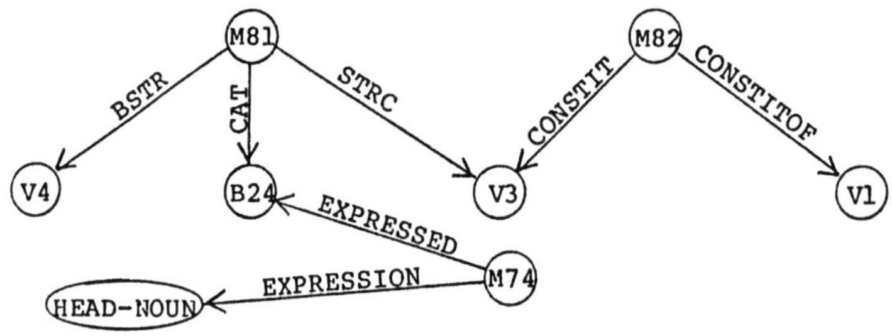

Fig. 28. Node V3 represents the interpretation of the CONSTIT-PHRASE

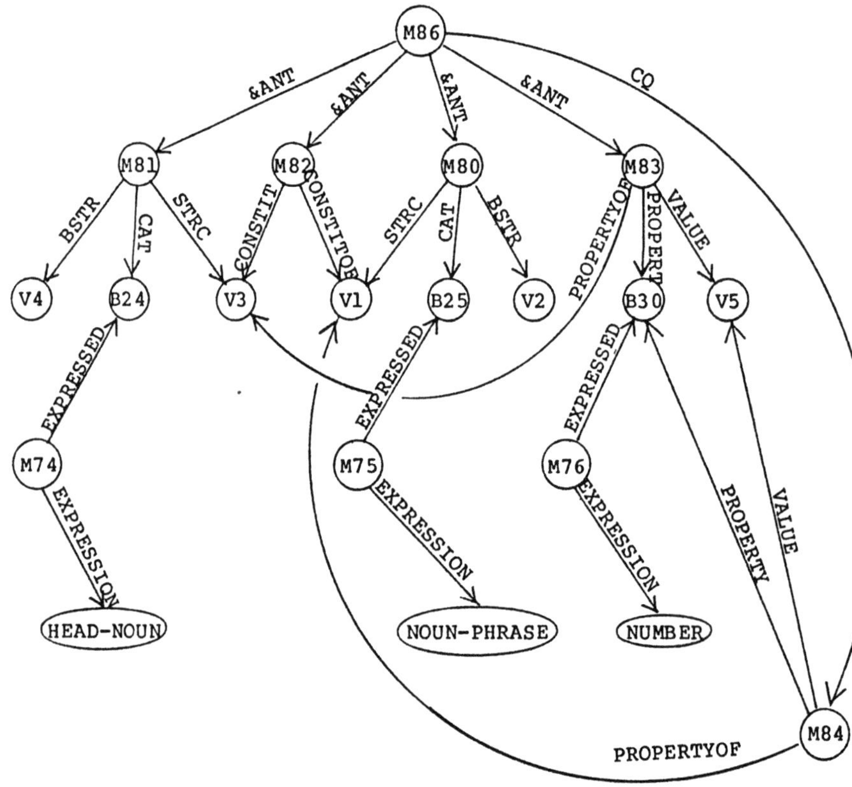

Fig. 29. Node M86 represents the interpretation of the input rule

V3, V4, and V5 are universally quantified (refer to Shapiro (1979 a) for the network representation of the quantification that is not shown in the figure and for more details on the rule structures of SNePS). The &ANT and CQ arcs are the SNePS system arcs used in the network representation of "&-entailment", the entailment of any of a set of consequents by the conjunction of one or more antecedents.

4 Language Use-Mention Distinction

In order for our system to treat linguistic knowledge as domain knowledge and to receive instruction in the use of this knowledge, it is essential for the system to distinguish between use and mention of language (Quine, 1951). We have already seen examples of this capability in our system. When words are entered into their appropriate lexical categories as in Section 2.5.2a, they are *mentioned*. Those lexemes that are themselves names of lexical categories are subsequently *used* to refer to their corresponding lexical categories. For example, the word 'VERB is *mentioned* when entered into the category L-CAT of lexical category names and is subsequently *used* to refer to the category of verbs (see Sect. 2.5.2). The word 'GOOSE is *mentioned* in the example sentence of Section 2.6 when specifying that its number is singular, but, in a similar sentence, the word 'GRADY is *used*.

As a more sophisticated example combining use and mention, we illustrate our system's processing of an equivalent version of the classic sentence of Tarski (1944) "'SNOW IS WHITE' IS TRUE IF AND ONLY IF SNOW IS WHITE". We do not treat truth relative to possible worlds. Our semantic network represents only the belief space of the system, and asserted propositions are those believed by the system.

We continue to build upon the language definition thus far input to the system in this article. The additional lexical entries that we input are:

L-CAT → 'MASS-NOUN   ADJECTIVE → 'TRUE
PROPERTY → 'TRUTH-VALUE   ADJECTIVE → 'FALSE
MASS-NOUN → 'SNOW

We explain to the system that

TRUE IS A TRUTH-VALUE
FALSE IS A TRUTH-VALUE

to be parsed and interpreted by the system as PROPERTY-CLASS-ENTRIES as shown in Section 2.6. Additional syntax rules such as the following are needed:

NOUN-PHRASE → MASS-NOUN
NOUN-PHRASE → LITERAL-STRING

Upon input of the sentence

If SNOW IS WHITE THEN "SNOW IS WHITE" IS TRUE

the system builds the parse tree shown in Figure 30 for the utterance.

Applying the teacher's rules, the system builds the network rule of Figure 31 as the interpretation of the input sentence. Node M92 represents the generic string "SNOW IS WHITE" and not just an instance of the string. Node M92 dominates a pattern that is matched by any instance of the string, with V8 a universally quantified variable node.

If the system believes that snow is white, then the rule shown in Figure 31 is used appropriately and if we query the system regarding any instance of the string "SNOW IS WHITE" it indicates that the string is true.

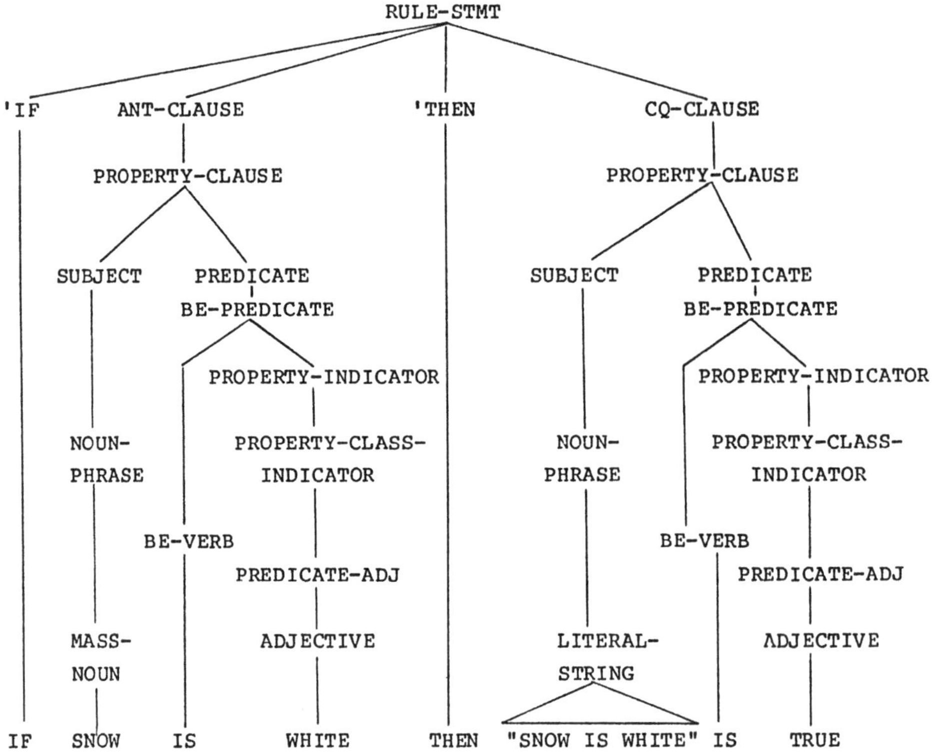

Fig. 30. Annotated parse tree

To complete the original bi-conditional statement, the converse statement

IF "SNOW IS WHITE" IS TRUE THEN SNOW IS WHITE

can also be entered the system and the converse of the rule of Figure 31 is built into the network as its interpretation.

5 Summary

This article has presented our approach to NLU: an approach that focuses on the capability of a natural langauge to be used as its own metalanguage. It is essential to this approach to have the system's parsing and linguistic knowledge be an integral part of its domain knowledge. It is our view that linguistic knowledge about a word or phrase is a part of its meaning or significance and, furthermore, there is no clear boundary line separating syntactic, semantic, and world knowledge. For these reasons we represent linguistic knowledge along with other domain knowledge in an integrated knowledge base. Furthermore, the linguistic rules of the system's knowledge base comprise the system's knowledge of language understanding in the same way that the rules of any rule-based system comprise that system's

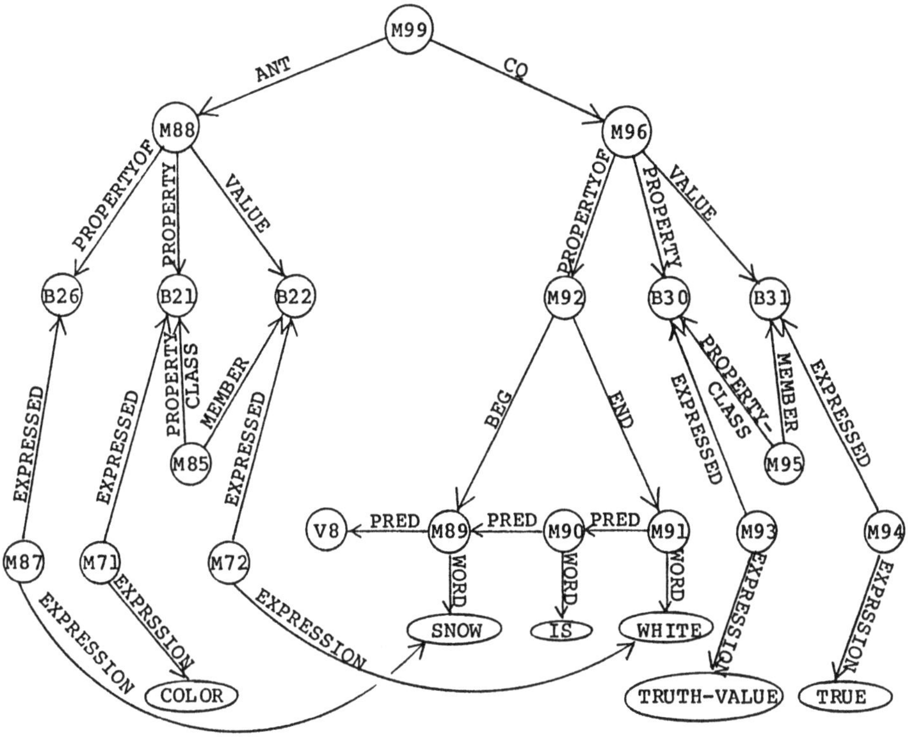

Fig. 31. Interpretation of the input utterance "IF SNOW IS WHITE THEN 'SNOW IS WHITE' IS TRUE"

knowledge of its domain of application. Our system also incorporates the use-mention distinction for language.

We are exploring the possibility of a NLU system's becoming more adept in its use of some language by being instructed in the use of the language. We wish this explanation to be given in an increasingly sophisticated subset of the language being taught. The system must start with some language facility, and we are interested in seeing how small and theory-independent we can make the initial kernel language.

In this chapter, we have discussed the core knowledge and representations of our system, including the kernel language, which consists of predefined terms, and syntactic and semantic rewrite rules with which to bootstrap into a more sophisticated language definition. We have demonstrated the capability of increasing the system's language facility by using the very same facility to instruct the system about language understanding. We built up the system's capability to the stage at which it processed the sentence "IF THE HEAD-NOUN OF A NOUN-PHRASE X HAS NUMBER Y THEN X HAS NUMBER Y". We presented additional examples of language being treated as the topic of discourse including the system's parsing and interpretation of the sentence "'SNOW IS WHITE' IS TRUE IF AND ONLY IF SNOW IS WHITE".

We discussed the system's parsing strategy, which is a combined bottom-up, top-down strategy. Our system's parser is a general rule-based inference system in which applicable rules are activated in parallel in the form of processes or demons. The inference system employs bi-directional inference to cut down the fan out of pure forward or backward chaining.

Acknowledgements. We would like to thank the SNePS Research Group of the State University of New York at Buffalo for their constructive comments and opinions during the course of this research. In particular, we thank William J. Rapaport for his comments on an earlier version of this chapter.

Appendix *Chronological Summary of Input to the System as Presented in This Chapter*

Section Number	Input
2.5.2	L-CAT → 'NOUN
2.5.2	L-CAT → 'PROPER-NOUN
2.5.2	L-CAT → 'DEF-DET
2.5.2	L-CAT → 'INDEF-DET
2.5.2	L-CAT → 'VERB
2.5.2	L-CAT → 'BE-VERB
2.5.2	L-CAT → 'ADVERB
2.5.2	L-CAT → 'ADJECTIVE
2.5.2	L-CAT → 'PREPOSITION
2.5.2	L-CAT → 'CONJ
2.5.2	L-CAT → 'PROPERTY
2.5.2	S-CAT → 'HEAD-NOUN
2.5.2	S-CAT → 'STRING
2.5.2	VARIABLE → 'X
2.5.2	VARIABLE → 'Y
2.5.2	NOUN → 'GOOSE
2.5.2	NOUN → 'GEESE
2.5.2	PROPER-NOUN → 'GRADY
2.5.2	PROPER-NOUN → 'GLADYS
2.5.2	DEF-DET → 'THE
2.5.2	INDEF-DET → 'A
2.5.2	VERB → 'HAS
2.5.2	BE-VERB → 'IS
2.5.2	ADVERB → 'THEN
2.5.2	ADJECTIVE → 'WHITE
2.5.2	ADJECTIVE → 'SINGULAR
2.5.2	ADJECTIVE → 'PLURAL
2.5.2	PREPOSITION → 'OF
2.5.2	CONJ → 'IF
2.5.2	PROPERTY → 'COLOR
2.5.2	PROPERTY → 'NUMBER
2.5.2	UNIQUE-MEANING-CAT → 'ADJECTIVE
2.5.2	UNIQUE-MEANING-CAT → 'PROPERTY
2.5.2	PROPERTY-CLAUSE → SUBJECT PREDICATE

Section Number	Input
2.5.2	SUBJECT → NOUN-PHRASE
2.5.2	NOUN-PHRASE → LITERAL
2.5.2	NOUN-PHRASE → VARIABLE
2.5.2	NOUN-PHRASE → PROPER-NOUN
2.5.2	PREDICATE → RELATION-PREDICATE
2.5.2	PREDICATE → BE-PREDICATE
2.5.2	RELATION-PREDICATE → RELATION PREDICATE-ADJ
2.5.2	BE-PREDICATE → BE-VERB PROPERTY-INDICATOR
2.5.2	RELATION → 'HAS PROPERTY-INDICATOR
2.5.2	PROPERTY-- INDICATOR → PROPERTY-CLASS-INDICATOR
2.5.2	PROPERTY-INDICATOR → PROPERTY
2.5.2	PROPERTY-CLASS-INDICATOR → PREDICATE-ADJ
2.5.2	RULE-STMT → 'IF ANT-CLAUSE 'THEN CQ-CLAUSE
2.5.2	RELATION PREDICATE-ADJ → RELATION ADJECTIVE
2.5.2	RELATION PREDICATE-ADJ → RELATION VARIABLE
2.5.2	BE-VERB PREDICATE-ADJ → BE-VERB ADJECTIVE
2.5.2	'IF ANT-CLAUSE → 'IF PROPERTY-CLAUSE
2.5.2	'THEN CQ-CLAUSE → 'THEN PROPERTY-CLAUSE
2.5.3	PROPERTY-CLAUSE : : PROPERTY SUBJECT
	PROPERTY PROPERTY-INDICATOR
	VALUE PREDICATE-ADJ
2.5.3	ANT-CLAUSE : : PROPERTY-CLAUSE
2.5.3	CQ-CLAUSE : : PROPERTY-CLAUSE
2.5.3	SUBJECT : : NOUN-PHRASE
2.5.3	NOUN-PHRASE: : LITERAL
2.5.3	NOUN-PHRASE: : VARIABLE
2.5.3	NOUN-PHRASE: : PROPER-NOUN
2.5.3	PROPERTY-INDICATOR : : PROPERTY-CLASS-INDICATOR
2.5.3	PROPERTY-INDICATOR : : PROPERTY
2.5.3	PREDICATE-ADJ : ADJECTIVE
2.5.3	PREDICATE-ADJ : : VARIABLE
2.5.3	PROPERTY-CLASS-INDICATOR > >
	[MEMBER ADJECTIVE PROPERTY-CLASS +]
2.5.3	INDEF-S-PHRASE > > [BSTR STRING CAT S-CAT STRC +]
2.6	GRADY HAS COLOR WHITE
2.6	'GOOSE HAS NUMBER SINGULAR
2.6	PROPERTY-CLASS-ENTRY → ADJECTIVE 'IS 'A PROPERTY
2.6	PROPERTY-CLASS-ENTRY : : MEMBER ADJECTIVE
	PROPERTY-CLASS PROPERTY
2.6	WHITE IS A COLOR
2.6	PLURAL IS A NUMBER
2.6	GLADYS IS WHITE
2.6	'GEESE IS PLURAL
3.2	DEF-S-PHRASE → DEF-DET S-CAT
3.2	INDEF-S-PHRASE → INDEF-DET S-CAT
3.2	MAIN-APPOS-PHR VAR-NAME → INDEF-S-PHRASE VARIABLE
3.2	VAR-APPOSITION-PHR → MAIN-APPOS-PHR VAR-NAME
3.2	SUP-STRING-REF → VAR-APPOSITION-PHR
3.2	CONSTIT-REF → DEF-S-PHRASE
3.2	CONSTIT-PHRASE→ CONSTIT-REF 'OF SUP-STRING-REF
3.2	NOUN-PHRASE → CONSTIT-PHRASE

Section Number	Input
3.2	CONSTIT-PHRASE > > [CONSTIT + CONSTITOF SUP-STRING-REF] [BSTR STRING CAT DEF-S-PHRASE STRC +]
3.2	SUP-STRING-REF : : VAR-APPOSITION-PHR
3.2	MAIN-APPOS-PHR : : INDEF-S-PHRASE
3.2	NOUN-PHRASE : : CONSTIT-PHRASE
3.2	DEF-S-PHRASE : : S-CAT
3.3	IF THE HEAD-NOUN OF A NOUN-PHRASE X HAS NUMBER Y THEN X HAS NUMBER Y
4	L-CAT → 'MASS-NOUN
4	PROPERTY → 'TRUTH-VALUE
4	MASS-NOUN → 'SNOW
4	ADJECTIVE → 'TRUE
4	ADJECTIVE → 'FALSE
4	TRUE IS A TRUTH-VALUE
4	FALSE IS A TRUTH-VALUE
4	NOUN-PHRASE → MASS-NOUN
4	NOUN-PHRASE → LITERAL-STRING
4	IF SNOW IS WHITE THEN "SNOW IS WHITE" IS TRUE
4	IF "SNOW IS WHITE" IS TRUE THEN SNOW IS WHITE

References

Allen, J. (1978): Anatomy of LISP. McGraw-Hill, New York

Bever, T. G. (1970): The Cognitive Basis for Linguistic Structures. In: Hayes, J. R. (ed.): Cognition and the Development of Language. Wiley, New York pp. 279-352

Bever, T. G. (1973): Serial Position and Response Biases do Do Not Account for the Effect of Syntactic Structure on the Location of Brief Noises During Sentences. Journal of Psycholinguistic Research **2**, 187-288 (1973)

Bobrow, R. J. (1978): The RUS System. BBN Report No. 3878

Bobrow, R. J. and Webber, B. (1980): Knowledge Representation for Syntactic/Semantic Processing. Proc. AAAI-80, pp. 316-323

Brachman, R. J. (1977): What's in a Concept: Structural Foundations for Semantic Networks. Int. J. Man-Machine Studies **9**, 127-152 (1977)

Brachman, R. J. (1978a): A Structural Paradigm for Representing Knowledge. BBN Report No. 3605

Brachman, R. J., Ciccarelli, E., Greenfeld, N., and Yonke, M. (1978b): KLONE Reference Manual. BBN Report No. 3848, July 1978

Brachman, R. J. (1979): On the Epistemological Status of Semantic Networks. In Findler, N. (ed.): Associative Networks. Academic Press, New York, pp. 3-50

Brown, G. and Yule, G. (1983): Discourse Analysis. Cambridge University Press, Cambridge

Bruce, B. (1975): Case Systems for Natural Language. Artificial Intelligence **6**, 327-360 (1975)

Burge, W. H. (1975): Recursive Programming Techniques. Addison-Wesley, Reading

Charniak, E. (1981): A Common Representation for Problem-Solving and Language-Comprehension Information. Artificial Intelligence **16** (3), 225-255 (1981)

Dahl, V. (1979): Quantification in a Three-Valued Logic for Natural Language Question-Answering Systems. Proc. IJCAI 79, pp. 182-187

Dahl, V. (1981): Translating Spanish into Logic Through Logic. AJCL **7** (3), 149-164 (1981)

Fillmore, C. (1968) : The Case for Case. In: Bach, E. and Harms, R. (eds.): Universals in Linguistic Theory. Holt, Rinehart, and Winston, pp. 1-90

Fodor, J.A. and Garrett, M.F. (1967): Some Syntactic Determinants of Sentential Complexity, Perception and Psychophysics **2**, 289-296 (1969)
Hayes, P. (1977): On Semantic Nets, Frames and Associations. Proc. IJCAI 77, pp.99-107
Hendrix, G.G. (1978): The Representation of Semantic Knowledge. In: Walker, D.E. (ed.): Understanding Spoken Language. Elsevier North-Holland, Amsterdam
Hendrix, G.G. (1979): Encoding Knowledge in Partitioned Networks. In: Findler, N. (ed.): Associative Networks. Academic Press, New York
Kaplan, R.M. (1973): A Multi-processing Approach to Natural Language. Proceedings of the National Computer Conference. AFIPS Press, Montvale, NJ, pp.435-440
Kay, M. (1973): The Mind System. In Rustin, R. (ed.): Natural Language Processing. Algorithmics Press, New York, pp.153-188
Levelt, W.J.M. (1970): Hierarchical Chunking in Sentence Processing. Perception and Psychophysics **8**, 99-102 (1970)
Levelt, W.J.M. (1974): Formal Grammars in Linguistics and Psycholinguistics, Vol.3: Psycholinguistic Applications. Mouton, The Hague
Maida, A.S. and Shapiro, S.C. (1982): Intensional Concepts in Propositional Semantic Networks. Cognitive Science **6**, 4 (1982)
McCord, M.C. (1982): Using Slots and Modifiers in Logic Grammars for Natural Language. Artificial Intelligence **18** (3), 327-367 (1982)
McKay, D.P. and Shapiro, S.C. (1980): MULITI - A LISP Based Multiprocessing System. Conference Record of the 1980 LISP Conference, Stanford University, pp.29-37
Pereira, F.C.N. and Warren, D.H.D. (1980): Definite Clause Grammars for Language Analysis - A Survey of the Formalism and a Comparison with Augmented Transition Networks. Artificial Intelligence **13**, 231-278 (1980)
Pollack, J., and Waltz, D. (1982): Natural Language Processing Using Spreading Activation and Lateral Inhibition. Proc. Conf. of Cognitive Science Society, pp.50-53
Quillian, R. (1968): Semantic Memory. In: Minsky, M. (ed.): Semantic Information Processing. MIT Press, Cambridge
Quillian, R. (1969): The Teachable Language Comprehender: A Simulation Program and the Theory of Language. CACM **12**, 459-476 (1969)
Quine, W.V. (1951): Mathematical Logic. Harper and Row
Quine, W.V. (1948): On What There Is. Review of Metaphysics **2**. Reprinted in: Linsky, L. (ed.): Semantics and the Philosophy of Language. University of Illinois Press, Chicago, 1952, pp.189-206
Robinson, J.A. (1965): A Machine-oriented Logic Based on the Resolution Principle. JACM **12**, 23-41 (1965)
Roussel, P. (1965): Prolog: Manuel de Reference et d'Utilisation. Groupe d'Intelligence Artificielle, Universite de Marseille-Luminy, September, 1975
Rumelhart, D. and Norman, D. (1973): Active Semantic Networks as a Model of Human Memory. Proc. IJCAI 73, pp.450-457
Schubert, L. (1976): Extending the Expressive Power of Semantic Networks. Artificial Intelligence **7** (2), 163-198 (1976)
Schubert, L.K., Goebel, R.G., and Cercone, N.J. (1979): The Structure and Organization of a Semantic Net for Comprehension and Inference. In: Findler, N. (ed.): Associative Networks. Academic Press, New York
Schubert, L.K. and Pelletier, F.J. (1982): From English to Logic: Context-Free Computation of 'Conventional' Logical Translation. AJCL **8** (1), 26-44 (1982)
Shapiro, S.C. (1971): A Net Structure for Semantic Information Storage, Deduction and Retrieval. Proc. IJCAI **71**, pp.512-523
Shapiro, S.C. (1979a): The SNePS Semantic Network Processing System. In: Findler, N. (ed.): Associative Networks - The Representation and Use of Knowledge by Computers. Academic Press, New York, pp.179a-203
Shapiro, S.C. (1979b): Using Non-Standard Connectives and Quantifiers for Representing Deduction Rules in a Semantic Network. Invited paper presented at Current Aspects of AI Research, a seminar held at the Electrotechnical Laboratory, Tokyo
Shapiro, S.C. and the SNePS Implementation Group (1981): SNePS User's Manual. Department of Computer Science, SUNY at Buffalo, NY

Shapiro, S.C. and Neal, J.G. (1982): A Knowledge Engineering Approach to Natural Language Understanding. Proc. ACL, pp. 136-144
Shapiro, S.C., Martins, J., and McKay, D. (1982): Bi-Directional Inference. Proc. of the Cognitive Science Society, pp. 90-93
Simmons, R. (1973): Semantic Networks: Their Computation and Use for Understanding English Sentences. In: Schank, R. and Colby, K. (eds.): Computer Models of Thought and Language. Freeman
Tarski, A. (1944): The Semantic Conception of Truth. Philosophy and Phenomenological Research **4**. Reprinted in: Linsky, L. (ed.): Semantics and the Philosophy of Language. University of Illinois Press, Chicago, 1952, pp. 13-47
Warren, D.H.D., and Pereira, F.C.N. (1982) An Efficient Easily Adaptable System for Interpreting Natural Language Queries. AJCL **8** (3-4), 110-119 (1982)
Woods, W.A. (1975): What's in a Link: Foundations for Semantic Networks. In: Bobrow, D.G. and Collins, A.M. (eds.): Representation and Understanding. Academic Press, New Xork, pp. 35-82

Using Declarative Knowledge for Understanding Natural Language

J. Pitrat

1 Introduction

Declarative knowledge includes no information prescribing when and how it can be used. For instance, "the article agrees with the noun in gender and number" is declarative knowledge: we can use it at the beginning of the parsing of a sentence, at the end, or not at all. We can check the gender, then the number, or the other way round, or only the gender. We can use it when we find an article, when we find a noun, in both cases, or when we have completed the parsing of a noun group.

Using declarative knowledge is beneficial because of its convenience and efficiency. It is easier to give declarative rather than procedural knowledge, because, since we do not indicate how the knowledge must be used, the amount of knowledge is smaller. The components of the knowledge are independent, so we can remove, add, or modify them independently of each other. It is also easier to use declarative knowledge for several applications. This is especially useful during work on natural languages in which the same knowledge can be used for both understanding and generating texts. Moreover, programs using declarative knowledge may be more efficient than programs using procedural knowledge. A procedural system is obliged to use the knowledge in a prescribed order. It may be difficult to find this order, and the best order may change according to the data. In some cases, Laurière's general program [12] solved a problem faster than a program specifically written to solve this problem. But unfortunately, to achieve this speed, we must have a very clever interpreter which knows when it is appropriate to utilize a piece of knowledge. If we have a combinatorial interpreter, the performances may be very poor; for this reason, general interpreters of declarative knowledge have a poor reputation in situations when we do not want to waste computer time.

The first programs which understood or generated natural language used procedural knowledge. For instance, Winograd [23] created a programming language "PROGRAMMAR" for defining syntactic knowledge. Also, the meaning of complex words such as "the", "be", "have", "one", ... was described in LISP subroutines. The pragmatic knowledge was given in a third procedural language, MICROPLANNER. In the same way, the systems using ATN semantic or syntactic grammars [2, 24] received their knowledge in a procedural form.

Curiously, it is often difficult to determine if a program received declarative or procedural knowledge. Some authors give a comprehensive description of the knowledge used, but do not accurately indicate how this knowledge is given to the program. We can have a clear idea of all the steps necessary for building the meaning representation, but have nothing clear about the representation of the knowledge. However, it is likely that in such cases, the knowledge is procedural.

Many programs used declarative knowledge for understanding and for generating natural language. We can classify them in three sets:

1. Some programs use a general interpreter of declarative knowledge, where we find mainly work done with PROLOG. See, for instance, Pereira and Warren [17], McCord [15], Norton [16]. All the knowledge which has been given to the program is often stated in these papers. This approach has produced some interesting results, but there are some difficulties. The language used for describing the knowledge is predicate calculus, and it is not highly effective in its description of the syntactic, semantic, or pragmatic knowledge. The human expert who gives the knowledge may prefer a formalism suitable for each kind of knowledge because the interpreter is general and cannot use the special characteristics of this domain. However, if a large amount of knowledge is given, then the system will not be very efficient. If the expert knows how the interpreter works, he can give the knowledge in such a way that it can be efficiently used; however, we lose an advantageous aspect of using declarative knowledge if we define it according to the procedure which will use it. An interesting improvement would be to give some metaknowledge in the same formalism (Gallaire and Lasserre [7], Dincbas [6]) so that the interpreter can adjust itself to the characteristics of the domain. However, much work must be done in this direction before efficient application to natural language.
2. In other cases, the author defines a special language for declarative knowledge, but only for part of the necessary knowledge. For instance, Charniak [3] is interested in the use of pragmatic knowledge, but he does not explore the other kinds of knowledge: the program receives a semantic representation, but not English sentences. This approach is useful for experimenting with methods, but it cannot enable one to study the difficult problem of simultaneously using various types of knowledge. Also, it may happen that the author uses the meaning representation of another, already-existing program, which creates exactly the same drawbacks.
3. The author defines a declarative representation convenient in defining the knowledge which is necessary for understanding natural language. He also develops an interpreter for this knowledge. This interpreter may be efficient because its author knows the kind of problem to be solved: processing natural language.

Arens [1] and Wilensky [22] experimented with the PHRAN and PHRED systems. The first is a language analyzer and the second a language production mechanism. They use pattern-concept pairs which indicate the relationship between a part of a sentence and a part of the meaning representation. Their program worked on simple sentences, effectively using the same knowledge for analyzing and for producing language. However, they mainly use semantic knowledge and in order to process more complex sentences this method must be improved.

A very interesting method has been defined by Kay [8-11] where syntactic and semantic knowledge is given in a functional grammar. Kay has implemented an interpreter with many interesting ideas for improving the efficiency of the system. It has been used for English, where word order is essential, and for Finnish, where word order is of less importance. This method has been used mainly for syntactic analysis. Recently, Rousselot [20] has experimented with stories in French. His interpreter also uses quite a bit of semantic and pragmatic knowledge.

My program belongs to this third class. There are two main differences from Kay's work. Kay defines one formalism and all the knowledge is given in the formalism. I preferred to define many formalisms, even inside one type of knowledge, for instance, syntactic knowledge. The advantage of Kay's method is that the interpreter is simpler, but on the other hand, it is difficult for a human expert to give his knowledge in various domains in only one formalism. If we accept several formalisms, we can choose for each specific type of knowledge a formalism convenient for the expert. Another difference in the realization of the interpreter is when a different strategy is used for dealing with the ambiguity.

In Section 2, I shall describe the various kinds of knowledge used by the system. To understand this part, it is not necessary to know the interpreter, and also, the human expert who gives the knowledge does not need to care about its use. This knowledge can be used for understanding and producing natural language. However, I have only implemented the first interpreter.

Section 3 will be devoted to a description of the interpreter, which uses knowledge to understand a text. I had to make a choice, since it is possible to develop very different interpreters for the same knowledge. This interpreter contains knowledge for utilizing the knowledge of the language and of the domain. Unfortunately, this metaknowledge is given in a procedural form, and this is the main weakness of the interpreter: if declarative knowledge is to be used efficiently then a lot of metaknowledge must be used, and it is interesting to use declarative metaknowledge exactly for the same reasons that it is interesting to use declarative knowledge.

French commentaries on chess games have been experimented on with this program; however, nothing in the interpreter depends either on French or on chess.

2 The Knowledge

The system receives knowledge on:
- lexicography
- syntax
- semantics
- pragmatics.

2.1 Lexicographic Knowledge

There are three subsets of lexicographic knowledge.

2.1.1 The Words

Each entry contains:
- the name of the words, used for communicating with the expert,
- the name of its conjugation, which is described in the third subset,
- the ordered sequence of its roots. A root is a string of characters which may be empty.

For instance:
être, être, s,, e, ét, f. The word "être" uses the conjugation "être" and has five roots, the second one being the empty string.
tenir, venir, tien, ten, tienn, tin, tîn. The word "tenir" uses the conjugation "venir" and has five roots.
créer, aimer, cré. "Créer" has the same conjugation as "aimer" and has only one root.

2.1.2 The Ending Sequences

Each entry contains:
- the name of a particular sequence of endings,
- an ordered sequence of endings: an ending is a string of alphabetic characters which may be empty.

For instance:

vsi, sse, sses, t, ssions, ssiez, ssent
vf, drai, dras, dra, drons, drez, dront
vps, s, s, t, mes, tes, rent

The first sequence is named "vsi". Its fifth ending is "ssiez".

2.1.3 The Conjugations

Actually, here we have the description of the various forms of a word, including the conjugations, the declensions, and the knowledge for determining noun plurals. It is useful to break up a conjugation into several groups, for instance, each tense of a verb, or if the language has declensions, each combination of gender and number. Each group represents a number of forms which is dependent on the part of the conjugation it describes: 6 for the present indicative in French, 1 for the present infinitive in French, 8 for the present indicative in Greek, 6 for a group of a Latin noun or adjective (there are six cases), 4 for a French noun or adjective (singular masculine and feminine, plural masculine and feminine).

A conjugation contains a name which is used in the description of the words and a set of groups. Each group contains a name which indicates its place in the conjugation, for instance, "ip" for the present indicative and "si" for the imperfect subjunctive. Then we have the name of the sequence endings and the list of n numbers of roots if the group has n components. The sequence endings must also have n components. If all the roots have the same number, we write this number only once. If a form is defective, the corresponding number of the root is 0. If all the elements of a group are defective, we do not include this group in the conjugation. If a group has several forms (such as the future of "asseoir", the present indicative of "payer", ...), we include several groups with the same name, each one describing one of these forms.

For instance, the conjugation "venir" is:

> venir, ip, 1, 1, 1, 2, 2, 3, ii, vii, 2, ps, vps, 4, 4, 4, 5, 5, 4, if, vf, 1, cd, vc, 1, sp, vsp, 3, 3, 3, 2, 2, 3, si, vsi, 4, 4, 5, 4, 4, 4, imp, vip, 0, 1, 0, 2, 2, 0, pp, vpp, 2, inf, vinf, 2, pprt, vpt, 2.

If we want to find the first person plural of the "passé simple" of "tenir", the information with the word "tenir" indicates that its conjugation is "venir". The name of the group describing the: "passé simple" is "ps". We have in "venir" the group: ps, vps, 4, 4, 4, 5, 5, 4. The first person of the plural is the fourth element. So the root is 5. In the word "tenir", we see that the fifth root is "tîn". The name of the sequence endings is "vps". The fourth element of "vps" is "mes". So we obtain the result by the concatenation of the root and of the ending: "tînmes".

It is easy to create these three sets of knowledge. For the conjugations, we collect the information in specialized books such as Bescherelle for French. We can choose where we separate the word into its root and its ending. It is usually better to restrict the number of roots, even if this increases the number of sequence endings. There are thousands of words in a language, and if each word has many roots, it is difficult to give them. On the other hand, however, the number of sequence endings is small, only about one hundred in French.

In French, the conjugation of a noun has only one group. We can manage special cases, such as "orgue" which is masculine when singular and feminine when plural. So, for the word, we have:

> orgue, amour, orgue

and the conjugation:

> amour, nom, nn, 1001

if "nn" is the name of the sequence endings: nn,,, s, s (the first two endings are the empty string). We see that the masculine singular of "orgue" is "orgue", its feminine plural is "orgues" and the feminine singular and masculine plural do not exist since there is a zero in the corresponding places.

This method is not completely general, because it is not convenient for languages such as English where a word has few inflexions or for languages such as Arabic where the modifications are not usually at the end of the word. However, it has been used successfully for French, Spanish, German, Latin, Russian, Italian, Polish, and Rumanian.

2.2 Syntactic Knowledge

There are five sets of syntactic knowledge.

2.2.1 Syntactic Markers

Syntactic markers are associated with words. For instance, "rester" has the marker AUXILIARYETRE: it does not use the auxiliary "avoir", but "être": "je suis resté" and not "j'ai resté". "Repentir" has the marker ESSENTIAL: it is a verb "essentiellement pronominal". This knowledge is useful for the agreement rules of the past participle.

2.2.2 Graphs

These indicate the knowledge of word order in a sentence. It is convenient to divide them into subgraphs, one for each important unit of a language: noun group, adjective group, clause, ... There are four kinds of nodes:

a) nodes corresponding to a word,
b) nodes which merge several nodes. It is useful if many nodes have the same set of successors, as in Figure 1. If each N_i may be followed by any P_j, it is convenient to introduce a node R, and we have only 11 arcs instead of 30.
c) nodes indicating the beginning of a subgraph. The order of the words at that place is described by another graph. We indicate its name and the name of the node where we must begin. This graph may be called recursively.
d) nodes indicating the end of a graph. In this case, the order of the following words is indicated in the graph which called the present graph. If we are at the first level, we have the end of the sentence.

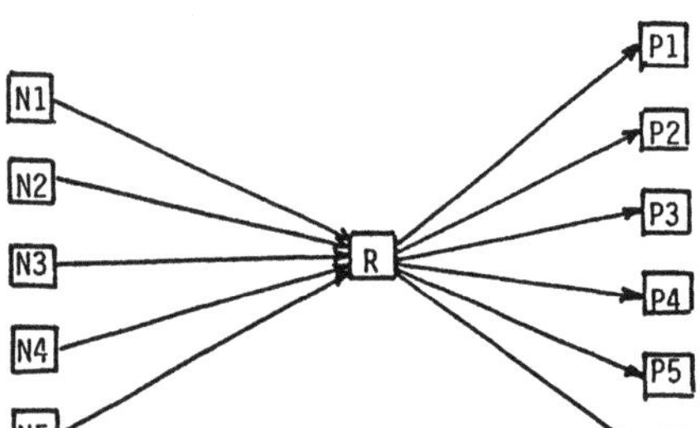

Fig. 1

Each node has a name, which can be used in the list of successors of the other nodes or in the other types of syntactic or semantic knowledge. Further, more information can be connected to a node:

a) conditions. When a condition is false, we cannot have this node in a correct sentence.

b) a set of arcs. This is mandatory except for the end nodes. Each element is a pair which consists of the name of a following node and a condition (which may always be true). If the condition is false, we cannot have the associated node after the present node.
c) when the node calls another graph, we have the name of this graph, and the name of the first node to consider. Moreover, we can indicate the value of a parameter which can be tested when we use the information of the subgraph. It is convenient to use the same graph for describing structures which are similar, but which may differ on some minor points. For a French clause, this parameter can be used to indicate if we have:
   - an ordinary clause
   - a relative clause
   - a relative clause with a preposition
   - a clause with a verb at the present participle
   - a clause with a verb at the past participle
   - etc.

In the same way, the value of the parameter may indicate if the same graph represents a noun group or a preposition group.

A condition is a conjunction of disjunctions of unit conditions, or of their negations. A unit condition may be:

a) a node is present.
   The node AUXETRE is present.
   The node AUXAV is absent.

These conditions occur in the description of the past participle agreement rules of French; AUXAV is the node corresponding to the place of the auxiliary "avoir" and AUXETRE to the auxiliary "être".

b) at some node we have:
   - some word: the word "le" is at node DET
   - some syntactic marker: the word at the node VERB has the syntactic marker AUXILIARYETRE (which means that a verb uses the auxiliary "être" in the active voice).
   - some value for one of the morphological characteristics of the word: the word at node NOUN has the value FEMININE for its characteristic GENDER.

Later, we shall see some other kinds of unit conditions associated with a node.

c) the value of a parameter of the present graph or of one of its ancestors.

In a condition associated with a node N1, we can refer to another node N in several ways:

- its name. Implicitly, it is a node of the same graph as the node N1
- its name and the indication of a level: SUP for the graph which called the present graph, SUPSUP for its grandfather. SUP.NOUN refers to the node NOUN in the father of the present graph.

A condition may refer to any node of the present graph or of any of its ancestors. It is possible that the node it refers to is after the node N. In that case, and if the interpreter chooses to begin at the first word of the sentence, it cannot evaluate the condition when it finds the node N. But the human expert does not concern himself with how the knowledge will be used. For instance we can put at node DET (determiner) a condition about a characteristic of the word at node NOUN.

2.2.3 The "Traits"

It may be convenient to define new objects for a graph: the description of the conditions and of the meaning of the words will be easier. For instance, in the meaning of a verb, it is important to indicate which objects may be the semantic subject of this verb. However, we have to define what is a semantic subject (the syntactic subject if the voice is active or a noun group with the preposition "par" if the voice is passive). In the same way, we have to define what is a voice. Thus, a "trait" defines these new concepts and more.

A trait is defined by a name and a set of pairs. The order of these pairs has no significance. Each pair consists of a value and a condition. The name can be used anywhere for referring to this definition: in a condition, or in the description of the meaning of a word or of an agreement rule. A trait is associated with a graph: there are traits for the clause, others for the noun group, etc. The traits SUJ (semantic subject) and VOICE are associated with the graph clause.

If only one condition among those in the set of pairs is true, then the value of the trait in the present context is the value associated with this condition. If several conditions are true, and the same value is associated with all of them, then the value is this common value. If several conditions are true, and the associated value is not always the same, then there is either a mistake in the grammar or the sentence structure is wrong. If no condition is true, the value of the trait is not defined.

The value of a trait may be a constant or a node. The value of the trait VOICE of a graph clause is a constant which may be ACTIVE, PASSIVE, or PRONOMINAL. The value of the trait SUJ (semantic subject) of a clause is a node. If the value of a trait is a node, we can use the name of this trait anywhere a node can be used except in the list of successors of a node, but it can be used as the possible value of another trait. In the definition of the trait SUJ, we can use as a possible value the trait SUBJECT (syntactic subject) with the condition that the trait VOICE have the value ACTIVE. Indeed, a new type of condition tests the value of a trait; but it is possible that the value of the trait SUJ is not defined, for instance, in "La tarte a été mangée" (the cake has been eaten).

The value of a trait of a graph may be a node of another graph. In "j'aime manger", the trait SUBJECT of the second clause "manger" is the trait SUBJECT of the first clause "j'aime".

In a simplified version of the definition of the trait VOICE, we have among its pairs:

ACTIVE The node AUXETRE is not present.

ACTIVE The word at node VERB has the syntactic marker AUXILIARYETRE (which means that, normally, this verb uses “être” as auxiliary).

PASSIVE The node AUXETRE is present and the word at node VERB does not have the marker AUXILIARYETRE.

2.2.4 The Agreement Rules

Their general form is:

Node 1. Node 2. Set of characteristics. Condition.

If the condition is true, the words at Node 1 and Node 2 must have the same value for all the given characteristics. So, the order of Node 1 and Node 2 does not matter.

DET - NOUN - GENDER, NUMBER.

The determiner and the noun always agree in gender and number since there is no condition. If we wanted to use a rule where there is agreement only if there is an article in DET, we would add a condition.

DET-NOUN-GENDER, NUMBER-SYNTACTIC MARKER. DET= ARTICLE.

The determiner must have the marker ARTICLE.

VERB - PRAC - GENDER, NUMBER. - PRESENT.AUXAV.

If the auxiliary “avoir” is present, the pronoun which is the object and before the verb (as “l'” in “je l'ai mangé”) agrees with the verb (which is necessarily at the past participle since “avoir” is present; it is possible, but useless, to add this condition). This rule is a part of the French past participle agreement rules.

We can have a trait at N1 or N2:

SUBJECT - VERB - NUMBER, PERSON - MOOD.VERB ≠ PARTICIPLE
MOOD.VERB ≠ INFINITIVE

SUBJECT is the syntactic subject of the clause. It agrees with the verb in person and number if the verb is neither at the participle nor at the infinitive.

If node N1 or node N2 is not present, the rule is not used. For instance, if there is no determiner, we do not use the first rule.

2.2.5 The Conjunctions

For each graph G, we have another graph G' which indicates the various ways in which to use conjunctions of graphs G. In the new graph G', we have nodes representing words which are conjunctions, nodes with a syntactic marker, nodes calling the graph G.

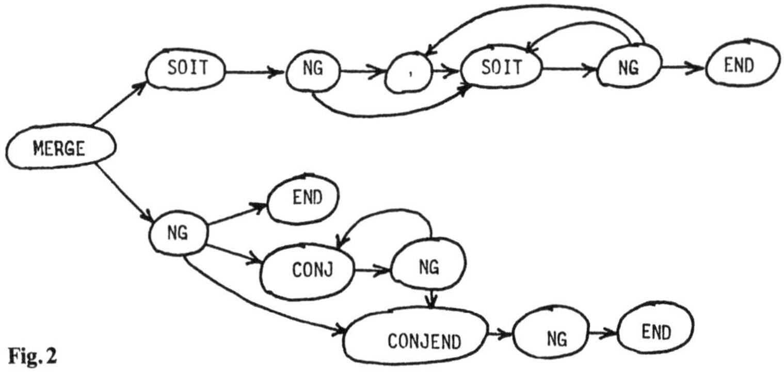

Fig. 2

For instance, the graph of Figure 2 is a simplified version of the graph associated with a noun group. NG indicates a call to the noun graph. SOIT is a syntactic marker which belongs to "soit", "et", "ou": the conjunctions which may begin a conjunction of noun groups such as in "Les Blancs prendront et la Tour et le Fou". CONJEND is a syntactic marker belonging to "et", "ou". CONJ belongs to "et", "ou", and the comma. MERGE is a merging node. Conditions must be added to the arcs and to the nodes, in order to avoid generating incorrect sentences such as "Les Blancs prennent soit le Cavalier et le Fou".

2.2.6 Comparison Between This Formalism and ATN Grammars

In both cases, we use a set of graphs for conveying knowledge. But an ATN is procedural, as opposed to my system where the knowledge is in a declarative form. The graph gives knowledge of the word order, but it does not prescribe an order for processing a sentence. The interpreter is not obliged to begin with the first word. It can begin with the last word, or even in the middle of the sentence. Natural language has been created to make it possible for human beings to understand it when speaking. It is usually better to follow this order; however, it is a choice made during the defining of the interpreter and the expert need not know it or worry about it during graph definition.

This declarative aspect appears in several cases:

- a condition associated with some point of the graph may use what happens at nodes after this node. It is possible that we may not be able to evaluate a condition when we arrive at a node, even if we have begun at the first word.
- we do not indicate when we must use the agreement rules; the interpreter chooses the appropriate time - when it has found both nodes, later, or not at all.
- the traits show some likeness to the registers of an ATN. However, they are completely different. A register has two purposes in an ATN.
- - for storing an intermediary result which will be necessary later. This augments the power of the automaton. The value of a register may be replaced later by another value. For me, this is not necessary, because everything of the

preceding and following nodes is supposed to be already known. It is impossible to change the value of a trait because it has a determined set of values with possible ambiguities. However, we cannot add a new value to the present set of values.

- - for building pieces of the syntactic and/or the meaning representation of the sentence. Here, the goal of the graph is not to create a structure, but only to give information on word order. The interpreter may build a structure, if its author thinks that it is useful and he is free to choose any kind of structure. Moreover, nothing in our graphs prescribes such a structure.

The expert gives knowledge of the language, but no information on how a program can utilize this knowledge. So he does not define a method for parsing a sentence.

2.3 The Semantic Knowledge

The meaning of a word has two main parts:

- a pattern part which indicates whether the meaning may or may not be present in a text.
- an action part which indicates how the meaning will act during the creation of the meaning representation.

These definitions of the two parts of a meaning are related to their use during analysis. But if we want to produce a text, the action part indicates the possibility of choosing a meaning to describe a piece of the meaning representation; the pattern part indicates how we use the word corresponding to a meaning. During an analysis, a meaning has some similarity with the rule: pattern ⇒ action; if we are producing a sentence, it is the rule: action ⇒ pattern. However, this is declarative knowledge. It is possible that several meanings may be considered for a word and semantic knowledge does not indicate how we can choose between them. The various meanings of a word are given independently. When the interpreter cannot find the correct meaning using the pattern part, it must use other kinds of knowledge to remove this ambiguity.

When we want to build the various meanings of a word, it is difficult to define how many meanings it has. For instance, in the examples:

Pierre attaque Paul en justice.
Le Cavalier attaque la Dame.

we have two different meanings of the word "attaquer". Moreover, in English we translate it by two different verbs: "to prosecute" and "to attack". But in the following examples:

Le Cavalier, en venant en f3, attaque la Dame e5.
Les Blancs attaquent l'aile Dame.

We can wonder if "attaquer" has the same meaning in these two sentences. There is no definite answer. It depends on the chosen meaning representation. If this representation is very accurate, we consider many meanings for each word: we must create as many meanings as there are possible action parts. It is possible that we have different action parts in two meanings, when pattern parts are exactly the same. In that case, it is very difficult to remove the ambiguity: we have to use pragmatic knowledge or the meanings of other words which may require in this position some characteristics which are in only one of the pattern parts.

In the preceding example, we many consider that "attaquer" has the same meaning in both sentences: the subject creates a danger for the object. But we can also consider two meanings. The first is the preceding meaning and is present in the second sentence. The second indicates that the subject may capture the object. It is the meaning of "attaquer" in the first sentence. Naturally, we can infer that the object is in danger.

2.3.1 The Pattern Part of a Meaning

This includes several optional components, except for the first two which must have at least one element.

1. The set of words which have this meaning. These words are partly synonymous. It is possible that they may not be synonymous for their other meanings. For instance, "gonfler" and "enfler" are synonymous in French when we say "mon doigt gonfle" and "mon doigt enfle", but not for "je gonfle un ballon". "J'enfle un ballon" is incorrect.
2. The node names where the words may be found.
3. A set of semantic markers. A condition can specify that, at some node, there is a word which has a meaning with a particular semantic marker. This new type of condition may be used anywhere. The expert has to define a set of semantic markers suitable for his application. In the chess domain, I defined the following markers:
   - piece (which may also be a set of pieces)
   - area of the board (a square or a set of squares such as a line, the center, etc.)
   - player (Black, White, both of them),
   - expert (one of the people who is playing a game, the author of a book, any chess player, etc.)
   - opinion (a move is fine, a player is good, an opinion is wrong, a knight is strong, etc.)
4. A condition. If it is not true, the meaning is not present in the sentence.
5. A set of triples, which describe the surroundings of the word. A triple has the following components:
   a) its necessity. It has three possible values:
      - mandatory. If the information in the descriptive part does not agree with the sentence, the meaning is not present.
      - optional. The information may not be there.
      - exclusive. The node may be absent, but if it is present, the words at this node must agree with the information in the third part of the triple.

   b) The name of the nodes where the following information can be found. It is a node of the present graph (graph of the present word) or of one of its ancestors.

c) the description of the situation at the node. It is a set of possibilities, and one of these must be satisfied. Each of them may be:
   - the name of a word which must be at this node
   - the semantic marker of a meaning of the word
   - if the node corresponds to a subgraph, a new set of triples which characterize some elements of this subgraph. If a mandatory triple is not present in the subgraph, then the possibility is not satisfied. These new triples may also correspond to a subgraph. So, we can describe very complicated structures.
   - a variable. The value of a variable is the object which is at the node given in the second part of the triple. A variable is a sequence of alphanumeric characters, the first one being a letter. The same variable may appear once or several times in the pattern part, and in the action part. However, it must appear at least once in each part. This mechanism is useful because it enables us to gather the meanings of several representations in one more complex representation. The scope of a variable is restricted to one meaning.

If the same variable occurs several times in the triples, and if they are present in the sentence, the system will merge the corresponding objects. The objects are represented by a frame which is a set of pairs - attribute-value - of this attribute. The merging operation is similar to Kay's unification [10]. If we want to merge the objects O1 and O2 into one object O, and if O1 and O2 have the same attribute A, and if they have the same value for A, the merging succeeds. But if they have different values for A, it fails. If both values are objects, we apply the same method for these objects. For instance, let O1 and O2 be squares. If O1 has the value 2 for its ordinate and O2 the value 5 for its ordinate, the merging fails. If the object O1 has an attribute and O2 does not have this attribute, we add to O the attribute with its value in O1. For instance, if O1 has the ordinate 2 and O2 the abscissa E, O will be the square E2.

This may be useful for removing ambiguities. If we have to understand "Ce coup amène le Roi en d5", "ce coup" may refer to several moves in the preceding part of the text. All the moves when the piece moving is not a king, or when the arrival square is not d5 are eliminated as possible references for "ce coup". If only one move remains, without the prior knowledge of the king moving to d5, then this is added to its description.

6. Examples of pattern parts. Let us give the pattern parts for two meanings of "attaquer". (In the following "man" is used to mean "chess piece".)
   a) The man P1 of player K1 has been moved to its present square by move Q1. P1 can capture the man P2.

```
WORD: ATTAQUER
NODE: VERB
TRIPLES : EXCLUSIVE, SUJ, VAR:K1, VAR:P1, VAR:Q1
          MANDATORY, OBJ, VAR:P2
          OPTIONAL, ADVERB, WORD:DIRECTEMENT.
```

SUJ and OBJ are traits. Their values are, respectively, the semantic subject and object. ADVERB represents all the nodes where an adverb may be found in a clause.

b) The man P1 of player K1 has been moved to its present square by move Q1. P1 creates a threat for the set of men P2, which are in the set of squares Z2.

WORD : ATTAQUER
NODE : VERB
TRIPLES : EXCLUSIVE, SUJ, VAR:K1, VAR:P1, VAR:Q1
EXCLUSIVE, OBJ, VAR:P2, VAR:Z2
OPTIONAL, GPREP, STRUCTURE :
MANDATORY, PREP, MARKER:PLACE
MANDATORY, NOUN, VAR:Z2
OPTIONAL, ADVERB, WORD : INDIRECTEMENT.

GPREP represents all the nodes where a preposition group may be found in a clause. The semantic marker "place" is a marker of prepositions such as: "à", "sur", "en" ...

Only the first meaning is present in:

Le Cavalier attaque directement la Dame.

Only the second meaning is present in:

Les Blancs attaquent. (The object is mandatory for the first meaning)
Les Blancs attaquent l'aile Dame. (The object must be a chess piece for the first meaning.)
Tarrasch attaque au centre. (The object is mandatory for the first meaning.)
Les Blancs vont attaquer sur l'aile Dame.
Le Cavalier attaque indirectement la Dame.

Both meanings may be present in:

Le Cavalier attaque la Dame.
La Th4 attaque le Cd4.

We must use other knowledge to remove these ambiguities.

7. The pronouns. I have only studied the Proref pronouns, which refer to an object in the preceding part of the text. The pattern part may contain:
- conditions about the object the pronoun refers to. For instance, it must have the same gender as the pronoun.
- limitations of the places where we can look for the object; for instance, a number of words N. Then we consider only the last N words.
- the name of the node where the object is. For instance, the pronoun "qui" refers to an object which is at the NOUN node of the noun group, which is father of the clause including "qui".

A pronoun has no action part. If a pronoun may refer to several objects, the meaning of another word may eliminate some of them: if the pronoun "le" may refer to a man or to a move, according to the pattern part, and if it is the object of a verb which requires a man there, the second possibility is removed. If several references are still possible, the pragmatic knowledge will try to remove some of these possibilities.

8. If several words occur in a circumlocution, the expert must choose a word which will appear in the first component of the pattern part which describes the meaning of this circumlocution. Several criteria may be helpful:
   - we must choose a word whose presence is mandatory. We cannot tie the first meaning of "attaquer" to "directement" which is optional.
   - it is better to choose an unusual word: the meaning will be considered each time the word appears. For "attaque à la baionnette", which describes a chess concept, we could tie the meaning of this expression to the word "la". But each time we find the definite article, we will look for "baionnette" and "attaque"; usually, we remove the meaning because they are not present. The best solution would be to leave the system to automatically find the word it ties with a meaning. This is possible, but has not yet been implemented.

2.3.2 The Action Part of a Meaning

We have considered two kinds of actions:

- those which define an object which represents the meaning of a set of words.
- those which describe how the presence of a word modifies the representation of the meanings of the other words.

1. Usually, the action part defines an object which is a part of the meaning representation. It may be necessary to also define some auxiliary objects. Each object is represented by a set of pairs: attribute-value of this attribute.

The first meaning of "attaquer" is represented by an opinion D1 and there are two auxiliary objects: a move Q1 and a man P1:

D1 = TYPE : ATTACK, WHO : P1, WHAT : P2, AFTER : Q1
Q1 = MOVINGMAN : P1
P1 = PLAYER : K1

P1, P2, Q1, K1 may be defined by the pattern part. When this meaning is present, the word "attaquer" describes a situation. Its type is "attack". This means that the man in the "WHO" slot may capture the man in the "WHAT" slot. The position is the position after the move Q1. This position is perfectly defined, because a move also has a slot "AFTER", whose value is the preceding move. So, when we arrive at the initial position, we have a list of all the moves from this position to the present one: we have the possibility to create it. This is essential for using pragmatic knowledge. If the subject is a move, we know that P1 is the man in the slot "MOVINGMAN" of this move. If the subject is a player, we only know that P1 is one of the men of this player.

For the second meaning of "attaquer" we have:

D1 = TYPE : DANGER, DEGREE : HIGH, FORWHOM : P2, AFTER : Q1
P2 = PLACE : Z2
Q1 = MOVINGMAN : P1
P1 = PLAYER : K1.

The man P2 is in danger after move Q1. If P2 is not in the sentence, then P2 is the set of men in the Z2 area.

2. Words such as “très”, “beaucoup”, “assez” do not define an object, but rather indicate that the value of an attribute of an object must be modified. The action part has the following structure:

Name of the attribute-variable representing the object to modify = list of pairs (old value→new value).

For instance, “très” can modify an adjective which represents an opinion D1 on the position for one player:

DEGREE.D1 = WEAK→VERYWEAK; HIGH→VERYHIGH; VERYWEAK→WORTHLESS; ...

In “Ce coup est très bon”, we evaluate the value of a move. Instead of “high” (corresponding to “bon”), the value of its degree will be “very high”.

Some words may contain both action types. “Trop” indicates two things:

- an opinion. An object has a negative appreciation because one of its property values is too high or too small.
- we must modify the value of the opinion represented by the adjective or the adverb after “trop”. The rule for changing the value is the same as that given for “très”.

2.3.3 Meaning of the Symbols Which Are Not Words

In any domain, we can find sequences of symbols which are not words of a natural language. This is particularly important in commentaries of chess games where we can find:

- numbers : 1983
- lines : a2-g8 (the diagonal from a2 to g8)
- squares : e5 (the square e5)
- men : Td4 (the rook on square d4)
  CD (the queen knight
  PTR (the king rook pawn)
- moves : Td4 (the rook moves to d4)
  e5 (a pawn moves to e5)
  0-0-0 (long castling)
  Rg8-g7? (the king moves from g8 to g7 which is an unwise move)
  Cd-e7+ (a knight moves from a square in the column d to the square e7 and the king is in check)

In some cases, there may be an ambiguity between two categories:

- Td4 may be a man or a move
- e5 may be a square or a move

or inside one category: for Td4, it may be possible that both rooks can move to d4.

I wrote an ATN grammar which automatically builds the representation of objects corresponding to these sequences of symbols. For the moves, I defined only the algebraic notation, always used in French commentaries. It would also be easy to add descriptive notation.

When there is an ambiguity between two categories, the grammar generates both possibilities. If there is an ambiguity inside a category, the program does not see it: it only generates a description of the object's characteristics which are present. If we have the move Td4+, it creates the following object:

MOVINGMAN	: →NATURE:ROOK	
ARRIVAL	: →X	:d
CHECK	: YES	

The pragmatic knowledge will try to complete this description and, in some cases, find the ambiguity.

This is the only knowledge given in procedural form. It would be possible to give it in declarative form; however, since it was a minor point, and the results of the ATN were excellent, I decided not to transform this knowledge.

2.4 *Pragmatic Knowledge*

This knowledge is clustered in several expertises which we can find in [18, 19]. An expertise is a set of productions. A production may contain variables with a scope restricted to an expertise. The value of a variable may be a numerical constant, an object, or a set of objects or numerical constants. It is possible that a production has no antecedents.

An expression may be:

- an object
- a numerical constant
- a variable
- an attribute of an expression
- a function of an expression, e.g., ADD for addition, ABS for absolute value. There is a database for representing the present state of the world and, with functions, we can access this database. For instance, we can know the name of the man on square e5.

An antecedent is a condition which includes two expressions and a relation which may be: $=$, $\neq$, $>$, $\geqslant$, $<$, $\leqslant$, $\in$. In the last case, the value of the second expression must be a set.

The consequence of a production may be:

1. a condition. In that case a production is: $c_1, c_2, \ldots c_n => d$ which may be used in several ways:

If the c_i are true and d is false, we have a contradiction.
If the c_i are true and d is unknown, then d is true. If d is:

variable = expression, if the expression can be evaluated, we have the possibility of defining the value of the variable.
If d is false, c_1, c_2, ... c_{i-1}, c_{i+1},... c_n are true and c_i is unknown, then we know that c_i is false.
Examples: K∈ §WHITE, §BLACK

§ indicates that the following name is the name of an object. If there is no §, we have a variable (such as K). So we know that the variable K may have two values: white or black.

ENPASSANT∈§YES, §NO
CAPTURE∈§YES, §NO
ENPASSANT=§YES = > CAPTURE = §YES

If the variable ENPASSANT has the value "yes", the variable CAPTURE also has the value "yes". If CAPTURE has the value "no", ENPASSANT also has the value "no" since it does not have the value "yes" and it has two possible values: "yes" or "no". (ENPASSANT has the value "yes" if the move is a capture en passant).

CASTLING=§YES, XA=7 => CASTLINGTYPE=§SHORT
MAN=§KING, ABS (XD-XA)>1 = > CASTLING=§YES

If there is a king move, and if the absolute value of the difference between the abscissas of the departure (XD) and arrival (XA) squares is larger than one, then there is castling. If the abscissa of the arrival square is 7, and if there castling, then it is short castling.

2. Variable = attribute 1: expression 1, attribute 2: expression 2, ..., attribute *n*: expression *n*.

We have another way of defining the value of a variable. We give the set of its attributes and their value. For instance:

OPINION=ONWHAT:Q, TYPE: §GENERAL, DEGREE : VAL,
INFERREDFROM : KS, AUTHOR : AUTHOR (DES).

We create a variable OPINION which has five attributes. The first, indicates the object of the opinion. It is the value of the variable Q (a move in the present expertise). Its type is general, as opposed to specific opinions of the aesthetics, the temerity or the originality of a move. Its value may be: excellent, good, poor, very bad, etc. In the present case, it is the value of the variable VAL. This opinion is inferred from another fact which is the value of the variable KS. The author of this opinion is the same author of another opinion, which is the value of the variable DES.

3. DEFAULT variable = expression. If we cannot discover another way of finding the value of the variable, its value is the value of the expression:

PROMOTION = §TRUE => DEFAULT NEWMAN = §QUEEN

If there is a promotion, the default value for the new piece is queen.

4. EXPERTISE name of an expertise $e_1 \rightarrow v_1$ $e_2 \rightarrow v_2$ ... $e_n \rightarrow v_n$ $w_1 \leftarrow f_1$ $w_2 \leftarrow f_2$ ... $w_p \leftarrow f_p$, where $e_1, e_2, \ldots, e_n$ are expressions evaluated in the current expertise, $f_1, f_2, \ldots, f_p$ are expressions evaluated in the new expertise, $v_1, v_2, \ldots, v_n$ are variables of the new expertise, and $w_1, w_2, \ldots, w_p$ are variables of the current expertise. The values of the e_i define the values of the v_i. When we have found all that was useful with the new expertise, we can transmit some information to the initial expertise by defining the values of the w_j. An expertise may use itself in one of its productions. For example, in determining if two moves are or are not the same, the expertise for verifying this will see that the departure and arrival squares are the same. If there is a promotion, the new man is the same. Both moves must be played in the same position. So we use the same expertise in checking to see that the preceding moves are the same in both cases.

I described this formalism more accurately in [18, 19]. I used it for giving several types of pragmatic knowledge:

- expertise for verifying if a move is a legal move and if necessary, for completing it. Usually, a chess commentary gives a minimal description of a move (après avoir roqué - les Blancs jouent Td4 - le pion e avance ...) and the pragmatic knowledge is useful for removing the ambiguity (if there is only one rook or if only one rook can move to d4) and for normalizing the moves. We can suppose that in the other expertises, we always know the departure and arrival squares of a move.
- expertise for finding the value of some characteristic: evaluating the development of each player; finding if the game is open or closed, etc.
- expertise for making inferences: it is likely that a move frequently used by experienced players is good; how can we understand a contradiction between two opinions.
- expertise for finding whether two objects are or are not the same: two moves, two players, two opinions, two experts, two numbers. It may be very difficult. Let us take a simple case. We have two numbers. A number N may be defined in two ways:

  by an interval: $N > A$ and $N < B$

  by a word such as "beaucoup", "peu", "plusieurs", "quelques uns", etc. which gives a very vague indication.

  In "Bien peu de joueurs sont des grands maîtres", "Bien peu" represents about 200. In "Il y a encore beaucoup de pièces sur l'échiquier", "beaucoup" represents about 30. The meaning depends on the nature of the object. It is difficult to see if two numbers defined in that way may or may not be the same. It is also difficult to discover if a number defined by an interval may be the same as a number defined by a sketchy indication. However, the problem of finding whether two objects may be the same is essential when we try to merge their descriptions. Let us suppose that a pronoun may refer to two objects O1 and O2. If this pronoun is the object of a verb, we may know a partial description D which comes from the meaning of this verb, of its subject, of its preposition groups, etc. If we are sure that D and O2 cannot be the same object, we have removed the ambiguity.

Pragmatic knowledge is useful in two ways:

- it fulfills an incomplete description of an object. This is especially useful for moves where the authors give as little information as possible. It simplifies the work of the other expertises which use normalized data.
- it verifies a possible interpretation. If it is false for the pragmatic knowledge, this possibility is removed: if we have "après ce coup, les Blancs auront un temps d'avance" and if "ce coup" may refer to two moves Q1 and Q2, we consider the position after Q1, and we evaluate the white advance for their development, and then we evaluate it after Q2. If, for one of them, this advance is not one unit, the corresponding reference is removed. However, there is a real problem. Everybody may agree on what is a legal move in chess, but each expert would have his own opinion of a player's development.

3 The Interpreter

The interpreter is independent of the knowledge. The expert who provides the knowledge need not know of the interpreter. It is possible to develop a wide variety of interpreters which use the same set of knowledge. An interpreter which is not well devised may require a large amount of time, and that is the main difficulty when using declarative knowledge. But it is not a systematic consequence of its use. On the contrary, Laurière [13] has shown that in some cases general systems using declarative knowledge may be more efficient than specific programs.

When we develop an interpreter using declarative knowledge, we must keep in mind two ideas:

- we must structure the knowledge when we receive it, so that the interpreter may use it efficiently. If we use the same knowledge for different goals, it may be necessary to structure it in a way convenient for each of them.
- when we are using the knowledge for solving a specific problem, it is important to carefully choose the piece of knowledge which will be used first. In some cases, we can avoid backtracking, in other cases we explore a space much smaller than the initial one. A general method for this is to build a structure concisely representing all the possible solutions. This structure summarizes a part of the constraints of the problem. With the other constraints, we prune this structure. The difficulty is to choose the first set of constraints so that the initial structure is not too large.

We have realized three interpreters:

- an interpreter for lexicographic knowledge,
- the main interpreter which builds the meaning representation.
  It directly uses syntactic and semantic knowledge and utilizes the results of the other two interpreters,
- an interpreter for pragmatic knowledge.

3.1 An Interpreter for Lexicographic Knowledge

This knowledge is given in a form suitable for generating a word. It is necessary to modify the knowledge so that we can use it efficiently in the analysis of a word. It stores each ending in a tree, beginning with the last letter of this ending. With the first letter, it also stores the pair: name of the ending sequence and position of this ending in this sequence. For instance, for the sequence vps, s, s, t, mes, tes, rent we have the tree of Figure 3.

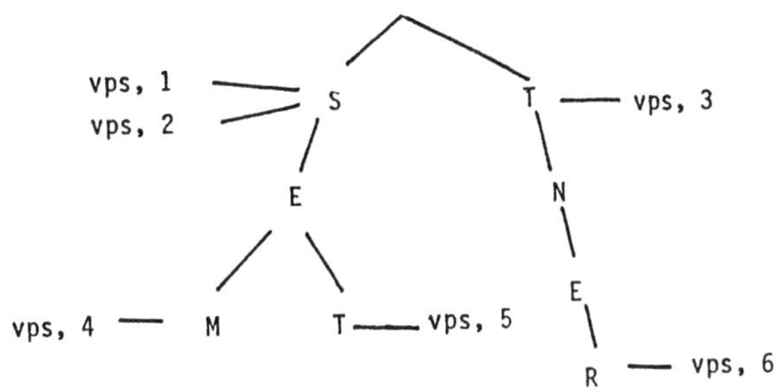

Fig. 3

The roots of a word are also stored in a tree; we begin at the first letter of a root and with the last letter, and we store the name of the word and the root position in the root sequence of this word. If we want to analyze the word $a_1a_2 \ldots a_n$, we cut it in two parts: $a_1a_2 \ldots a_{i-1}a_i$ and $a_{i+1}a_{i+2} \ldots a_n$. We want to see if $a_1 \ldots a_i$ is a root of a word W and $a_{i+1} \ldots a_n$ an ending and if the conjugation of the word W allows this. We begin with $i=n$, i.e., with the empty ending. We search in the tree of endings for $a_{i+1} \ldots a_n$. There are three possibilities:

1. The string $a_na_{n-1} \ldots a_{i+2}a_{i+1}$ is in the tree, but no pair (name of sequence, position in the sequence) is stored with the last letter a_{i+1}. So $a_{i+1} \ldots a_n$ is not a known ending. We decrease i and we resume the procedure.

2. The string $a_n \ldots a_{i+1}$ is in the tree and p pairs (name of sequence, position in the sequence) are stored with a_{i+1}. Let (S_j, P_j) be the jth pair. Now we look for $a_1a_2 \ldots a_{i-1}a_i$ in the tree of roots. If it is not in this tree, there is a failure, so we decrease the value of i and we resume the procedure. If $a_1 \ldots a_i$ is in the tree, let (W_k, R_k) be the kth element among the q pairs (name of word, position of root) stored with a_i. For each W_k, we look in the file of words for the name of its conjugation: C_k. In C_k, we look for a group G with an ending sequence named S_j. Thus, if the P_j^{th} position in this group has the value R_k, we have an analysis of the word: we have the word W_k, the tense is given by the name of group G, the "person" by P_j. For instance, let us analyze "tînmes". We start with $i=6$, but we do not have the empty string in Fig. 3, so we consider $i=5$. "s" is a possible string in Fig. 3, but "tînme" is not a root. With $i=4$, "se" is not a possible ending: no pair is stored with "e". With $i=3$, "sem" is in the tree and we have one pair: $j=1$, $S_1=$vps, $P_1=4$. In the tree of roots "tin" is a root with one associated pair: $K=1$, $W_1=$"tenir", $R_i=5$. As we have seen in Sect. 2.1 the name of the conjugation of

"tenir" is "venir". In "venir" we look for a group with the ending sequence "vps"; the group "passé simple" has this sequence. Its fourth element is 5, which is the value of R_1. So "tînmes" is the first person plural ($P_1 = 4$) of the "passé simple" of "tenir".

After finding a possibility, we must proceed with the next possibility: we look for the other groups of the conjugation and for the other words W_K. For instance "moule" has nine possible analyses:

- masculine noun (mould)	
- feminine noun (mussel)	
- verb "mouler" (to cast):	
- - present indicative	1st person singular
	3rd person singular
- - present subjunctive	1st person singular
	3rd person singular
- - imperative	2nd person singular
- verb "moudre" (to grind)	
- - present subjunctive	1st person singular
	3rd person singular

3. The sequence $a_n a_{n-1} \ldots a_{i+1}$ is not in the tree. We stop the process because we have all the possible analyses.

It is possible to improve the efficiency of the method; however, the short computer time renders this useless.

For generating word, we receive the name of a word W, the name of a group, and a pair (person, number) for a verb or (gender, number) for a noun or an adjective. Let n be the position corresponding to this pair. With the name of the same word, we find the conjugation, then the group with the given name. Let S be the name of the ending sequence and r the nth element of S. We concatenate the rth root of W and the nth element of S.

3.2 The Main Interpreter

There are three sets of programs:

- when the system receives the knowledge, it modifies it so that it can be used more easily when parsing a text. I do not give a distinct description of the various treatments made in this step, however I will indicate what modifications have been made to each type of knowledge when describing how this knowledge is used.
- when the system receives a text, first, it builds a structure which is ambiguous, and secondly, it prunes this structure to remove these ambiguities.

3.2.1 Building the Structure

During this step, we only use part of the syntactic knowledge: the traits, the agreement rules, and some conditions are not used. We want to represent concisely all the possible syntactic analyses. If there is an ambiguity, we consider all the possibilities. If later we find the same node of the same graph for the same word of the text, we merge both paths. If we are at the first node of a similar graph (for instance a clause) in both cases, but not in the same graph, we perform only one analysis for this graph, but the analyses diverge again at the end of the common graph. Kay [8] has independently developed a method which has the same advantages: if an ambiguity is local, we know that at some place there are two possibilities, but the part of the sentence after the ambiguity is parsed only once. Figure 4 indicates the representation of a node which indicates the beginning of a subgraph. It is broken up in two nodes N1 and N2, N2 before the new graph and N2 at the end of this graph. At each level, the nodes are given in order of occurrence in the text.

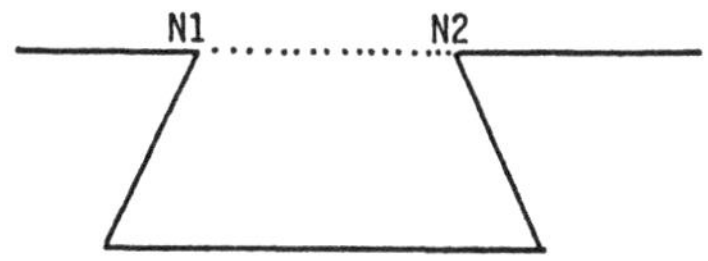

Fig. 4

Figure 5 gives the representation of "le pilote ferme la porte" which has two interpretations ("the pilot closes the door" and "the strong pilot carries her"); "ferme" may be verb or adjective; "la": article or pronoun; "porte": noun or verb. There are two paths between "pilote" and the period. For "Le Cavalier de la Dame qui est menacé va en d7.", we have Figure 6; "qui est menacé" can be an element of the preposition group "de la Dame" and we have the path FGHIJKLM or an element of the noun group "Le Cavalier" and we have the path FSTHIUM. In both cases, we use the same analysis for the clause "qui est menacé". This possibility is very useful in French for the relative clauses, the preposition groups and the conjunctions. For instance in "Les Cavaliers attaquent les Dames et les Fous et les Tours menacent les Pions" (The knights attack the queens and the bishops and the rooks threaten the pawns), each noun group will be analyzed only once. However, there are two paths between "attaquent" and "menacent". In one case, the knights attack the queens and the bishops when the rooks threaten the pawns. In the other case, the knights attack only the queens; but the bishops and the rooks threaten the pawns.

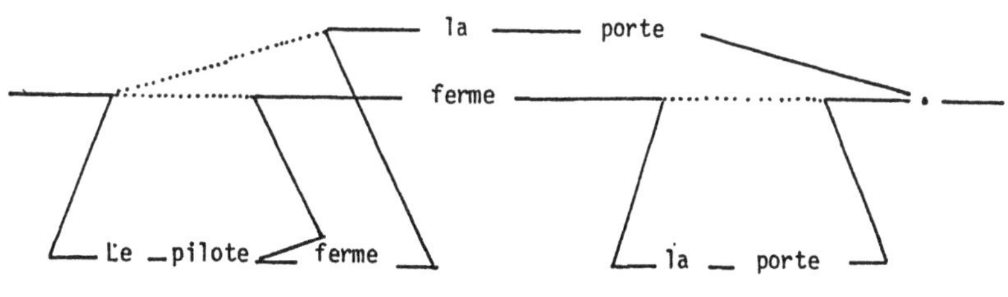

Fig. 5

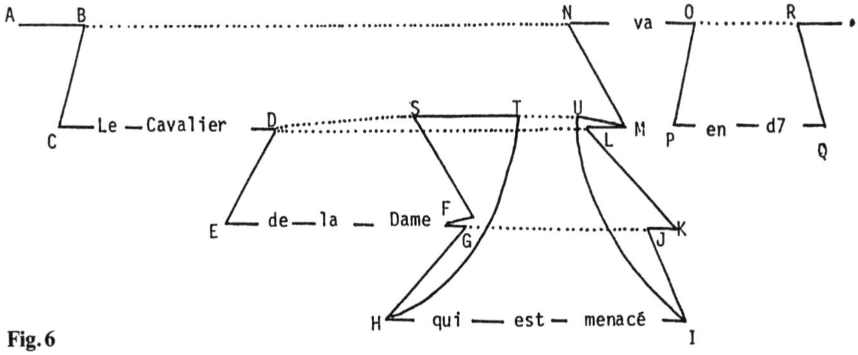

Fig. 6

To build the structure, we mainly use two kinds of knowledge:

- the order of the words, given by the graphs,
- the nodes of the graph where a meaning can be found. When we try adding a node to the structure, at least one meaning of the current word in the text must be associated with this node.

The interpreter partially uses a third type of knowledge: the conditions associated with the nodes or the arcs of the graph. It is not possible to use all the conditions for two reasons:

1. the condition may use elements which are as yet unknown, such as the traits. We never use such conditions at this stage.
2. the condition may not be evaluated at this stage, because a node which appears in this condition has not yet been developed. For instance, if we have a condition: Node N is present, and if we do not find node N, it may be dangerous to conclude that the condition is false, because later node N will perhaps be built. But it is a pity not to use this kind of information which removes many nodes. So, when the program receives the graphs, it automatically determines if a condition can or cannot be evaluated when the interpreter meets these conditions, when it begins with the first word of the sentence. It marks the conditions that may be evaluated, and later the interpreter uses only marked conditions. I chose to analyze the sentence from the beginning; the human expert need not know of this choice. I must modify the knowledge so that the interpreter processes it efficiently even if the expert does not foresee such a use. When using declarative knowledge, it is usually better that the system organizes it, so that the interpreter can use it in a convenient form. In the preceding example, this is very simple: for each condition of a node N, or of an arc beginning with N, the system determines whether a node appearing in this condition may occur after the node N. If this may never happen, for all these nodes, it marks that this condition can be evaluated even in the first phase. The system analyzes the graphs when it receives them for another reason: its goal is to avoid creating too many subgraphs. For instance, some groups (such as the adverb group) may be found in many places within a sentence and much time would be wasted if we tried to determine if such a group was present in each place. Instead, the system deter-

mines, when it receives the graphs, a list of all the nodes belonging to all the possible graphs which may contain the first word of this graph (for instance, the first word of a clause may be a determiner, a relative pronoun, etc.). Before building a new group G, the interpreter will find out if the following word has at least one meaning which can be at a node belonging to the set of nodes which may begin the new group G. If this is not the case, the group is not considered. We avoid building substructures which will be erased later. The expert still does not know of this concept. The program finding the list of the possible nodes for the first word is very simple. It systematically develops all the nodes and it stops when it finds a node corresponding to a word. Then it stores it and it backtracks to the last choice. This is necessary to avoid loops: a graph clause may begin with a graph clause, so we keep the names of all the graphs considered and we do not try then twice.

The system builds a compact structure, although there are still some ambiguities. For instance:

1 e2-e4 1 ... d7-d5. Attaquant le Pe4. Bien que pratiquée par des maîtres, cette poussée précoce, en ouvrant immédiatement le jeu, sert la cause des Blancs qui disposent d'un temps d'avance.

There are three ambiguities:

1. "des Blancs" is a preposition group which may be tied to "cause" or to "sert".
2. "qui disposent" is a relative clause which may be tied to "cause" or to "Blancs".
3. "d'un temps d'avance" is a preposition group which may be tied to four words: "disposent", "blancs", "cause", and "sort".

The structure has 146 nodes. The semantic, pragmatic, and syntactic knowledge, which has not yet been used, will remove all these ambiguities. Then, the structure will have 120 nodes. So these ambiguities which give $2\times2\times4=16$ possibilities add only 26 nodes to the structure. Building the structure of the preceding example required only 0.6 second of Amdahl V/7.

3.2.2 Using the Graphs Representing the Conjunctions

For each graph, we have another graph which indicates how several elements may be tied with conjunctions. If the conjunction (such as "soit") is before the first group, the interpreter knows that it has to build several groups of the same nature. But usually it finds a conjunction at the end of the first group. The system always assumes that there is a conjunctions of groups. If, at the end of the first group, there is no conjunction, the interpreter erases all the nodes which have been created at the conjunction level. Figure 7 gives the structure for "La Dame prend la Tour et le Fou et les Cavaliers prennent des Pions". There are two paths from L to f. In the first path: LMNOPQRSTUVWXYZabcdef, the queen captures the rook and the bishop when the knights capture some pawns. In the second path: Lmnopqrstuvwxyzf, the queen captures only the rook when the bishop and the knights capture some pawns.

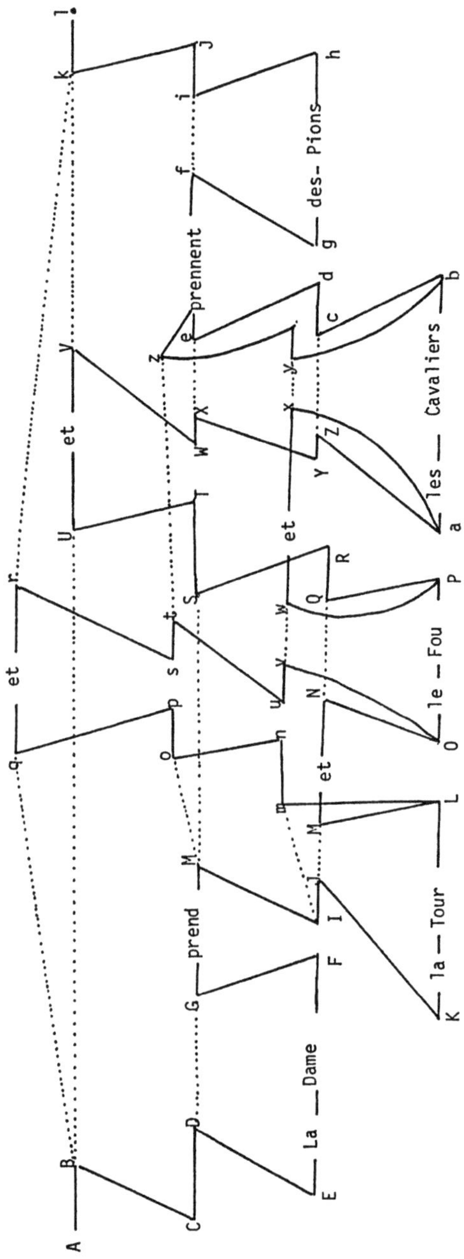
La
Dame
prend
la
Tour
et
le
Fou
et
les
Cavaliers
prennent
des-
Pions
et
et

Fig. 7

Unfortunately, conjunctions are frequent in a text; it is mainly the commas which are ambiguous: one of their meanings is a conjunction ("and" or "or") such as in "Les Blancs vont prendre le Pion a7, le Cavalier e5 et la Tour d6". But the system does not waste much time, because the elementary graphs without conjunction are analyzed only once. In Figure 7, only two conjunctions "et" are shown twice in the structure. If there is no conjunction at all, we waste time creating the beginning of a structure with conjunctions and we also waste time removing it.

3.2.3 Achieving the Building of the Structure

We add to the nodes which correspond to a word, all the possible meanings of this word and the possible values of its morphological characteristics. If the word is a pronoun, we determine all the words it may refer to. In the other cases, we consider all the triples of each meaning. For each triple, we find the words which agree with its description, and we tie in both directions the triples and the corresponding word. If a triple is not tied to a node, it is removed. If it is a mandatory triple, and if it is in a father triple, we resume the procedure for the factor. If we have a triple which is at the first level of a meaning, then we remove the meaning. If a node has no meaning left, it is removed. Later, if we remove a node, we also remove the meanings still associated with this node. When we remove a meaning, we remove all the ties in both directions between its triples and the other parts of the structure.

3.2.4 Pruning the Structure

Ambiguity has many facets:

- a node may have several successors
- a node may have several predecessors
- several meanings may be tied to a node
- a trait may have several possible values
- a word may have several values for one of its morphological characteristics
- etc.

The concept of certainty is important, because it shows the places where there is no ambiguity. Near those areas, the interpreter can prune more drastically, and thus certainty spreads.

A node is certain if the graph is disconnected when we remove it. To find whether a node N is certain, we start at the beginning of the structure and we try to reach its last node without crossing N. If we succeed, N is no certain. We improve the algorithm if we do not start from the initial node of the structure, but from the nearest certain node before N. Later, if we remove some parts of the structure, we must bring the remaining parts up to date. It is sufficient to consider only the nodes between the last certain node N1 before the modified area, and the first certain node N2 after this area. Moreover, a node N is not certain if there is a path between N1 and N2 which does not cross N.

A meaning is certain if it is the only meaning tied to a certain node. A trait is certain if one of its values is associated with condition which is always true. It is possible that the condition used characteristics of nodes which are not certain. But if, for each choice, the condition is true, the trait is certain.

Each piece of knowledge can create constraints. It is clear for the conditions of a node, an arc, or a meaning. But an agreement rule can produce several constraints. A meaning gives one constraint for each mandatory triple. For each kind of constraint, a subroutine is able to verify if the corresponding condition is true or false. When executing this subroutine, we may have to choose: if, in Fig. 6, we consider the agreement of "qui" and the word to which it refers, we see that two backward paths are possible from "qui". One of them leads directly to "Dame", the other climbs to the upper level and leads to "Cavalier". For each choice, we store its characteristics. When we have completed an evaluation of the constraints, we use the result of the evaluation (true or false) and the present choices to possibly prune the structure. Then we backtrack to the last choice, and we stop the evaluation only when we have considered all the possibilities. Now we will describe how we can prune. This method is independent of the nature of the constraint (condition, agreement rule, triple of a meaning, pragmatig constraint, etc.).

3.2.4.1 Pruning with False Conditions. If the evaluation of a constraint gives the value "true", we do nothing. The constraint cannot eliminate anything in the set of choise which leads to the present state. If the evaluation is true, whatever choice we take, then the constraint is removed. For instance, in Figure 6, let us assume that we have already found that "qui" is singular. The constraint is the agreement of "qui" with the noun it refers to. The number of "qui" agrees with the number of "Dame" and with the number of "Cavalier", which are the only two possibilities. So the agreement in number is removed.

If the evaluation gives the value "false", we have three possibilities:

1. No choice has been made. So there is a mistake somewhere: either the author of the text has produced an incorrect sentence, or there is an error in the knowledge given to the system: when everything is certain, all the conditions must be true.

2. Only one choice has been made. We remove the possibility of making this choice, whatever it is. In Figure 6, let us consider the agreement in gender and number of "qui" and "menacé". There is only one path between these words; "menacé" is definitely masculine singular. But "qui" may be masculine or feminine, singular or plural. Let us look at the agreement in number. If "qui" is singular (first choice), we have the value true, so there is nothing to do. If "qui" is plural (new first choice), we have the value false. We have made only one choice, we remove it: now "qui" is definitely singular. In the same way, we remove the feminine possibility for "qui".

Now, we consider the agreement in gender of "qui" with the noun it refers to. We have just seen that "qui" is definitely masculine, so there is no choice present. There are two paths backward from "qui". One of them leads to "Cavalier" following HTSD. This word is also masculine; the condition is satisfied. But if we take the other path, then after HGF, we arrive at "Dame" which is definitely feminine. The condition is false. We remove the only choice: taking HG instead of HT. After removing HG, the system will automatically prune arcs which do not have at least one arc starting from each of their extremities, for instance, FG because there is now nothing after G. In the same way, it removes successively GJ, JK, IJ, KL, LM. We stop the process at nodes F and M which still have a departure and an arrival arc. The system also brings up to date the certainties. In that case, the nodes S, T, and U will become certain. The nodes between H and I were already certain. So now, all the nodes in Figure 6 are certain.

The same constraint, agreement in gender between two nodes, may have very different consequences:

- removing a morphological ambiguity,
- removing a path in the structure.

If the constraint is associated with a node which is not certain, considering this constraint is already one choice. If there is no other choice and if it is a failure, we remove the node. For instance, let us consider the sentence "le pilote ferme le porte" which is very similar to that of Figure 5. The initial structure is given in Figure 8. Let us apply the agreement rule between the article and the noun of the noun group between K and L. No node between D and G is certain. We are making a first choice when we choose to consider this noun group.

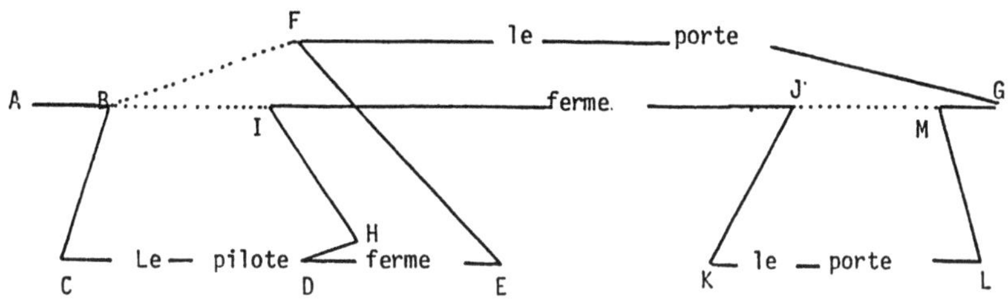

Fig. 8

The agreement in gender between "le" and "porte" gives the value false: "le" is masculine and "porte" is feminine. There is no other choice since there is only one path between "le" and "porte". We remove the only choice, considering the substructure KL. Then, the subroutine will also remove DH, HI, BI, IJ, JM, LM and MG. The ambiguity in the sentence disappears when using this agreement rule.

When we have successfully completed the pruning, it is unnecessary to keep the constraint which is now always true.

3. More than one choice has been made. Something must be removed, but we do not know what. "Les Tours des deux joueuses qui sont menacées sont au centre" is represented in Figure 9; "Tours" is ambiguous. It may be masculine (a round) or feminine (rook). "qui" may refer to "joueuses" or to "tours".

The agreement between "qui" and "menacées" indicates that "qui" is feminine plural. If "qui" refers to "tours" and if "tours" is masculine, the condition is false. But which possibility should we remove, the path between "qui" and "tours", or

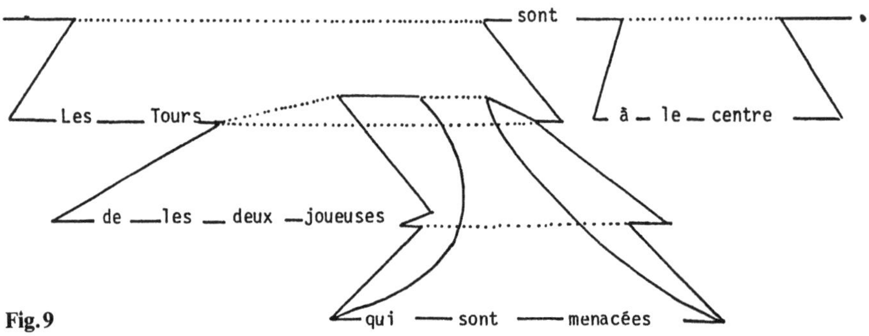

Fig. 9

that "tours" is masculine, or both of them? In this case, we keep the condition with the two choices which have been made. If later the pruning removes the other possibility at one of these choices, the interpreter will automatically consider this constraint a second time.

Let us consider Figure 6 again: "le Cavalier de la Dame qui est menacé va en d7". It is possible that the interpreter chooses to verify the agreement of "qui" and the noun it refers to, before the agreement of "qui" and "menacé". "qui" may be masculine or feminine. If we choose "qui" masculine and the path which leads to "Dame", the condition is false, but two choices have been made. So, we store the condition with these two choices. When later we verify the agreement of "qui" and "menacé", we will remove the possibility "qui" feminine. But we will also see that there was a condition waiting with a choice on the gender of "qui". So it is put on the agenda once again and, since there is now only one choice, the path between "qui" and "Dame" will be erased.

It may happen that the condition is false and that there are more than two choices. To be completely correct, it would be necessary to keep the n choices and reconsider the condition when $(n-1)$ choices disappear. But it is easier to store only two among the n choices, no matter which. If one of these two choice possibilities disappears, we reconsider the condition. If the n-2 other possibilities have also been removed, we have only one choice left and we can conclude. If some of the $(n-2)$ possibilities are still present, we again store the condition with two of the remaining possibilities. The process will stop since each time the number of choices decreases. It may happen that we consider a condition and store it again without removing anything. However, this seldom happens, and so we gain in simplicity what we lose in efficiency.

Let us summarize. A condition may lead to several types of elimination:

- an arc of the structure
- a node of the structure
- a possible value for a trait
- a possible value for a morphological characteristic of a word
- a possible meaning of a word
- a possible triple in the meaning of a word
- a possible reference for a pronoun

A condition may come from:

- an arc of the graph
- a node of the graph
- an agreement rule
- a trait
- a meaning of word
- a triple of a meaning
- a pragmatic constraint

Any condition may lead to any type of elimination. Later, we will see the constraints coming from pragmatic knowledge.

3.2.4.2 Pruning with the Knowledge That an Object Must Be Present. This method is similar to the pruning with false constraints. It may happen that there is an ambiguity between *n* objects $O_1, O_2, \ldots O_n$, but for some reason we know that the good object is O_1, which becomes certain. Then we can eliminate everything which leads to $O_2, O_3, \ldots O_n$.

- If the objects are meanings of the same word, we remove all the other meanings and the node these meanings are tied to, also becomes certain.
- If the object O_1 is a node, we remove all the arcs of the structure which could allow it to be gone around. For instance, in Figure 10, if we know that N is certain, the interpreter removes the paths BFG and AIJD.

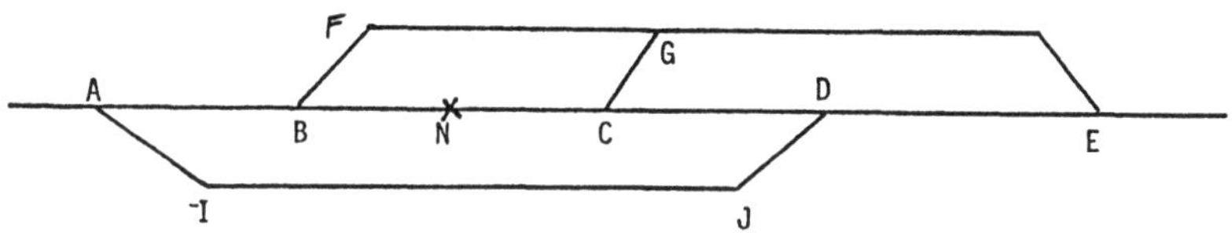

Fig. 10

- If the object O_1 is a possible reference of a pronoun, we remove the other references.
- If the object O_1 is the value of a trait, we remove all the other possible values, and so their associated conditions must be false. We will see in Sect. 3.2.4.3 that this creates a new type of pruning: pruning with true conditions.

But when can be sure that an object is certain? In the present state of the interpreter, this happens in only one situation: we have a meaning M_1 which is certain, this meaning is tied to no other meaning by its triples, and only one other meaning M_2 has a triple tied to M_1. We have seen in Sect. 3.2.3 that we have built all the possible ties in the structure. In that case, the tie between M_2 and M_1 becomes mandatory. If a text is coherent, we cannot have a word which has no bind to the other words of this text. So the triple on M_2 tied to M_1 becomes certain, M_2 itself becomes certain, and the node tied to M_2 also becomes certain. If there is a condition which is still ambiguous (for instance in that node or in the meaning M_2), it must be true and we apply the methods seen in Sect. 3.2.4.1 for pruning with false conditions. This fact does not happen frequently. However, when it happens, it drastically affects the structure. This is the main method for using the optional knowledge in the triples of a meaning.

For instance, we have seen two meaning of "attaquer". The first one foresees the possibility of finding the adverb "directement". Let us suppose that this word has no triple in its meaning, a situation which frequently occurs with words whose meaning depends mainly on the other words. If we have "Les Blancs attaquent directement la Tour", "attaquer" has two meanings. The first one is tied to "directement" by its optional triple. The second one only foresees the adverb "indirectement". So there is only one connection between "directement" and the rest of the sentence. However, since "directement" is effectively in the sentence, it must be tied to another word. This one tie becomes certain. The triple of "attaquer" foreseeing "directement" becomes mandatory, the first meaning of "attaquer" is also certain: we can remove the other meaning. The ambiguity has disappeared.

I have implemented this method only for this weak form. It would be possible to generalize the method when several words W_i have many ties between then, but when only one tie goes away from or towards this set of words in the rest of the sentence. This unique tie would also be certain if some elements among the words W_i were also certain. However, the search for such situations would be very expensive in computer time, whereas in its weak form, it is quite inexpensive.

We will see in Sect. 3.2.4.3 another case which could lead to the same type of pruning, but it has not yet been implemented.

3.2.4.3 Pruning with True Conditions. When we know that something must be certain, it may also happen that we know some conditions must be false. So, when we evaluate and when we find the value to be true, we remove the choice which has been made if there is only one choice. If there are several choices, we store only two choices, and then wait until one of them disappears before reconsidering the condition. This method is similar to the method of pruning with false conditions: we only have to exchange the words "true" and "false". This does not happen when we know that a node is absent: the conditions on the nodes and the arcs of the graphs must be true if the node is present. This is necessary but not sufficient. It is possible that the node may be absent although the conditions are true. But, for the traits, if a condition is true, the associated value must be the value of the trait. So, if we know that a trait has the value V, all the conditions associated with values different from V must be false. So, we can prune with true conditions. For instance, if we know that the trait VOICE must have the value ACTIVE, all the conditions associated with the value PASSIVE must be false. We have seen in Sect. 2.2.3 that one of them is: the node AUXETRE is present and the verb at node VERB does not have the syntactic marker AUXILIARYETRE. If we have a situation when one of these two unit conditions is definitely true (without making a choice), we conclude that the other condition must be false. If the verb does not use the auxiliary "être", the second condition is true. So, the first condition must be false. If the node AUXETRE is present, it must be removed. Conversely, if we know that the trait VOICE must have the value PASSIVE, all the conditions associated with the value ACTIVE must be false. Among them, we have: the node

AUXETRE is absent. Because this condition is false, the node AUXETRE must be present. If there is no other choice, we apply the method described in Sect. 3.2.4.2 and eliminate any path which circumvents AUXETRE.

If a condition tied to a rejected value V of a trait T is: the trait T' has the value V', this condition must be false, so the trait T' does not have the value V', we resume the same procedure for all occurrences of the value V' in the list of pairs defining the value of the trait T'.

3.2.4.4 Performances of the Method. Only pruning with false conditions and pruning with the knowledge that an object must be present have been implemented. It is not difficult to implement pruning with true conditions: the method is exactly the same, after exchanging the values "true" and "false". I did not include it, because it was infrequently used, but it is certainly an interesting improvement of the method.

When all the conditions have been considered, and if the program has received the knowledge necessary for understanding a sentence, we have the meaning representation of this sentence and, as a byproduct, the syntactic analysis of this sentence. If there are still some places with several possibilities, either some important knowledge has not been given, or the system has ineffectively used the knowledge. Earlier, we saw that in some cases I did not implement useful methods, for instance, pruning with true conditions. Some cases exist where the system does not remove all the ambiguities, although this would be possible, for instance, in trying to systematically backtrack to prove that, at the end, we can obtain only one solution. However, this is completely against the spirit of the method: we can avoid backtracking if we use the constraints in good order. Anyway, the main reason for failure in the removal of ambiguities does not come from poor use of the knowledge, but it stems from a lack of knowledge, mainly of pragmatic knowledge.

3.2.4.5 Ordering the Conditions. The system has an agenda on which are the conditions to be considered. Two principles enable it to order them:

- First choose the constraints which work on small areas of the structure.
- Then prefer the places in the structure which are certain.

If we do not want the system always to examine the same conditions, we must choose conditions with only one choice. At the beginning of the process, there are many ambiguities, so it is likely that a condition which utilizes information at many places of the structure will find many choices. Conversely, if it is a local constraint, it is likely that there will be few choices. The system used the following order:

- conditions of the arcs
- conditions of the nodes
- conditions of the traits
- agreement rules
- condition of the meanings
- conditions arising from the triples in the meanings
- conditions using pragmatic knowledge

So, syntactic knowledge is used preferably first, and pragmatic knowledge last. But there is not a syntactic phase followed by a pragmatic phase. So a syntactic constraint cannot be used because there are several choices. It is stored and when we consider the pragmatic knowledge, we can remove one of these ambiguities. So, we again consider the syntactic constraint. When there are several conditions of the same type, the system prefers conditions tied to a part of the structure which is certain. Indeed, if the part is not certain, we have already made one choice, and if we find another ambiguity, we cannot prune.

It is not necessary to use sophisticated methods for ordering the trials. Almost all the tasks must be done, as we only stop when we have removed all the ambiguities. The preceding order is sufficient. The more important point is to use pragmatic knowledge as late as possible: evaluating pragmatic knowledge requires much computer time, and it is usually necessary to use information from many parts of the sentence. So it is likely to find only one choice when most of the ambiguities have been removed.

3.2.4.6 The Pruning Mechanism. Each part of the structure which is liable to be removed is autonomous: a node; an arc; a meaning; a triple in a meaning; a possible value for a trait; a possible reference for a pronoun. It includes references to all the other independent parts where this part of the structure is used. For instance, a node has a list of its predecessors, its successors, its meanings (if it is a node associated with a word), the traits which have this node as a possible value, etc. If we have to eliminate a node, we know all the places where this node is referred to, so it is easily eradicated. But, when we remove something, it may remove a choice in a list of possibilities where this element was present. For instance, when we remove a node N, one of its possible successors N' may now have only one predecessor. If that happens, we look in the set of waiting conditions to see if there is a choice of the predecessors of N'. If we find such a condition, we remove it from this set and we put it onto the agenda so that it will be considered again.

Moreover, if we remove a part of the structure, leaving only one choice, we try to discover if the remaining object is certain. If two meanings M1 and M2 were associated with a node N, and if we remove M2, we look to see if N is certain. If so, M1 becomes certain as well as some of its triples, and the system will find all the consequences of this new fact. For each type of elementary part of the structure, there is a procedure which draws new facts when we remove such a part. Possibly, it will call the same procedure or another one for other parts of the structure.

3.3 The Interpreter of Pragmatic Knowledge

This interpreter receives the pragmatic knowledge and the value of several variables. The value of the variables is defined by the meaning representation which is itself built from the action part of the meanings (in which the value of the variables is known from the triples which are certain). If we have the move Bd5, we will initialize the following variables:

MOVINGMAN = (NATURE : §BISHOP)
XA = 4 (for d)
YA = 5

If the move is described by "Après De3, les Blancs vont promouvoir leur pion", we have:

PLAYER = §WHITE
PROMOTION = §YES
MOVINGMAN = (NATURE : §PAWN)
AFTER = (MOVINGMAN : (NATURE : §QUEEN), XA : 5, YA : 3)

This is created when we use the action part of the meanings, and we replace the variables by the objects they represent. If we have the description of a move, we use the pragmatic knowledge of a legal move, and we verify if this move is legal. If it is not, we have a value "false" and if only one choice has been made, it is removed. If several choices have been made, we do not prune as long as more than two choices remain. So we have the next type of condition, and its consequences are exactly the same as those of the other conditions. However, pragmatic knowledge is also useful for completing the meaning representation. The author of a text usually gives only minimal information: the reader has to infer the other characteristics of the objects. For instance, the author writes that a player castles without specifying short or long castling. The interpreter uses the knowledge for finding it. This is easy if only one of them is a legal move. Then, it indicates the type of castling, the arrival and departure squares of the king, the fact that there is no capture and no promotion in this move, etc. Completing the description is useful for defining other parts of the pragmatic knowledge: we can assume that we always know when a move is or is not a capture, its departure square, etc. After completing the description, we may have for Bd5:

PLAYER : §WHITE
MOVINGMAN : (PLAYER : §WHITE, NATURE : §BISHOP, NAME-OF-THE-MAN : §KING) (for King Bishop)
XD : 7
YD : 8
XA : 4
YA : 5
PROMOTION : §NO
CAPTURE : §NO
CASTLING : §NO
ENPASSANT : §NO
CHECK : §NO

It is easy to find all this information when we know the position, and if only one bishop can move to d5. But, if several men of the same nature can move to a square, inferences must be made. This is very difficult, because a lot of chess knowledge is necessary, so consequently I did not give this kind of knowledge.

To use the knowledge, it is important to know the position in which a move has been played, or when we must evaluate a chess characteristic (such as the development of a player). In some cases, it is explicitly given in the sentence, but it frequently happens that we have indication of a move Q, but not of the preceding move. The program uses very simple heuristics. If the comment is on move R which is the nth move of player P, if the move Q is also a move of player P, and if there is no other move at the beginning of the sentence, then Q is played after the move preceding R. If it is an opponent's move, it is played after R. When the interpreter knows the last move, it uses the expertise to build the situation after this move. If it cannot infer the last move or some of its predecessors, it cannot build the position. In that case, many things cannot be checked. For instance, is Bf1-a6 a legal move? This cannot be determined without knowing the position. However, it can find some information from that part of the knowledge which does not use the situation on the board. It could find that Bf1-a5 is not a legal move. It can partially complete a move. After "Les Blancs ont roqué", the meaning representation would include:

PLAYER : §WHITE
CASTLING : §YES

The final description will be:

PLAYER : §WHITE
MOVINGMAN : (PLAYER : §WHITE, NATURE : §KING)
XD : 5
YD : 1
YA : 1
CAPTURE : §NO
CASTLING : §YES
PROMOTION : §NO
ENPASSANT : §NO

In the pragmatic knowledge, we have a complete definition of legal moves, including capture en passant, and the fact that the king must not pass over any square on which be would be in check when he castles.

The interpreter works in a rather combinatorial way. If there is a production a_1, $a_2, \ldots a_n = > b$, if all the a_i are true, if b is v = expression, and if the value of the expression is E, then the variable v will have the value E if it was not already defined. If it has had a value $E' \neq E$, there is a contradiction, and we return to the last choice. If b is false, $a_1, a_2, \ldots a_{i-1}, a_{i+1} \ldots a_n$ are true, if a_i is $v \neq$ expression, if the expression has the value E, then the value of v is E if it was not already defined. There is a contradiction if it has a value $E' \neq E$. If the a_i are true and if b is $v \in$ S, if the value of v is known, and if this value does not belong to the set S, there is a contradiction. If the value of v is not known, we give to v one of the values of S. If later there is a contradiction, we try another value of S. We never change the value of a variable, except in the case where it has been defined by $v \in$ S, or if the determination of its value has used directly or indirectly the value of such a variable. When we try another value of a set, the values of all the variables are defined since the last choice becomes unknown again. We define a variable as belonging to a set only when it is not possible to use another bit of knowledge. For instance we have:

CASTLING ∈ §YES, §NO
XD∈1, 2, 3, 4, 5, 6, 7, 8 (the abscissa of the departure square)
CAPTURE ∈ §YES, §NO

Such definitions may also be useful when there are only two possible values (such as CASTLING and CAPTURE). If we have:

CASTLING=§YES=>XD=5

and if XD $\neq$ 5, we can conclude: CASTLING=§NO and we have another method for finding the value of a variable.

The interpreter knows where each variable occurs. So when it finds the value of a variable, it knows which productions can be considered. If no production is left which is able to give a value to a variable, we can use a default value for this variable (if it exists).

It would be difficult to use the same knowledge in a procedural form. The main difficulty comes from the fact that a move may be partially described by any subset of a large set of parameters. For a procedure, we could try two solutions:

1. foresee all the combinations of parameters and write a subroutine for each of them. But there are too many of these combinations.
2. systematically generate all the legal moves and, for each of them, find the value of all its parameters. We eliminate the move if the value of a known parameter is different from the value of the same parameter of this move. This method is feasible for chess because there are not many legal moves. But in a case where we have a sufficient amount of information on the move, the interpreter will find the move directly without backtracking. Moreover, in a game with many legal moves, the combinatorial method will not work; on the other hand, the interpreter will find the solution quickly if the partial description of the move only corresponds to one legal move, even if there are many legal moves in a position for this game.

I took my examples mainly from the description of the legal moves, but the method was also applied successfully to some other kinds of pragmatic knowledge, as we saw in Sect. 2.4:

1. expertise for finding the value of some chess characteristic. This is used as a condition. If we know from a possible interpretation of the text that the value of some chess characteristic is V_1, if the interpreter computes the value of this characteristic on the present board and finds a value $V_2 \neq V_1$, then we have a false condition, and we can prune. For instance, if an interpretation of the text says that the game is closed, and the interpreter, using its expertise, concludes that the game is open, then this interpretation must be removed. If there is only one choice, we prune. The main difficulty is that most of the chess concepts do not have a perfect definition. In some cases, all chess players agree on the same value, but in other cases they only agree that the characteristics belongs to set of values. And it is difficult to define this set precisely. For instance, after 1.e2-e4 d7d5,2.e4xd5 Dd8xd5,3.Cb1-c3 Dd5-a5, an author considers that White has a development advance of one tempo. However, according to Tarrasch's definition, each player

has one man developed. It is evident that the queen is not on a good square. This explains the author's point of view. But the system, which uses Tarrasch's definition, finds in this case that the author is wrong, and as it is the only interpretation, it stops. Another problem arises because it is difficult to infer the position where a characteristic is evaluated. If it is evident for any chess player that a sequence of moves will be played, the author evaluates the position after they have been played. But nowhere does he mention that these moves have been played, and he uses the present indicative for a future position! It is well known to psychologists [4] that a chess player does not see the actual position, but the position after the evident moves have been played. So the programs must have the capability of an average chess player. However, I did not define this knowledge, which is very difficult to find.

2. expertise for performing inferences. This is useful for completing the meaning representation, and also for evaluating conditions. Let us assume that we have in the text a word indicating a contradiction such as "quoique", "bien que", etc. The program has to find which opinions are in contradiction. And it may happen that the contradiction cannot be found from facts in the sentence, but from facts inferred from the sentence. For instance: "Bien que pratiquée par des maîtres, cette poussée favorise la cause des Noirs" (Although played by masters, this pawn move is in favour of Black). Where is the contradiction marked by "Bien que"? A contradiction comes from two different opinions of the same characteristics. This is not the case in this sentence where the opinions are:
- Masters often play this move.
- This move is good for Black (the opponent).

But two inferences enable the interpreter to understand the contradiction:
- if a good player often chooses to play a move, this move is probably good,
- if a move is good for the opponent, it is bad for the player.

Now we have understood the contradiction. An intelligent understander must not only find from the text that there is a contradiction, but must also find the exact reasons for this contradiction. Anyhow, if in one interpretation, it does not find an explanation for a contradiction, the choice leading to the thought that there is a contradiction is removed.

3. expertise for finding whether two objects may be the same. This corresponds to the same need as Kay's unification. In some cases, it is not easy to find whether two objects are or are not the same. However, such cases frequently occur when there is a pronoun. A triple of another word, for instance of a verb, may give some information on the object referred to by the pronoun. All the possible candidates must agree with this information. If the expertise indicates that two objects cannot be the same, the possible reference is eliminated. This is not always easy; in "ce coup, qui amène une pièce au centre, est excellent", "ce coup" refers to a preceding move. But we have some knowledge on it:

- the moving man is a piece (not a pawn)
- the arrival square is in the center of the chess board
- the move is very good

It is easy to use the first element of information: we eliminate pawn moves. The second element is more difficult: e4 is certainly in the center, a1 is certainly not in the center, but f4? This problem is difficult and I have not yet solved it. In some cases I gave the necessary expertise for finding whether two objects are certainly not the same. If we cannot exclude their identity, the interpreter supposes that they may be the same. But, if there are several candidates, it is not capable of putting them in order. This characteristic is important for human beings. We are able to prefer an interpretation which is impossible according to the syntactic and semantic rules, but highly plausible for the pragmatics as supposed, to an interpretation which agrees with the rules, but which is very unlikely. Any French speaking person will understand "Pierre m'a donné une tarte; je l'ai mangé" as: I have eaten the tart. According to the syntax, this sentence is not ambiguous. Its only possible meaning is: I have eaten Pierre. This fact is certainly possible, but so improbable that we prefer any other interpretation, even if it violates the rules of the syntax. It would be important to give with the pragmatic knowledge some metaknowledge on the frequency and the plausibility of the knowledge. However, I did not give the program any knowledge of this type.

3.4 The Implementation

The interpreters are written in Fortran and the experiments have been made on the Amdahl V/7 of the C.I.R.C.E., the computer center of the C.N.R.S. List processing is made by the use of subscript variables. On the whole, there are more than 10000 Fortran instructions; 1500 are for the programs reading the various kinds of knowledge, 1500 are for helping the debugging, printing the results, or are subroutines for list-processing, such as a garbage collector. More than 7000 are for the three interpreters, the greatest number being for the second one. No knowledge at all of the language and the domain was included in the programs.

The computing time was acceptable - less than one second of CPU for a line of text. My main goal was to study how it would be possible to use declarative knowledge, which could be given in a convenient form by the expert who does not need to know how it will be used. Moreover, a general interpreter must use the knowledge in a reasonable amount of time. "General" does not mean that it can use any kind of knowledge, rather that it can efficiently use unknown knowledge in a known linguistic domain such as the order of the words, the agreement rules, or the morphology of the words.

The metaknowledge of how to use knowledge efficiently is inside the interpreter. This is the reason for its large size. It is difficult to improve it without using a completely different approach: the metaknowledge must also be given in a declarative form. If we want to improve performance, a large amount of metaknowledge is necessary, and it would be very difficult to write a procedural interpreter using it.

4 Discussion

I do not believe that human beings use only one method for understanding natural language, and I think that in the future, it will be necessary to realize systems which can choose between several methods. Certainly, some methods, such as those defined by De Jong [5] or Lebowitz [14], which use mainly pragmatic knowledge, are very interesting: they can understand a text even if these are some mistakes, they are fast, and men are probably working in a similar way on the parts of texts which are not essential for us, and for which a superficial understanding is sufficient. But there are other parts of some texts which convey essential information. For these parts, a precise understanding of the sentence is needed, and I believe that more sophisticated methods must also be developed. A difficult problem is the cooperation between these methods: it is not just a switch between methods M_1, M_2, ... M_n. The best solution may be to systematically use an inexpensive method, and if its results indicate that a paragraph contains some important information which it has been unable to extract, then the system must choose another method. But the second method will have better results if it can use the preprocessing of the first method. Schank [21] has already pointed out that it may be useful to use several levels of analysis for finding the interesting parts of a text.

The system efficiently used syntactic knowledge. It received a significant part of French grammar, and it was easy to add more information. The definition of the meanings was more difficult, since this kind of information is described nowhere. We must find the various meanings of a word, and the context in which each meaning can be found. It would be difficult to describe a reasonable number of the words of a language, but the difficulty does not arise in the method: it is in the nature of the problem. Each meaning has very precise constraints which rule when it can or cannot be used, there are many meanings, and neither the meanings nor the constraints have been well defined. Our method, which tries to simplify the definition of the meanings, is in the right direction. But the more serious problem comes from the pragmatic knowledge. It is really difficult to understand precisely real texts in a technical domain. The main difficulties are:

- the size of the knowledge necessary, even in a limited domain such as chess. We have shown that part of the knowledge must give the program the ability to play reasonably good moves at chess. It is not sufficient to use a program developing a large tree, as most chess playing programs do, and there is no satisfying chess program based on knowledge. Moreover, we need other kinds of chess knowledge, such as the definition of useful concepts (pinning a man, isolated pawn, etc.), knowledge about these concepts (if the concept is valuable, there is a danger, the opponent will try such a manoeuvre, we can make such an inference, etc.). This is a huge task, more difficult than providing the knowledge for playing chess, which is as yet an unsolved problem.
- the knowledge must be given with a special kind of metaknowledge: knowledge on the soundness of the knowledge. We must know that one event is normal and another infrequent. Without this, we cannot perform what human beings seem to do very easily: if there are mistakes in texts, very often we do not see them. When I was defining this system, I found sometimes that the author had said the opposite to what he actually wanted so say only when I tried to simu-

late the behavior of the system. However, when reading it, I had correctly understood the author's thinking. When we evaluate the value of a concept, it is not sufficient to have a result. We need a set of results; for instance, many people agree with a value, some people agree with another value, and nobody accepts any other possibility. Without this, a program would reject many good sentences because its knowledge is not identical to that of the author of the text. It must be tolerant to other knowledge, but it must not accept just anything.

I tried to realize a general system. It is general in the sense that nothing in the interpreters depends on French or on chess. But for different languages or different domains, the system could have serious difficulties because I did not implement mechanisms which were not essential for chess comments in French. For instance, the interpreter attaches great importance to the order of the words. It is a good method for languages such as French or English, but certainly not for Latin. A better solution would be to give the interpreter a set of strategies, and that for each language and domain it chooses the subset which will probable give the best results.

If we want to have a general interpreter of declarative knowledge which is also efficient, this interpreter must not be combinatorial, it must be clever. But a clever interpreter has to use declarative knowledge for the same reasons that a clever program uses it. The interpreter must use declarative metaknowledge: knowledge for efficiently using declarative knowledge. A part of this metaknowledge will structure the knowledge when the expert gives it. Another part will enable the interpreter to choose among the various pieces of knowledge which can be used for solving a problem. Many defects of the interpreter came from the fact that I knew what to do to correct a blunder, but it would have been necessary to put this metaknowledge in a program which was already complicated. If the failure was infrequent and/or minor, I did not add the metaknowledge to the interpreter. Naturally, we have a new problem: how do we efficiently use metaknowledge? But metaknowledge is knowledge for using knowledge, and it can be used for utilizing metaknowledge which is a special kind of knowledge. It is not necessary to create metametaknowledge! But during an execution, it may be necessary to consider several levels: some metaknowledge for using another metaknowledge, which uses the basic knowledge.

It was a pleasure to use and modify the syntactic knowledge. However, defining the meanings of the words was much more difficult. But real problems arose during the definition of the pragmatic knowledge. It was difficult to experiment with the program since for each new sentence, it was necessary to define the chess knowledge for all the concepts which were used in that sentence: knowledge about one single concept is very great. There is a problem in experimenting with programs which really understand technical texts. For each new line of text, many new concepts appear and the knowledge related to one concept includes many productions. Certainly, the process will converge, but only when we have gathered thousands of productions. For a small increase in the quality of the performances, there are huge increases in the quantity of the knowledge which we must give to the system. This fact limits the size of texts which can now be experimented on with such programs.

5 Conclusion

The goal of this program was not to study what kind of syntactic, semantic, or pragmatic knowledge is necessary for understanding natural language. I wanted to study how it is possible to give delarative knowledge so that the expert need not know how it is to be used in the future. And nevertheless, I wanted to show that it is possible to realize an efficient interpreter for this knowledge. The main difficulties came from two points:

- a large amount of knowledge is necessary. Certainly, it will be difficult to have human experts find it. We will not be able to avoid realizing systems which automatically find this knowledge.
- the interpreter also needs a large amount of metaknowledge, knowledge on how knowledge can be efficiently used. It will be necessary to gather this metaknowledge and to realize a general metainterpreter for using it.

References

1. Yigal Arens: Using Language and Context in the Analysis of Text. IJCAI 81, pp. 52-57
2. J. Brown and R. Burton: Multiple Representations of Knowledge for Tutorial Reasoning. In: Bobrow-Collins (ed.): Representation and Understanding. New York: Academic Press 1975, pp. 311-349
3. E. Charniak: On the Use of Framed Knowledge in Language Comprehension. Artificial Intelligence **11** (3), 225-265 (1978)
4. de Groot: Thought and Choice in Chess. The Hague: Mouton 1965
5. G. Dejong: Prediction and Substantiation: A New Approach to Natural Language Processing. Cognitive Science **3** (3), 251-273 (1979)
6. M. Dincbas: Contribution à l'étude des systemes experts. Thesis. Ecole Nationale Supérieure de l'Aéronautique et de l'Espace, Toulouse, 21. 1. 1983
7. H. Gallaire and C. Lasserre: Metalevel Control for Logic Programs. In: Clark and Tarnlund (eds.): Logic Programming. New York: Academic Press 1982, pp. 173-185
8. M. Kay: Morphological and Syntactic Analysis. In: A. Zampolli (ed.): Syntactic Structures Processing. Amsterdam: North-Holland 1977
9. M. Kay: Functional Grammar. Proceedings of the Fifth Annual Meeting of the Berkeley Linguistic Society, F-1979
10. M. Kay: An Algorithm for Compiling Parsing Tables from a Grammar. Xerox Report, 1980
11. M. Kay: Algorithm Schemata and Data Structures in Syntactic Processing. Xerox Report CSL-80-12, October 1980
12. J. L. Laurière: A Language and a Program for Starting and Solving Combinatorial Problems. Artificial Intelligence **10** (1), 29-127 (1978)
13. J. L. Laurière: Toward Efficiency Through Generality. IJCAI 79, pp. 519-521 (1983)
14. M. Lebowitz: Memory-based Parsing. Artificial Intelligence **21** (4), 363-404 (1983)
15. M. McCord: Using Slots and Modifiers in Logic Grammars for Natural Language. Artificial Intelligence **18** (3), 327-367 (1982)
16. L. Norton: Automated Analysis of Instructional Text. Artificial Intelligence **20** (3), 307-344 (1983)
17. F. Pereira and D. Warren: Definitive Clause Grammars for Language Analysis. A Survey of the Formalism and a Comparison with Augmented Transition Networks. Artificial Intelligence **13** (3), 231-278 (1980)
18. J. Pitrat: Un langage pour décrire les connaissances pragmatiques. In: Colloque Intelligence Artificielle de Toulouse. Publication 24. Groupe de Recherche 22 du C. N. R. S., Université Paris VI, July 1981, pp. 177-205

19. J. Pitrat: Un langage pour décrire les connaissances de façon déclarative. In: Utilisation des connaissances déclaratives. Publication 30. Groupe de Recherche 22 du C. N. R. S., Université Paris VI, September 1982, pp. 121-148
20. F. Rousselot: Un nouveau formalisme pour la compréhension des textes. In: Connaissances et metaconnaissances. Publication 38. Groupe de Recherche 22 du C. N. R. S., Université Paris VI, September 1983, pp. 185-217
21. R. Schank: Interestingness: Controlling Inferences. Artificial Intelligence **12** (3), 273-297 (1979
22. R. Wilensky: A Knowledge-based Approach to Language Processing; a Progress Report. IJCAI 81, pp. 25-30
23. T. Winograd: Understanding Natural Language. Edinburgh University Press 1972
24. W. Woods: Transition Networks Grammars for Natural Language Analysis. Communications of theACM **13** (10), 591-606 (1970)

Weighted Parsing

M. Thiel

1 The Need for Weighting

Certain relations hold good in the traditional scientific disciplines which ultimately determine the success of those sciences. For example, a hypothesis is established in order to explain an observation on the assumption that if the implications of that hypothesis are false then the hypothesis itself is false. Even if many of the implications are true, however, this is not proof that the hypothesis is true, but only support for it (cf. the introductions to the theory of science by Hempel and Oppenheim (1948), Stegmüller and Varga von Kibéd (1970), Hempel (1974), Braun and Rademacher (1978)).

Applying this to natural language, a linguist observes the behaviour of personal pronouns and their referents and establishes (or looks up in a grammar) the hypothesis that pronoun gender and number must agree with their reference group. For want of a test implication, which does not come to mind (or is that inherent in linguistics?), the linguist must resort to the permitted procedure of directly observing the hypothesis and verifying it experimentally. After a while he comes across the sentence "Alfo hielt die Zahnbürste in der Hand, als wäre es eine Waffe" in a short story. (Alfo held the toothbrush in his hand as if it were a weapon. "Zahnbürste" - toothbrush - is a feminine noun, whereas "es" - it - is a neuter pronoun.) The hypothesis is obviously refuted. In accordance with the principles of (natural) science he would have to conclude that pronouns do not follow their reference group in gender.

Our linguist must either introduce further restrictions (e.g. semantic rules), or content himself with classifying the phenomenon as an exception. As a computational linguist, he cannot do the latter. How, then, is a parser to identify the exception as such?

The integration of further, above all semantic (sub)grammars is no real solution for the computational linguist because the problem is obviously not: "There are cases where the available grammar is lacking in scope and exactitude", but "There are cases where it is necessary to make a distinction between the grammars of different text types". It is impossible to attribute absolute values in the Boolean sense of "true" and "false" to the applicability of a rule and the resulting grammatical structure while an analysis is running. In other words, one cannot proceed from the assumption that every rule (or subgrammar) of a natural language, once shown to be valid (by a recognised grammar or by verification on a text), everywhere and always applies in this same form. If we characterise this state of affairs as "the grammar varies", a comparison with Klein's "Varietätengrammatik" (grammar of varieties) suggests itself (Klein 1974). Klein's approach is a possible alternative, which was developed with a different objective in mind (spoken German for foreigners).

With linguistic phenomena it is necessary to proceed from probabilistic laws, which, as we shall examine below, can be taken into account by the introduction of weighting into computational linguistics, especially in parsers.

Approaches to this are to be found in Wilks (1973, 1976). The basic unit of Wilk's system is the "template", in which a unit of information is represented in the form of a sentence. Contained in the templates are "formulas" which reproduce the meaning of the words. Templates can be combined into "semantic blocks".

The system produces translations from English into French. The correct generation, for example, of the gender in pronominal references in French "makes quite clear whether or not the program has made the correct inferences in order to understand what it is tranlating" (Wilks (1976, p. 158). To solve problems of reference, preferences are used. In the sentence:

> Give the monkeys bananas although they are not ripe because they are hungry.

the problem is to establish the different references of the two occurrrences of "they". This is a trivial task for the system and can be achieved with so-called simple preference mechanisms. In the sentence:

> John drank the wine on the table and it was good.

the reference to "it" can no longer be decided with simple mechanisms, since both "the wine" and "the table" can be "good". Wilks must, therefore, introduce further preference processes, the "extended inferential mode". "In this mode, new template-like forms (called extractions) are inferred from existing ones, and then added to the template pool on which common sense inference rules then operate" (Wilks (1976, p. 167). Thus, for the sentence:

> John bought a car in the market and liked it immediately.

the templates

1 John bought the car
2 John in market

are produced. In order to solve the pronoun reference, extractions are first derived (here 1.1-1.3) and then further inferences are made about the new set of templates and 3 is derived. If there is more than one result the template which was reached by the shortest route is taken as the right one.

1.1 John has	a-car
1.2 John use	car
1.3 John paid	money
3 John immed-liked car	

If "... the 'preferential assumption' is that the shortest possible chain of such inferences will be the right one" (Wilks, 1976, p. 169), then the control of a Wilks parser will, in this case, solve an ambiguity. An analogous strategy is applied at a morphological level, when in the case of the analysis of compounds, that solution which involves the least divisions is accepted from a solution set.

We may consider this strategy as a possible approach to weighting although some important possibilities such as that of ordering of solutions and following up several solutions are absent. Wilks himself points out in his critical evaluation of the system that weighting represents a promising further development: "This difficulty may mean that preferences in the system will have to be weighted in a way they are not at present" (Wilks, 1976, p. 196).

The controlled partition grammar (Wotschke et al., 1976; Wotschke, 1976) is to be assessed similarly. A controlled partition grammar is a context free grammar with a regular control set over the grammar, implying the control of the application of rules supplementary to the grammar. A control set of a context free grammar is a subset of the productions contained in the grammar (Wotschke, 1976, p. 91). Thus there is an (alterable) extrinsic ordering of the rules.

By altering the control set one may alter the characteristics of the grammar. In this way the scope of the language generated may be varied, partially similar characteristics of the parser being available as with the use of weights, cf. text type dependent parsers (Section 7.1).

One of the most elaborated applications of weighting seems to be found in the machine translation system METAL; see Slocum (1984). METAL uses a plausibility factor "to select the 'best' interpretation from the available reading of an ambiguous sentence. We base our scores on both lexical and grammatical phenomena ..." (Slocum, 1984, p. 11). The use of scores in METAL traces back to the grammar DIAGRAM. "DIAGRAM makes frequent use of such general attributes in the subprocedures called factors that are used to assign likelihood scores to syntactic and semantic analysis. Instead of simply accepting or rejecting analysis, a rule can accept it with some assessments of the probability of its correctness" (Robinson, 1982, p. 30). For example, in the sentence

the man that I saw with the telescope

the interpretation of "with the telescope" as part of the relative clause is higher scored than the interpretation as attribute of "the man".

This approach is to be compared with Charniak's PARAGRAM parser (Charniak, 1983). As a deterministic parser Charniak takes the PARSIFAL parser of Marcus (Marcus (1980)) as a starting point of PARAGRAM. In PARAGRAM active rules are tested in parallel. These tests give "a numerical 'goodness rating' which, the higher the number, the better the fit between the rule and the buffer/stack. PARAGRAM then takes the rule with the highest number and runs it, ..." (Charniak, 1983, p. 123).

There is an important distinction between PARAGRAM's calculation of the goodness rating and the approach proposed here: PARAGRAM is a deterministic parser and it takes - in terms of production systems - only one production set into account, whereas here all production sets are involved (see Sect. 6.1.1). There are two further remarks on PARAGRAM: the goodness rating of a rule is the result of various atomic tests. The results of these atomic tests are added to or subtracted from the score of the rule. The following table gives an example (Charniak, 1983, p. 123):

Atomic test	Add if succeed	Subtract if fail
Category (e.g. NP)	4	15
Specific word (e.g. "to")	6	15
Semantic okay	0	8
Other (e.g. agreement)	2	15

It should be stated that there is no distinction between the different kinds of weights, compare Section 8. Further, semantics does not seem to support very much the decision whether a rule will be successful or not.

So, we can conclude that the need for weighting exists. In the following chapters an attempt is made to give the theoretical background for weighting, which the systems discussed above lack.

2 A Digression: Regulation Processes

If the scientist and the linguist had parts to play in the last scene, so now it is the turn of the engineer. He is certainly familiar with the following very simplified model:

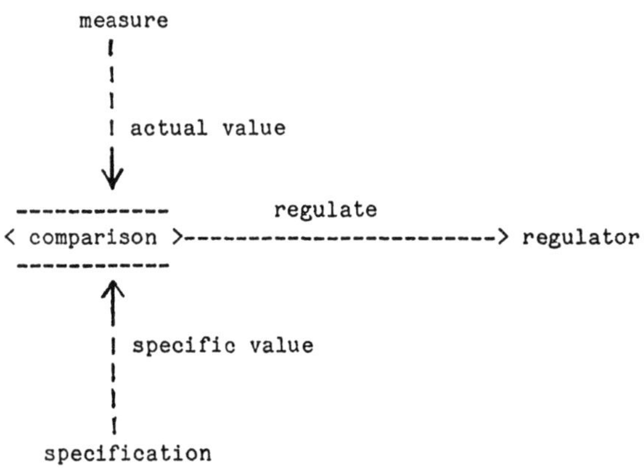

The regulator makes constant measurements of the actual values of a system and compares these with given specified values. If there is a difference between the actual and specified values the regulator receives a stimulus to intervene in the system in the necessary manner. This new setting remains as long as no new stimulus is sent.

3 Aspects of System Control

In this section we shall touch on some areas of the whole question of "system control" inasmuch as they are relevant to weighting. For the integration of controls into a complete system, see Section 6.1.1.

Independently of further characteristics (such as syntactic or semantic analysis, analysis strategies, etc.) every parser possesses, even if only implicitly, a feature which we may call "(analysis-)MODE". MODE should, for the purposes of the following discussion, embrace the two values "normal" and "rescue".

If MODE = normal the linguistic rules of the system are applied with maximum precision, almost "letter for letter". What "maximum precision" is, is to be seen in terms of the restrictions of the system in question. In most cases this is the only state in which a parser can be, which means that MODE usually does not have to be or cannot be explicitly declared. So one is aware of other states.

In rescue-MODE the restrictions of the linguistic rules are made looser. It must be assumed for simplicity's sake that restrictions are either loose or not and that degrees of looseness are not possible. This would be possible in principle but would unnecessarily complicate the issue.

Furthermore another feature which plays a role in the conception of rescue-MODE ought to be mentioned: the restrictions can be loosened for ever or only for a moment. There is a further alternative: they can be loosened in the whole grammar or only at points, i.e. in a single rule. In both cases, temporal and local, all intermediate stages are conceivable.

MODE is a system internal parameter, i.e. there is no scale for MODE which is independent of the individual system and which would allow a direct comparison of different parsers. The morphological analysis of a semantically controlled ATN can, for example, be so minimal that errors in the inflection of the input string may not be recognized in MODE = normal. In a (morpho-)syntactically oriented parser this (im)precision would only be reached with certainty in MODE = rescue.

What we have so far considered can be described in the following diagram:

```
             MODE = normal
                   !
   ---------->!
   !               ↓
   !
   !          ----------
   !          ! SYSTEM !
   !          ----------
   !               .
   !               .
MODE = rescue....
```

The dots show up the incompleteness of the present representation of the model: who is to monitor MODE, how can MODE be changed?

A decision stage mus be introduced which can refer to a measurement function. The measurement function measures and evaluates the result of the system and passes the result of the evaluation on to a decision function, which checks the result of the system, i.e. the evaluation thereof, for its acceptability and decides what, if any, MODE-change may be necessary. In general terms:

> The decision stage compares the actual and specified values and adjusts MODE accordingly.

Parallels with regulating processes are obvious - cf. the digression in Section 2 - even if some differences in detail should be noted. With regulating processes an asymptotic approximation to the specified value is aimed for. New control values are kept as long as no other control value is supplied. The specified value remains constant for the process to be measured for a given unit of time. In parsers, however, the specified value falls from the most to the least exacting value, i.e. the specified value for the next object to be measured (e.g. sentence, or more generally, units for analysis) cannot remain that of the preceding object but must be set to the highest expected value, say, MODE = normal. The parameter MODE can be described as "global" because it operates throughout the whole analysis. Furthermore MODE can control system internal local controls, so that we have a hierarchy of controls.

Let us take the example from Section 1 again. Supposing that the rules:

R1 = Agreement of gender
R2 = Agreement of number

and the control "both R1 and R2 successful" are given in MODE = normal, then if MODE goes over to rescue, the control of the subgrammar can be changed to "either R1 or R2 successful", in order to reach a result with weakened restrictions.

The incompleteness of the above representation, shown by the dashes, can be resolved. Since a further control stage must be introduced for the control of MODE we must assume that a hierarchy of controls is necessary for natural language parsers. This stage keeps a running check on the acceptability of the output structures throughout the analysis. "Acceptability" should not and cannot be defined here; it is up to the linguist to decide what and how he evaluates. However, the control stage to be developed must be capable of taking this freedom of decision into account.

The control stage postulated here can be realised by the weighting of output structures. What is understood by the term "weighting" will be explained in detail in the following sections. The concept of weighting is a heuristic to limit the search space. A heuristic is to be delimited from a blind search and "offers solutions which are good enough most of the time" (Feigenbaum and Feldman, 1963, p.6; quoted after Barr and Feigenbaum, 1983, p.29).

It remains open as to whether MODE is controlled by weighting alone. (This would lead to further questions concerning structuring of controls.) The representation for a unit being analysed can now be completed as follows:

```
                MODE = normal
                      !
     -------------->!<----------------
     !                |                !
     !                ↓                !
     !          ------------           !
     !          !  SYSTEM  !           !
     !          ------------           !
     !                |                !
     !                ↓                !
MODE = rescue     weighting        MODE = normal
     ↑                |                ↑
     !                ↓                !
     !          ------------           !
     ---------< comparison >----------
                ------------
```

The concept being developed here makes the solution of another unconnected problem more urgent. Error treatment deserves a mention here, especially error treatment during runtime, something which is not fully clarified in programming languages. In the present context this means that, when the control discovers that the weight of an output structure does not correspond to a specified value and changes MODE, it must execute an error analysis. It must be established if there was an error and, if so, where it occurred in order to then carry out an adequate error treatment.

Not nearly every problem which arises can be dealt with here. The attempts at a description in Section 4 are, therefore, the be looked at as a first approximation and certainly require a more general formulation. In the same way the list of examples cannot be complete as the possibilities for application do not form a finite set.

4 Types of Weighting

For the preparation of the typing of weightings, some terms are introduced: A grammar Gr consists of a sequence of n subgrammars Tg. A subgrammar consists either of a sequence of k subgrammars and a weight g or a rule r and a weight g. The rules consist of the description of the left hand side (ls) and the right hand side (rs).

The recursion of the definition has the consequence that subgrammars as well as rules can be weighted and that it is unimportant for the following definitions whether the weight comes from a subgrammar or from a rule.

$$
\begin{aligned}
Gr &:= Tg_1, \ldots, Tg_r, \ldots Tg_n \\
Tg_r &:= Tg_{r1}, \ldots, Tg_{rm}, \ldots, Tg_{rl}, g \\
Tg_r &:= r, g \\
r &:= ls, rs
\end{aligned}
$$

The expression

struct (t)

stands for a structure in the history of the derivation of a sentence. Saying

match (r, struct (t-1))

expresses the fact that the structure struct (t-1) is matched with the left side of the rule r. Match gives the value true if rule r can be applied to struct (t-1), and the value false if ls of rule r does not match with struct (t-1). In the case of true the struct (t) will be created out of struct (t-1) applying rule r.

The functions

pos (R, Tg_{rm})
pos (Tg_{rm}, Tg_r)

give the position (place value) of the rule and subgrammar, respectively.

The weight g of a structure struct (t) is calculated by the unary function "valuation":

g: = w (struct (t)).

Normally, this function will be realised as a reading operation.

4.1 Endogenous Weighting

An endogenous weighting exists if the weighting is carried out by the software system; this means the system user (a grammar writer, say) has no influence on the weighting. Several examples can be given here. For instance, the weight may result from the sequence of the applied subgrammars or rules. For this calculation, a binary function must be defined with the parameters

- weight of a structure (given by struct (t-1)) and
- position of a subgrammar or a rule applied to struct (t-1) in a sequence, given by the function pos.

If a subgrammar consists of a sequence of rules which are sequentially executed from the first to the last, and these rules are arranged according to the strictness of the restrictions expressed by the left side, we can proceed on the assumption that the application of the n-th rule is correcter than the application of the n + 1-th rule. (Compare this with the particular ordered transfer entries in METAL; see Slocum, 1984, p. 16.) Although the control calculates the weight from the ordering relation of the applied rule, the linguist can nevertheless influence this weighting from outside the system by the arrangement of the rules. Therefore, this example concerning endogenous weighting is a little problematic.

On the other hand, a weighting by reason of the number of applications of a rule or by reason of the number of the arcs or nodes produced by rules or subgrammars in the linguistic representation might be less problematic. Nevertheless these examples show the problems of the endogenous weighting, so that in practice, exogenous weightings are preferred.

4.2 Exogenous Weighting

An exogenous weighting exists if the weight is defined by the user (here: grammar writer) of a software system. Two ways of weighting can be distinguished: absolute and relative exogenous weighting.

4.2.1 Absolute Exogenous Weighting

We can talk of absolute exogenous weighting if, indepedent of an existing weight of a structure struct (t-1), a new weight for struct (t) is introduced by a rule or a subgrammar. Here, it really seems useful to suggest the reduction of a weight to the value 0, i.e. to forbid a structure totally. To set another absolute value only makes sense if this depends not on the other weights of the structure or the rules.

4.2.2 Relative Exogenous Weighting

The relative exogenous weight is calculated by a binary function including the parameters

- weight of a structure to which a rule or subgrammar is applied (given by w (struct (t-1))) and
- a modifying weight from the applied rule or subgrammar.

Because of the manifold possibilities of application, relative exogenous weightings are expected most frequently. A procedure for the construction of a network with weighted ways, which can be used in a homograph reduction system, is an example (compare SALEM, 1980). The chain of terminals on the way with the highest weight is the first for which one can expect a successful sentence analysis. The weighting of the ways is calculated from the weights of pairs of word classes. The weights are taken from a specific table. This is a variant of weighting by means of weights from rules.

Thus, it must be pointed out that the source of the weight is not restricted to rules; not only tables but also dictionary entries are possible.

As an example, weighting by means of dictionary entries can also be shown within the framework of the homograph analysis. The weighted pairs of word classes represent the "normal case" of the occurrence of the pair's word classes. But, for instance, it is not possible for all words of the word class "adverb" to have the same weight as not all adverbs occur with the same frequency (compare "mit" in German as adverb: Er ist mit der Beste - he is one of the best). Besides this, the modification of the default value also depends on the other interpretations of the word. Thus, the term of homograph class comes into play here, see Eggers et al. (1969).

Weights in the dictionary can also be used in another way because the probability of a certain word class is not only determined by the further word classes to which the word belongs, but also by the fact that this word belongs to the type and the specific subject of the text. Examples concerning this can be found in Luckhardt (1983). Again, this can be applied not only to morphosyntactic interpretations, but above all to classificational semantics and world knowledge data bases: in texts concerning computer technology, the meaning "gardens" for the German word "Anlage" will surely be very low weighted ("Anlage" can mean plant, installation, (stereo) system, apparatus, grounds, gardens, investment). The dictionary entry in the CTX-system (TRANSIT project, see Zimmermann et al., 1983), for instance, is used similarly. In Sect. 6, the problem of whether to compile text type or subject area specific dictionaries will be examined.

The ambiguity of the sentence

Im Garten spielen die Indianer
(the Indians are playing in the garden, or,
they are playing Indians in the garden)

can stand for an example concerning weights within rules. On the one hand, "die" can be a definite article (as in "die Indianer"), on the other hand, it can be a personal pronoun (as in "die spielen"). The latter solution certainly is less probable than the first one, which has effects on the weights of the particular rules.

And, last but not least, in the field of semantics, an immense number of such examples can be given.

5 The Application of Weighting in an MT-System

For more than 12 years the Sonderforschungsbereich "Elektronische Sprachforschung" (Special Research Unit: Electronic Language Research) has been engaged in machine translation. In one of its subprojects the MT-system SUSY has been developed. Today there exists a line of different stages of development of SUSY. The languages English, French and German are included in a way that allows one to characterise SUSY as a multilingual system. In this chapter we concentrate, above all, on those aspects of SUSY where concepts of weighting are integrated.

The analysis part of the MT-system uses a heterogenous parser. This means that for classes of problems different methods of solution are used. The whole analysis part (extensively described in SALEM, 1980) is subdivided into a sequence of three parts: a morphology driven part, a syntactics driven part and a semantics driven part.

The morphological analysis includes inflectional analysis, string compound analysis and (optional) homograph reduction. It uses dictionaries with up to 140000 (mostly) stems (e.g. for German). The homograph reduction uses a network whose nodes are labelled with morphosyntactic information and whose arcs are labelled with the weight of the transition from the left category to the right one. The algorithm computes the weight of every path through the network and passes the best ones to the syntactic analysis. It may be instructed to select between 1 and 12 paths per sentence. For German the algorithm selects two paths per sentence default, for English four. These paths could be treated in parallel by syntactic analysis.

In 1981 the project started to realise a new concept of the syntactic analysis, SUSY II. SUSY, SUSY II and the system environment common to both form the

SUSY-E system. In SUSY II the linguist defines his linguistic knowledge of the natural language in a procedural metalanguage. A program (compiler) translates this into an internal representation that is executed by a runtime system using a dictionary. The system interacts with a data structure of chart type. A control supervises all these components and their interactions. This model can be shown in a diagram:

```
-------------------------------------------------
!                                               !
!                    control                    !
!                                               !
!-----------------------------------------------!
!                                               !
! !------------!    !-----------!   !---------! !
! !            !    !           !   !         ! !
! ! grammar    !==> ! compiler  !   ! dictio- ! !
! !            !    !           !   !         ! !
! !------------!    !-----------!   !   nary  ! !
!                         ||        !         ! !
!                         ||        !         ! !
!                         \/        !         ! !
! !------------!    !-----------!   !         ! !
! !            !    !           !   !         ! !
! !   data     !    !  runtime  !   !         ! !
! !            !<==>!           ! <==!        ! !
! ! structure  !    !   system  !   !         ! !
! !            !    !           !   !         ! !
! !------------!    !-----------!   !---------! !
!                                               !
-------------------------------------------------
```

SUSY II is a production system using structured linguistic knowledge. This knowledge includes processes, grammars and rules and it is organised as a tree. The terminal nodes are called rules, the preterminal nodes are called grammars. All other nodes are processes. Rules contain a left hand side and a right and side. The left hand side consists of a path description which names only the elements of the path, followed by conditions on the single trees (i.e. on their structure and the decoration of the nodes) and relations between the trees. The right hand side describes the structure to be built. Some standard transductions can be formulated by using predefined functions. If-then-else statements are possible, but case- or loop-constructions are not supplied. Grammars contain an entry condition which is meant to select a path within the actual data structure. It consists of a description of properties of the top node of each tree and of restrictions on the right and left context. Moreover, grammars contain interpretation parameters for distinction between parallel, iterative, preferential and stratificational processing, an explicit value for marking used material or for its deletion, a parameter for invoking the garbage collector, etc. Grammars contain a list of rules identified by their names. The actual data structure is selected by a process and is described as a path of unspecified length by communicating the conditions of its first and last elements and a global restriction for all objects between. Moreover, context restrictions can be formulated. Processes consist of interpretation parameters (like grammars) and a list of grammars and processes identified by their names. These are meant to operate on the subgraphs identified by the entry condition. An exit condition on the material existing after termination of the process, i.e. the original subgraph minus structures which have been deleted by subprocesses plus new material, is tested only if new material has been produced. If a structure is found which fits the exit condition, all "wrong" structures will be destroyed, otherwise everything is accepted.

On the basis of this control structure the concept of weighting is being integrated. It is possible to weight rules, grammars and processes.

The generation of partial parsers, as described in Section 7.2, includes a runtime system that controls the tree of linguistic knowledge and chooses each time the next executable process or grammar contingent upon their weights.

Finally, the semantic analysis disambiguates word meaning, introduces thesaurus-like relations (e.g. synonymy) and analyses underlying semantic relations for nonvalency-bound prepositional noun groups. This analysis is semantics driven. The algorithm uses a knowledge base that contains rules using semantic features. For German, this data base contains 75000 entries; most of them feature attributing rules. The rules are ordered in sequence. A sequence $r_1, r_2, \ldots, r_n$ for the disambiguation of a lexeme is ordered in such a way that the conditions of rule r_i are stricter than the conditions of rule r_{i+1}. The process that operates on this sequence stops if a rule applies. So the rules are endogenously weighted.

The analysis part of the MT-system SUSY is used in some other projects, for example in the TRANSIT project for automatic indexing in the CTX system (see Zimmermann et al. (1983)). There, words are further disambiguated using a so-called "Differenzierungswörterbuch" (differentiating dictionary) that contains the definitions of the ambiguous words and a variable for each definition. The value of this variable is interpreted as weight. The German word "Medium", for example, is described as follows (Zimmermann et al., 1983, p. 105):

Weight	Definition
9	Mittel, Mittler: das Medium Fernsehen (means, mediator: the medium of television)
2	Physikalische Substanz: löslich im Medium Wasser (physical substance: soluble in (the substance) water)
0	Verbindung zur Geisterwelt: ein gutes Medium (Contact with the spirit world: a good medium)

The following chapters will give a more detailed description of the use of weighting in the parser. In each case an example showing the realisation of the concept in the system will be given.

6 Examples of the Application of Weighting

The complexity of controls has already been indicated; see also Thiel (1983) on this subject. Weighting can control MODE, and this, in turn, the application of rules. The purpose of weighting is then, on the one hand, control. On the other hand, weights result from linguistic data and are assigned to linguistic data (i.e.

structures); the ambivalent nature of weights has already been pointed out. More precisely, in exogenous weighting the weights are initially fixed in external linguistic data, i.e. not in the control structure. The control reads these weights, processes them and draws conclusions from them. So the regulation cycle ist complete. The grammar contains rules which are processed by the control in order to use them to control the processing of the grammar. This is the aspect to which this chapter is devoted.

6.1 Weights in the Control Structure

As an example of the plausibility of linguistic output structures in the case of ambiguity, the weighting of rules was suggested for relative exogenous weighting. However, no mention was made of how these weights are to be used. From the point of view of application in the control structure they are used to control the selection of alternative rules. In other words, if one describes the course of the analysis in the form of a tree, they steer the way through this tree and allow the selection of the most heavily weighted alternative rules or subgrammars. This makes an analysis strategy possible which can be described as a "best-first" strategy (cf. Wahlster, 1979). A fuller illustration of this now follows in the framework of production systems. In Wahlster (1982) preferential markers for ATNs intended for similar use are proposed.

6.1.1 Production Systems

Production systems have been developed on the basis of string substitution systems and formal grammars. In artificial intelligence and in language processing systems production systems are often called upon in models of system contexts. The following description of production systems refers mainly to Nilsson (1982) and Rosner (1983). References to further literature are to be found therein.

Production systems possess a global data base, a set of production rules and a control structure. Every rule has a precondition which is tested in the data base. If the precondition is fulfilled the rules may be applied, in the course of which the data base is changed. For a given data base the control system selects the applicable rules and determines which section of the data base is to be activated in relation to the rule. It also tests the final condition and terminates the calculation accordingly.

The data base is at the disposal of all rules and all rules communicate through the data base. For further clarification the concepts of production set and search tree must be introduced (Rosner, 1983, p.43: P-tree). A production set is the set of applicable rules on a given data base. Each of these rules changes the data base so that a further production set can also be produced for each of these new data bases. Thus we have a graph (normally a tree, a search tree), which represents the area of solution. See on this subject the diagram for the 8-puzzle in Nilsson (1982, p.28). (The 8-puzzle consists of a 3×3 matrix of 8 different movable elements and one empty element.)

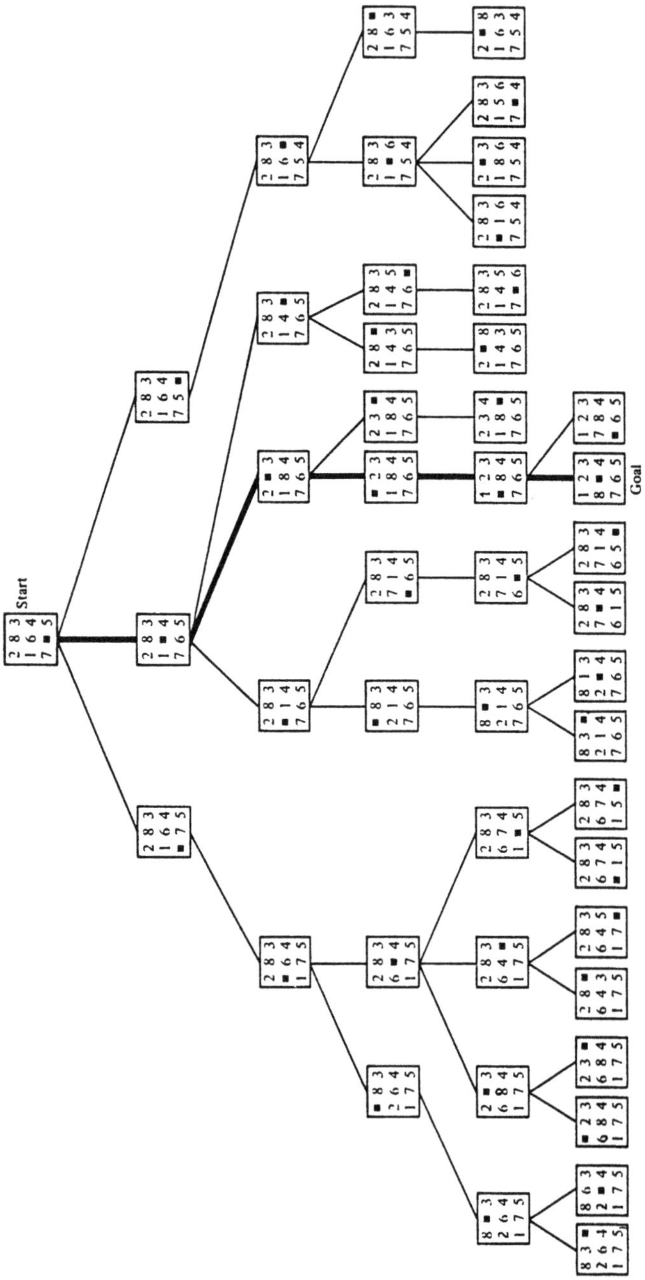
Start
Goal

Production sets can be commutative. The order in which the rules are applied is irrelevant in a commutative set of rules (cf. Nilsson, 1982, p.35). Any order will produce the same data base. In a noncommutative set of rules the application of one rule prevents the application of any other rules by producing an altered data base.

Here a distinction between different cases should be introduced:

(a) there is a production set with a rule which is applicable in several mutually exclusive sections of the data base.
(b) there is a production set with various rules which are applicable in the same section of the data base.
(c) there is a production set with various rules which are applicable in various mutually excluded sections of the data base.

Rule sets (a) and (c) are obviously commutative, whereas (b) needs to be noncommutative and produces ambiguities. Since the order in which the rules are applied with commutative production sets is arbitrary, (a) and (c) can be applied either sequentially (in any order) or in parallel. Sequential application of rules is not possible with noncommutative production sets.

Assuming that weighting belongs in the control, it is worth having a closer look at production sets on the control system. Nilsson (1982, p.21ff.), differentiates between two strategies: the irrevocable and the tentative.

An irrevocable strategy means that a rule is selected from a production set and applied without the decision being able to be revised by the choice of an alternative from the production set. (For this a search tree is not necessary.) This procedure can be called deterministic. It presupposes that the production set contains only one element or that the configuration of the rules does not affect the solution or that there is an intelligent decision function which selects the best applicable rule. This function could make use of weights.

In the tentative strategy as opposed to the irrevocable strategy, it is allowed to resume with a so far unused alternative from earlier production sets. So all alternatives are followed through. To achieve this there exist various strategies. Either an alternative is followed up in the search tree, backing up the present state of the system which is later activated to follow up another alternative from the production set at the same point, or, for all alternatives from the production set, a search tree is built up. In "blind" systems this can lead to structures with a very large scope. "An intelligent control strategy would grow a much narrower tree, using its special knowledge to focus the growth more directly towards the goal" (Nilsson, 1982, p.27). For solutions to this problem in artificial intelligence, see Nilsson (1982, Chap.2).

This is how the concept of weighting can be included in a best-first strategy. Weighting can be looked upon as a basis for an evaluating function which directs and limits the growth of the search tree but also establishes the best path through a search tree. The evaluation function f^* gives the minimal costs of a path through the search tree from the start node to the goal node. The cost from the start node to node n ist calculated by $g^*(n)$, and the cost from n to the goal node is calculated by $h^*(n)$. So

$$f^*(n) = g^*(n) + h^*(n),$$

where f(n), g(n) and h(n) are estimations of $f^*(n)$, $g^*(n)$ and $h^*(n)$ respectively.

As strategies for heuristic searches the staged search and limitation of successors are of importance (Doran and Michie, 1966; application to speech understanding: Lowerre, 1976; vision: Rubin, 1978). In the staged search those branches of the search tree whose f is minimal are lopped off (for example if the memory overflows). The search tree is further expanded from the remaining branches. This process can be repeated. There is no guarantee that the best path will be kept to. In the strategy of limitation of successors those successor nodes whose f(n) is minimal are not expanded. There is no way of stopping the long-term best nodes from being irreversibly eliminated.

The best-first strategy may be described as follows: Let all productions be weighted; then the maximum of weights of all production sets can be computed. Those productions with the maximal weight are collected in a so-called "hyperproduction set". All productions of the hyperproduction set are executed. Then the production sets for the newly generated nodes are computed. After this the algorithm iterates. Thus a parallel expansion of those nodes most promising at every instant is given. Because every node is always involved in the computing of the hyperproduction set, the algorithm always finds the best path through the search graph. This algorithm shows some analogies with the AO* algorithm (see Nilsson (1982), p. 104), which uses marked connectors. So the weight of a production in a production set (Wgt (prod (n))) is also included in h(n):

$$h(n) = h'(n) + \text{Wgt}(\text{prod}(n)).$$

The best-first strategy is not supposed to remove nodes from the search tree but merely to follow up those with the highest value from f(n). Thus it is garanteed that the best paths will be kept to in the long term. So the best-first strategy is tentative.

6.2 Weights in Linguistic Structures

Apart from the effect of weights of rules on the control structure, weights also give, of course, values to the linguistic structures. If all alternatives in an analysis tree are pursued and several alternative results produced, their comparison is possible.

This comparison, if it is carried out on interim results, allows the directed execution of garbage collection. The weights represent the necessary decision basis by which the garbage collector can decide about the acceptability or nonacceptability and therefore the rejection of an interim result. It should be noted that the garbage collector must be taken in a more complex sense than is normally the case. Its job is not to collect various bits of free memory but to clear memory by rejecting interim results. The search tree is made smaller by the decimation of the data base, which leads to more efficient analysis times.

So far we have only been dealing with linguistic objects in the narrow sense of rules and structures. Now we mention weighting in other areas connected with language. Here, for example, we should refer to the use of weights in inference rules of tasks in artificial intelligence.

6.3 Learning Systems

As has been shown, weights do not remain unchanged for all texts of a language. The text characteristics which have an effect here are described by the term "sublanguage": a sublanguage is defined by the specifications of text type, subject area and text function. Luckhardt (1984) defines text type and realization type (cf. the implementation in the project SUSY-BSA, described in Keil, 1982, p.35ff.) as the "Kennzeichnung von Texten, in denen bestimmte Strukturen vorherrschen, z.B. Sätze mit Anweisungen (vorwiegend Imperativsätze), Wortlisten, Nominalstrukturen" (the characteristic of a text, in which certain structures prevail, e.g. sentences with instructions (in German mostly imperative, in English infinitive), lists of words, nominal structures; Luckhardt, 1983). The text function predominantly gives the purpose for which a text was written, e.g. as an advert for a position, maintenance instruction, report, abstract, etc. This means a text is produced in its subject area in an appropriate form and for an intended purpose.

The accommodation of a parser to a sublanguage can be achieved by a learning system which approximates the weights to the characteristics of the sublanguage. For the present, we will proceed from an initial, intellectually executed entry of weights. The learning system will be realised by the parser, which is in the specific state of "learning", whereby an amount of text from a sublanguage, which is large enough, is analysed. Each rule (or word meaning) which leads to an acceptable result is increased in weight.

This procedure brings about two problems:

1. How does the function which increases the weight for the rule or the word meaning look? An answer to this question can be expected from empirical examinations.
2. How is it decided whether a rule leads to an acceptable result? We must proceed from the fact that, at the beginning of the procedure, the system does not have the optimal rules for the text and thus cannot give acceptable results. The solution of this problem seems to be possible in several ways. For example, using artificial intelligence concepts of expert systems, the conclusion from an existing results structure to the applied rules necessary to achieve this structure offer a starting point.

In general, we can say about learning systems that empirical work has to decide on their effectiveness, especially because the dimensions and number of the sublanguages have not been settled.

7 Computation of Weights

7.1 Weights and Sublanguage

The dependence of the weighting on the sublanguage to which a text belongs has been referred to quite often. This allocation is considered more closely in this chapter.

The dependence of the weighting on the sublanguage is directly understandable if one considers that in different sublanguages different subsets of the rules of a language are used. For this reason the weights also change if the sublanguage changes. From this, a more precise allocation automatically results by using the specifications of the sublanguage and the origin of the weights, because the linguistic descriptions are involved there. The text type, as the surface-oriented typification, is above all reflected in the selection of the morphosyntactic rules and thus influences the weights of these rules as far as they are used as a basis for the calculation of weights. The corresponding facts can be applied to the weights of the word meanings which are preferred in the subject area. The integration of thesauri in the project SUSY-BSA can be mentioned as the realisation of this context (compare Keil, 1982, p.40ff). This dependence is shown in the following diagram (→ means "determines"):

```
sublanguage                       origin of weights
     !                                          !
     !                                          !
     !                                          !
     !--- text type     ──→          rules ---!
     !                                          !
     !--- subject area ──→ word meaning ---!
     !
     !--- text function
```

If "$weight_R$" stands for a weight with the origin "rules" and "$weight_L$" describes a weight with the origin "dictionary", then two functions, f_R and f_L, which modify the weight to weight' for all rules and dictionary entries must be defined:

$$weight'_R := f_R\,(\text{text type}, p_R, weight_R)$$
$$weight'_L := f_L\,(\text{subject area}, p_L, weight_L)$$

These functions generate rules or dictionaries which are accommodated to the sublanguage.

In the functions for calculating the modified weights, the meaning of the parameters p remained open. Now these parameters shall be specified. The starting point for the discussion of p in

$$weight'_R := f_R\,(\text{text type}, p_R, weight_R)$$

is the consequence concerning the rules which results from the specification of a text as a special type. Consequently, the rules as holders for weights also hold the modified $weight'_R$. This means that p_R must be identified with the linguistic objects of the rules. The fact that certain structures are more or less preferred in a special text type means that the application of certain rules is preferred. Hence, in generation systems, the right side (structural change) of these rules must be used for the identification of p_R. The parameter p_R describes a structure which matches with the right side of a rule:

$$p_R = \text{struct}\,(t) \text{ with}$$
$$\text{match}\,(r, \text{struct}\,(t)) = \text{true}$$

For f_R results

$$weight'_R := f_R\,(\text{text type}, \text{struct}\,(t), weight_R).$$

Thus, according to the text type "instructions", for example, imperatives can be weighted higher than other finite forms of a verb.

In the following, an approach is developed for dictionaries (and knowledge bases) for semantic disambiguation, and especially the parameter p_L is specified. As the subject area is a text variable and the calculation of the weight must depend on the dictionary entry, or more precisely, on the meaning description of the dictionary entry, p_L must be a meaning description variable of the dictionary. Thus, f_L can be described more precisely:

$$\text{weight}'_L := f_L\ (\text{subject area, meaning description, weight}_L).$$

We must proceed from the fact that a parser with its dictionaries can be used in different subject areas. The content of the dictionaries as well as their organisational concept should be independent of a specific subject area. So a new subject area does not change the content of a dictionary. This means that the meaning description may not be identical with the subject area.

Finally, we show an example relating to the function f_L which simulates a possible realisation of the procedure. Suppose a German dictionary contains the entries:

	(meaning description)
Anlage	BOTANIC
Anlage	APPARATUS
Anlage	COMMUNICATION

A disambiguation rule which, in the case of "besichtigen" (to view, inspect, visit), for example, admits in the semantic relation "patient" an argument with the characterisation "large object", allows for the sequence "eine Anlage besichtigen" only the interpretations

		(meaning description)
besichtigen +	Anlage	BOTANIC
	Anlage	APPARATUS

In a text with a subject area "computer technology" only the interpretation "APPARATUS" can be expected. For this subject area, f_L may produce in the dictionary the weights

f_L (computer technology, BOTANIC, weight_L) = 0
f_L (computer technology, APPARATUS, weight_L) = 80
f_L (computer technology, COMMUNICATION, weight_L) = 20

Thus, the result of the disambiguation rule can be weighted:

		(meaning description)	
besichtigen +	Anlage	BOTANIC	with g = 0
	Anlage	APPARATUS	with g = 80

and "Anlage" as an apparatus is accepted.

7.2 Weights and Partial Parsers

In computer science, partial parsers are constructed by proceeding from a given grammar. This grammar defines, and this is what is meant by "partial", a part (subset) of the (natural) language which is determined a priori. See, for example, Seelbach (1975) or Rostek (1979).

The conception on which this procedure is based does not seem to be the only one possible, for it proceeds from the fact that, to repeat this in other words, the parser can analyse nothing other and not more than just this subset of the language. Another conception which can be followed in a positive way takes the opposite course: Proceeding from a global parser, several partial parsers are derived. A global parser is a parser which is not restricted to a certain subset of natural language. The advantages of this procedure are that, by less expenditure, more partial parsers can be constructed and development work is not repeated. Moreover, such a system is open to new subsets of the natural language, which were not planned during development.

By means of weights, and using a procedure similar to that shown in Section 7.1 in connection with sublanguages, a global parser can be restricted to a partial parser by allocating the value zero to the absolute exogenous weights which generate structures that do not belong to the specific language subset. This means that the rules and subgrammars weighted in this way are deleted from the grammar. (An implementation in the Sonderforschungsbereich 100, project A2, verified this concept.) Further details can be looked up in Section 7.1, in which the dependence of the text type and weights is discussed, because according to the comprehension of the sublanguage a partial parser is above all a parser for a specific text type.

In this connection, however, we must refer to a difference: parsers are accommodated to a specific sublanguage by modifying relative weights, whereas partial parsers are realised by absolute weights. Both procedures can certainly be understood as differing variations of the same principle.

8 Evaluation of Weights

Within the reflections concerning the concepts of weighting, we did not deal with the problems of at what time weightings should be made and how they are to be stored. These are not only questions of realisation, but are above all questions of conception: the moment of execution of the weighting decides upon the structure and the behaviour of the system as shown in the following.

The possibilities of use described in Sections 5 and 6 and the computation of weights described in Section 7 must also be distinguished as regards the evaluation moment of the weights.

The use of weights for the control of parsing - compare best-first strategy, garbage collector, etc. - only permits weighting during runtime. So far, no problems occur. The determination of the computation moment of weights, however, is much more important. Intuitively, a preprocessor without computation during runtime seems to be a solution. The preprocessor solution, however, brings about some disadvantages for text specific parsers, as the preprocessor would create a separate parser and separate dictionaries for each text type by substituting the original weight by a modified one. Alternatively, a multiple weight without multiplication of the parser and the dictionaries should be accepted. But, as only a finite number of variables with modified weights as value can be used in a dictionary entry, this procedure brings about disadvantages as well.

Consequently, there exist reasons to make computations of weights during runtime. In particular, this means that, firstly, during the dictionary access, the function f is applied and, secondly, during rule application, the selection of the rule/subgrammar is influenced by the call-in of f_R, above all when alternatives exist.

But even here, at least two critical aspects result: firstly, the performance of the parser is definitely affected. But this can only be stated finally after exhaustive practical tests. First implementations show that the waste of time is justifiable. Secondly, the case may occur that for the same subgrammars/rules and dictionary entries, the functions f_R and f_L must be evaluated several times. But this may be controlled by (possibly complicated) organisation.

The question concerning storage can be reformulated as a question concerning the kinds of weights and the consequences resulting from them. The kinds of weights - in contrast to the ways of weighting, see Section 4 - can be distinguished through what they value. If the weight g_m, for example, values a word meaning and the weight g_n weights a syntax rule, then the weight g_r, which is calculated by a function of g_m and g_n, cannot be allocated an appropriate interpretation. What should be the meaning of g_r and how should the different kinds of weights be included in the calculation? Consequently, the different kinds are not compatible with each other.

Therefore, only accumulation of weights of the same kind is allowed. For example, if the weight of the resulting structure is calculated from the weight of the structure in the data base and the weight of a production rule, both belong to the same kind, but not the weights concerning semantics and morphosyntactic probabilities.

For further reflection, the weights referring to morphology, syntax, semantics and pragmatics are distinguished. (Other classifications may also be possible.) For n kinds, the actual total weight for each kind is noted separately in an array of length n. This seems to be the most acceptable solution because it offers more differentiated information and because the final (i.e. after finishing the analysis) global valuation remans calculable, if this is desired. The most important characteristic is the fact that during the search in the solution tree different control strategies can be realised, depending on the kinds of weights. In connection with ATNs, Wahlster (1979) discusses control mechanisms for navigation through the network. In this connection, he makes a difference between syntactically, semantically and semantic-pragmatically controlled ATNs. According to the best-first strategy developed above, the paths through the solution tree are determined by the weights. As syntactic, semantic and semantic-pragmatic weights are kept separately, they can also be used spearately from each other for the calculation of the optimal path through the solution tree. In this connection, whether production systems or ATNs are dealt with has less relevance.

References

Barr, A. and Feigenbaum, E.A. (1983): The Handbook of Artificial Intelligence, Vol.1, London: Pitman
Bibel, W. and Siekmann, J.H. (1982): Künstliche Intelligenz. Frühjahrsschule 1982. In: Informatik Fachberichte 59. Berlin-Heidelberg-New York: Springer
Braun, E. and Rademacher, H. (1978): Wissenschaftstheoretisches Lexikon. Graz-Wien-Köln: Styria
Charniak, E. (1983): A Parser with Something for Everyone. In: King (1983), pp.117-149
Charniak, E. and Wilks, Y. (1976): Computational Semantics. An Introduction to Artificial Intelligence and Natural Language Comprehension. New York-Amsterdam: North-Holland
Christaller, T. and Metzing, D. (eds.) (1979): Augmented Transition Network Grammatiken. 2 Vols. Berlin: Einhorn
Doran, J. and Michie, D. (1966): Experiments with a Graph Transverser Program. Proc. Soc. (London) **294,** 235-259 (1966)
Eggers, H., Dietrich, R., Klein, W., Rothkegel, A., Weber, H.J., and Zimmermann, H.H. (1969): Elektronische Syntaxanalyse der deutschen Gegenwartssprache. Tübingen: Niemeyer
Feigenbaum, E.A. and Feldman, J. (eds.) (1963): Computers and Thought. New York: McGraw-Hill
Hempel, C.G. (1974): Philosophie der Naturwissenschaften. München: dtv
Hempel, C.G. and Oppenheim, P. (1948): Studies in the Logic of Explanation. In: Philosophy of Science. Vol.15, pp.135-175
Keil, G.C. (1982): System Conception and Design. Forschungsproject SUSY-BSA, Universität des Saarlandes, Saarbrücken. Mimeo
King, M. (1983) (ed.): Parsing Natural Language. London-New York: Academic Press
Klein, W. (1974): Variation in der Sprache. Kronberg: Scriptor
Kuhlen, R. (1979): Datenbasen Datenbanken Netzwerke, Vol.1. München-New York-London-Paris: Saur
Lowerre, B.T. (1976): The HARPY Speech Recognition System. Technical Report. Computer Science Department, Carnegie-Mellon University
Luckhardt, H.-D. (1983): Erste Überlegungen zur Verwendung des Sublanguage-Konzepts in SUSY. Multilingua **3** (3) 135-142 (1984)
Marcus, M. (1980): A Theory of Syntactic Recognition for Natural Language. Cambridge-London: MIT Press
Nilsson, N.J. (1982): Principles of Artificial Intelligence. Berlin-Heidelberg-New York: Springer
Robinson, J.J. (1982): DIAGRAM: A Grammar for Dialogues. CACM **35** (1), 27-47 (1982)
Rosner, M. (1983): Production Systems. In: King (1983), pp.35-58
Rostek, L. (1979): Methoden des partiellen Parsing für das automatische Indexing - Syntaxgraphen zur Analyse von Sprachmustern. In: Kuhlen (1979), pp.251-282
Rubin, S. (1978): The ARGOS Image Understanding System. Proceedings of the ARPA Image Understanding Workshop, Carnegie-Mellon University, pp.159-162
SALEM (1980): Ein Verfahren zur automatischen Lemmatisierung deutscher Texte, ed. by Sonderforschungsbereich 100 "Elektronische Sprachforschung". Tübingen: Niemeyer
Seelbach, D. (1975): Computerlinguistik und Dokumentation. München: Verlag Dokumentation
Slocum, J. (1984): METAL: The LRC Machine Translation System. Working Paper LRC-84-2. Linguistic Research Center, University of Texas
Stegmüller, W. and Varga von Kibéd, M. (1970 and 1973, 1983, 1984): Probleme und Resultate der Wissenschaftstheorie und Analytischen Philosophie. 4 Vols. Berlin-Heidelberg-New York: Springer
Thiel, M. (1983): Die Systemarchitektur von SUSY unter benutzerspezifischem Aspekt. Sprache und Datenverarbeitung **12,** 20-24 (1983)
Wahlster, W. (1979): ATN und semantisch-pragmatische Analysesteuerung. In: Christaller and Metzing (1979), pp.167-185
Wahlster, W. (1982): Natürlichsprachliche Systeme. In: Bibel and Siekmann (1982), pp.203-283
Wilks, Y. (1973): Preference Semantics. In: Memoranda from the Artificial Intelligence Laboratory 206. Stanford University, Stanford
Wilks, Y. (1976): Parsing English II. In: Charniak and Wilks (1976), pp.155-184

Wotschke, E.-M. (1976): Controlled Partition Grammars as a Basis for a Syntactic Analysis of English. In: Sonderforschungsbereich "Elektronische Sprachforschung": Internationales Kolloquium Automatische Lexikographie, Analyse und Übersetzung. Saarbrücken: SFB 100. Preprints

Wotschke, E.-M., Wotschke, D., and Downey, P. (1976): Size, Index, and Context-Sensitivity of CPGs. IBM RC 5867 (No. 24639). New York

Zimmermann, H. H., Kroupa, E., and Keil, G. (1983): CTX. Ein Verfahren zur computergestützten Texterschließung. BMFT Forschungsbericht ID 83-006. Bonn: Bundesministerium für Forschung und Technologie

A Distributed Word-Based Approach to Parsing*

S. L. Small

Abstract. People have an incredible facility for organizing and selecting word senses in arriving at the intended meaning of sentences in context. The process takes place with such unnoticed and subconscious ease that it has been often overlooked in the study of language. To those building computer programs to understand language, however, this phenomenon represents a central problem. While many syntactic constructions and conceptual relations can be described through systems of rewrite rules, the word sense selection problem remains. The reason for this lies in the incompatibility of the sense discrimination problem and the rule-based problem-solving method.

The computational theory of **Word Expert Parsing** approaches natural language understanding as a non-uniform distributed process of interacting words. An expert process for each word actively pursues its intended meaning in the context of other word experts and real-world knowledge. The theory perceives understanding as a behavior of memory interactions, and the computer model emphasizes process rather than output structures.

The *Lexical Interaction Language* (LIL) formalizes the interactions among individual word experts, and the *Sense Discrimination Language* (SDL) specifies their actions to determine intended word senses in context. These languages constitute the formal theory of Word Expert Parsing, and permit the representation of all linguistic knowledge in terms of active word-based distributed agents. An existing computer program translates word experts represented in these languages into executable processes that interact to cooperatively analyze sentences.

This chapter makes a number of claims about the processes of natural language comprehension and its computational realization. A formal theory is developed and a computer model constructed to provide evidence to support those claims. Word Expert Parsing explains the understanding of sentences containing highly ambiguous words and complex structures. The distributed word-based approach is advanced as a framework for a full-scale theory of discourse comprehension.

* The preparation of this manuscript has been supported by the National Science Foundation under Grants IST-8208571 and MCS-8209971. Their support of this basic research is gratefully acknowledged.

1 Introduction

The *Word Expert Parser* (WEP) is a computer program that analyzes fragments of natural language text in order to extract their meaning in context. The system has been developed with particular attention paid to the wide variety of different meaning roles of words when appearing in combination with other words. The character of such lexical relations runs the gamut from the simple direct knowledge that some word sequence represents some remembered concept to the more analytical knowledge that particular kinds of lexical sequences often represent certain classes of conceptual notions.

An underlying perspective of the research about the nature of individual words recasts them as active processes which make inferences to determine their individual roles in the overall sentence, and which communicate with their neighbors to both acquire and provide the information necessary for such local inference to take place. Words do not have meaning per se, but rather, contribute to understanding through their effects on the ongoing interactions of memory. Sequences of lexical items mean something only through the interactions (a) among experts for their component words; and (b) between individual word experts and other memory processes. Lexical relations are thus viewed not as static functions, but as active processes causing words to combine together through dynamic interrogation and inference. The overall parsing process converges at their eventual agreement on a mutually acceptable interpretation for a fragment of text.

Note the fundamentally different perspective advanced by WEP compared to traditional computer parsing systems. The interpretation of natural language discourse cannot take place in isolation from other memory processes and have a reasonable chance of success at difficult applications (e.g., ones that can be said to require some sort of understanding to achieve). WEP does not separate comprehension into distinct phases, and the parser operates through constant interaction with other (currently simulated) parallel programs concerned with attention, reference, discourse structure, and reasoning about beliefs. The role of the parser is to participate in this mutual inference process; WEP does not build a syntactic or semantic structure to be used at some later time by some independent computer system. A parsing system is an expert language program which executes at the same time as many other expert programs, and which contributes to understanding by its interactions over time with the other modules. By the time the parser has examined an entire sentence, a large proportion of the effects of reading that sentence should already be felt by the rest of the overall computer system.

2 Background Motivations

2.1 Linguistics

The evolution of this perspective started with the observation that the understanding of a particular fragment of text depends fundamentally on the disambiguation of the individual words composing it. Knowing the contextual meanings of the words is tantamount to understanding the meaning of the overall fragment.

Another way of saying the same thing (Rieger, 1977) is that language interpretation can be ultimately viewed as a process of word sense discrimination. Unfortunately, this perspective does not eliminate the classic problems of deciding the nature of a distinct word sense, and the difference between different usages, word senses, and idioms. The solution to these problems comes in realizing that the process of understanding the meaning of words in context requires no reference to those notions at all.

The organization of WEP is founded on the belief that the grouping together of words to form meaningful sequences is an active process which succeeds only because of highly idiosyncratic application of lexical knowledge. That is, we fragment text and understand the meaning of the pieces because we know how the particular words involved interact with each other. Clearly, the first time we see a word, none of these interactions can be idiosyncratic (from the point of view of that word), and a parser must appeal more to general linguistic processing and to hypothesis-driven processing controlled by surrounding words than it might otherwise do to understand the meaning of the fragment. If many of the words are new, processes to apply general knowledge must do what they can.

Sometimes sequences of two or more words interact together to such an extent that they seem to behave as a single lexical item. Linguists have labelled such sequences *idioms*. The notion to which this definition gives rise, however, causes several problems for linguistic theory. First of all, rarely does such a sequence hold together so tightly that it can be truly treated theoretically as a single lexical item. Secondly, rarely does such a sequence have a unique meaning. More often than not, the meaning of an idiomatic expression must be determined by disambiguation. The sequence must be analyzed in context and be treated by comprehension processes as being either (a) a cohesive whole with idiosyncratic meaning, or (b) a sequence having meaning through the application of more general language knowledge (i. e., typical "parsing"). There is no a priori way of knowing the meaning of the sequence to be the one or the other.

The notion of *idiom* falls at the idealized end of a continuum. Lexical sequences can be *more or less idiomatic,* in the sense that the process interactions constituting the understanding of them includes greater or fewer idiosyncratic interactions. The WEP way of looking at the most idiomatic sequences is that the special interactions among the participating words take priority over any other potential interactions involving those words. The disambiguation of idiomatic expressions, i. e., the understanding of the sequences as either idioms or non-idioms (to use the popular distinction), generally requires expert interactions with high-order memory processes in addition to the strictly word-specific ones. The understanding of an idiom thus differs insignificantly, from the perspective of WEP theory, from comprehension of any other kind (according to whatever classification scheme) of lexical sequence.

The notion that all fragments of language are more or less idiomatic, while radical in some linguistic quarters, has been previously suggested. In his introductory textbook, *Aspects of Language,* Dwight Bolinger asks "whether everything we say may be in some degree idiomatic; that is, whether there are affinities among words that continue to reflect the attachments the words had when we learned them, within larger groups" (Bolinger, 1975). After working within what he calls "the prevailing reductionism," Bolinger began to suggest a positive answer to his pedagogical question, choosing to take "an idiomatic rather than an analytical view" (Bolinger, 1979) of language. The contribution of artificial intelligence in general, and of *Word Expert Parsing* in particular, is to develop theory from this informal view. The notion of process, and of process interaction, allows us to begin to do just that.

2.2 Psychology

The Word Expert Parser is being developed as one part of a uniform memory model that represents understanding through interactions among its large number of fairly small distributed elements. By distributed processes, we mean simultaneous non-uniform procedures that are not synchronized. These elements are seen as processors, rather than as static structures, and communicate by transmitting among themselves some kind of symbolic messages or signals. While the existing WEP system operates through the transmission of symbol structures (Newell, 1980), there may be good psychological reasons to restrict word and concept experts to the transmission of activation (Feldman and Ballard, 1982). The nature of the human intelligence, as a serial symbol manipulating system or as a highly parallel system of activation propagating connections, must influence profoundly the architecture of computer systems to understand. The work described in this paper consists of a highly distributed system of symbol transmitting connections. As the research proceeds, it will be necessary to decide whether or not the experts should be allowed this symbolic communication, or whether they should be constrained to communicate by weighted activation levels only. Recently, our research group has embarked on a project explicitly directed toward neurolinguistic modeling. (Note that the goals of WEP are multi-faceted, involving both cognitive modeling and computational understanding.) Initial results from this neurolinguistic effort are reported in Cottrell and Small (1983).

The present research takes a stand on a number of ongoing debates in psycholinguistics. In particular, just as WEP disputes the sharpness of the linguistic notion of idiom, so it argues that the psycholinguistic concept of *function words* does not help one to understand the phenomena under study. Such *function words* make up a class of words that indicate which parts of a sentence go together and how. They are usually distinguished from *content words,* which are the meaningful elements (e.g., objects, events). In our view, the words of language can be *more or less functional,* in the nature of their effects in directing the language comprehension process. Some words (morphemes) have no roles other than functional ones (e.g., a, *-ing*), while others make significant contributions on a number of fronts including functionality (e.g., *deep, in*). The representation of function words in WEP does not differ in structure from the representation of typical content words. The difference lies simply in the amount of certain kinds of word expert processing that are performed in each case. It would be interesting to see if neurological evidence (in comprehension, rather than production) supports the WEP contention.

A second psychological question involves the effects of context on the processes of word and sentence interpretation. Are these processes "of a highly interactive, directable nature" or are they "basically isolable and autonomous" (Swinney, 1979)? This question has been studied often with experiments involving the processing of lexical ambiguities during comprehension. These experiments have tested whether (a) context prevents access to inappropriate word senses (the *prior decision hypothesis*); or (b) context has its effect only after access to all word senses (the *post decision hypothesis*). The design of WEP has been based on the latter idea, that word sense disambiguation takes place through the application of context after retrieval of all senses. While we considered constraining word experts by prior pruning (Rieger and Small, 1981), and even built an early version of WEP to perform that way (on several examples), the parser now operates in accord with the post decision hypothesis.

2.3 Computer Science

It has been recognized for some time that the most difficult applications of computers in the processing of natural language (e.g., machine translation) require significantly more than syntactic analysis alone. The structure of most natural languages does not lead straightforwardly to simple semantic interpretation of sentences based on their syntax. The unfortunate metaphor that suggests viewing people as Von Neumann computers (Small et al., 1982) has led to mistaken approaches to the analysis of natural languages as if they were similar to computer (or logical) languages. While the structure of ALGOL statements or sentences of the first-order predicate calculus may lead directly to interpretations of their meaning, this same mechanism just does not work for highly ambiguous, context-dependent sentences of evolved human languages.

It seems further to be the case that the processes of syntactic, semantic, and even pragmatic (general and discourse-specific context) analysis are very much interrelated. There are many feedback situations involving each of these aspects of processing. The body of this paper discusses a variety of these interdependencies as they relate to parsing: how objects mentioned in previous sentences can affect the meaning of the current sentence (even its structural analysis); how knowledge about the actors and objects, apart from that explicitly represented in a text can do the same; how the structure of idiosyncratic fragments often has nothing to do with their meaning. In developing a computer program to participate in dialogues with a person, many analogous feedback situations at the levels of plan recognition (speech actions and overall user goals), plan generation, and language production (Allen and Small, 1982) are prevalent.

The only computationally effective way to accommodate these fundamental interactions across the many inferential tasks of natural language comprehension appears to be in modular distributed computer systems. Such systems are both difficult to construct and inherently different in design from those intended to be sequential and non-interacting. While other programs account for the significant feedback cycles in language processing (Riesbeck and Schank, 1976), and the procedural deterministic nature of parsing (Marcus, 1979), no system yet takes into consideration both of these phenomena and the inherent parallelism and interdependence over time of all comprehension process. The work described here is intended to be a first step in that direction. Within the next several years, and in conjunction with the work in planning and goal recognition of Allen (1979) and the representation of naive human knowledge about the world (Hayes, 1978), an initial prototype of such a computer system should become a reality.

3 The Parsing System

The distributed parsing scheme of the Word Expert Parser works as follows. The WEP reader examines a word of text and retrieves its word expert from memory. The word expert starts processing, trying to determine the meaning role of its word in context, i.e., interacting with other word experts and with higher-order model processes to acquire the appropriate conceptual knowledge to make the correct inferences. Finally, all the word experts for a particular fragment of text come to mutual agreement on the meaning of the fragment, and the local distributed process terminates - local, in the sense that as long as there remains input text, the overall parsing process continues, while the disambiguation of individual lexical sequences making up the larger text completes.

The individual word experts have a dual responsibility in the model to coordinate two interconnected facets of the parsing process. Each active word expert must (a) determine its own meaning or function role in the larger text, and (b) provide conceptual and control information to other experts to enable them likewise to coordinate this complex task. Isolated word sense discrimination is not possible, since much of the dynamic knowledge required to complete that task must come from other experts. Thus each expert must both ask questions of other experts and and answer ones posed to it. The parser contains mechanisms for the passing of messages among word experts, in order to achieve this basic interaction.

3.1 Model Organization

The decentralized representation of parsing knowledge in word experts leads to an overall model organization to support (a) exchange of information and (b) distributed decision-making (i.e., agreement on overall meaning). The executing word expert is temporarily the coordinator of the entire parsing process, changing structures and invoking procedures in its environment. These structures and procedures make up the model organization illustrated in Figure 1. We refer to the control structure of the parser as a *lexical interaction* control structure. The basic aspects of this distributed control for a particular word expert include (a) suspending execution while waiting for needed information and (b) resuming execution when that information becomes available. When word sense discrimination requires some word expert to ask a question of another expert, it must wait to receive the answer before proceeding. When the information arrives, the word expert continues processing where it left off. Eventually, the word expert completes its sense discrimination and determines the intended meaning of its word in context.

The control flow that results from this coroutine control environment can be viewed as the movement of a window across the input stream. Inside the window,

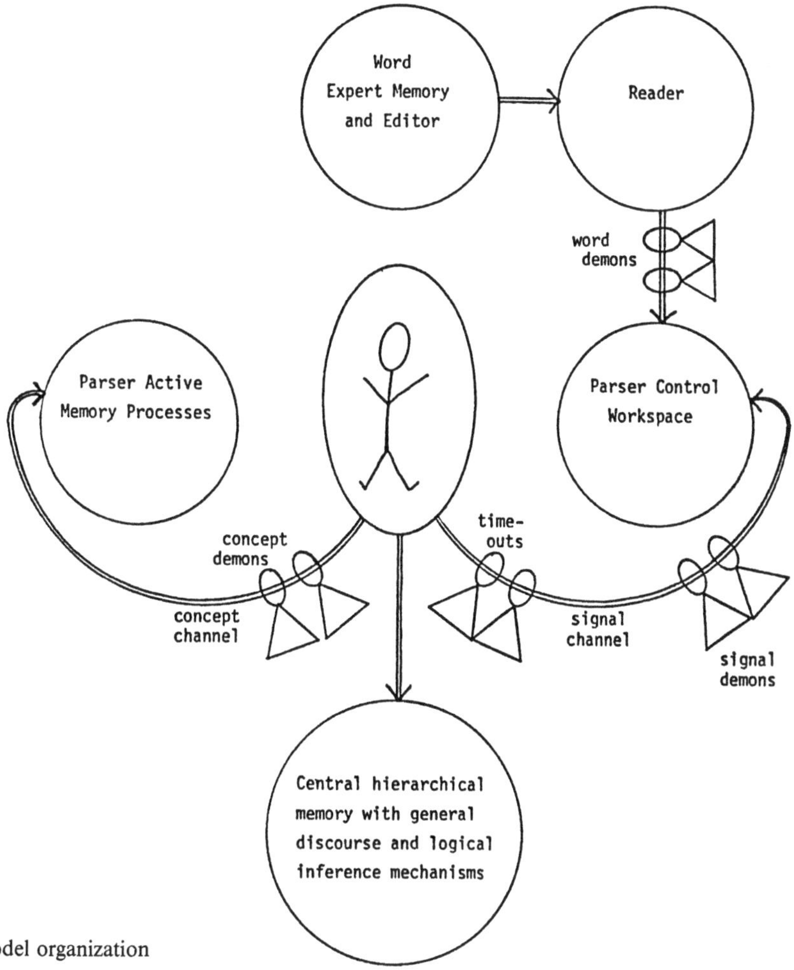

Fig. 1. Model organization

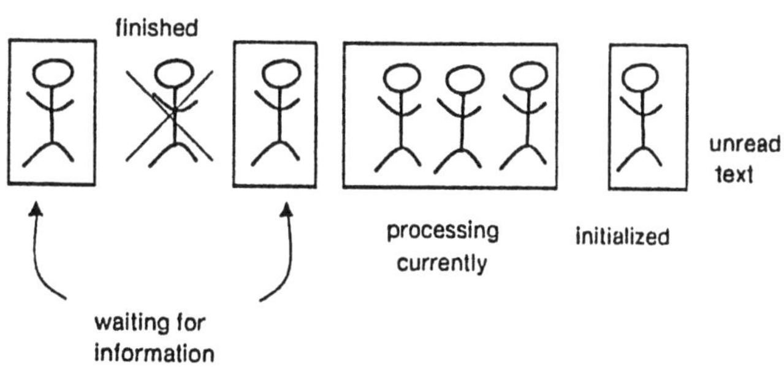

Fig. 2. Flow of control in the parser

control passes from word expert to word expert and back again, but the hearing of new words and the termination of old experts causes the overall processing window to move ahead. Figure 2 illustrates the control structure of the model in terms of this metaphor. The hearing of new words expands the right side of the window as the termination of word experts contracts the left side. Eventually, the window includes the last word of the input text, and the process terminates.

3.2 Control Mechanisms: Expert Suspension and Resumption

3.2.1 Restart Demons

Any word expert that desires some piece of information through interaction with one of its neighbors specifies the nature of that information in a data structure called a *restart demon*. The demon has the responsibility of monitoring the data transmissions on the two central pathways in the model. When the requested datum appears, the restart demon provides it to its associated word expert, which continues where it left off. The exact structure of restart demons is kept hidden from individual experts - an expert executes a statement stating that it wishes to receive information of a particular kind from another (specified or unspecified) expert. The interpretation of the statement involves constructing the specified restart demon, and putting it on the appropriate channel to await the anticipated data.

The execution of the statement does not cause the suspension of the expert. The expert continues its processing as if nothing had happened. Of course, it cannot make use of the needed data until it arrives, and thus often it must choose to suspend its execution at the time of demon creation. Note, however, that the expert might simultaneously create several restart demons, all awaiting different information. When a piece of awaited data arrives, the expert can process it. Part of the specification of the restart demon is the name of an entry point within the expert at which processing can continue when the desired information appears. Our use of the term *entry point* to describe the subgraphs of expert networks derives from this control aspect of their use.

3.2.2 Timeouts

The limitations of human working memory, of whatever extent they are determined to be, must be accounted for in constructing cognitive models. The traditional view of short-term memory as a data (or knowledge) store leads to models with a fixed-length buffer of quickly accessible short-term data, and general procedures for replacing items in that buffer with other items. Another vantage point on this question comes from viewing this memory in terms of the active problem-solving processes of the model. This perspective suggests building models with time-limited processes that may not remain active indefinitely. Just as the size of an individual constituent in a fixed-length buffer may depend on the nature of that item, so the time limit on an active process (even the units of time employed) must be allowed to depend on the nature of its functioning. A more complete discussion of timeout demons is given by Small (1981b).

As a completely procedural distributed model, the Word Expert Parser does not contain some finite fixed-length buffer to represent a short-term memory, but models the memory limitation with processes that have a strictly limited life span. The human understander does not wait indefinitely for information that could aid his/her understanding, and the model cannot either. When a word expert posts a restart demon to await some piece of information from another expert, a companion *timeout demon* is initiated to monitor the duration of the wait. In the ideal case, the desired information quickly becomes available in the model, and the awaiting expert promptly receives it. If the information does not appear within a certain time, however, the special timeout demon must command the awaiting process to go on without it. The timeout demon specifies both how long the expert is willing to wait for the information it desires and the name of an entry point within the awaiting expert where processing should continue if the associated restart demon times out instead. The units of measurement for timeouts are based on certain model events, including

(a) the number of syntactic groups created,
(b) the number of words read,
(c) the number of sentence breaks encountered, and
(d) the termination (as opposed to suspension) of particular word experts.

This control strategy has enormous significance: the processing of individual experts can depend on either the existence or the non-existence of relevant information. In terms of human problem-solving, this is analogous to our basing some decision on the explicit knowledge that we do not know something. Often the knowledge that we do not know something can be as useful to solving a problem as any other sort of knowledge.

3.3 Message and Memory Objects: Expert Interaction Data

The restart demons and timeouts of WEP coordinate the interaction among cooperating word experts. This interaction involves sending and receiving messages of only two (well-defined) types:

concept structures
control signals

Concept structures represent the meaning of fragments of text, referents, relations, conceptual expectations, and all other conceptual knowledge in the system, and can be thought of as case frameworks, frames, or KRL units (Bobrow and Winograd, 1977). Control signals represent syntactic and idiosyncratic lexical cues, query/reply handshaking between experts, cues to accompany concept structures and to indicate their significance, and similar kinds of stereotypic information. Control signals are currently just unstructured atomic symbols. Every interaction in the parser involves the transmission of a single message, which includes one concept structure and one control signal.

3.3.1 Control Signals

Message interactions in WEP consist of one control signal and one concept structure. Often the signal can be viewed as an accompaniment to the concept, telling the recipient how the sender meant the concept to be interpreted. This does not mean that the recipient of such a message must use it in the way the sender intended it to be used. For the message to be meaningful, however, its recipient must know (a) something about the sender of the message, and (b) what the sender thinks the message means. For example, one word expert might say to another, "If the words coming after you in the sentence could be seen to more closely represent X than Y, please let me know, because in that case we as a larger group of words probably mean Z". Its reasons for inferring Z are its own, and open to interrogation. The important point for understanding the role of control signals in WEP is that some atomic symbol, accompanying a concept structure, could convey to certain experts the entirety of the above message.

A typical kind of standard language knowledge that people have concerns passive sentences. We know that the words *is* or *was,* when followed by a word having *en* affixed to its end, must be interpreted in a particular way. The following sentences illustrate this construction.

1) "Giscard was beaten by Mitterand."
2) "Giscard was beaten by four o'clock."

The experts cooperating to understand the meaning of these fragments must exchange messages in a manner prototypic for particular known constructions. Note that they never reference directly any prototype; rather, the prototypic aspect of passive sentences is modeled by interaction patterns recognized by certain word-based processes.

The expert processes modeling the words in the example sentences cooperate through interaction to infer their meaning. They begin executing one after another, with the *en* expert coordinating the particularities of the passive voice. The *en* expert must tell the expert for *beat* not to attempt for itself to find the concept structures it ordinarily needs (e.g., for its meaning role discrimination), and instead to await them from *en,* which will provide them. Furthermore, the *en* expert expects the word *by* to appear in the text, and anticipates certain interactions with its expert process. The interactions between the *en* expert and that for *by* determine that in one case, the lexical sequence beginning with *by* designates the agent of the main action of the sentence (i.e., *by Mitterand*), and in the other, it represents the time that this action takes place (i.e., *by four o'clock*).

The message from *en* to beat would consist simply of the signal *EN*. This control signal causes *beat* to await the signals *AGENT* and *OBJECT* that *en* is in effect promising to send later. The message from *en* to *by* would consist of the control signal *PASSIVE* and a concept structure that *beat* and *en* have together decided might represent the meaning of the words appearing after *by.* The *by* expert must use this concept structure as a preference filter - if the word sequence it finds more closely represents a location or a time (even if neither of these) than an agent for a beating (e.g., a person), it should reject *en*'s request, with a *REJECT* signal. Otherwise, it should send an *ACCEPT* signal, along with the requested concept (which *en* will then send to *beat* with the *AGENT* signal). Each interaction involves either a control signal alone, or the combination of a particular static type concept of concept structures.

3.3.2 Concept Structures

For purposes of this discussion, a concept structure CONCEPT1 will be considered to have

(a) a *VALUE* slot containing a single value representing the most particular static type concept of which CONCEPT1 is an instance;
(b) an *UP* slot containing a single value representing the dynamic concept of which CONCEPT1 is a refinement;
(c) a *ONE-OF* slot containing a disjunct of concepts of which CONCEPT1 is an instance of at least one;
(d) a *NONE-OF* slot containing a conjunct of concepts of which CONCEPT1 is an instance of none; and
(e) a number of ASPECTS, concepts representing various roles vis-à-vis CONCEPT1.

Note that the *ONE-OFs* and *NONE-OFs* of a concept are particularly significant (especially for pattern-matching) when it has a very general *VALUE* (e.g., the concept C#ANYTHING, which represents any object in the world).

As an example of a concept structure, examine the representation of the main action in the sentence "The fellow kicked the bucket" in a context appropriate to the idiomatic interpretation. The central action is that of dying, reflected in the *VALUE* (or static type) cell of the concept. The dynamic *UP* cell, reflecting the previous unrefined value of the concept, contains the lexical notion of a person *kicking* (in the strictly linguistic sense; a person "kicking" as opposed to a person kicking). The following structure represents this action in the WEP model:

```
concept: c00179
  value: C#DIE
  up: c00122
concept: c00122
  value: C#L#PERSON-KICK
  up: c00078
  aspects: agent: c0043
           object: c0099
```

This latter concept has a dynamic concept link to a simple lexical kicking structure, which points up to the most general action node. Note that the DYING concept must get its case fillers by the dynamic refinement links, and that certain of the cases become irrelevant at more specific levels of the dynamic concept hierarchy (i.e., the bucket fills a case at one level, but not at the more specific level, in which its contribution is already included in the concept value itself).

Such concept structures are the uniform way to represent meanings in WEP, whether expectations, filters, transmissions to external mechanisms, or end results.

As another example of a concept structure, take the expectation of the *beat* and *en* experts in the above example about the nature of the words following *by* in those sentences. The *en* expert expects the word *by* to appear, because of its linguistic knowledge of its contexts (i.e., passive sentences). Interactions with the *beat* expert lead to the construction of a concept structure to represent the kinds of things that can perform "beatings". Such a concept includes a *VALUE* slot containing nothing very specific, perhaps the name of a concept denoting any object at all, perhaps one designating something slightly more specific. The *ONE-OF* slot, by constrast, contains specific notions, such as people (perhaps even particular ones from the domain of discourse) and other things. Later, when the by expert gets hold of the concept, it augments it, especially by adding notions to the *NONE-OF* slot.

3.3.3 Signal and Concept Filters

The local interactions among word experts involve the transmission of control signals and concept structures. An expert must specify one of these message types as the nature of the desired information, even though the transmission mechanism will provide the expert with both on continuation. The particular datum awaited will trigger continuation, though it might be accompanied by another datum of the other type. The organization of the system can be viewed as consisting of two data channels (Rieger, 1977), one conveying control signals and the other concept structures. Each restart demon can be seen as watching the transmissions on a single one of the channels.

The nature of the triggering datum can be restricted through the specification of filters. Concept structures are filtered by concept filters, themselves simply other concept structures. A restart demon on the concept channel often contains a concept structure to filter the acceptable triggers. The filtering process takes place through a typical symbolic pattern-matching operation, in which the various components of the concept structures to be matched must be compatible. A signal filter does the same for demons on the signal channel. Such a filter is no more than a list of acceptable triggering control signals. Thus, in the above example (i.e., Mitterand was beaten), the word expert for *beat* awaits an *AGENT* control signal (to be provided by *en* with help from *by*), and this triggering signal will arrive with an accompanying concept structure.

3.4 Word Expert Structure

The active agents of WEP are the word experts, cooperating distributed processes which interpret by mutual agreement the meaning of fragments of English text. The individual activity of word experts can be broken into two facets, word sense discrimination (i.e., local expert processing), and active lexical interaction (i.e., message transmission and reception). Word experts are represented as networks composed of a collection of subnetworks called entry points (or *entries*). Each entry point contains a number of nodes, and has no cycles. The actions of the word expert are coordinated at the individual nodes. Figure 3a provides a graphic illustration and Figure 3b a formal description of word expert structure.

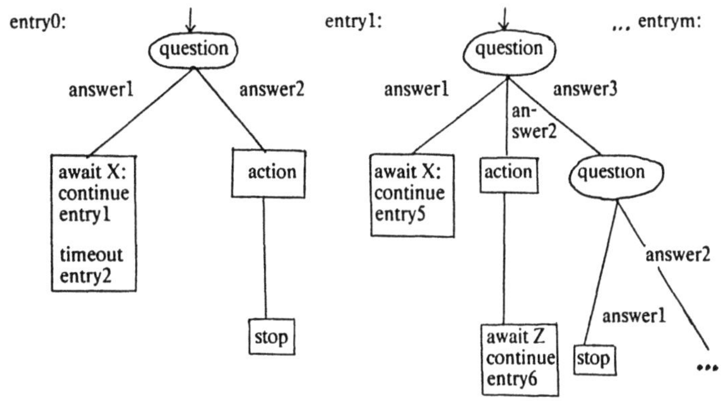

(a)

```
<expert <name>
  [entry0
     (node0 <node type> <node body>)
     (node1 <node type> <node body>)
     (noden <node type> <node body>)  ]
  [entry1                              ]
  [entrym                              ]>
```

Fig. 3. Word expert structure (b)

There are five kinds of nodes in the Word Expert Parser. The *ACTION* and *QUESTION* nodes perform functions for inferring the role of the word in the overall fragment in which it appears, and comprise a *Sense Discrimination Language* (SDL) for word-based parsing. The *AWAIT* and *SEND* nodes coordinate word expert interactions within the parser, and make up the *Lexical Interaction Language* (LIL). The *BINDC* node is used for interaction between a word expert and one of the higher-order memory processes required for the operation of the parser. Note that except for simple pattern-matching functions, the results of these higher-order memory processes are simulated by user input in the current computer model.

4 Example: "The man throws in the towel"

The following example trace of the Word Expert Parser was made at the University of Rochester with a version of WEP very similar to that described by Small (1980) and Small and Rieger (1982). The text which follows was altered only in the following trivial ways from the exact output of the parsing program:

(1) All data typed by the user have been set in bold face;
(2) all simulated interactions with parallel inference modules (i.e., queries to the user about such topics as focus of attention) have been set in italics; and
(3) the spacing and indentation were changed to facilitate the commentary in the right hand column.

Each part of the trace separated by a boldface line of asterisks represents an execution of a word expert. Since these are coroutines simulating parallel processes, a particular expert may execute several times before finally terminating. Each expert has a name indicated on the first line of the trace; for example, the first occurrence of the word *the* is called e00009 by the model. The next line of the trace for a particular execution of some word expert contains (a) the name of the entry point (the modular subpiece of an expert) where execution resumes, and (b) the name of the word expert responsible for sending its input data (on the next line). This data includes a *concept structure* and a *control signal* (as described in a previous section of this chapter). Note that sometimes one or both of these inputs are empty.

The rest of the trace shows the execution of each entry point. Most of the word expert actions and model events are left out of this short execution trace, as the details of the WEP theory have not been described here. The important aspects of the trace for current purposes are (a) the general flow of activity in the model, including the suspension and resumption of experts, and (b) the interactions of word experts with each other and with external knowledge sources. These latter lexical interactions are easily spotted in the example by their appeal to the user for input. Recall that the parallel comprehension processes required by WEP are currently simulated by the user.

```
Script started on Thu Oct 1 18:32:35 1981
$ ipclisp
/usr/lisp/ipclisp 11/16/80.
1. (loadwep)
Word Expert Parser loaded
t
2. (w%wep)
          Word Expert Parser
            Micro-WEP 5.2
    IRCAM/Paris VIII/Rochester/Maryland
[wep] trace 5
[wep] parse
```

This is a version of Franz Lisp running on the VAX-780 at the University of Rochester. All WEP research is now being conducted with this system. Other versions of WEP include one running in VLISP on the PDP-10 at *IRCAM* in Paris and one running in Maryland Lisp at the University of Maryland.

Version 5.2 of WEP has been developed at *IRCAM*, the Université de Paris VIII (Vincennes), the University of Rochester, and the University of Maryland.

The trace is set at level 5 (the highest setting is level 20) to print just the minimum of information.

```
    WORD EXPERT PARSER
text> The man throws in the towel.
    > ←
              reading: the
              initializing: the/e00009
****************************************
```

The WEP reader requires more text. The parser does not work on whole sentences at a time, but rather on individual words and phrases as they are read. Textual analysis completes only when the user explicitly states that there will be no additional input.

```
* e00009 ** entry/initentry * expert/nil
* the    ** concept/nil     * signal/break
>entry: initentry
>entry: e0
****************************************
* e00009 ** entry/e1     * expert/wep
* the    ** concept/nil * signal/pause
```

The *the* expert executes first, receiving no concept structure as input, but receiving the BREAK control signal, which indicates a preceding sentence break. The expert starts the construction of a concept structure (to represent the mapping of the recognized noun phrase), and then pauses execution. The pause allows any suspended experts to resume execution on the basis of the new information just broadcast by the expert. When WEP becomes fully parallel (i.e., experts as processes rather than as coroutines), certain details of this control will change. The *the* expert finally suspends its execution and awaits the report of the anticipated conceptual entity.

```
>entry: e1
      reading: man
      initializing: man/e00023

****************************************
```

```
* e00023 ** entry/initentry * expert/e00009
* man    ** concept/nil     * signal/entity-
                              construction
>entry: initentry
>entry: e0
>entry: e1
****************************************
```

The word expert for man begins executing with the ENTITY-CONSTRUCTION control signal reflecting the inference from the *the* expert about the processing state of the parser. The *man* expert determines immediately that *man* denotes a human adult male (this word is not currently disambiguated), and reports the concept structure representing this to the rest of the system.

```
* e00009 ** entry/e2          * expert/e00023
* the    ** concept/c00037    * signal/nil
>entry: e2
q> *******> Discourse Focus <*******
q>
q> c00037: c# human-adult-male c# l# man
           c# anything
q> **lexical: the man
q>
q> Is such a concept in focus? no
      reading: throws
      initializing: s/e00055
      initializing: throw/e00056
****************************************
```

Only a single word expert was awaiting this concept report, the *the* expert, and it now continues its processing. It must now determine, in consultation with the focus of attention process, whether or not the new description has a referent in the existing context. If so, *the* reports this referent concept to the rest of the model; otherwise it sends along the concept just constructed. In the example, we assume that there is no previous referent (or we shall have to provide it!) and answer **no** to the query.

```
* e00055 ** entry/initentry * expert/e00023
* s      ** concept/nil     * signal/complete-
                              entity
>entry: initentry
>entry: e0
****************************************
```

The next word expert to execute is that for the suffix s. Experts for suffixes always execute before the root words to which they are attached. Context analysis by the *s* expert determines that the input is starting to describe an action, and thus it broadcasts the relevant control signal, the ACTION-CONSTRUCTION signal, to the rest of the system.

```
* e00056 ** entry/initentry * expert/e00009
* throw  ** concept/nil     * signal/action-
                              construction
>entry: initentry
>entry: e0
>entry: e2
q> *******> Multiple Perspective <*******
q>
q> c00037: c# human-adult-male c# l# man
           c# anything
q> **lexical: the man
q>
q> c00079: c# anything
q>
q> Can the former be viewed as the latter? yes
```

The *throw* expert is the most important process involved in the analysis of the example fragment. It consists of many entry points (subprocesses) and executes several times. On this first execution, *throw* starts the construction of an action concept, and then attempts to refine its meaning to be as precise as possible given the existing discourse context and surrounding lexical constraints. Its first action toward this goal is to search the local active memory for a concept structure potentially representing the agent of the designated action. The system queries the user as part of the matching process, after *throw* finds a prospective match. Next, *throw* uses this prospective agent to

```
>entry: e1
q> *******> Conceptual Proximity< *******
q>
q> c00037: c# human-adult-male c# l# man
         c# anything
q> **lexical: the man
q>
q> view concepts:
              c# machine c# horse c# person
                c# organization
q> Which views apply (best first) c # person
>entry: e70
>entry: e50
>entry: e3
      reading: in
      initializing: in/e00137
```

begin its disambiguation. The conceptual relationship between the concept in the subject position and various known agents (i.e., machines, people, horses, and organizations) leads to inferences by *throw* about its meaning. In this case, we tell WEP that a man is more like a person than like the other possibilities.

The *throw* expert asks that the next word be read, since often its immediate successor affects fundamentally its meaning (as in this case). The *in* expert thus begins executing with the PARTICLE control signal. This signal requests that *in* decide if it plays the role as verb particle. The incoming concept gives *in* the advice of *throw* about the decision. Note that the system is robust enough that a non-response by *in* within a certain time is treated as a rejection.

```
***************************************
* e00137 ** entry/initentry  * expert/e00056
* in     ** concept/c00145  * signal/particle
>entry: initentry
>entry: e0
      reading: the
      initializing: the/e00169
```

The *in* expert must await the execution of subsequent experts. If the next expert begins construction of an entity concept structure (i.e., representing a noun phrase), *in* awaits the report of that structure. If the next expert does anything else, *in* continues its processing.


```
***************************************
* e00137 ** entry/initentry  * expert/e00056
* in     ** concept/c00145  * signal/particle
>entry: initentry
>entry: e0
      reading: the
      initializing: the/e00169
```

The *in* expert must await the execution of subsequent experts. If the next expert begins construction of an entity concept structure (i.e., representing a noun phrase), *in* awaits the report of that structure. If the next expert does anything else, *in* continues its processing.


```
***************************************
* e00169 ** entry/initentry * expert/e00015
*the     ** concept/nil     * signal/setting
>entry: initentry
>entry: e0
```

In this example, the *the* expert immediately broadcasts the awaited ENTITY-CONSTRUCTION signal, and then pauses. Note that the pause is significant here, as the *in* expert resumes execution.

```
***************************************
* e00137 ** entry/e1     * expert/e00169
* in     ** concept/nil  * signal/entity-
                           construction
>entry: e1
```

The *in* expert prepares to receive the forthcoming concept structure and suspends itself once again.

```
***************************************
* e00169 ** entry/e1     * expert/wep
* the    ** concept/nil  * signal/pause
>entry: e1
      reading: towel
      initializing: towel/e00191
```

The pausing *the* expert now continues its processing, and begins the construction of the new concept structure (representing the meaning of the noun phrase). The reader examines the next word, *towel*, and initializes its expert.

```
***************************************
* e00191 ** entry/initentry * expert/e00137
* towel  ** concept/nil     * signal/entity-
                              construction
>entry: initentry
>entry: e0
>entry: e1
***************************************
```

The word expert for *towel* builds the very much awaited concept structure, which it reports to the model as a whole. This particular broadcast causes great fireworks in the system, as many suspended word experts await the concept.

```
* e00169 ** entry/e2          * expert/e00191
* the    ** concept/c00205    * signal/nil
>entry: e2
q> *******> Discourse Focus < *******
q>
q> c00205: c# towel c# l# towel c# anything
q> **lexical: the towel
q>
q> Is such a concept in focus? no
****************************************
```

The *the* expert resumes execution, and along with the reference mechanism, tries to find a referent for the towel description. Again playing the part of this mechanism, we answer that there is no matching description in the focus of attention of the system. This causes the just created structure (intercepted by *the*) to be sent along to other awaiting experts.

```
* e00137 ** entry/e41         * expert/e00169
* in     ** concept/c00205    * signal/nil
>entry: e41
>entry: e2
q> *******> Multiple Perspective < *******
q>
q> c00205: c# towel c# l# towel c# anything
q> **lexical: the towel
q>
q> c00145: c# anything
q> ** oneof: c# physobj c# idea c# gear
              c# machine
q> ** noneof: c# time c# state c# volume
q>
q> Can the former be viewed as the latter? yes
****************************************
```

The *in* expert resumes, now equipped to determine whether or not it plays the role of verb particle to *throw*. The process it goes through to determine this involves comparing the expectations of *throw* in the existing context with those normally associated with *in*. Thus, *in* the morning would cause *in* to reject a role as particle, while *in the tractor* would lead to acceptance of that role. The query to a simulated knowledge base mechanism asks whether the reported concept more closely resembles a physical object, an idea, a gear, a machine, a time, a state, or a volume. The first four cases cause acceptance of the particle role; the latter three cause rejection. We answer that indeed towels can be viewed as physical objects better than as times, states, or volumes.

```
* e00056 ** entry/e4          * expert/e00137
* throw  ** concept/c00205 * signal/accept
>entry: e4
****************************************
```

The broadcast of the ACCEPT signal thus causes resumption of the *throw* expert, which can now continue its own disambiguation task.

```
* e00056 ** entry/e5       * expert/wep
* throw  ** concept/nil    * signal/pause
>entry: e5
q> *******> Conceptual Proximity< *******
q>
q> c00205: c# towel c# l# towel c# anything
q> **lexical: the towel
q>
q> view concepts:
   c# physobj c# idea
q> Which views apply (best first) c# physobj
q> *******> Discourse Focus < *******
q>
q> c00259: c# anything
q> ** oneof: c# area c# volume
q>
q> Is such a concept in focus? no
q> *******> Conceptual Proximity< *******
q>
q> c00205: c# physobj c# towel c# l# towel
              c# anything
q> **lexical: the towel
```

After pausing with no intermediate resumptions, *throw* now pursues its complex task of deciding among the various possible meanings of *throw in the towel* in the current context. The first step, shown in the first user query, decides between *throwing in ideas* and *throwing objects into places*. The second query actually determines, without a particular volume or area specified for the *throwing in* action, whether or not one can be located within the focus of attention (e.g., *Rick jumps in the pool. Joanie throws in the towel.*). Thirdly, *throw* asks about the concept to see if it can be some kind of machine being put into operation (e.g., *Rick threw in the tractor*). And lastly, the *throw* expert tests whether or not some bargaining action (e.g., *Rick and Joanie are bargaining over the price. Rick throws in a dollar*) or some charitable action (e.g., *Rick receives the plate in church. He throws in a dollar*) are within the focus of attention. Since the results of all these external lexical interactions, both discourse

```
q>
q> view concepts:
  c# physobj c# gear c# machine
q> Which views apply (best first) c# physobj
q> *******> Discourse Expectation < *******
q>
q> c00271: c# anyaction
q> ** oneof: c# charitable-action
            c# bargaining-action
q>
q> Concept not expected locally.
q> Is such a concept expected? no
      reading: *period*
      initializing: *period*/e00287
```

and logical interactions, came out the way they did, the *throw* expert chooses the idiomatic meaning of *throw in the towel*, as can be seen below in the structures built to represent the meaning of the fragment.

```
****************************************
* e00287    ** entry/initentry  * expert/e00056
* *period* ** concept/nil       * signal/complete
                                  -entity
>entry: initentry
>entry: e0
```

Lastly, the word expert for the period ending the sentence executes, sending a sentence BREAK signal to the rest of the model. This signal often causes some final bookkeeping to be done within certain experts.

```
      WORD EXPERT PARSER
text> ←
```

We provide the system with no more text, and after executing any spontaneous expert resumptions (none in the example), the parsing process terminates.

```
[wep] memory
*** Active Memory ***
```

The active memory contains the constructed meaning representations. Note that WEP is a process model, and the trace of its execution contains far more relevant information about WEP and its value than do these fairly ad hoc case frameworks.

```
concept: c# anyaction
```

The concept representing the most general action in the knowledge hierarchy.

```
concept: c00075
  value: c# 1 # throw
  isa: c# anyaction
  type: action
  lexical: (s throw)
  aspects: ((agent . c00037))
```

The concept underlying the linguistic entity throw.

```
concept: c00101
  value: c# person-throw
  isa: c00075
  type: action
```

A concept structure representing the action of a person throwing.

```
concept: c00241
  value: c# 1 # throwin
  isa: c00101
  type: action
  aspects: ((object . c00205))
```

A concept structure to represent the linguistic fragment *throw in* in the knowledge hierarchy.

```
concept: c00203
  value: c# 1 # towel
  isa: c# anything
  type: entity
```

An underlying conceptual representation of the lexical item *towel*.

```
concept: c# anything
```

The most general conceptual entity (e.g., as opposed to action) in the hierarchy of system knowledge.

concept: c00035
  value: c#1#man
  isa: c#anything
  type: entity
	The conceptual entity represented by the word *man* in the lexicon.

concept: c00283
  value: c#give-up
  isa: c00241
  type: action
	The representation of the conceptual notion of conceding defeat in a competitive situation. This is the underlying representation for the idiomatic meaning of *throw in the towel.*

concept: c00205
  value: c#towel
  isa: c00203
  type: entity
  lexical: (the towel)
  roles: ((object . c00241))
  role: object
  allof: (c#physobj)
	The structure representing the conceptual notion of a towel.

concept: c00037
  value: c#human-adult-male
  isa: c00035
  type: entity
  lexical: (the man)
  roles: ((agent . c00075))
  role: agent
  allof: (c#person)
	The concept structure representing a human adult male, and hence, the person underlying the syntactic subject of the example sentence.

[wep] **exit** $ script done on Thu Oct 1 18:35:00 1981	

5 Word Expert Definition

5.1 Overview of Expert Functions

The primitive functions of individual word experts comprise the theory of Word Expert Parsing, and fall into the three classes mentioned above, local word sense and role discrimination, expert/expert interaction, and expert/memory interaction. Each of these classes consists of a number of different primitive actions. The behavior of a word expert when it executes and performs a particular (idiosyncratic) sequence of these actions represents the crux of the WEP theory of understanding. Figure 4 summarizes the actions that may be performed by an individual word expert in performing its task.

These word expert behaviors presented succinctly here are carried out by a small number of primitives (about twenty to thirty depending on how they are counted). These primitive actions are summarized in Figure 5 and described in detail in the next section. The most complete account of the theory of Word Expert Parsing appears in the dissertation of Small (1980).

SIDE EFFECT ACTIONS:
- Ask that the next word be read and its expert initialized;
- Build a concept structure to represent some meaning or to use as a filter;
- Change the global state of the system (a description of the syntactic focus of the system);

MULTIPLE CHOICE QUESTIONS:
- Ask about the system state description;
- Ask about the word represented by a particular expert;
- Ask about the lexical origins of some concept structure;

LEXICAL INTERACTIONS:
- Report new information to the model at large or to a particular word expert making a request;
- Post a timed demon to await some piece of needed information;
- Suspend execution until some information arrives (or relevant demons time themselves out);
- Terminate execution after completing its diagnosis as to its role;

MEMORY INTERACTIONS:
- Request information from a discourse tracking process;
- Request an inference from a general semantic memory mechanism;
- Request a constrained pattern-matching operation.

Fig. 4. Word expert functions

5.2 Lexical Interaction Language

There are basically two nodes that are concerned with expert/expert interactions in the system, the *AWAIT* node, which posts timed restart demons, and the *SEND* node, which transmits control signals and concept structures to the demon queues and to the global interpreter processes. The AWAIT node actually consists of three different nodes in one, depending on the nature of the data awaited by the posted restart demon. We will therefore describe it as separate nodes. The SEND node also performs several actions, depending on whether the data being transmitted is intended for a demon queue or a particular expert, and which one.

5.2.1 AWAIT

The AWAIT node causes a demon to be posted on one of the data channels that connect different processes of the system. The CONCEPT channel contains those demons awaiting the report of a concept structure by an executing word expert; the SIGNAL channel contains demons that trigger on the transmission of particular control signals; and the WORD channel has associated demons awaiting the initialization of word experts for particular words. An AWAIT node schema is shown in Figure 6.

The CHANNEL field of the AWAIT specifies the type of restart demon to be created, this depending on the kind of object that can trigger it (every word expert

LEXICAL INTERACTION
Posting Restart Demons for Receiving Messages
AWAIT CONCEPT: Posting a demon on the concept channel;
AWAIT SIGNAL: Posting a demon on the signal channel;
AWAIT WORD: Posting a demon to trigger on reading;
Lookahead
PEEKW: Getting the name of the next word expert;
READW: Absorbing the next word expert;
Sending Messages on Channels
SEND CONCEPT: Transmit a message on the concept channel;
SEND SIGNAL: Transmit a message on the signal channel;

WORD SENSE DISCRIMINATION
Syntax and Control Signals
OPENG: Initiate a lexical sequence;
DECLAREG: Participate in the current lexical sequence;
BREAKG: Transmit a sentence break signal;
LINK: Associate a lexical sequence and a concept structure;
CLOSEG: Terminate a lexical sequence;
Semantics and Concept Structures
CREATEC: Create a new concept structure;
REFINEC: Refine the value of a dynamic concept structure;
BUILDC: Create a concept structure to act as a filter;
ASPECTC: Specify role fillers for a concept structure;
ROLEC: Specify the role of a concept;
Questions about Incoming Messages
SIGNAL: Probe incoming concept signals;
LITERAL: Probe words associated with incoming expert names;
IDIOM: Query concept structure/lexical sequence associations;
Internal Control Flow
NEXT: Branch within an entry point;
CONTINUE: Concurrently execute another entry point;
PAUSE: Continue after pausing to let demons fire;
ALIAS: Creating entry point variables;

MEMORY INTERACTION
Multiple Choice Perspectives
VIEW: Test the relative closeness of various concepts;
Receiving Concepts from Other Mechanisms
BINDC IMMEDIATE: Concept pattern match;
BINDC LOCAL: Find a matching concept in active memory;
BINDC ASPECT: Find a match in a slot of a concept structure (CS);
BINDC DISCOURSE: Ask a discourse process to find a needed CS;
BINDC REAL-WORLD: Ask a real-world knowl. mech. to find a needed CS;

Fig. 5. Word expert primitives

```
[<node name> AWAIT
    (CHANNEL <channel> <type filter> <filter>)
    (BINDCONCEPT <local concept structure name>)
    (BINDSIGNAL <local control signal name>)
    (BINDEXPERT <local word expert name>)
    (FROM <word expert name>)
    (REPORT <report constraint>)
    (WAIT <signal type> <number of ticks>)
    (CONTINUE <entry point>)
    (ELSE <entry point>)]
```

Fig. 6. Schema for the AWAIT node

resumption includes an input of each type, a control signal, a concept structure, and the name of another word expert; only one of these, however, could have triggered the resumption). The special type filter contained in this specification allows the demon to make a quick type check on the perceived data. For example, a concept might be of type ENTITY or ACTION, and a signal of type SEQUENCE. These types allow a quick type check to eliminate matches immediately between concepts or signals of different fundamental types. If this quick check does not rule out the demon, it must perform a more extensive pattern-matching operation. Concept filters are other concept structures, signal filters are lists of specific signals, and word filters are lists of words. These are examined more closely below.

The BINDCONCEPT field tells the demon what name to give the incoming concept so that it can be referred to in the restarted word expert. In the case of a concept demon, this concept represents the triggering concept. The BINDSIGNAL slot permits the demon to name the control signal that is input to the restarted word expert, and the BINDEXPERT slot permits the demon to give the resumed expert the name of a word expert (e.g., the sender of the other data).

The FROM field of the AWAIT contains a filter on the particular word expert that can send a triggering concept to that demon. The REPORT field contains either *HERE* or *NORMAL,* depending on whether or not the demon gobbles up a transmitted concept before other demons can be triggered by it. If the WAIT field of an AWAIT node is specified, it identifies the type of companion timeout to associate with the restart demon. As an example, suppose the WAIT slot specifies one single tick of the SEQUENCE timeout type. Such a specification causes the posted demon to time out automatically at the transmission of the first signal on the SIGNAL channel of the system that indicates the initiation of a new syntactic sequence. Such a timeout causes the restart demon to be killed and a timout restart to be generated for the awaiting expert; the restart causes the expert to continue processing at a predetermined entry point, with the new knowledge that some desired piece of data has not arrived within the specified time. The CONTINUE field of the demon indicates the entry point for word expert resumption on normal restart, and the ELSE field specifies the entry for expert resumption on timeout.

AWAIT CONCEPT. A restart demon on the concept channel will fire and resume the suspended word expert if three conditions are met:

(a) some word expert has used SEND to direct a concept structure to the CONCEPT channel;
(b) no restart demon on this channel has chosen to absorb the concept before it makes its way to the given demon; and
(c) the concept filter that forms part of the demon definition matches the transmitted concept.

Of course, if these conditions are not met before a certain number of counted model events take place (specified in the WAIT field), the demon times out, and its associated word expert resumes execution in a predetermined sequence of default activities.

```
[node4 AWAIT
    (CHANNEL CONCEPT ENTITY CONCEPT3)
    (BINDCONCEPT CONCEPT2)
    (BINDSIGNAL)
    (BINDEXPERT)
    (FROM)
    (REPORT HERE)
    (WAIT SEQUENCE 1)
    (CONTINUE ENTRY3)
    (ELSE ENTRY2)]
```

Fig. 7. Example AWAIT node

Before invoking the AWAIT CONCEPT mechanism, a word expert ordinarily creates a concept structure to act as a filter on the allowable trigger concepts. For example, when the *deep* expert executes and cannot discriminate its intended contextual meaning, it creates the following filter concept (locally referred to as CONCEPT3) for the restart demon it posts:

ONEOF: C # PERSON
C # ARTISTIC-ENTITY
C # VOLUME
C # ANYTHING

Note that this concept contains the token C # ANYTHING, the most general entity concept, which does not really filter anything except non-entities (e.g., actions). The reason for this is that these filters are used as expectations by the model. That is, a word expert can ask as part of its sense disambiguation whether something or other is expected by some previously executing (though not necessarily terminated) word expert. For example, the expert for the ambiguous word *pit* uses the expectations of preceding word experts *peach* or *deep* to determine which of its possible meanings is indended in a sentence (i.e., the pit of a fruit or a hole in the ground).

In fact, the pit expert uses the filter concept shown above in concluding that *pit* means "a hole in the ground" in the phrase *the deep pit*. The AWAIT specification of the *deep* expert is shown in Figure 7. Note that the restart demon it constructs is filtered by the quick type check for ENTITY concepts. The CONCEPT3 filter shown above permits this AWAIT to provide other experts with useful conceptual hypotheses. The system decouples expectation from control flow by using such non-binding filters that serve only as suggestions. The *deep* expert does not insist on being awakened by certain classes of concepts, but rather expects certain ones and will accept anything.

AWAIT SIGNAL. The control signals of the model are atomic flags that are used by word experts to describe aspects of model processing to other experts. For example, when the *a* word expert starts executing, it transmits the *ENTITY-CONSTRUCTION* signal on the global SIGNAL channel of the model, which contains demons that trigger on particular control signals, just as the CONCEPT channel contains demons triggered by concept structures. In this simple case, a special model process simply forwards this signal to the next expert as it runs for the first time. In other cases, control signals cause expert resumptions and timeouts. Note that most timeouts are caused by the transmission of a certain number and type of signals on the SIGNAL channel.

Control signals are also used to accompany the passing of concept structure messages between two experts as they carry out a dialogue for some specific reason. This occurs between *take* and *in,* for example, as they determine through mutual consent whether or not they form a cohesive pair as verb and verb particle (as in *take in a stranger* but not in *take in pain an aspirin*). The *PARTICLE* signal coordinates this dialogue. The current set of about a dozen different signals must be expanded to over twice that number in a more complete theory.

The *AWAIT SIGNAL* node allows an expert to post a restart demon to trigger on the tranmission of particular control signals on the SIGNAL channel. In the example of verb particles, the *take* expert waits for the next word expert to be initialized by the model (see AWAIT WORD below), sends it the *PARTICLE* message, and then uses AWAIT SIGNAL to post a restart demon to trigger on one of a set of possible control signal replies, either *ACCEPT* or *YOU-DECIDE* or *REJECT*. Note that none of these signals is forcing to the expert that receives it; the design of WEP has insured that the control structure and the hypothesis-generation remain mutually helpful, without tight coupling. After a certain amount of processing, including execution of word experts for words following it in the input stream, the *in* expert sends the appropriate message along the SIGNAL channel, reawakening the *take* expert with some new information. The *take* expert then uses that information to complete its processing (and undoubtedly much of the processing of the entire sentence).

AWAIT WORD. When some executing word expert expects some particular word to appear later in the input sequence, and can use that fact to determine its meaning or role, it creates an *AWAIT WORD* demon. If the awaited word is read by the model, the (possibly timed) demon fires, and delivers the name of the expert responsible for that word to the restarted expert, which can now start up a dialogue with the other expert. For example, when the *-en* expert runs and diagnoses a passive construction, it awaits possible future interaction with the *by* expert by posting an AWAIT WORD demon. Upon encountering the *by* expert (i.e., receiving its name), the *-en* expert can then interact with *by* to determine the role of *by* in the larger fragment, and accept information assembled by *by* to forward it back to the verb expert with whom *-en* has been interacting. The AWAIT WORD format is similar to the other two AWAIT formats.

5.2.2 PEEKW and READW

Often a word expert needs to know the identity of an adjacent word in order to make correctly some decision. The most common examples involve the comprehension of compound verbs and idiomatic expressions, when a peek ahead for some particular lexical item could lead to the most reasonable decision path. For example, the *throw* expert always takes a peek at the word to its right to determine whether or not this word is on its list of known particles. The *throw* expert does

```
[node0 ACTION
    (PEEKW EXPERT1)
    (NEXT node1)]
[node1 QUESTION
    LITERAL EXPERT1
    (AWAY node3)
    (UP node4)
    (IN node5)
    (OUT node6)
    (* node2)]
[node3 ACTION
    (READW EXPERT1)
    (NEXT node9)]
[node9 SEND
    (TO EXPERT EXPERT1)
    (SIGNAL *PARTICLE*)]
```

Fig. 8. Illustration of peeking and reading

not bother to strike up a conversation with its neighbor if it has no reason; the *PEEKW* primitive allows an expert to take a peek at its neighbor without disturbing it.

Sometimes a word expert must actually preempt the normal execution of the next word. A verb expert can prevent the normal execution of the expert for its neighboring particle by reading this word itself and thus preventing the model at large from doing so. By effectively using *READW*, an expert may completely dominate its right neighbor; the controlled expert ends up in a state wherein it can only execute on receipt of an appropriate control signal from the dominating expert. Note that the action of READW can be easily performed using a word demon (created with AWAIT WORD) permitted to match anything.

An illustration of these two primitives can be seen in the nodes from the *throw* network shown in Figure 8. The expert looks to see if the word to its right is one of its known particles. If this is indeed the case (which it tests with the LITERAL question described in the next section), then *throw* goes ahead and absorbs this word expert, gaining complete control over its execution. In the example, the word *away* occurs to the right of *throw*.

5.2.3 SEND

The transmission of messages by word expert takes place simply and straightforwardly. The *SEND* node specifies either (a) a data channel the message takes to reach the awaiting word experts, or (b) the name of the particular expert for which the message is intended. The two channels (currently) part of WEP are the SIGNAL channel and the CONCEPT channel. The restart demons are associated with one channel or the other and monitor the transmissions on that single data pathway. The schema of Figure 9 illustrates the syntax of SEND nodes.

An expert SENDs to the SIGNAL channel to announce a control state or to perform idiosyncratic and linguistic interactions with other experts, as illustrated in an example above. The control signal can be accompanied by a concept struc-

```
[<node name> SEND
    (TO CHANNEL <channel>)
    (SIGNAL <control signal>)
    (CONCEPT <concept structure>)]
```

Fig. 9. SEND node schema

```
[node3 SEND
  (TO CHANNEL SIGNAL)
  (SIGNAL *PASSIVE*)
  (CONCEPT CONCEPT2)]
```

Fig. 10. Example SEND node

ture, which one expert may wish to make available to the receiving expert. Figure 10 shows the full form of such a SEND as it appears at one point in the *-en* expert. The *-en* expert informs *by* (which *-en* knows as EXPERT1) to consider its role in passive sentences and to expect to hear about an agent matching filter concept CONCEPT2. Note that this CONCEPT2 represents an expectation that is not binding on the decision-making of the *by* expert.

An expert SENDs to the CONCEPT channel to report a comprehension result, when it is confident that the structure it has built correctly represents the meaning of some lexical sequence. Concept structures so reported are introduced into the concept channel, where they can trigger AWAIT CONCEPT demons. Concepts not consumed by a demon are sent to the active memory of the WEP model. Transmissions to this channel work the same as to the other, differing only in the demon population it can trigger. A SEND to a particular word expert contains the following line instead of that indicating the transmission channel.

(TO EXPERT <expert name>)

Such a SEND works the same as those to model channels, except that it does not trigger awaiting restart demons. Figure 8 illustrates an inter-expert transmission of this kind.

5.3 Sense Discrimination Language

The range of actions and question categories available to an expert as it probes its lexical and comprehension contexts is defined by a subset of the word expert primitives called the *Sense Discrimination Language* (SDL). The primitives of this sublanguage for word sense discrimination are shown in the middle section of Figure 5. By invoking SDL questions and branching on their outcomes, the decision logic of an expert unfolds in a given context. By invoking SDL actions, the expert builds concepts and concept filters, posts restart demons and expectations, and announces state information to the parser at large using control signals. We give a brief account in the following sections of the approximately twenty SDL primitives.

5.3.1 Syntax and Control Signals

OPENG. Concepts generally arise from lexical sequences (e.g., noun groups, idioms). When the probing of an expert leads it to conclude that it begins a new lexical sequence, it invokes an OPENG to open a new group, and to send a descriptive sequence signal to the parser at large (i.e., the signal channel) announcing the type of the new sequence. (This signal will typically be forwarded to the next expert as it is first read and started.) Since concepts and lexical sequences are distinct data structures in the model, a concept is not automatically associated with a lexical group. Instead, concept-group associations must be specifically established via the LINK primitive described below.

DECLAREG. When a word expert determines that it should be participating in the currently open group, it must declare its membership. Since every expert other than a sentence break must declare its participation in some group (unless it has been consumed by another expert and never actually runs), OPENG is always immediately followed by a DECLAREG. Of course, an expert does not have to open a group in order to participate in one. The word expert for *a* has a very simple role as the initiator of a new group, as the following node from that expert shows.

```
(node1 ACTION
       (OPENG *ENTITY-CONSTRUCTION*)
       (DECLAREG))
```

As with OPENG, DECLAREG makes no contribution to a concept structure; it performs the simple structural function of declaring an expert to be a participant in the current lexical sequence.

BREAKG. Some words do not participate in any group, but rather terminate the current thought (sentence). Invoking the BREAKG primitive sends the special sentence breaking signal *BREAK* and increments the sentence time counter. The word expert for a period contains the following node.

```
(node0 ACTION
       (BREAK))
```

LINK. At some point during a lexical sequence, a participating expert will decide to declare (via BUILDC) a concept which it believes represents or contributes to that sequence. Using the LINK primitive, it can then establish the association between the current lexical group and this concept, a fundamental operation that maps lexical structure onto meaning. Any or all of the experts participating in a sequence can create and LINK their concepts to that sequence.

CLOSEG. The last of the primitives dealing with lexical sequences, the CLOSEG statement, terminates the currently active lexical sequence. Specifically, it sends a designated signal to the parser at large and permanently incorporates the finished sequence in all concepts that have LINKed to it. LINK and CLOSEG are illustrated by the man expert at a point where it has decided that it means "a human adult male".

```
(node8 ACTION
       (REFINEC CONCEPT0 =C#HUMAN-ADULT-MALE)
       (LINK CONCEPT0)
       (CLOSEG *COMPLETE-ENTITY*)
       (NEXT node11))
```

5.3.2 Semantics and Concept Structures

CREATEC. An expert invokes the CREATEC primitive to create a new concept structure. The most general conceptual category of the concept must be specified, and an instance of the appropriate type will be constructed. An expert typically invokes CREATEC to begin construction of the concept the expert believes will be its ultimate contribution to the comprehension of the overall fragment (sentence) in which it occurs. The BUILDC primitive, described below, allows the expert to begin construction of a filter or expectation. The following statement in some node causes the system to build a new instance of an action concept.

```
(CREATEC CONCEPT3 ACTION)
```

The effect of this is to create a concept structure with general category ACTION, and locally to call it CONCEPT3 (it also has a unique global name). The concept is not made public unless and until the expert reports it with a SEND to the concept channel, as described earlier.

REFINEC. The REFINEC primitive constructs a new dynamic concept structure containing a value slot that further specifies the nature of the concept. The new concept contains a pointer to the old one it refines. In a typical sequence, an expert creates a new concept, refines its meaning to be something less general than the "any action" or "any entity" it started with, and then SENDs it down the channel as a meaning report, or uses it internally. The *eat* expert, for example, might initially declare that it represents some form of "ingesting", as shown in the following.

```
(node7 ACTION
        (CREATEC CONCEPT2 ACTION)
        (REFINEC CONCEPT2 =C#INGEST)
        (LINK CONCEPT2)
        (CLOSEG *COMPLETE-ACTION*))
```

The *eat* expert arrives at this node in its decision logic, which creates an action concept, refines its meaning to membership to the C#INGEST category (from membership in the C#ANYACTION category), declares its participation in the current lexical sequence, and closes that (verb) group. The new CONCEPT2 could then be reported to the model, or held privately by the *eat* expert as it continued the refinement process.

Further sense disambiguation could lead the *eat* expert to refine its meaning again (before SENDing its report) from this very general "ingesting" notion. Suppose, for example, that *eat* determines itself to designate the "eating a meal" action. It might then refine again the meaning of CONCEPT2 and, certain not to receive any further information about this concept, report it to the concept channel and the other word experts.

```
(node14 ACTION
        (REFINEC CONCEPT2 =C#DINE)
        (NEXT node15))
```

```
(node15 SEND
        (TO CHANNEL CONCEPT)
        (CONCEPT CONCEPT2)
        (SIGNAL *ACTION*))
```

BUILDC. The BUILDC primitive can actually build concept structures with a certain amount of initial refining information already present, in addition to special conjunctive and disjunctive combinations of other concepts. The purpose of BUILDC is to allow the construction of concept filters to accompany the expert's restart demons; these are incompletely specified concepts describing expected information. Should the *deep* expert wish to intercept any concepts (on the concept channel) with which it might interact, it uses BUILDC to construct a concept to accompany its restart demon. Note the special disjunction created for this purpose in the following specification.

```
[node8 ACTION
       (BUILDC CONCEPT1 ENTITY
               (ONEOF =C#VOLUME
               =C#ARTISTIC-OBJECT
               =C#PERSON))]
```

Besides the special ONEOF slot in concept structures, the BUILDC primitive can be used to specify a conjunctive NONEOF slot as well. It seems important to language understanding that concepts be constrained by expectation to be an instance of one of a certain set of concepts at the same time it is not an instance of any of (none of) another set of concepts.

ASPECTC and ROLEC. When a word expert considers itself to be the controlling expert of the lexical sequence (and hence concept) under construction, it will generally make efforts to seek out information from other experts in that group or elsewhere and weave that information together through the concepts it has constructed. An expert who believes it is the main action will seek out its agent and other conceptual cases in order to knit those concepts into its main action concept. Similarly, experts in charge of objects (i.e., noun-like concepts) and object describers (i.e., adjective-like concepts) will attempt to make linkages with other members of their groups. ASPECTC and ROLEC make such connections for an expert.

The ASPECTC primitive links one concept into a case framework being constructed by another (the model makes no distinction between regular concept structures and such case frames). The ROLEC statement informs the linked-in concept of its participation there. For example, if an expert has CONCEPT3 under construction as an action concept, it will usually look in the WEP active memory (the final destination for structures sent down the concept channel and not blocked by some demon) for concepts qualified to fill its various roles. If, say, it finds that CONCEPT6 can and should play its AGENT role, the expert establishes this relation by including the following statements in an appropriate ACTION node.

```
(ASPECTC CONCEPT3 (AGENT CONCEPT6))
(ROLEC CONCEPT6 AGENT)
```

This adds the relationship to the structures for both concepts. ASPECTC and ROLEC are kept as distinct operations because, while CONCEPT3 can have only one AGENT, CONCEPT6 might be playing several roles within the sentence, and may eventually be linked into other concepts by ROLEC calls from other experts.

5.3.3 Questions About Incoming Messages

SIGNAL. The SIGNAL question causes a branch depending on the value of an incoming control signal. For example, the word expert for *throw* needs to know if its incoming control signal indicates (a) a noun group under construction; (b) a completed noun group (at least to the best knowledge of the previous word); (c) an open verb group; or (d) a passive sentence. The following node illustrates this situation.

```
[node1 QUESTION
       SIGNAL SIGNAL1
       (*ENTITY-CONSTRUCTION* node2)
       (*COMPLETE-ENTITY* node3)
       (*ACTION-CONSTRUCTION* node4)
       (*EN* node5)
       (* node6)]
```

The word experts for inflectional suffixes of verbs always execute before the root words to which they are attached. The *throw* expert uses this node1 to make its initial hypotheses about its role in the larger fragment in which it participates.

LITERAL. The LITERAL probe asks whether some particular expert represents one of a set of specific words, and then branches accordingly. For example, after PEEKing to its right neighbor (which it will then bind internally as EXPERT1), it might ask to know what word that expert designates. This sequence of actions is illustrated in the following nodes.

```
[node0 ACTION
       (PEEKW EXPERT1)
       (NEXT node1)]
[node1 QUESTION
       LITERAL EXPERT1
       (EN node2)
       (ING node3)
       (*node4)]
```

The latter node forces a branch to node2 if EXPERT1 represents *en*, to node3 if *ing*, and to node4 otherwise. This example in fact comes from the was expert at a point where it takes a peek downstream.

IDIOM. The IDIOM query permits a type of lookahead for concepts expressed by specific lexical sequences (or close derivatives) of potential interest to the running expert. However, rather than performing literal pattern-matching on the lexical sequence to the right, IDIOM instead poses the following type of question: Is the concept to my right represented by any of the following lexical sequences? This is considerably different from literal matching, because it will involve the running of the neighboring experts and their collective wisdom about how to group themselves into the concept whose surface form is under scrutiny.

The *take* expert can illustrate the use of IDIOM. To *take a puff,* to *take a break,* to *take someone for an idiot,* to *take five,* and so forth, are all idiomatic expressions (to one degree or another; see the next section for more discussion of idiomaticity). The take expert must take a peek to the right for one of these; the following node illustrates the required action.

```
(node4 QUESTION
        IDIOM CONCEPT1
        ((A PUFF) node5)
        ((A BREAK) node6)
        ((FIVE) node10)
        ((A PEEK) node12)
        ((FOR A) node7)
        (* node8))
```

This node causes a branch to one of nodes node5, node6, node7, node10, or node12 on the basis of the lexical structure of CONCEPT1 (or to node8 if none seems applicable). The local concept variable CONCEPT1 was previously bound in the decision logic of the *take* expert to the right neighboring concept. Of course, even after branching, the decision logic might ask further questions to confirm the presence of the idiomatic expression before finally adopting it (and not adopting it if it were *took five ounces* or *took the man for a vaccination*).

5.3.4 Control Flow

This group of four SDL primitives affects the path of execution through the expert's decision logic, where that path is not already implied by one of the other decision-making primitives.

NEXT. The NEXT action causes a branch within a single entry point of an expert. As such, this control primitive often occurs as the last instruction in an ACTION node that has taken other structure-building actions. Since the lack of such a branching instruction causes termination of the entry point containing the node, NEXT directs the expert to its next node. Imagine the following as the last statement in some ACTION node.

```
(NEXT node3)
```

CONTINUE. The CONTINUE control primitive allows an expert to remind itself of other chores to be performed, without actually doing them immediately. By CONTINUEing a node in its logic, the expert essentially causes an internal entry point to be queued up to run after its main line of execution has terminated. For example, an expert believing itself to be the main verb might pursue the object and agent slots directly, but queue up pointers to other parts of its logic, say node17 and node19, that will deal with its other possible conceptual cases. The following could appear in sequence in some ACTION node of an expert.

(CONTINUE node17)
(CONTINUE node19)

After the current line of decision logic has terminated, these other regions of the expert's logic will be started up in turn. Many nodes can be queued for eventual execution.

Note that CONTINUE exists primarily in anticipation of true parallel hardware, where several of the tasks of an expert could be tended to concurrently. We refer the reader interested in this parallel implementation to the ZMOB hardware (Rieger et al., 1980) that has been designed in part for this application. However, this primitive is a convenient tool even in the current system, because it allows the writer of the experts flexibility in sequencing the internal actions of a word expert.

PAUSE. The PAUSE primitive resembles CONTINUE in that it queues up another node of the expert for eventual running, but differs in that the continuation will not occur until the system has processed all the run requests of other experts currently on the master RUN-ME queue. This is mostly useful after an expert has made and announced some discovery, and wants other experts to have a chance to react (i.e., their restart demons to fire) before it itself continues its processing.

ALIAS. Branching decision logic is awkward when two distinct lines of reasoning share common substructure. For example, if *sequence1* is a sequence along one line of reasoning and it follows through *sequenceX* along to *sequence2,* and if *sequenceA* is a sequence that also requires *sequenceX,* but then moves along to *sequenceB,* then *sequenceX* must be shared by two paths through the expert. Without some additional provisions, *sequenceX* would have to be duplicated, an undesirable state of affairs.

The control primitive ALIAS solves this problem by allowing *sequence1* and *sequenceA* to declare "aliases" before entering *sequenceX,* as shown in Figure 11. At the end of *sequenceX,* there is a continuation instruction. Instead of taking literally the destination node of the continuation, the CONTINUE function recog-

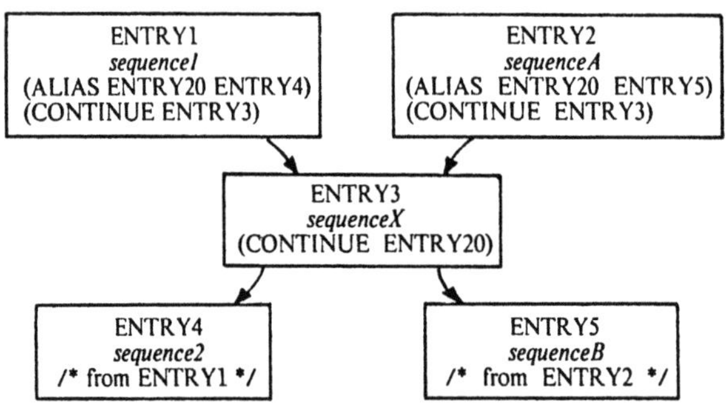

Fig. 11. Illustration of ALIASing

nizes the alias and successfully continues where it should. The ALIAS mechanism can be thought of as a rudimentary form of intra-expert subroutine call. The aliases themselves are simply variables that are assigned to refer to entry points (i.e., designated substructures) of word experts.

5.4 Memory Interaction

Expert decision logic must have access both to real-world knowledge and to dynamically changing discourse and real-world context. The sense discrimination primitives in this category interact with a pattern-matching mechanism which helps experts make the best choice among specific alternatives based on "closeness" of real-world matching. As we have already pointed out, most of the elaborate pattern-matching requests are routed to the human, and are not implemented in the current parser. While much work remains to be done here, the WEP theory has at least helped us bring into focus the extent and forms of interaction with real-world pattern-matchers. We consider this a good first step toward a more autonomous model.

5.4.1 Interaction Requirements

While it is clear that certain lexical sequences cannot be understood solely through recourse to syntax and semantics, namely those fragments for which idiosyncratic interactions are required (i.e., specific remembered contexts), why do we need other kinds of general knowledge? In trying to understand the meaning of *throw in the towel,* i.e., discriminating between its literal and idiomatic meanings in context, the relevant word experts must find out some things about the person performing the described action before knowing what action he/she is in effect performing.

Discourse Knowledge. If the discourse describes some sort of competition between two people (or teams), for example, *throw in the towel* could indicate a concession of defeat by one of them. The following fragment illustrates such a contextual situation.

Rick and Joanie play chess. Rick throws in the towel.

On the other hand, if the discourse has recently made reference to a place where one might dispose of a towel, throw in the towel might be signifying the putting of some towel in that place. The following example illustrates this case.

Joanie drops a penny into the pit. Rick throws in the towel.

It is not the claim that knowledge of the discourse context is sufficient to disambiguate the meanings of the example sentence, but rather, that such knowledge is required to understand it.

The discourse interactions required to interpret the above example take place (a) between the *throw* expert and a higher-order process modeling the *activity context,* i.e., monitoring the ongoing activities in the text, and (b) between the *in* expert and a process modeling the discourse *focus of attention*. There are two aspects to the processing of the activity mechanism, the unsolicited sending of control signals to indicate the anticipation of certain actions in the text and concept structures to represent them, and the more data-directed interactions with word experts (and other understanding processes) to determine the nature of the actions that actually do occur. The *throw* expert must carry on *activity context interactions* to determine if the discourse could be seen as discussing some competitive activity. If so, the "concession of defeat" interpretation of the example sentence is plausible. The *in* expert carries on focus of *attention interactions* to find out if some location has recently been described in the text *in which* something might be thrown.

Real-World Knowledge. The understanding of fragments of natural language text *by a particular individual* (or computer program) often requires knowledge of the beliefs of that individual. How can this be true given the fact that, even when the discourse context has not been made to render a particular fragment unambiguous, the majority of readers still interpret it the same way? The answer lies in the common experience brought to understanding by readers from the same culture. This notion carries over to the common experiences of people in all sorts of subcultures as well, such as scientific communities (e.g., linguists, psychologists), religious groups, age and class groups (e.g., college students, ghetto youth), and so forth. There are pieces of text that would be understood in common by members of these groups and not by people outside these groups, and other fragments that would be understood in common by almost everyone.

The comparison of new concepts with previously seen ones is a fundamental method of interpretation in the Word Expert Parser. Individual word experts interact with a memory of real-world knowledge to determine whether certain conceptual notions can be perceived as other ones. The paradigm for these interactions is based on multiple choice: of all the fragments of text that have already been understood (the finite choice), which most closely resembles the one now being examined? Suppose the model were given the following sentence.

Rick throws a seminar.

This sentence must be understood by analogy with the previously assimilated notion of "throwing organized activities". The question in WEP would be put forth by the *throw* expert and would be some variation on the following (depending on the knowledge of *throw* stored in the *throw* word expert): "Is a seminar better viewed as a party, a tantrum, a chess game, a legal case, or a baseball?" This multiple choice VIEW question, described below, is a basic expert primitive for sense discrimination through memory interaction. The importance of multiple choice in inference is discussed by Rieger (1978).

Another class of memory interactions takes place between individual word experts and a process maintaining beliefs about the world. A word expert may interact with this belief modeling process to determine the *relative plausibility* of two propositions. Consider the following sentences, both of which have been successfully interpreted by the existing WEP system (with the user simulating the belief modeling process).

The man eating tiger growls.
The man eating shrimp growls.

The difference between these two fragments from the perspective of WEP involves the relative plausibility of *tigers that eat men* and *men who eat tigers* in the first case, and of *shrimp that eat men* and *men who eat shrimp* in the second. Of course, in certain contexts, the problem is resolved through discourse interactions; the activity context or focus of attention could make clear the appropriate meaning without any need for more general knowledge. Clearly, however, we can understand these fragments perfectly well without any guiding discourse context.

5.4.2 VIEW

Frequently, an expert will have narrowed itself down enough to have some clear expectations about what other concepts with which it must group, and will wish to determine which of those are, in fact, present. Since it cannot hope to anticipate precisely, it issues a VIEW question to the real-world processor. This VIEW question contains a reference to the concept in question, and a menu of possibilities which corresponds to the expert's range of expectations about the nature of the concept in question. VIEW selects the most reasonable characterization of the concept in question from the multiple choice of possibilities, and the expert branches on this result. VIEW is thus a "best fit" type of pattern-matching.

```
(node2 QUESTION
       VIEW CONCEPT2
       (=C#ANYTHING node10)
       (=C#MEAL node9)
       (=C#GARBAGE node8)
       (=C#ABSOBJ node7)
       (=C#SMALL-PHYSOBJ node6)
       (=C#PERSON node5)
       (=C#CONTEST node4)
       (=C#PARTY node3))
```

Fig. 12. VIEW query to semantic memory

Figure 12 shows a VIEW question taken from the *throw* network. Here, *throw* is asking that CONCEPT2 (a previously bound local expert variable referring to the concept to the right of *throw*) be characterized with respect to a choice of eight items, whose order is unimportant. The VIEW mechanism will prefer the most specific and closest possible binding, and *throw* will then branch to one of the named nodes.

5.4.3 BINDC

The BINDC primitive is essentially a way of requesting that some module external to the parser itself search for an appropriate concept; the needed concept must come from particular specified origins and must match a provided concept structure template. As such, it is the basic mechanism by which an expert gains access

```
[<node name> BINDC <concept variable>
   (MODULE <module specification>)
   (WHERE <search space>)
   (FILTER <concept filter>)
   CONTINUE <entry point>)
   (ELSE <entry point>)]
```

Fig. 13. BINDC request schema

to other concepts in the comprehension environment as it constructs its own concepts and inter-concept relationships. The general form of the BINDC node is shown in Figure 13.

The <concept variable> is the local name used by the expert to refer to the result of the BINDC attempt. The concept structure returned to the requesting expert often participates in some sort of structure-building action after its binding. The search for the desired structure takes place with a pattern-matching constraint specified in the ⟨concept filter⟩ field of the BINDC instruction. Any bindable concept in the search space must match this structure. The ⟨external module⟩ description must be one of IMMEDIATE, ASPECT, LOCAL, DISCOURSE, and REAL-WORLD. The programs to search for matches of the first three kinds are implemented in the model. The external discourse and real-world memory modules are currently simulated by appeal to the user. The ⟨search space⟩ field is particular to the module specification, and should become clear in the forthcoming discussion.

BINDC IMMEDIATE. The BINDC IMMEDIATE form allows the expert to establish a second pointer to (name for) an existing, accessible concept. This new binding action could be made to take place unencumbered, or alternatively, a concept filter could be provided to constrain it. In the latter case, this primitive represents an invocation of the local concept pattern-matcher. For example, the following word expert node will cause CONCEPT2 to be bound to CONCEPT1, providing CONCEPT1 is an instance of CONCEPT3, built here to represent "a man eating":

```
[node14 ACTION
        (BUILDC CONCEPT3 ACTION
                (VALUE =C#PERSON-EAT)
                (ASPECTS (AGENT =C#MAN)))
        (NEXT node19)]
[node19 BINDC CONCEPT2
        (MODULE IMMEDIATE)
        (WHERE CONCEPT1)
        (FILTER CONCEPT3)
        (CONTINUE ENTRY4)
        (ELSE ENTRY6)]
```

BINDC ASPECT. This primitive enables the expert to establish a pointer to an aspect (e.g., role filler) of another concept, provided it passes a specified concept filter. For example, to gain a pointer to a concept which is an instance of a dog, and which is playing some sort of role in action concept CONCEPT5, the expert includes the following node.

```
[node11 ACTION
        (BUILDC CONCEPT7 ENTITY
                (VALUE =C#DOG))
        (NEXT node4)]
[node4  BINDC CONCEPT6
        (MODULE ASPECT)
        (WHERE CONCEPT5)
        (FILTER CONCEPT7)
        (CONTINUE ENTRY7)
        (ELSE ENTRY2)]
```

BINDC LOCAL. The BINDC LOCAL instruction requests the special active memory process of the parser to search the local concept memory for a concept passing a set of constraints. This is the local memory to which all experts forward their generated concepts when they suspect those concepts to be of potential interest to other experts. Examine the following expert node.

```
[node21 ACTION
        (BUILDC CONCEPT2 ENTITY
                (ONE-OF =C#PERSON
                        =C#ANIMAL
                        =C#MACHINE
                        =C#ANYTHING)
                (ROLE AGENT))
        (NEXT node8)]
[node8  BINDC CONCEPT1
        (MODULE LOCAL)
        (WHERE ACTIVE)
        (FILTER CONCEPT2)
        (CONTINUE ENTRY2)
        (ELSE ENTRY1)]
```

BINDC DISCOURSE. A word expert calls on the discourse module of the system when it must gain access to a concept using discourse criteria, rather than basic (semantic) features of the sought-after concept. While this mechanism is not fully implemented, word experts incorporate such requests, which must for the moment be answered by the user. Our approach toward building the model has always been to determine the necessary interactions required by an expert to achieve sentence comprehension successfully, regardless of whether or not every auxiliary module could be implemented immediately.

The current model requests DISCOURSE binding attempts involving the focus of attention and the current activity context. An expert might request a concept variable be bound to the one concept of a multiple choice list that best describes the current topic of discourse; the pit expert does this when its other (more local) gauges do not discriminate enough. The pit expert asks if the current activity context is best described as a musical event, car racing, digging, or eating. The following node performs this binding request.

```
[node13 ACTION
        (BUILDC CONCEPT2 ACTION
                (ONE-OF =C#MUSICAL-EVENT
                        =C#CAR-RACING
                        =C#DIGGING
                        =C#EATING))
        (NEXT node25)]
[node25 BINDC CONCEPT1
        (MODULE DISCOURSE)
        (WHERE ACTIVITY)
        (FILTER CONCEPT2)
        (CONTINUE ENTRY9)
        (ELSE ENTRY1)]
```

The BINDC DISCOURSE primitive also includes binding requests based on discourse-related expectations and on anaphoric references. The word expert for *in,* for example, decides whether or not to participate in the idiosyncratic sequence *throw in the towel* based (in part) on the existence of a volume or area within the focus of attention. The following node would perform this query.

```
[node3  ACTION
        (BUILDC CONCEPT2 ENTITY
                (ONE-OF =C#VOLUME
                        =C#AREA))
        (NEXT node15)]
[node15 BINDC CONCEPT1
        (MODULE DISCOURSE)
        (WHERE FOCUS)
        (FILTER CONCEPT2)
        (CONTINUE ENTRY8)
        (ELSE ENTRY16)]
```

While this BINDC mechanism is regarded as a black box in the current system, relying completely on input from the human, some of the actions it must perform are constrained by the known interactions it must have with word experts.

BINDC REAL-WORLD. When an expert wishes to receive a binding based on the most plausible real-world possibility, independent of explicit knowledge from the comprehension of the text at hand, it requests a REAL-WORLD memory binding. Examples of such requests include asking for the name of an instrument frequently associated with eating, or requesting the best description of Rick's age from a multiple choice of possibilities - very old, old, middle-aged, young, or very young? Such binding attempts may be viewed as (inferential) lookups of defaults from a large world knowledge base. As with the discourse BINDC form, this form is currently a black box which relies entirely on the human.

The model currently invokes the BINDC REAL-WORLD primitive in a few cases, with the required inferences provided manually. Sometimes, a word expert needs to know which of two competing propositions is more plausible, given the nature of the world. The above example of one *man eating shrimp* and one *man eating tiger* illustrates the relevant situation. The word expert for the suffix *-ing* actually requests that the REAL-WORLD inference module determine in each case the relative plausibility of one thing eating the other. Suppose that CONCEPT1 represents a man eating a tiger, and that CONCEPT2 represents a tiger eating a man. Then the following node illustrates the REAL-WORLD plausibility query of the *-ing* expert.

```
[node11 ACTION
        (BUILDC CONCEPT5 ACTION
                (ONE-OF CONCEPT1
                        CONCEPT2))
        (NEXT node7)]
[node7  BINDC CONCEPT1
        (MODULE REAL-WORLD)
        (WHERE PLAUSIBLE)
        (FILTER CONCEPT5)
        (CONTINUE ENTRY19)
        (ELSE ENTRY4)]
```

The existing Word Expert Parser successfully disambiguates both possibilities in each of the two X eating Y examples, with the user answering the difficult inference question. The experimental constraint of computer science is the construction of working programs. The next stage in the development of the Word Expert Parser must be to make a convincing statement that the required DISCOURSE and REAL-WORLD memory mechanisms can be constructed. In each case, we feel that we have correctly compartmentalized these two open-ended processes within the WEP framework. While both defer to the human, their demands on the human are quite specific, and do not require any specific knowledge about the internal machinery of the program.

6 Summary and Conclusions

We have mapped out a theory of organization and control for a meaning-based language understanding system. In this theory words rather than sentence-level rules are the organizational units of knowledge, and assume the form of procedural entities that execute as coroutines. Parsing a sentence in context demands a control environment in which these experts can ask questions of each other and of higher-order memory processes, forward advice and expectations to each other, and suspend and resume on the occurrence of certain control state and conceptual information. The Word Expert Parser has a number of characteristics that make it desirable both as a computationally efficient and psychologically plausible model. By way of conclusion, we enumerate what we feel are the important theoretical and practical characteristics of the theory.

1) Individual words of language carry the bulk of human knowledge about the parsing process; sentence comprehension is coordinated by modular word experts incorporating this knowledge.
2) Word experts are modular graph structures that are easily augmentable (though executable). The model represents linguistic competence in terms of the different primitive actions that can be performed by the individual word experts. Language acquisition involves adding additional substructure to these word expert graphs.
3) The idiosyncratic nature of individual lexical functions comes across in the study of ambiguity resolution and idiom comprehension. All of language can be viewed as idiomatic to some degree; the Word Expert Parser is a model that focuses on this idiomaticity through the idiosyncratic contributions of individual words to the process of determining sentence meaning.
4) The word-based scheme and the emphasis on ambiguity lead to a model that interacts highly with general memory mechanisms. In fact, the overall processing of WEP is best viewed as a pattern of interactions, *idiosyncratic* and *linguistic* interactions among word experts, and *discourse* and *logical* interactions between word experts and external processes.
5) The model has enabled the development of a credible psychological theory of language comprehension. As such, it has provided a new perspective on some old problems that is consistent with the data in a broad range of areas. For all these areas, the WEP view of the comprehension process as actively inferential, highly interactive, and context-sensitive has been supported by the experimental evidence. This, without the need to segment the comprehension process into the traditional divisions of syntax, semantics, and pragmatics.

The Word Expert Parser represents a first attempt at a psychological model of language understanding and a computationally useful system. As with all artificial intelligence systems for language processing, the underlying theory needs further development and refinement. The word expert primitives must be evaluated and changed, with additions undoubtedly required. The model represents to some degree a promissory note on a viable and adequate system of language comprehension.

References

Allen, J.F. (1979): A Plan-based Approach to Speech Act Recognition. Ph.D. Thesis. Department of Computer Science, University of Toronto, 1979

Allen, J.F. and Small, S.L. (1982): The Rochester Discourse Comprehension Project. SIGART Newsletter **79,** January 1982

Bobrow, D. and Winograd, T. (1977): KRL: A Knowledge Representation Language. Cognitive Science **1,** 1 (1977)

Bolinger, D. (1975): Aspects of Language. Harcourt Brace Jovanovich 1975

Bolinger, D. (1979): Meaning and Memory. In: Haydn (ed.): Experience Forms. The Hague: Mouton 1979

Caramazza, A. and Zurif, E.B. (1976): Dissociation of Algorithmic and Heuristic Processes in Language Comprehension: Evidence from Aphasia. Brain and Language **3,** 572-582 (1976)

Collins, A.M. and Loftus, E.F. (1975): A Spreading Activation Theory of Semantic Processing. Psychological Review **82,** 407-428 (1975)

Cottrell, G.W. and Small, S.L. (1983): A Connectionist Scheme for Word Sense Disambiguation. Cognition and Brain Theory **6**, 1 (1983)
Feldman, J.A. and Ballard, D.H. (1982): Connectionist Models and Their Properties. Cognitive Science **6**, 205-254 (1982)
Gigley, H.M. (1982): A Computational Neurolinguistic Approach to Processing Models of Sentence Comprehension. COINS Technical Report 82-9. University of Massachusetts, Amherst, March 1982
Gordon, B. and Caramazza, A. (1982): Lexical Decision for Open- and Closed-class Words: Failure To Replicate Differential Frequency Sensitivity. Brain and Language **15**, 143-160 (1982)
Hayes, P.J. (1978): The Naive Physics Manifesto. Working Paper 34. Institut Dalle Molle pour les Etudes Semantiques et Cognitives de l'Université de Genève, 1978
Marcus, M.P. (1979): An Overview of a Theory of Syntactic Recognition for Natural Language. AI Memo 531. Artificial Intelligence Laboratory, Massachusetts Institute of Technology, 1979
McClelland, J.L. and Rumelhart, D.E. (1981): An Interactive Activation Model of Context Effects in Letter Perception: Part 1: An Account of Basic Findings. Psychological Review **88**, 375-405 (1981)
Newell, A. (1980): Physical Symbol Systems. Cognitive Science **4**, 2 (1980)
Norman, D.A. (1981): A Psychologist Views Human Processing: Human Errors and Other Phenomena Suggest Processing Mechanisms. Proceedings of the 7th International Joint Conference on Artificial Intelligence, pp.1097-1101, Vancouver, B.C., August 1981
Pylyshyn, Z.W. (1978): Computational Models and Empirical Constraints. The Behavioral and Brain Sciences **1**, 93-127 (1978)
Rieger, C. (1977): Spontaneous Computation in Cognitive Models. Cognitive Science **1**, 3 (1977)
Rieger, C. (1978): The Importance of Multiple Choice. Proceedings of the Conference on Theoretical Issues in Natural Language Comprehension, Urbana, Illinois, 1978
Rieger, C. and Small, S.L. (1981): Toward a Theory of Distributed Word Expert Natural Language Parsing. IEEE Transactions on Systems, Man, and Cybernetics **11**, 1 (1981)
Rieger, C., Bane, J., and Trigg, R. (1980): ZMOB: A Highly Parallel Multiprocessor. TR-911. Department of Computer Science, University of Maryland, May 1980
Riesbeck, C.K. and Schank, R.C. (1976): Comprehension by Computer: Expectation-based Analysis of Sentences in Context. Research Report No.78. Department of Computer Science, Yale University, 1976
Small, S.L. (1980): Word Expert Parsing: A Theory of Distributed Word-based Natural Language Understanding. Ph.D. Dissertation. Department of Computer Science, University of Maryland, 1980
Small, S.L. (1981a): Viewing Word Expert Parsing as Linguistic Theory. Proceedings of the 7th International Joint Conference on Artificial Intelligence, Vancouver, B.C., August 1981; TR 93, Department of Computer Science, University of Rochester, 1981
Small, S.L. (1981b): Demon-Timeouts: Limiting the Life Spans of Spontaneous Computations in Cognitive Models. Proceedings of the 3rd Annual Meeting of the Cognitive Science Society, Berkeley, CA, August 1981
Small, S.L. and Rieger, C. (1982): Parsing and Comprehending with Word Experts (A Theory and Its Realization). In: Lehnert, W. and Ringle, M. (eds.): Strategies for Natural Language Processing. Englewood Cliffs: Erlbaum 1982
Small, S.L., Cottrell, G.W., and Shastri, L. (1982): Towards Connectionist Parsing. Proceedings, 1982 National Conference, American Association for Artificial Intelligence, Pittsburgh, PA, August 1982
Swinney, D.A. (1979): Lexical Access During Sentence Comprehension: (Re)Consideration of Context Effects. Journal of Verbal Learning and Verbal Behavior **18**, 645-660 (1979)

Parsing by Means of Uppsala Chart Processor (UCP)

A. Sågvall Hein

1 Introduction

Uppsala Chart Processor (UCP) is a *linguistic processor* of the General Syntactic Processor (GSP) family, making use of the *active chart mechanism*. The language competence required for turning it into a parser is formulated in the *procedural UCP formalism*. It embodies process-oriented actions, such as initiating and promoting processes and storing results, and thus functions as the driving force of the processing. UCP supports both morphological and syntactic analysis.

The historical background of UCP is outlined in Section 2. In Section 3 we present the UCP formalism and demonstrate its use in the parsing process. During the development of UCP we have, basically, been working with Finnish and Swedish morphology, and with Swedish syntax. For that reason, we choose to use Swedish examples throughout the presentation. The reader will, no doubt, appreciate the applicability of the proposed strategies for the analysis of other languages as well. In Section 4 we say some words about current applications, and in Section 5 we summarize our experience, so far, of working with UCP.

2 Background

2.1 General Syntactic Processor

By the General Syntactic Processor (GSP), Ronald Kaplan introduced the concept of a linguistic processor, as a logical and computational framework in which the behavior of various syntactic analyzers and generators can be emulated (Kaplan 1973). A linguistic processor, thus, represents a level of abstraction above that of an individual parser or generator.

GSP includes

- a representation for the initial, intermediate, and final structures of the linguistic expression subject to processing, the *chart,*
- a number of *process primitives* for the formulation of a *network grammar,* and
- a *scanning algorithm,* making use of a number of additional *control structures* for keeping track of the processing.

Given a syntactic grammar in the internal grammar format, GSP behaves as a syntactic processor. If the grammar is directed towards analysis and the initial chart represents the output of a previous word recognition procedure, then GSP should work as a syntactic analyzer. In the reverse case, with a generation tuned grammar and the initial chart representing a syntactic description, GSP is supposed to produce a sequence of words corresponding to that structure, i.e., to work as a generator. The potential of GSP for emulating various parsing algorithms is discussed by Kaplan (1973) with regard to the ATN parser (Woods 1969) and the Kay powerful parser (Kay 1967). As for generation, the example chosen illustrates the implementation of transformational rules.

Kaplan thinks of syntactic processing as "many-to-many mappings of strings of trees into strings of trees" (op. cit., p. 194). A string of trees is considered to be the general representation format for a sentence at various levels of processing, i.e., after dictionary look-up and morphological analysis as well as after syntactic analysis. Due to lexical and structural ambiguities in natural language, mapping between these two levels is not one-to-one but many-to-many. By *families of strings of trees* Kaplan refers to the set of alternative linguistic descriptions at a given processing level, each family representing a member of the set.

The chart is a compact representation for families of strings of trees, arrived at by successive expansions of ordinary linguistic trees. Figure 1 shows GSP's chart representation of the sentence *I saw the log* prior to syntactic analysis. It is a directed graph with labeled edges and numbered vertices, and it expresses three kinds of relations, i.e., *dominance* (--- >), *precedence* (→), and *alternation* (see vertex 6 in Fig. 1). Alternative edges are considered to be members of different families.

The chart in Figure 1 can be traversed in two ways, corresponding to the alternative readings of *saw*. Through a chart resulting from a dictionary look-up procedure, there are, however, often ways for which there are no interpretations. It is the job of the grammar applied in the syntactic analysis to rule out these ungrammatical readings. For an illustration, let us assume that the dictionary consulted in constructing the chart in Figure 1 would have supplied an additional interpretation of *saw* as a noun. With this addition, the chart would presumably look like the one in Figure 2.

The ungrammatical PRO-N-DET-N reading represented by the chart in Fig. 2 is to be rejected by the syntactic rules. Syntactic analysis in the GSP framework amounts to matching a chart structure, representing the output of a dictionary look-up procedure, to a grammar formulated as a network. The grammar arcs specify operations, formulated by means of a number of process primitives. Roughly, the grammar operations can be categorized as logical operations, control operations, and chart modifying operations.

At all times GSP's attention is fixed on a particular edge in the chart and arc in the grammar, and the operations specified by the arc in focus are executed with regard to the edge in focus.

The logical operations specify the conditions for transition from one state-vertex combination, or configuration, to a succeeding one such as arc and edge symbol matching (cf. CAT in ATN). GSP, basically, leaves it to the user to supply the necessary logical operators.

For a systematic scanning of the GSP chart three kinds of moves must be accounted for: transition from one vertex to an immediately succeeding one, from

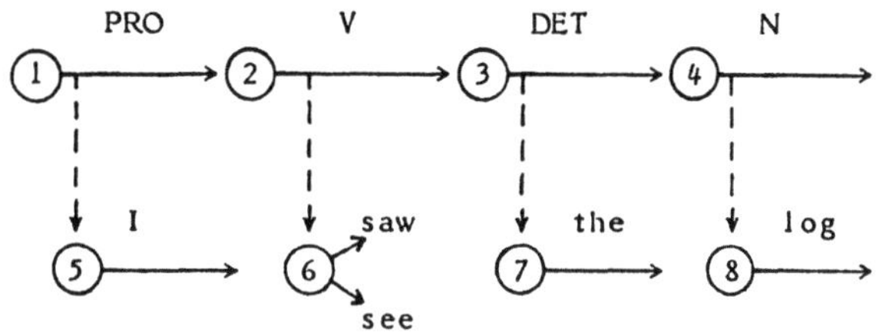

Fig. 1. (From Kaplan, 1973)

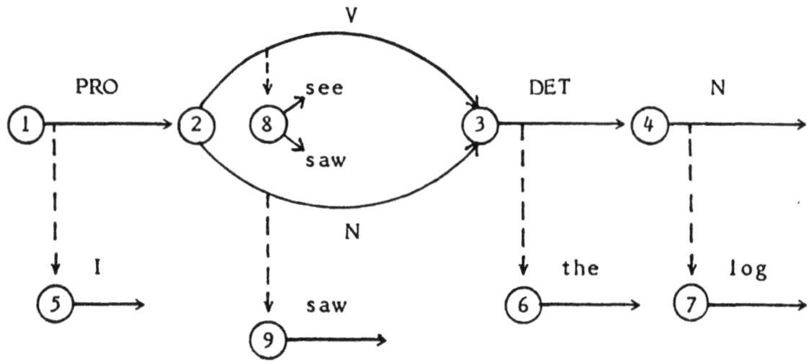

Fig. 2

one edge to its daughter edge, and from one edge to its closest alternating edge. Analogous actions are required for exploring the grammar. The responsibility for specifying these moves is shared between the grammar and the scanning algorithm in the following way.

Transition moves, i. e., changing chart and grammar focuses, from one state/vertex configuration to a succeeding one are specified in the grammar. Primitives for these operations are provided, e.g., (NEWVERTEX vert.spec), (NEWSTATE state.name). It is the job of the scanning algorithm, SYNTAX, to see to it that all legal arc-edge combinations of a configuration are tried. SYNTAX operates upon a list of configurations, initially containing only the first one, i.e., vertex 1 and state 1. For this (and the following configurations) it enumerates and evaluates all possible combinations of alternating arcs and edges one by one. Each arc-edge evaluation succeeds or fails. The outcome of the evaluation has to be returned to the scanner as a true or false signal, explicitly set by a primitive grammar operation. Success means transition to a new state, i.e., the creation of a new configuration according to the operations of the arc being evaluated. Alternative configurations are kept in a backtracking list, from which they are fetched and executed by the scanner. This is how GSP simulates nondeterministic behavior. It should be noted, however, that backtracking is not automatically accounted for but has to be specified in the grammar. At the disposal of the grammar writer there is an operator (NDPUT), which, when included in an arc, will have the effect of saving current chart and grammar focuses as a configuration on the backtracking list. For complete nondeterminism, this operation has to be included in every arc of the grammar. Controlling recursion, i.e., the scanning of a daughter of an arc/edge is also the job of the grammar writer. It consists in manipulating a recursion level stack by means of an operator taking three arguments. The history of a scan is

```
(ATN):  (PUSH NP/ T (SETR SUBJ *) (TO S/NP))


(GSP):  (NDPUT) (LPUT NIL T ((SETR SUBJ EDGE) (TO S/NP SIS)))
        (TO NP/ NIL)
```

Fig. 3. (From Kaplan, 1973)

recorded in registers, essentially equivalent to an ATN register. Accordingly, the setting and accessing of registers is grammar controlled. Finally, the grammar writer has to care about various chart modification operations. The nature of these modifications is not quite clear to us. However, they seem to allow for the modification of edges already part of the chart. "The standard elementary transformations (add-left-sister, erase, substitute, etc.) operate on chart sections held in registers and physically change edge properties" (Kaplan 1973, p. 218).

Just to give an impression of what a grammar arc might look like in the internal GSP format, we show an ATN arc and the corresponding GSP formulation (Fig. 3).

The rule in Figure 3 is used to identify the subject in active declarative clauses by pushing for an initial NP and storing the result, if successful, in the SUBJ register. The operations of the ATN PUSH arc are decomposed into the following GSP operations:

NDPUT (saves the current configuration, chart and grammar focuses, on the backtracking list)

LPUT (puts an element on the push-down store used to keep track of levels of recursion in the chart and the grammar; the element thus created specifies current register value, continuation arc in the grammar, S/NP, and continuation vertex in the chart, i.e., succeeding SISter vertex)

TO NP/ NIL (transfers control to the NP/ subnetwork of the grammar, while remaining in the current position of the chart)

The GSP TO-operator has been constructed in analogy with the ATN TO-operator. It compiles into the following sequence of primitive operations: (NEWSTATE state. name) (NEWVERTEX vert. spec) (SIGNAL T).

An impressive burden is laid upon the grammar writer, and the buildingstones at his disposal are very primitive. To use Kaplan's own words: "But creating a large grammar in this way would be as tedious as programming a large system in a conventional assembly language" (op. cit. p. 209). The solution to the problem that he advocates is defining a high-level grammar formalism compilable to the primitive GSP grammar format along with a compiler (cf. the TO-operator in Fig. 3). We know of no such grammar formalism for the computational machinery outlined above. The reason for this should be that it is not an easy task to design an attractive grammar formalism that has to include means for stepping through the chart and the grammar, extending the chart, controlling recursion and backtracking, and signalling the outcome of the evaluation of an arc-edge combination. In other words, the processing machinery is too complex in the original version of GSP and too much of its control rests upon the grammar.

The basic issue of GSP is the chart. With the further development of the chart the problems indicated above have been reduced. Below we will outline this development.

2.2 *The Development of the Chart*

The chart was originally conceived of by Martin Kay as a natural representation for ambiguous lexical strings. In his article on the MIND System (Kay 1973), for which GSP was developed as the syntactic processing component, he interprets the chart as a transition network. The chart presented by Kay differs, however, from that of GSP in a substantial way. For a comparison we present Kay's chart representation of the ambiguous sentence *They are flying planes* before (Fig. 4 a) and after (Fig. 4 b) morphological analysis, respectively.

The chart in Figure 4 b is an extension of that in Figure 4 a. Seven edges have been added and none deleted. It displays the ambiguity of two words, e.g., *are* and *flying*. The word *are* is recognized as a present tense form of either the auxiliary *be* or of the main verb *be*. The word *flying* is identified as a present tense participle of the verb *fly* or as an adjective *flying*. If the word edges are disregarded, there are four different paths through the chart, i.e.,

a) (CAT PRO) (CAT TENSE) (CAT AUX) (CAT PRESP) (CAT NOUN)
b) (CAT PRO) (CAT TENSE) (CAT AUX) (CAT ADJ) (CAT NOUN)
c) (CAT PRO) (CAT TENSE) (CAT VERB) (CAT PRESP) (CAT NOUN)
d) (CAT PRO) (CAT TENSE) (CAT VERB) (CAT ADJ) (CAT NOUN).

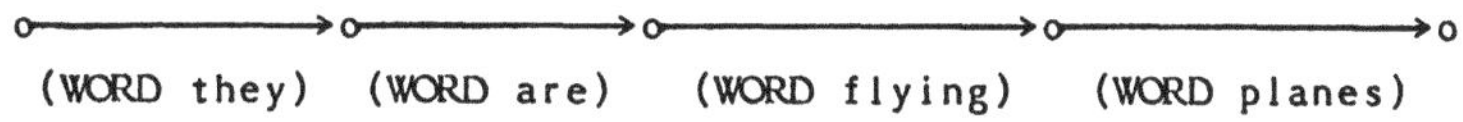

Fig. 4 a. (From Kay, 1973)

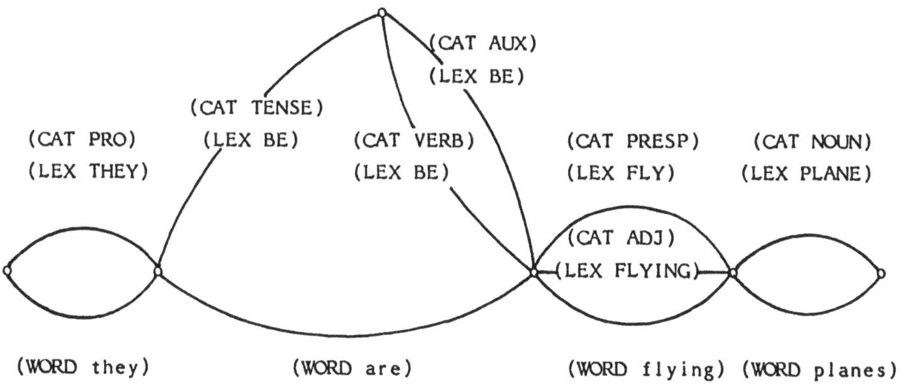

Fig. 4 b. (From Kay, 1973)

Subsequent syntactic analysis is responsible for ruling out b) and c), and for presenting two alternative descriptions of the sentence, based on a) and d). As should be evident from a comparison between the simple listing of the alternatives above and Figure 4b, the chart presents an economic way of representing and processing ambiguous strings, common parts being represented and processed only once (cf. (CAT PRO), (CAT TENSE), and (CAT NOUN)), cf. a Well-Formed Substring Table. (The same is true of the GSP chart.)

Kay aims at nondeterministic processing. Thus, he imposes the restriction that the chart can undergo one kind of change only, i.e., extension by the insertion of new edges (and vertices when required). Once inserted into the chart, an edge can never be deleted (or its label modified).

The GSP and the Kay chart representations differ further with regard to the kinds of relations they express in their basic structure. The dominance relation of the GSP chart is not expressed in the basic structure of the Kay chart, the edge structure of the latter one reflecting precedence and alternation only. The absence of the dominance relation calls for some alternative means for expressing recursion levels and for guaranteeing nondeterminism in recursive processing.

For the expression of recursion levels in a chart of the Kay type, there seem to be two possibilities, i.e., to make an interpretation of the order between the alternating edges of an edgeset, or to reflect levels in the edge labels. Kay chooses the latter alternative, elaborating the edge label structure. Thus edge labels are structured as trees of attribute-value pairs (see further Fig. 8 below). Allowing for structured edge labels as an alternative to hierarchically organized edges (cf. GSP) simplifies the control structure, as will be shown below.

For guaranteeing nondeterminism in recursive processing, Kay further elaborates the vertex structure of his chart. In the GSP chart a vertex is defined by its edgeset, its outgoing edges. Kay, in addition, includes an extra field in the data structure of the vertex, a so-called *waitlist-entry*. The function of the waitlist-entry is to keep a record of rules that have been unsuccessfully applied. It specifies the vertex at which the rule was initiated, its *anchor*, current register values, and the rule itself. If the scanning algorithm sees to it that the rules of the waitlist-entry of a certain vertex are applied to all new edges outgoing from that vertex as they are being generated, then full nondeterminism is achieved.

Based on the computational framework outlined above, Kay presented schemes for two subprocesses of the morphological analysis, i.e., morphographemic rewriting and dictionary look-up, and for syntactic analysis (see Kay 1977a).

2.2.1 The Chart and Morphographemic Rewriting

Morphographemic rewriting denotes a process in which strings are rewritten to allow for a linguistically motivated segmentation of word forms into morphs. It is called for by orthographic and morphophonemic variation. If the rewriting technique is applied in the morphological analysis, the dictionary look-up procedure will have to deal with sets of strings. Using the chart for representing such sets, certainly, is an attractive suggestion. For an illustration, we present a chart representing the Russian word form *plaču* after due morphographemic rewriting (Fig. 5).

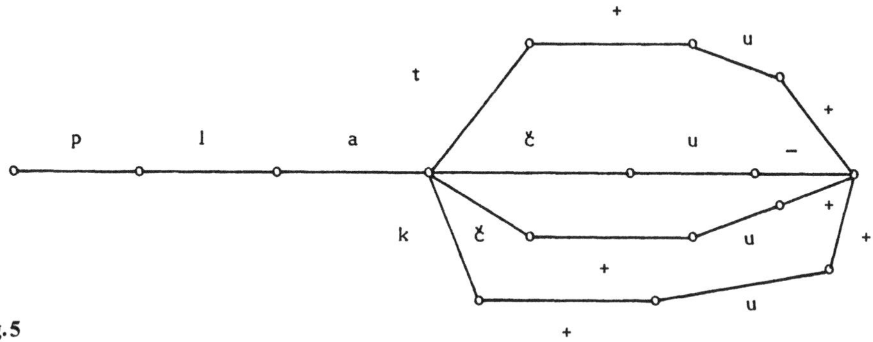

Fig. 5

In the rewriting process the following rules were applied:

R1: ču_ → t+u+
R2: ču_ → k+u+
R3: ču_ → č+u+

Note: + denotes morpheme boundary and _ the space sign. The string *plaču* is threefold ambiguous denoting:

a) a verb (*plat+u* /R1) in the present tense, 1st person (Engl. *pay*)
b) a verb (*plak+u* /R2) in the present tense, 1st person (Engl. *cry*)
c) a noun (*plač+u* /R3) in the dative singular (Engl. *cry*)

The rewriting rules are expressed as a transition network. In Figure 6 we present the Russian rules discussed so far, in the grammar format proposed by Kay.

The character field of an arc specifies the condition for transition to a successor arc, and the replacement field of the final arcs contains the character string to be inserted into the chart (one edge per character). With this declarative rule format, the rewriting algorithm alone will be responsible for scanning the chart and the grammar.

The rewriting grammar has to be initiated at each vertex of the initial chart, since rewriting, basically, may occur anywhere in the string. Initiating the grammar at a vertex means creating an arc-edge combination, a *task,* in which the first arc of the grammar is applied to the first edge of the vertex. The rewriting algorithm further enumerates and evaluates all possible tasks of a state-vertex configuration, and accounts for advancement through the chart and grammar, task by task. It

Arc No.	Character	Alternate	Successor	Replacement
1	č	0	2	
2	u	0	3	
3	_	4	0	t+u+
4	_	5	0	k+u+
5	_	0	0	č+u+

Fig. 6

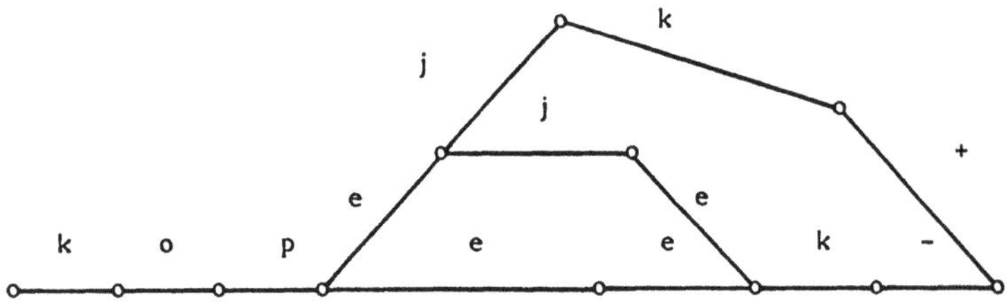

Fig. 7

creates new paths through the chart in accordance with the replacement specifications. As in GSP, when a task has been evaluated, it is removed from the backtracking list, the *agenda*. Processing comes to an end when the agenda is exhausted.

The procedure described so far holds for irrecursive rule application. There are, however, cases where a rewriting rule has to apply to the output of another one. In Figure 7 we show such an example from Russian.

Figure 7 represents *kopeek,* i.e., the noun *kopejka* (Engl. *kopeck*) in the genitive plural form after due rewriting. Two rules have been applied, i.e.,

R1: ee → eje
R2: jek_ → jk+

R1 is an orthographic rewriting rule. It generates an explicit representation of /j/ (implicitly expressed by the Russian spelling convention in vowel contexts). R2 is a phonologically based rewriting rule. It eliminates the secondary stem vowel, motivated by the stem final consonant cluster. (When the stem is followed by an ending, which is the case in the remaining forms, its appears as *kopejk+*). R2 has to apply to the result of R1. If both rules are part of a common rewriting grammar, this is an example of recursive rewriting.

To allow for recursive application of rewriting rules in the general case, the procedure described above has to be extended in two respects. The first extension is evident, i.e., initiating the grammar at new vertices as they are being created. The other problem concerns a situation which may arise as a consequence of the insertion of new edges. An edge may be inserted 'too late', i.e., when the arc which it would match has already been matched to the edgeset in question and the tasks accordingly removed from the agenda. In other words, there is no guarantee that the edgesets are exhaustively being examined since, at the time of evaluation, the processor doesn't know whether they are finally complete or not. Strictly ordering the rules is one possible approach, which is, though, incompatible with the generality of the scanning algorithm that Kay is aiming at. His alternative is the waitlist device. When a new edge is inserted at a given vertex, a task is created for this edge and the arcs of the waitlist of the vertex. Hereby, full nondeterminism is achieved. Various degrees of nondeterminism can be arranged for by various uses of the waitlist device in the design of the rewriting algorithm.

As concerns the proposed rewriting grammar, it has to be extended. The fact that a string has been subject to rewriting, and also by which particular rule(s), has to be recorded. Rewriting a string without further notice means degenerating it. The Russian word *banka* (Engl. *pot*) may serve as an illustration. Its stem appears as *banok+*, with the secondary vowel *o* in the genitive plural, and as *bank+* in the remaining forms. The traditional treatment of such words is to regard the non-secondary-vowel stem alternant, i.e., *bank+* as the lexical form of the stem. Using the rewriting technique we may follow this tradition and retrieve *banok+* from the lexical stem. However, there is also a Russian word *bank* (Engl. *bank*) whose stem doesn't alternate. Further, the inflectional paradigms of both stems include the zero-ending. Consequently, if the application of a secondary-vowel-deleting rewriting rule is not properly controlled, we may falsely analyze *banok* as a form of *bank*, and *bank* as a form of *banok*.

The machinery required for verifying compatibility between morphs when various kinds of rewriting rules have been applied turns out to be fairly complex (cf. Sågvall 1973). A record of the rewriting rules that were applied is crucial not only at the retrieval of a tentative stem but also during the rewriting process itself, since recursive rewriting cannot apply irrestrictedly. Consequently, the proposed rewriting scheme has to be further elaborated. To be specific, the condition part and the replacement part of the grammar arcs have to be extended. In addition to character matching, the condition part must cope with the verification of criteria concerning previous rewriting operations. The replacement field must include a subfield for stating the type of rewriting taking place.

Further, if rewriting rules for phonologically based alternations have to be formulated in terms of graphemes only, the set of rules tends to become large and unperspicuous. This was our experience from an attempt to formulate rewriting rules covering secondary-vowel deletion and consonant palatalization in Russian according to the proposed scheme. From this we concluded that a means for expressing the rules in phonetic terms such as consonants and vowels, velars, alveolars, liquids, etc. was required. Our treatment of morphemic alternation will be presented in Section 3.3.1 below.

2.2.2 The Chart and Dictionary Search

If the dictionary keys are organized as a string of letter trees, the dictionary search process can be regarded as the mapping of a chart structure to a transition network. If so, a dictionary search task amounts to matching a (character) edge in the chart to a (character) arc in the dictionary tree. An outline of a such a scheme has also been proposed (Kay 1977a). Our extensions of this basic scheme will be presented in Section 3.2 below.

2.2.3 The Chart and Syntactic Analysis

A procedure for carrying out syntactic analysis, task by task, according to the same basic strategy as the rewriting and dictionary look-up procedures was also outlined. According to this scheme, recursion is taken care of by the waitlist facility, the administration of which is handled by the syntactic algorithm. The algorithm accounts for full nondeterminism. The grammatical descriptions being built are successively recorded in registers (cf. ATN). The descriptions have a treelike structure. In Figure 8 we show the analysis of *The cat that was chased by the dog*

```
S [ACTIVE
   NP [THE
      CAT
      S [PASSIVE
         NP [THE DOG]
         VP [AUX [PAST]
            chase
            NP [The cat]]]]
   VP [TENSE [PAST]
      VERB [escape]]]
```

Fig. 8. (From Kay, 1977 a)

escaped. The structure of the edge labels allows for the representation of feature-sets as trees. Thus, there is, and quite naturally so, a formal similarity between the structure of the edge labels and that of the registers. A waitlist entry contains a grammar arc and a record of the history of the scan, i. e., current register contents. A compulsory part of the register contents is a reference to the vertex from which the rule was initiated, its anchor. A syntactic task specifies an arc, an edge, and current register contents. A set of grammatical operators were defined, which, embedded in an ALGOL-like framework, constitute a grammatical notation on a higher level than that of GSP. They account for the creation of new tasks and edges, for the setting and accessing of registers, and for logical operations.

2.3 The Active Chart

In 1975 Kay outlined a refined chart notion which draws upon the analogy between an edge and a waitlist entry (Kay 1975). Waitlist entries are considered to be edges of a special kind, i. e., *incomplete* or *active* edges as opposed to the (historically) original ones which are called *complete* or *inactive.* Reconsidering a waitlist entry, from being a property of a vertex to having the status of an edge, implies defining its span and direction. The vertex, holding the former waitlist entry, will be the endpoint of the active edge, the starting point of which will be the anchor of the waitlist entry. Former registers will be contained in the edge labels. The creation of new tasks will be entirely based upon the relation between incomplete and complete edges. According to a general law, henceforth referred to as the *active chart law,* a task will automatically be created for every path in the chart consisting of an incomplete edge followed by a complete one. For initiating rules, incomplete edges going from and to the same vertex must be allowed for. The chart and the agenda completely encapsulate the state of the processing at a given moment. Below, this version of the chart and associated control structure will be referred to as the *active chart mechanism.*

In an active chart parser processing is ultimately driven by those mechanisms that are responsible for inserting edges into the chart. What is their place and nature in a parser? Different answers to this question imply the design of different parsers in the common framework.

3 Uppsala Chart Processor

We think of a parser as a processing machinery (e.g., GSP), assigning a grammatical description to an utterance in a given language in accordance with a description of that language (a grammar and a dictionary). If the language description is clearly delimitable from the processor and, thus, exchangeable, the processor will have to embody the universally valid phenomena that hold for grammatical analysis. The distinction between the processor and the language competence in such a model will reflect our opinion about what is universal and what is language specific.

The insertion of new edges into the chart in an active chart parser simulates the invocation and promotion of rules (active edges) and the closing of constituents (inactive edges). Since elements of the particular language being analyzed provide important signals for these operations (see further Kimball 1973), we consider them to be part of the language specific component. Next we will have to decide on their place within the language description. We may conceive of a subcomponent which embodies the edge-generating mechanisms, and which is separate from the grammar and the dictionaries, as an alternative to integrating them with the grammar rules and the dictionary entries. In our work on UCP the latter alternative has been chosen, as the one that offers the greatest flexibility and hereby also the best experimental environment. (For an alternative view, see, e.g., Thompson 1981). The total of the language description of a UCP parser is formulated in the procedural UCP formalism, including means for the successive extension of the chart. Figure 9 illustrates our general parsing concept.

UCP accounts for processing at various linguistic levels, using a common chart structure. The active edges represent the application of dictionary search rules, phonological rules, morphological rules, and syntactic rules. The inactive edges represent characters, morphs, words, phrases, clauses, and sentences.

If the active chart law is allowed to operate without any restrictions in the common chart, an abundance of inherently unproductive tasks is bound to be generated such as, e.g., attempts to apply syntactic rules to characters, dictionary search rules to phrases, etc. For the avoidance of such a situation, the chart law has been modified to take linguistic level into consideration. The responsibility for distinguishing between the levels rests upon the grammar writer. The mechanisms available will be demonstrated in connection with the presentation of the formalism.

The UCP formalism includes a format for representing grammatical descriptions, a set of operators for expressing grammar rules and dictionary entries, and some conventions for organizing the grammar and the dictionaries.

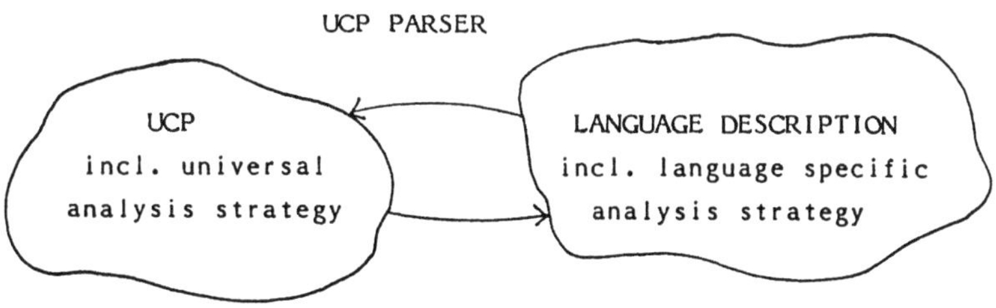

Fig. 9

3.1 The Format of the Grammatical Descriptions

The format of the grammatical descriptions, GDs, is a slightly extended version of Kay's *structure* (Kay 1977b). In other words, GDs are expressed as unordered, hierarchical sets of attribute-value pairs. For a first illustration of this format, we present a GD of the Swedish noun *kvinnorna* (Engl. *the women*) (Fig. 10). The whole GD in Figure 10 is expressed as the value of the formal attribute *. It is a set of five attribute-value pairs, descriptors. (Descriptors will be referred to by their attribute names.)

The first descriptor, WORD.CATegory, has a single symbol, NOUN, as its value. The value of the second descriptor, NOUN.FEATures, however, is in itself a description, consisting of 5 simple descriptors. The LEX descriptor provides a lexeme reference. GENDER, NUMB, SPEC, and DECL state gender, number, species, and declension type. The fact that the value of a descriptor may be a description itself makes it possible to express hierarchical relations in this format. The third descriptor gives information about the stem including a record of its surface representation (CHARacterS). Since the descriptors are unordered, special means must be taken to reflect order when required. UCP does it by explicitly enumerating them.

```
(* = (WORD.CAT = NOUN
      NOUN.FEAT = (LEX = !KVINNA
                   GENDER = UTR
                   NUMB = PLUR
                   SPEC = DEF
                   DECL = -OR)
      STEM = (CHARS = (1 = K
                       2 = V
                       3 = I
                       4 = N
                       5 = N)
              MORPH.CAT = NOUNSTEM
              NOUNSTEM.FEAT = (GENDER = <* NOUN.FEAT GENDER>
                               DECL = <* NOUN.FEAT DECL>
                               LEX = <* NOUN.FEAT LEX>))
      NUMB.SUFF = (CHARS = (1 = O
                            2 = R)
                   MORPH.CAT = NUMB.SUFF
                   DECL = -OR
                   NUMB = <* NOUN.FEAT NUMB>)
      SPEC.SUFF = (CHARS = (1 = N
                            2 = A)
                   MORPH.CAT = FORM.SUFF
                   NUMB = PLUR
                   SPEC = <* NOUN.FEAT SPEC>)))
```

Fig. 10

The formulation of the NOUNSTEM.FEAT value of the STEM descriptor illustrates a third way of expressing a descriptor value, i.e., by referring to some other value in the GD. For reference, the path through the GD from its formal attribute * to the value referred to is given within angle brackets, <...>. For instance, in Fig. 10 the value of the GENDER descriptor of the NOUN-STEM.FEAT descriptor of the STEM descriptor is stated as identical to the value of the GENDER descriptor of the NOUN.FEAT descriptor.

Names of descriptors can be chosen freely[1], excluding * and & which have special functions. * names the GD of an inactive edge and & that of an active one. Thus the GD in Fig. 10 belongs to an inactive edge.

The format of the GDs is similar to a tree representation, and with this analogy in mind, we will sometimes refer to the 'top-level' attributes of a GD, cf. WORD.CAT, NOUN.FEAT, STEM, NUMB.SUFF, and SPEC.SUFF in Fig. 10. It differs, however, from a linguistic tree in two respects. First, the descriptors are *unordered*. Secondly, the description format does not allow for identical descriptor names on one and the same level, and thus fulfills the *uniqueness* condition. For a discussion of the formal properties of this representation format and its relation to the LFG representation format (Kaplan and Bresnan 1982), see Ahrenberg (1984).

3.2 Dictionary Search

We will start our presentation of the UCP chart, formalism, and processing mechanisms by a demonstration of the dictionary search process.

Whatever process we want UCP to carry out must be specified in its grammar. For the purpose of dictionary search only, one rule will do; see Figure 11.

The rule displayed in Figure 11, named START.RULE, has a *rule body* specifying the operation PROCESS(SVE.DIC). It further includes a *domain specification*. The domain of the rule is CHARacters, which means that the rule applies to character edges. A START.RULE is a compulsory rule of a UCP grammar. Its invocation at the beginning of the expression to be processed is the first action taken by UCP, also responsible for representing the input expression as a chart of character edges.

For an illustration, suppose that SVE.DIC is the name of a dictionary, whose keys are organized as a string of letter trees (one for each initial character). Suppose further, that SVE.DIC contains the Swedish preposition *med* (Engl. *with*), as shown in Figure 12.

If so, we may illustrate the operation of UCP, tracing the effects of the function call:

(Process "med" (rulestep)).

---

[1] In naming descriptors, other than those denoting function, the following conventions are applied. Attributes denoting morphosyntactic category are suffixed with *.CAT.* Attributes expressing morphosyntactic features are collected under a descriptor name suffixed by *.FEAT,* preceded by a category name.

```
START.RULE
    PROCESS(SVE.DIC);
      Domain: CHAR;
```

Fig. 11

```
MED
  <& LEX> ::: 'MED,
  <& WORD.CAT> ::: 'PREP,
  ADVANCE,
  <* CHAR> ::: ' ',
  STORE;
```

Fig. 12

Fig. 13

The expression to be analyzed is given to the function PROCESS as a string of characters. Its second (optional) argument RULESTEP activates the trace package which allows us to have the processing displayed task by task.

As a result of the function call the processor starts building an initial chart and invokes START.RULE at vertex 1. Figure 13 shows the graphical representation of the chart after the execution of these first two tasks.

For a distinction between inactive and active edges in the graphical representation of the chart, inactive edges are drawn on and above the 'horizon', and active edges below it. Active edges from and to the same vertex are displayed as vertical bars. Direction is constantly left-to-right and thus not explicitly marked.

The print function (TYPE chart) gives us, in addition, the contents of the edge labels and the numbering of the vertices. The printed version of the chart in Figure 13 is shown below.

1→1 Creator: 1
Rule: START.RULE;

1→2 Creator: 2
GD: (* = (CHAR = M))

It should be read as follows. There is an active edge from and to vertex 1. It was created by task number 1. It represents the rule START.RULE. Further, there is an inactive edge from vertex 1 to vertex 2. It was created by task number 2. It represents a linguistic construct, with the description (CHARacter = M). Active edges are distinguished from inactive ones by their rule specification.

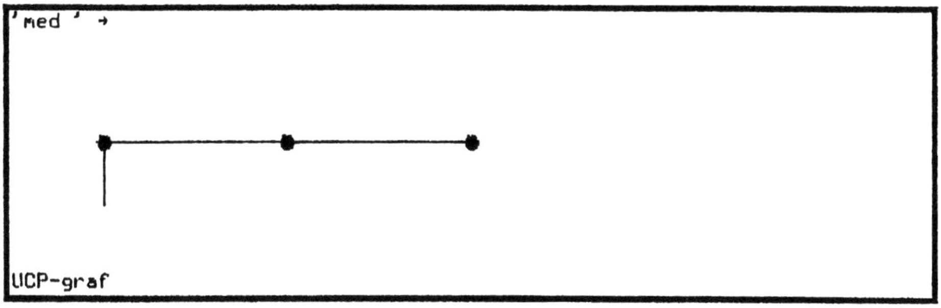

Fig. 14

The chart in Figure 13 contains a pair of an active edge followed by an inactive one. Since, further, the inactive edge fulfills the domain specification of START.RULE, i.e., CHAR, the two edges will create a task in accordance with the UCP chart rule. It will be assigned number 3.

The trace of a task displays its subtasks, accordingly subnumbered. The first subtask states the name of the rule, and the following ones its operations, one by one.

3.1 START.RULE[2];
3.2 PROCESS(SVE.DIC);

The PROCESS operator inserts an active edge from and to the final vertex of the active edge of the current task, in our example vertex 1. Given a dictionary name as its argument, it initiates search in the dictionary named by it. After the execution of task number 3, the chart looks like the one in Figure 14.

The new vertical edge, resulting from the execution of subtask 3.2 is reflected in Figure 14 by a lengthening of the vertical bar of vertex 1. Furthermore, the chart includes a new inactive edge, from 2 to 3, which has been inserted by the processor without explicit trace. It was generated by task number 4, see below.

1→1 Creator: 1
Rule: START.RULE;
1→2 Creator: 2
GD: (* = (CHAR = M))
1→1 Creator: 3
Rule: Consult dictionary SVE.DIC
2→3 Creator: 4
GD: (* = (CHAR = E))

The new active edge from 1 to 1, *Consult dictionary SVE.DIC* will form a task, task number 5, with the following character edge from 1 to 2. This is the first proper dictionary search task, so far. It amounts to matching the value of the attribute

[2] Each task is preceded by its sequential number. Tasks which are built into the processor, for instance, those that account for building the initial chart, are not displayed. They are, however, assigned sequential numbers, by which their effects can be recognized in the trace.

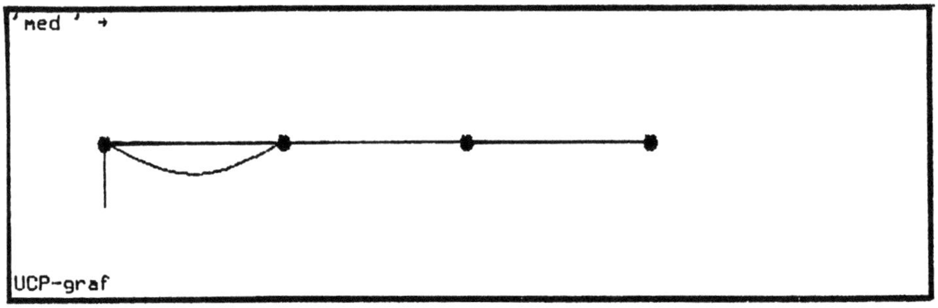

Fig. 15

CHAR, i.e., M, of the inactive edge, with an initial character arc of the dictionary tree of SVE.DIC[3]. Since *med* is in the dictionary, the task will succeed. For the recognition of the succeeding character of the input, E, a new task must be created in which this character is matched against the succeeding arcset in the dictionary tree. This can be arranged for if we create a situation in which the inactive edge is preceded by an active dictionary search rule, anchored in the same vertex as the one that initiated the dictionary search process, i.e., vertex 1. We may think of this action as 'lengthening' the active edge by one character edge. ADVANCE is the name of the operator with this effect. It is defined in a global meta entry of the dictionary. (We will return to the meta entries of the dictionary in Section 3.2.1). The ADVANCE operation is part of task 5 and displayed in the trace. Figure 15 shows the chart after the execution of task number 5.

5.1 ADVANCE;

The chart displays two new edges, the active edge resulting from the advancement operation, and the inactive character edge from 3 to 4 automatically built by the processor.

1→1 Creator: 1
Rule: START.RULE;
1→2 Creator: 2
GD: (* = (CHAR = M))
1→1 Creator: 3
Rule: Consult dictionary SVE.DIC
1→2 Creator: 5
Rule: Consult dictionary SVE.DIC
2→3 Creator: 4
GD: (* = (CHAR = E))
3→4 Creator: 6
GD: (* = (CHAR = D))

---

[3] The matching operation of a dictionary search task is built into the processor, and thus not displayed in the trace.

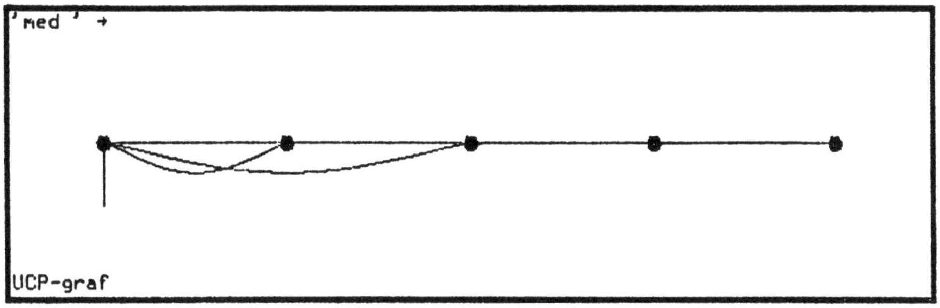

Fig. 16

The active edge from 1 to 2 forms a successful dictionary search task with the inactive edge from 2 to 3, i.e., task number 7.

7.1 ADVANCE;

The effects of task 7 (Fig. 16) are quite analoguos to those of task 5. Except for the addition of a new active edge representing the continued dictionary search process, the last initial edge has appeared, i.e., the one representing the final space.

1→1 Creator: 1
Rule: START.RULE;
1→2 Creator: 2
GD: (* = (CHAR = M))
1→1 Creator: 3
Rule: Consult dictionary SVE.DIC
1→2 Creator: 5
Rule: Consult dictionary SVE.DIC
1→3 Creator: 7
Rule: Consult dictionary SVE.DIC
2→3 Creator: 4
GD: (* = (CHAR = E))
3→4 Creator: 6
GD: (* = (CHAR = D))
4→5 Creator: 8
GD: (* = (CHAR = ' '))

The dictionary search edge from 1 to 3 will form a task with the inactive edge from 3 to 4, task number 9. This task will succeed. It represents the recognition of the last character of the dictionary entry, MED. At a total hit, the operations specified by the dictionary entry will be appended to those of the dictionary search edge and evaluated one by one. For an illustration, let us look at the trace of task 9.

9.1 <& LEX> : = : '!MED,
<& WORD.CAT> : = : 'PREP,
ADVANCE,
<* CHAR> : = : ' ',
STORE;

9.1 lists the rule specified in the dictionary entry of MED (cf. Fig. 12). It is a *conjunction* of three operations, separated by , . Before each operation is evaluated it is displayed in the trace, accordingly subnumbered.

9.2 <& LEX> : = : '!MED

9.2 assigns the value !MED[4] to the LEX descriptor of the current active arc. The assignment is carried out by means of the *unification* operation (: = :). It is the first assignment to the GD of the active arc, and thus there may be no conflicting LEX value, and the operation succeeds. Consequently, 9.3 is evaluated.

9.3 <& WORD.CAT> : = :'PREP;

9.3 assigns the value PREP to the WORD.CATegory descriptor of the active arc, and the unification operation succeeds. Before accepting *med* as the preposition *med,* we want to inspect the following character to verify that we are at the end of a word. For this purpose, the dictionary rule specifies an advancement operation.

9.4 ADVANCE;

An active edge resulting from an advancement operation inherits the GD, if any, of the active edge of the task in which it was created. In Figure 17 we show the chart after the execution of 9.4, and a printout of the new active edge from 1 to 4.

A new task is created, task 10, displayed below.

10.1 <* CHAR> : = : ' ',
STORE;

In 10.2 the character edge from 4 to 5 is tested by a unification operation.

10.2 <* CHAR> = ' ';

10.2 returns a true value, and the next and final operation is carried out.

10.3 STORE;

A STORE operation has the effect of inserting an inactive edge into the chart. The edge inherits its GD from the active edge of the current task. Its startpoint is the startpoint of the active edge of the current task, and its endpoint is the endpoint of the inactive edge of the current task. Thus, the STORE operation of 10.3 will insert an inactive edge from 1 to 5, with the same GD as that of the active edge from 1 to 4. Figure 18 displays the chart after the execution of subtask 10.3, and a printout of the new inactive edge from 1 to 5.

Because the new inactive edge will be preceded by the active edge from 1 to 1, a dictionary search edge, the active chart law will make an attempt to create a new task of these two edges. However, since the inactive edge is not a character edge, the attempt will not lead to the creation of a new task. In Section 3.2.1 we will return to the issue of how the domain of a dictionary search rule is specified.

With the execution of task 10, the agenda will be exhausted and the processing finished. Processing is considered to be successful when there is an inactive edge

---

[4] Lexeme references, or lemmas, are by convention prefixed by *!*, for uniqueness, since they function as the entries (atoms) to the base of lexemes.

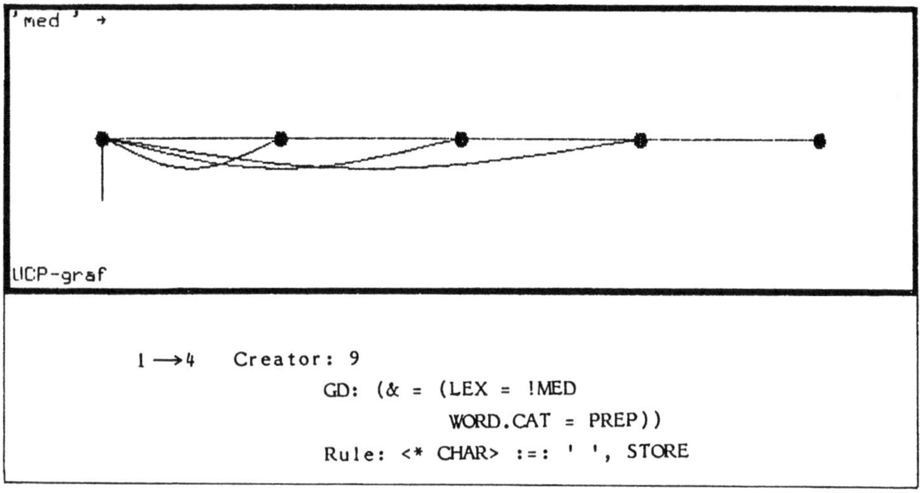

Fig. 17

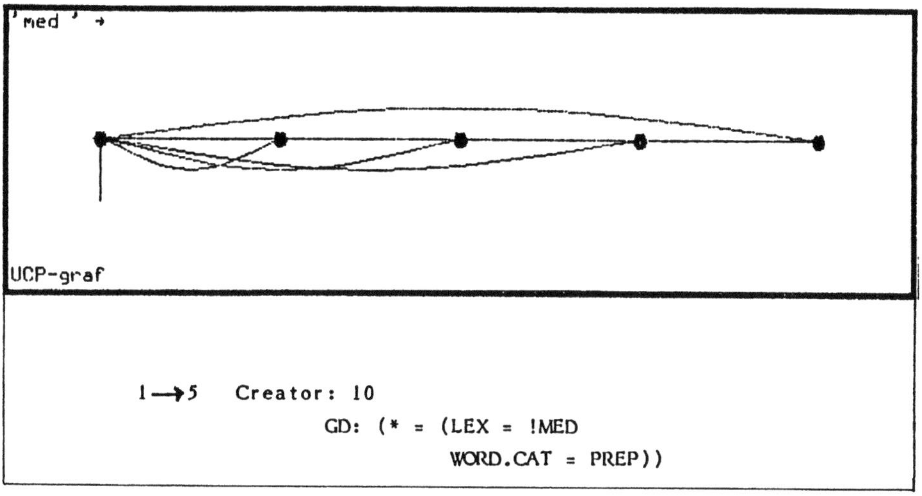

Fig. 18

spanning the whole chart, and the result of the processing is found in that edge. The function (PRINTRESULT) returns its GD.

Our example has demonstrated the basic principles of UCP, and also some of its vital operators, i.e., the edge-generating and thus process-oriented operators PROCESS, ADVANCE, and STORE, and the logical, or GD-oriented, unification operator. Next we want to demonstrate how the dictionary search process can be modified in various ways.

```
SVE.DIC
-------
            DOMAIN
                CHAR;

            FORWARD-ACTION
                ADVANCE;

            GATHERING-RULE
                CONTINUE;

...
```

Fig. 19

3.2.1 Influencing the Dictionary Search Process

A UCP dictionary consists of three compulsory meta entries and any number of ordinary entries. The search keys of the ordinary entries are represented as character trees. The lexical information associated with them is expressed in the general, procedural formalism. At the retrieval of an entry, its operations are appended to the current dictionary search arc and automatically executed, as demonstrated in Section 3.1. Figure 19 shows the meta entries of SVE.DIC as they were defined in this example.

The DOMAIN of the dictionary search process is explicitly defined in the first meta entry of a UCP dictionary. The domain specification in Fig. 19 signifies that dictionary search edges will form tasks only with those inactive edges which include CHAR as a top-level descriptor in their GDs. In our Swedish parser, the domain is CHAR for all dictionaries. The fundamental dictionary search operation amounts to matching the value of the domain attribute of an inactive edge with a dictionary arc label. The arcs of the dictionary trees of the Swedish parser are all labeled by graphemes. The basic dictionary search operation is considered to be universally valid, and, consequently, built into the processor. If a dictionary search task fails, the processor sees to it that alternative arcs are tried one by one. If, on the other hand, the matching operation succeeds, actions are taken in accordance with the operations specified in FORWARD-ACTION and GATHERING-RULE.

FORWARD-ACTION specifies an advancement in the chart, as demonstrated in Section 3.2, and in the dictionary tree. (The active edge keeps track of the position in the tree.) The fact that the advancement operation of FORWARD-ACTION is performed as soon as a matching operation succeeds, regardless of whether it is a partial or a total hit, implies full nondeterminism in the dictionary search process.

GATHERING-RULE in Figure 19 specifies the general truth condition, expressed as CONTINUE in the UCP formalism (cf. T in LISP). In this meta entry, we are, however, free to specify any operations that we want to integrate with the search process. Basically, two kinds of actions are motivated, i. e., record-

```
GATHERING-RULE
    <& CHARS>, <& CHARS :NEW> ::: <& CHARS :LAST> <* CHAR>/
    <& CHARS :NEW> ::: <* CHAR>;


MED             <& LEX> ::: '! <& CHARS :LAST>,
                <& WORD.CAT> ::: 'PREP,
                ADVANCE,
                <* CHAR> ::: ' ',
                STORE;


    1→1         Creator: 3
                Rule: Consult dictionary SVE.DIC

    1→2         Creator: 5
                GD: (& = (CHARS = (1 = M)))
                Rule: Consult dictionary SVE.DIC

    1→3         Creator: 7
                GD: (& = (CHARS = (1 = M
                                   2 = ME)))
                Rule: Consult dictionary SVE.DIC

    1→4         Creator: 9
                GD: (& = (CHARS = (1 = M
                                   2 = ME
                                   3 = MED)
                          LEX = !MED
                          WORD.CAT = PREP))
                Rule: <* CHAR> ::: ' ', STORE;
```

Fig. 20

ing the characters as they are being scanned, and rewriting the chart to cope with orthographic and morphographemic alternation.

3.2.1.1 Recording the Characters as They Are Being Scanned. When dictionary keys are organized as character trees, only the final character of the search key is available when an entry is found, unless special means are taken, which is why we included the operation <& LEX> : = : '!MED in the lexical rule of *med* in the previous example. We would rather like to generate such a lexeme reference automatically, prefixing the dictionary key, with *!*. In order to do so, we need access to the dictionary key in the task representing a final hit. This can be arranged for if the characters are recorded in the GDs of the dictionary search edges as they are being scanned. In Figure 20 we present a GATHERING-RULE with this effect, an accordingly modified version of the dictionary entry MED, and the corresponding dictionary search edges.

In the formulation of GATHERING-RULE in Figure 20 some operators and formal variables are used which have not so far been introduced, i.e., *dependent disjunction, presence, concatenation,* :NEW, and :LAST.

The rule is a dependent disjunction of two sequences of operations, separated by /. A dependent disjunction behaves like a Boolean disjunction. The first sequence of operations applies to the case when the GD of the active edge includes a CHARS descriptor (see 1→2, 1→3, and 1→4 in Figure 20), and the second one to the case when there still is no such descriptor, i.e., the recognition of the first character (see 1→1 in Figure 20). Let us start by examining the latter alternative first.

This consists of a unification operation, in which the :NEW descriptor of the CHARS descriptor of the GD of the active edge is assigned the value of the CHAR descriptor of the GD of the inactive edge. :NEW is not in itself a descriptor name, but a variable over integers. It enumerates the integers, starting with 1 at the first instantiation, and adding 1 to its value at each new call. The effect of this unification operation is illustrated in the edge from 1 to 2 in Figure 20.

In the first operation of the first conjunction the *presence* of a CHARS descriptor in the GD of the active edge is tested by a path-expression. If the evaluation of the path expression returns a NIL value, the execution of the conjunction is interrupted and the alternative sequence is evaluated. If, on the other hand, the operation succeeds, the following unification operations will be executed. Its right-hand side is a *concatenation* operation, in which the value of the :LAST descriptor of the CHARS descriptor of the GD of the active edge is concatenated with the value of the CHAR descriptor of the inactive edge. As is the case with :NEW, :LAST is a variable over descriptor names. It evaluates to the last top-level descriptor of the GD of the active edge. The unification operation sees to it that the result of the concatenation operation is assigned to a new member of the CHARS set of the active edge. The results of this operation, executed twice in the current example, are displayed in 1→3 and 1→4 in Figure 20. The effect of concatenation is achieved by simply juxtaposing an atomic symbol and a path expression evaluating to an atomic symbol.

Finally, the GD of the edge from 1 to 4 in Figure 20, displays the lexeme reference !MED, generated by the first operation of the lexical rule in Figure 20.

3.2.1.2 Formulating the Dictionary Rules in a Compact Way. The rather primitive nature of the UCP operators calls for some means for formulating the rules in a compact and perspicuous way. The *subrule facility* is such a means. By subrules we refer to sequences of operations that are part of other rules, but listed as separate entries under their own names in the grammar. The name of a subrule substitutes the sequence of operations that it specifies. When the processor encounters the name of a subrule during the interpretation of a rule, it retrieves the operations specified by it and evaluates them. As subrules we treat sequences of operations commonly used. The operations constituting the rule body of *med* (see Fig. 20) is an example of such a sequence, holding for all prepositions. Naming it PAT-

```
SVE.DIC
-------
MED     PATTERN.PREPOSITION;
...
TILL    PATTERN.PREPOSITION;
...
```

```
SVE.GRAM
--------
PATTERN.PREPOSITION
    <& LEX> :=: '! <& CHARS :LAST>,
    <& WORD.CAT> :=: 'PREP,
    ADVANCE,
    <* CHAR> :=: ' ',
    STORE;
...
```

Fig. 21

TERN.PREPOSITION would give the formulation and organization of the language data presented in Figure 21.

Since subrules are not real rules but rather an organizational convention, they should be referred to rather as 'pseudo-rules' or 'meta-rules'. However, for ease of presentation we stick to the word 'subrule', it being a handy word to which we are used. In their formal expression, subrules differ from ordinary rules in that they have no explicit domain specification. They are automatically specified for the same kinds of linguistic elements as the rules of which they are part. For instance, PATTERN.PREPOSITION applies to characters only.

3.2.1.3 Processing Numerical Expressions. The use of the procedural formalism in expressing the dictionary rules provides a basis for analyzing numerical expressions in a general manner. The processing of *1986* will demonstrate how this can be done.

The integers from 0 to 9 are stored in the dictionary. The entry of *1* illustrates their common formulation (Fig. 22).

```
1    PATTERN.DIGIT;
```

Fig. 22

The fragment of the grammar specifying the operations of PATTERN.DIGIT and its subrules is presented in Figure 23.

The result of the processing is presented in Figure 24.

The first digit *1* is recognized in the dictionary, and the operations of PATTERN.DIGIT are carried out. The first operation is an advancement operation for an inspection of the succeeding character. END.OF.WORD names an operation in which the TYPE of the character is tested. This operation needs an explanation. Along with the dictionary and the grammar, the language description includes a *base of characters*. In the character base, the characters are classified with regard to type as *separators, digits, vowels,* or *consonants*. Prefixing the last symbol of a path expression with :, excluding :NEW and :LAST, indicates to the processor

```
SVE.GRAM

  PATTERN.DIGIT
     ADVANCE,
     (END.OF.WORD,
      (<& CHARS :LAST> ::: '1, <& NUMB> ::: 'SING/<& NUMB> ::: 'PLUR),
      STORE.QUANT/
      MORE.DIGITS);

  END.OF.WORD
     <* CHAR :TYPE>:::'SEP;

  STORE.QUANT
     <& WORD.CAT> ::: 'QUANT,
     <& LEX> ::: '! <& CHARS :LAST>,
     (<* CHAR> = ' ', STORE/ MINORSTORE);

  MORE.DIGITS
     <* CHAR :TYPE> ::: 'DIGIT,
     <& CHARS :NEW> ::: <& CHARS :LAST> <* CHAR>,
     ADVANCE, MORE.DIGITS/
     END.OF.WORD, <& NUMB> ::: 'PLUR, STORE.QUANT;
```

Fig. 23

```
1986 :
  (* = (CHARS = (1 = '1'
                 2 = '19'
                 3 = '198'
                 4 = '1986')
        NUMB = PLUR
        WORD.CAT = QUANT
        LEX = !1986))
```

Fig. 24

that the symbol denotes a property stored in the base. The path expression returns the value associated with that property. The preceding part of the path expression should evaluate to the atom under which the property is stored. The space sign and the punctuation marks are typed as SEP for separator. Due to this device, we may test for the end of a word in one single operation instead of having to take into account all the individual separators.

If a separator follows the first digit, the numerical expression consists of one digit only, and its GD should be stored. In it we want to include information about number which is handled by the succeeding disjunction operation:

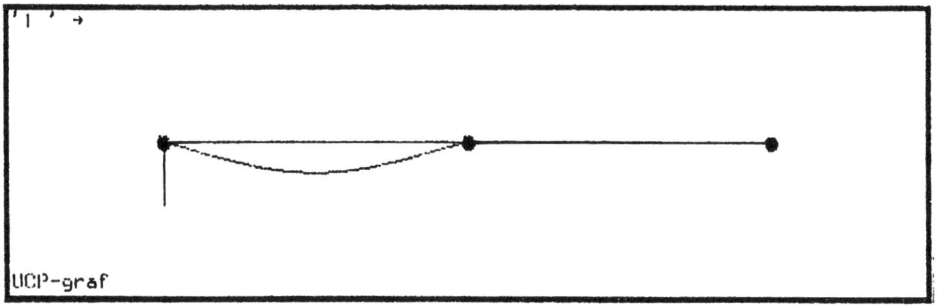

Fig. 25

(<& CHARS :LAST> :=: '1, <& NUMB> :=: 'SING/<& NUMB> :=: 'PLUR)

If the digit is identical to 1, its number is singular. Otherwise it is plural.

STORE.QUANT specifies the operations by which its word category and lexeme reference are assigned. The storing operation is expressed as a disjunction for the following reason. The active edge of the current task spans vertices 1 and 2, and the inactive edge vertices 2 and 3, representing the separator (see Fig. 25).

A STORE operation in the current task will lead to the creation of an inactive edge from 1 to 3, including the separator. This is reasonable, provided that the separator is identical to the space sign. If, however, the separator is a punctuation mark, it is not motivated to have it included in the representation of the numerical expression. This is avoided if the operator MINORSTORE is used instead. MINORSTORE inserts an inactive edge spanning the same vertices as the active edge only. Its GD behaves like STORE in that it inherits by default the GD of the active edge. Thus, in this example MINORSTORE will insert an inactive edge from 1 to 2, hereby excluding the punctuation mark from the representation of the numerical expression.

Let us go back to PATTERN.DIGIT. If the character succeeding the first digit is not a separator, the operations of MORE.DIGITS will be performed (Fig. 23). MORE.DIGITS starts its operations by testing for a character typed as a DIGIT. If this is the case, the character is accordingly recorded, an advancement is made to the next character, and MORE.DIGITS is *recursively* called until the end of the word is found and the operations of STORE.QUANT performed. If any character other than a separator or a digit were recognized, the evaluation of PATTERN.DIGIT would be interrupted, and no final analysis presented.

As mentioned above, STORE and MINORSTORE inherit by default the GD of the active edge. We may, however, specify path expressions as their arguments if motivated. For instance, the CHARS descriptor in the GD in Figure 24, may seem superfluous. Modifying STORE.QUANT as shown in Figure 26 would give the GD presented in the same figure.

```
1986 :
    (* = (WORD.CAT = QUANT
          QUANT.FEAT = (LEX = !1986
                        NUMB = PLUR)))


  STORE.QUANT
        <& OUT WORD.CAT> ::= 'QUANT,
        <& OUT QUANT.FEAT LEX> ::= '! <& CHARS :LAST>,
        <& OUT QUANT.FEAT NUMB> ::= <& NUMB>,
        (<* CHAR> = ' ', STORE(<& OUT>)/ MINORSTORE(<& OUT>));
```

Fig. 26

3.3 *Morphological Analysis*

The morphological analysis amounts to the *recognition of the constituent morphs* of the word, and the *building of a GD* corresponding to its interpretation. The recognition process includes the segmentation of the word into tentative morphs, and the verification of the segmentation via the application of morphotactic rules.

In UCP, the segmentation process is carried out via dictionary search, including devices for handling morphophonemic alternation. The verification of the segmentation resulting from the dictionary search process is handled by the application of morphotactic rules. The building of the final GD is integrated with the segmentation process and with the application of the morphotactic rules. The segmentation process can be made *predictive* as will be demonstrated below.

3.3.1 Predictive Segmentation into Tentative Morphs

For the morphological analysis, the lexical material should be organized as a dictionary of stems or roots, and a number of affix dictionaries. We will outline the basic principles of the segmentation process using the Swedish example *kvinnorna,* cf. Figure 10. The segmentation of the word is based on a dictionary of stems (SVE.DIC), a dictionary of nominal number affixes (NUMB), and a dictionary of nominal species (form) affixes (FORM). Figure 27 presents those entries of SVE.DIC, SVE.GRAM, NUMB, and FORM that are relevant for the current discussion.

Figure 28 presents the chart resulting from the dictionary search process.

The example illustrates how search in the relevant affix dictionary is initiated from the dictionary entry of the preceding morph by means of the PROCESS operator. (The three edges created by this operator are included in Figure 28.) A well-considered organization of the dictionary into mini-dictionaries (cf. Koskenniemi 1983) will lead to a highly predictive dictionary search process in the nondeterministic framework. There is still one more device available, the use of which

```
SVE.DIC

    KVINN  PATTERN.FLICKA;


SVE.GRAM

    PATTERN.FLICKA
        <& MORPH.CAT> ::= 'NOUNSTEM,
        <& NOUNSTEM.FEAT GENDER> ::= 'UTR,
        <& NOUNSTEM.FEAT DECL> ::= '-OR,
        <& NOUNSTEM.FEAT LEX> ::= '! <& CHARS :LAST> 'A,
        STORE,
        ADVANCE,
        PROCESS(NUMB);

NUMB

    OR     <& MORPH.CAT> ::= 'NUMB.SUFF,
           <& DECL> ::= '-OR,
           <& NUMB> ::= 'PLUR,
           STORE,
           ADVANCE,
           PROCESS(FORM);

FORM

    N      <& MORPH.CAT> ::= 'FORM.SUFF,
           <& NUMB> ::= 'SING,
           <& GENDER> ::= 'UTR,
           <& FINAL> ::= 'VOWEL,
           STORE.FORM;

    NA     <& MORPH.CAT> ::= 'FORM.SUFF,
           <& NUMB> ::= 'PLUR,
           STORE.FORM;
```

Fig. 27

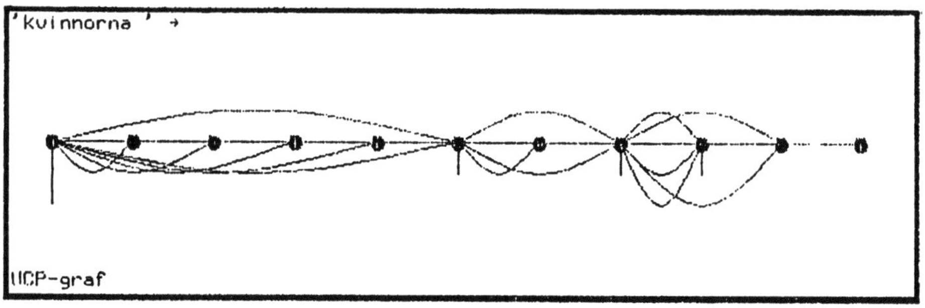

Fig. 28

```
1→1    Creator: 3
       Rule: Consult dictionary SVE.DIC

6→6    Creator: 15
       Rule: Consult dictionary NUMB

6→8    Creator: 19
       GD: (* = (MORPH.CAT = NUMB.SUFF
                 DECL = -OR
                 NUMB = PLUR))

8→8    Creator: 21
       Rule: Consult dictionary FORM

8→9    Creator: 23
       GD: (* = (MORPH.CAT = FORM.SUFF
                 NUMB = SING
                 GENDER = UTR
                 FINAL = VOWEL
                 SPEC = DEF))

8→10   Creator: 26
       GD: (* = (MORPH.CAT = FORM.SUFF
                 NUMB = PLUR
                 SPEC = DEF))
```

Fig. 29

further contributes to the predictability of the search process. What we have in mind is the possibility of *bringing arguments along with the* PROCESS *operator* as will be demonstrated in the current example.

In the dictionary search process, two species affixes were recognized, see the edges 8→9 and 8→10 in Figure 29. They differ with regard to number, the first one associating with singular nouns, the second one with plurals. Now, if we could bring along the information that the preceding number affix denotes plural, the singular species affix would never have to be recognized. To achieve this aim we modify the number affix entry, as shown in Figure 30.

The chart resulting from this modification of the OR-entry is displayed in Figure 31, with the relevant edges printed.

The N-affix will be found in the FORM dictionary, but the number unification operation of its rule will fail, and the affix never be stored in the chart.

3.3.1.1 Morphemic Alternation. The segmentation process is complicated by the phenomenon of morphemic alternation, in specific, alternating stems. Basically, two kinds of alternations have to be dealt with, i.e., stem internal alternation concerning one character (cf. one segment alternation, Koskenniemi 1983), and stem

```
NUMB

    OR      <& MORPH.CAT> ::= 'NUMB.SUFF,
            <& DECL> ::= '-OR,
            <& NUMB> ::= 'PLUR,
            STORE,
            ADVANCE,
  ——>       <& COPY NUMB> ::= <& NUMB>,
            PROCESS(FORM, <& COPY>);
```

Fig. 30

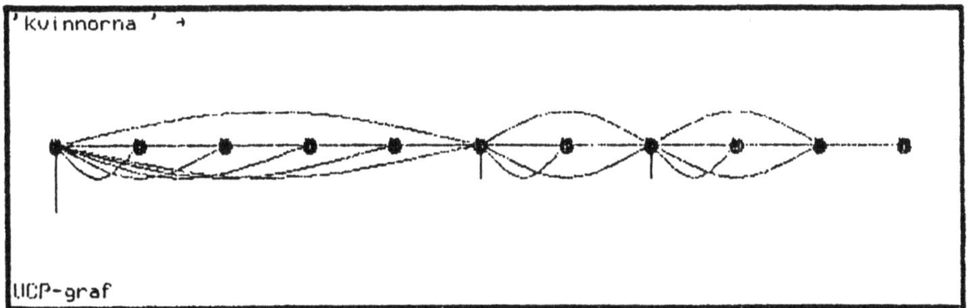


```
8——>8    Creator: 21
         GD: (& = (NUMB = PLUR))
         Rule: Consult dictionary FORM

8——>10   Creator: 24
         Rule: (* = (NUMB = PLUR
                     MORPH.CAT = FORM.SUFF
                     SPEC = DEF))
```

Fig. 31

final alternation concerning one or several characters. In UCP, stem internal alternation is handled by means of rewriting rules (cf. Section 2.2.1), whereas stem final alternation is accounted for by the dictionary and the dictionary search rules.

3.3.1.1.1 Stem Internal Alternation. A common case of stem internal alternation is that of phonologically based vowel insertion, such as *cykel* (Engl. *bicycle*) and *cyklar* (Engl. *bicycles*). For the recognition of the secondary vowel stem alternant, we may formulate a rewriting rule transforming the stem to its non-vowel form, and have this rule integrated with the dictionary search process invoking it from the gathering-rule meta entry of the dictionary. In Figure 32 we present a gathering-rule in which we integrated such a rule call with the character recording operations discussed above (Section 3.2.1.1), and the rule (SEC.VOC) itself.

```
SVE.DIC:        GATHERING-RULE
                    <& CHARS>,
                    <& CHARS :NEW> ::= <& CHARS :LAST> <* CHAR>,
           -->      (<* CHAR :MODE> = 'OBSTR, PROCESS(SEC.VOC)/ CONTINUE)/
                    <& CHARS :NEW> ::= <* CHAR>;

SVE.GRAM:       SEC.VOC
                    <& FIRST> ::= <*>,
                    <& FIRST SEC.VOC> ::= '+,
                    ADVANCE,
                    <* CHAR> ::= 'E,
                    ADVANCE,
                    <* CHAR :MODE> ::= 'SONOR,
                    <& SECOND> ::= <*>,
                    <& SECOND SEC.VOC> ::= '+,
                    STORE(<& FIRST>, <& SECOND>);

                        Domain: CHAR , not SEC.VOC;
```

Fig. 32

In GATHERING-RULE, if the character being inspected is classified as an obstruent with regard to articulation mode, the secondary vowel rule is invoked, else processing simply goes on. In SEC.VOC the following actions are taken. The character being inspected is assigned to the descriptor FIRST. This descriptor is further marked with + for SEC.VOC, denoting that it has been generated by the secondary vowel rule. An advancement is made to the succeeding character which should be an *e* for the rule to go on. The following character is specified as a sonorant. It is assigned to the descriptor SECOND which is further marked with + for SEC.VOC. In the final operation of the rule two inactive edges are specified by the arguments of the store operator (cf. Fig. 26). Once inserted into the chart, they will span the same vertices as the three character edges to which they correspond. A new vertex, though, has to be created; this is the endpoint of the first new edge and the startpoint of the second new one. The domain of SEC.VOC is CHAR and *not* SEC.VOC to prevent its recursive application. In Figure 33 we present a graphical display of the chart after the application of the secondary vowel rule to *cykel,* and a printing of the two new edges.

The number of the new vertex is 8. The dictionary search edge from 1 to 3 will apply to the new edge from 3 to 8, and the dictionary entry *cykl* will eventually be retrieved. The pattern rule associated with this entry will take the application of the secondary vowel rewriting rule into proper consideration, and mark the stem alternant with the secondary vowel as *singular,* and the other one as *plural.* Other types of internal stem alternation well apt to be treated by rewriting rules are *umlaut* and *palatalization.*

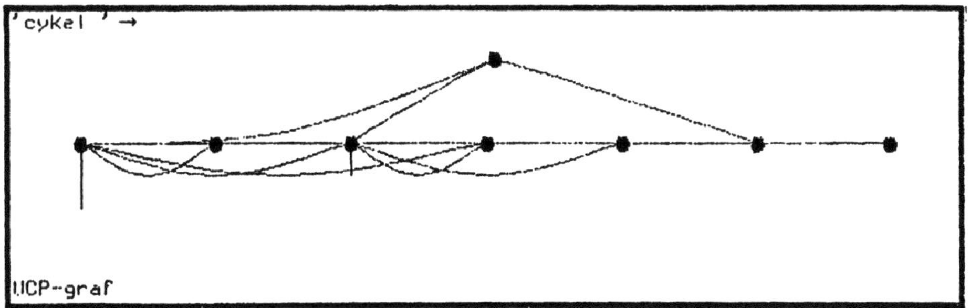


```
3→8   Creator: 17
            GD: (* = (CHAR = K
                      SEC.VOC = +))

8→6   Creator: 17
            GD: (* = (CHAR = L
                      SEC.VOC = +))
```

Fig. 33

3.3.1.1.2 Coping with Stem Final Alternation in the Dictionary. Invoking rewriting rules from GATHERING-RULE means that the rules will be generally applied with due impact on the processing resources as a consequence. Alternations concerning the final part of the stem only can be more economically handled in the dictionary. We think of cases such as the noun stem alternation in words like *ganglion* (Engl. *ganglion*) and *ganglier* (Engl. *ganglions*). For such words, we enter the common part of the stem *gangli* in the dictionary, and carry on the search for the succeeding segment by operations specified by the pattern rule. Figure 34 displays the dictionary entry *gangli,* and the pattern rule associated with it.

Since the dictionary key of words behaving like *ganglion* is not identical to its lemma (or lexeme reference), the rule must include an operation in which the lemma is generated from the dictionary key and the final segment. This is done in the third operation of PATTERN.GANGLION. In the next operation an advancement is made to the succeeding character. If it is an *o,* we advance further in search for an *n.* If one is found, the stem is marked for singular, and processing goes on in the regular manner via the subrule STORE.NOUN.STEM. If no *o* is found the stem constituent will be closed in the same subrule, and search for a succeeding affix will be initiated from there. (The stem won't be marked for plural, since this stem alternant may appear not only in plural forms but also in the definite singular form.)

```
SVE.DIC

        GANGLI   PATTERN.GANGLION;


SVE.GRAM

        PATTERN.GANGLION
            <& NOUNSTEM.FEAT GENDER> :=: 'NEUTR,
            <& NOUNSTEM.FEAT DECL> :=: '-ER,
            <& NOUNSTEM.FEAT LEX> :=: '! <& CHARS :LAST> 'ON,
            ADVANCE,
            (<* CHAR> = 'O, ADVANCE,
             <* CHAR> = 'N, <& NOUNSTEM.FEAT NUMB> :=: 'SING, ADVANCE/
             CONTINUE),
            STORE.NOUN.STEM;
```

Fig. 34

3.3.2 The Application of Morphotactic Rules

It is the job of the morphotactic rules to verify the segmentation resulting from the dictionary search process, and to build the corresponding GD of the word. In demonstrating how morphotactic rules are initiated and applied in UCP, we continue to use the example in Section 3.3.1. The recognition of a noun stem is a strong prediction of a noun. Consequently, the morphotactic noun rule should be invoked upon recognition of a noun stem. In UCP terms this means that a noun rule initiating operation should be included in the lexical rules of the noun stems. Further, the morphotactic rule should start its operation at the beginning of the stem. So far, we have presented only one rule-initiating operator, i.e., PROCESS. As a matter of fact, this operator takes rule names as well as dictionary names as its first argument, and is thereby capable of initiating the application of a grammar rule[5]. It won't do the job, however, for the following reason. PROCESS inserts its active edge at the final vertex of the inactive edge of the current task, which in our example would mean to initiate the morphotactic noun rule at the end of the nominal stem. Instead we need an operator inserting its active edge at the beginning of the inactive edge of the current task. This is how MAJORPROCESS is defined. In other respects it behaves in the same manner as PROCESS. In Figure 35 we present a simplified version of the Swedish noun rule holding for our example, and the modification of PATTERN.FLICKA, initiating this rule.

The last operation of the noun rule (Fig. 35) needs an explanation. As mentioned above (see Sect. 3.2), the active edge resulting from an ADVANCE opera-

[5] UCP has some self-knowledge enabling it to distinguish between a dictionary name and a rule name.

```
NOUN
  <& WORD.CAT> ::: 'NOUN,
  <* MORPH.CAT> ::: 'NOUNSTEM,
  <& NOUN.FEAT> ::: <* NOUNSTEM.FEAT>,
  ADVANCE,
  <* MORPH.CAT>::: 'NUMB.SUFF,
  <& NOUN.FEAT DECL> ::: <* DECL>,
  <& NOUN.FEAT NUMB> ::: <* NUMB>,
  ADVANCE,
  <* MORPH.CAT> :::'FORM.SUFF,
  <& NOUN.FEAT SPEC> ::: <* FORM>,
  ADVANCE(CLOSE.WORD);

      Domain: MORPH.CAT;

CLOSE.WORD
      END.OF.WORD,
      (<* CHAR> = ' ', STORE/ MINORSTORE);

         Domain: CHAR;

 PATTERN.FLICKA
      <& MORPH.CAT> ::: 'NOUNSTEM,
      <& NOUNSTEM.FEAT GENDER> ::: 'UTR,
      <& NOUNSTEM.FEAT DECL> ::: '-OR,
      <& NOUNSTEM.FEAT LEX> ::: '! <& CHARS :LAST> 'A,
      STORE,
      MAJORPROCESS(NOUN),
      ADVANCE,
      PROCESS(NUMB);
```

Fig. 35

tion without an argument inherits the domain specification of the current active edge. If, however, we want to change the domain of a rule in connection with an advancement operation, we may do so giving a rule name as an argument to the ADVANCE operator and specifying the new domain in that rule (see CLOSE.WORD in Fig. 35). The use of the *advance with an argument* facility in the noun rule allows us to change the domain from MORPH.CAT (for morphological category) to CHAR for the inspection of the delimiting character.

The result of the analysis according to these rules is presented in Figure 36.

3.3.2.1 Handling Zero-Realizations of Morphemes. The noun rule in Figure 35 won't recognize, e.g., indefinite forms of the noun, since the rule requires the presence of an explicit species affix, and the indefinite form is signalled by the absence

```
KVINNORNA :          (* = (WORD.CAT = NOUN
                           NOUN.FEAT = (GENDER = UTR
                                        DECL = -OR
                                        LEX = !KVINNA
                                        NUMB = PLUR
                                        SPEC = DEF)))
```

Fig. 36

of such an affix in Swedish. The demand for a species affix is expressed by the operations ADVANCE, <* MORPH.CAT> :=: 'FORM.SUFF. Let us examine what would happen if the number affix were followed by a delimiting character. If so, the advance operation wouldn't take place since there would be no inactive edge available fulfilling the domain specification of the rule (MORPH.CAT at this state). Consequently, for the rule to cope with non-explicit species affixes it must be reformulated to provide for an advancement to a character edge. In Figure 37 we show how this can be done, introducing at the same time the *independent disjunction* (or *parallel processing*) operator *(. . ./. . .)*.

Having recognized a number suffix, we advance in parallel to a species suffix and to CLOSE.WORD for the retrieval of a delimiting character. Before advancing to CLOSE.WORD, we assign the value INDEF to the species descriptor. As should be clear from what has been said so far, the independent disjunction operator inserts one active edge for each alternative.

In Swedish, not only the species category, but also the number and the case categories exhibit zero realizations. To cope with this, the independent disjunction operator will have to be extensively used in the formulation of a complete noun rule for Swedish, with a substantial impact on the processing as a consequence. Below we will demonstrate an alternative solution, according to which more of the job is handled by the dictionary search process.

The basic idea behind this alternative approach is to inspect the succeeding character at the retrieval of a morph, and, if it turns out to be a separator, to draw the necessary conclusions to avoid nondeterministic parallel processing in the noun rule. In Figure 38 we present the relevant fragment of a Swedish language description illustrating the alternative handling of zero-morphs. The fragment concerns the example discussed above.

If the number affix is followed by a separator, we know that the form is indefinite and may as well assign this value to the form descriptor at the retrieval of the number affix. The presence of a form descriptor in the GD of the number affix will be used by the noun rule to signal the end of the word. For an economic structuring of the information in the number affix dictionary, we define a STORE.NUMB.SUFF subrule as shown in Figure 39.

In the same way we handle zero realizations of the number and the case categories.

```
NOUN
  <& WORD.CAT> :=: 'NOUN,
  <* MORPH.CAT> :=: 'NOUNSTEM,
  <& NOUN.FEAT> :=: <* NOUNSTEM.FEAT>,
  ADVANCE,
  <* MORPH.CAT>:=: 'NUMB.SUFF,
  <& NOUN.FEAT DECL> :=: <* DECL>,
  <& NOUN.FEAT NUMB> :=: <* NUMB>,
→ (ADVANCE, <* MORPH.CAT> :=: 'FORM.SUFF,
   <& NOUN.FEAT SPEC> :=: <* FORM>, ADVANCE(CLOSE.WORD)//
   <& NOUN.FEAT SPEC> :=: 'INDEF, ADVANCE(CLOSE.WORD));

     Domain: MORPH.CAT;
```

Fig. 37

```
NUMB

          OR
             <& MORPH.CAT> :=: 'NUMB.SUFF,
             <& DECL> :=: '-OR,
             <& NUMB> :=: 'PLUR,
             ADVANCE,
      →      (END.OF.WORD,
              <& FORM> :=: 'INDEF/
              <& COPY NUMB> :=: <& NUMB>,
              PROCESS(FORM, <& COPY>)),
              MINORSTORE;

          NOUN
            <& WORD.CAT> :=: 'NOUN,
            <* MORPH.CAT> :=: 'NOUNSTEM,
            <& NOUN.FEAT> :=: <* NOUNSTEM.FEAT>,
            ADVANCE,
            <* MORPH.CAT>:=: 'NUMB.SUFF,
            <& NOUN.FEAT DECL> :=: <* DECL>,
            <& NOUN.FEAT NUMB> :=: <* NUMB>,
      →     (<* FORM>, <& NOUN.FEAT SPEC> :=: <* FORM>/
             ADVANCE, <* MORPH.CAT> :=: 'FORM.SUFF,
             <& NOUN.FEAT SPEC> :=: <* FORM>),
            ADVANCE(CLOSE.WORD));

               Domain: MORPH.CAT;
```

Fig. 38

```
NUMB
          OR  <& DECL> ::: '-OR,
              STORE.NUMB.SUFF;


SVE.GRAM

      STORE.NUMB.SUFF
              <& MORPH.CAT> ::: 'NUMB.SUFF,
              <& NUMB> ::: 'PLUR,
              ADVANCE,
              (END.OF.WORD, <& FORM> ::: 'INDEF/
               <& COPY NUMB> ::: <& NUMB>,
               PROCESS(FORM, <& COPY>)),
              MINORSTORE;
```

Fig. 39

```
(* = (WORD.CAT = NOUN
      NOUN.FEAT = (GENDER = NEUTR
                   DECL = -
                   LEX = !UNIVERSITET!BIBLIOTEK
                   NUMB = SING
                   SPEC = DEF
                   COMPOUND = +)
      STEM = (MORPH.CAT = NOUNSTEM
              NOUNSTEM.FEAT = (COMPOUND = <* NOUN.FEAT COMPOUND>
                               GENDER = <* NOUN.FEAT GENDER>
                               DECL = <* NOUN.FEAT DECL>
                               LEX = <* NOUN.FEAT LEX>)
              PREF = (MORPH.CAT = NOUNSTEM
                      NOUNSTEM.FEAT = (GENDER = NEUTR
                                       DECL = -
                                       LEX = !UNIVERSITET))
              HEAD = (MORPH.CAT = NOUNSTEM
                      NOUNSTEM.FEAT = (GENDER = <* NOUN.FEAT GENDER>
                                       DECL = <* NOUN.FEAT DECL>
                                       LEX = !BIBLIOTEK)))
      FORM.SUFF = (MORPH.CAT = FORM.SUFF
                   NUMB = <* NOUN.FEAT NUMB>
                   SPEC = <* NOUN.FEAT SPEC>)))
```

Fig. 40

```
SVE.DIC

     UNIVERSITET     PATTERN.BORD;

     BIBLIOTEK       PATTERN.BORD;


SVE.GRAM

     PATTERN.BORD
               <& NOUNSTEM.FEAT GENDER> :=: 'NEUTR,
               <& NOUNSTEM.FEAT DECL> :=: '-,
               <& NOUNSTEM.FEAT LEX> :=: '! <& CHARS :LAST>,
               ADVANCE,
               (STORE.NOUN.STEM//COMP.TEST);

     COMP.TEST
               NOT END.OF.WORD,
               MAJORPROCESS(STEM.COMP),
               (MINORSTORE, PROCESS(SVE.DIC)//
                <* CHAR> = 'S, STORE, ADVANCE, PROCESS(SVE.DIC));
```

Fig.41

3.3.3 Derivational Analysis

So far, we have only discussed inflectional analysis in the UCP framework. However, by means of the operators and conventions already introduced, derivational analysis can also be handled. For a demonstration, we present the analysis of the compound *universitetsbiblioteket* (Engl. *the university library*) (Fig. 40), and the corresponding rules (Fig. 41).

The GD of the compound in Figure 40 displays its constituent structure, the stem being analyzed as consisting of a prefix followed by a head. From its head the stem inherits declension and gender descriptors, whereas the value of its lexeme descriptor is the result of concatenating the lexeme value of the prefix with that of the head. The stem is further marked as *compound*. The epenthetic *s* is not reflected in the GD of the stem, and below we will demonstrate how it has been handled. As is the case in the analysis of simple nouns, the morpho-syntactic features of the noun are assigned from the stem and the inflectional affixes.

The first operation of COMP.TEST (Fig. 41) makes use of the *negation* operator to verify that the stem is not word final. If the negation operation returns a true value, the compound stem rule (STEM.COMP) is invoked at the beginning of the stem[6]. The second alternative of the independent disjunction of COMP.TEST rec-

[6] All the process-oriented operators, i.e., PROCESS, MAJORPROCESS, ADVANCE, STORE, and MINORSTORE return true values.

```
(* =
(WORD.CAT = NOUN
 NOUN.FEAT = (GENDER = UTR
              DECL = -
              LEX = !METALL!ARBETARE
              SPEC = INDEF
              COMPOUND = +)
 STEM = (MORPH.CAT = NOUNSTEM
         NOUNSTEM.FEAT = (COMPOUND = <* NOUN.FEAT COMPOUND>
                          GENDER = <* NOUN.FEAT GENDER>
                          DECL = <* NOUN.FEAT DECL>
                          LEX = <* NOUN.FEAT LEX>
         PREF =  MORPH.CAT = NOUNSTEM
                 NOUNSTEM.FEAT = (GENDER = UTR
                                  DECL = -ER
                                  LEX = !METALL))
         HEAD = (MORPH.CAT = NOUNSTEM
                 NOUNSTEM.FEAT = (DER = +
                                  LEX = !ARBETARE
                                  GENDER = <* NOUN.FEAT GENDER>
                                  DECL = <* NOUN.FEAT DECL>)
                 STEM = (MORPH.CAT = VERBSTEM
                         CONJ = I
                         LEX = !ARBETA)
                 SUFF = (MORPH.CAT = NOUN.SUFF
                         NOUN.SUFF.FEAT =(GENDER = <* NOUN.FEAT GENDER>
                                          CBLTY = +
                                          DECL = <* NOUN.FEAT DECL>))))))
```

Fig. 42

ognizes the epenthetic *s*, and steps by it without further notice. The first alternative takes care of cases without an epenthetic element. STEM.COMP recognizes the compound stem and builds its GD.

Figure 42 shows an analysis of the compound *metallarbetare* (Engl. *metal worker(s)*), the head of which is a nomen agentis. The word consists of a stem only, without an affix. The constituents of the stem are a prefix, and a head which in turn consists of a verbal stem and a nominal derivational suffix. The noun is unmarked with regard to number, and in such cases we refrain from stating a number descriptor.

The search for a constituent morph of a compound can be constrained in the same manner as the dictionary search for an inflectional affix (see Section 3.3.1). We illustrate this by the analysis of *1600-talet* (Engl. *the 17th century*).

The analysis presented in Figure 43 is based on an extension of the MORE. DIGITS subrule presented above (Fig. 23). The extension consists in invoking

```
(* = (WORD.CAT = NOUN
      NOUN.FEAT = (GENDER = NEUTR
                   DECL = -
                   LEX = !1600!TAL
                   NUMB = SING
                   SPEC = DEF
                   COMPOUND = +)
      STEM = (MORPH.CAT = NOUNSTEM
              NOUNSTEM.FEAT = (COMPOUND = <* NOUN.FEAT COMPOUND>
                               GENDER = <* NOUN.FEAT GENDER>
                               DECL = <* NOUN.FEAT DECL>
                               LEX = <* NOUN.FEAT LEX>)
              PREF = MORPH.CAT = QUANTSTEM
                     LEX = !1600)
              HEAD = MORPH.CAT = NOUNSTEM
                     NOUNSTEM.FEAT = (GENDER = <* NOUN.FEAT GENDER>
                                      DECL = <* NOUN.FEAT DECL>
                                      LEX = <* NOUN.FEAT LEX>)))
      FORM.SUFF = MORPH.CAT = FORM.SUFF
                  NUMB = <* NOUN.FEAT NUMB>
                  GENDER = <* NOUN.FEAT GENDER>
                  FORM = <* NOUN.FEAT SPEC>)))
```

Fig. 43

```
          MORE.DIGITS
               <* CHAR :TYPE> ::: 'DIGIT,
               <& CHARS :NEW> ::: <& CHARS :LAST> <* CHAR>,
               ADVANCE, MORE.DIGITS/
          ---> <* CHAR> ::: '-,
               <& MORPH.CAT> ::: 'QUANTSTEM,
               MAJORPROCESS(STEM.COMP),
               STORE,
               <& NEXT NOUNSTEM.FEAT LEX>::: '!TAL,
               PROCESS(SVE.DIC,<& NEXT>)/
               END.OF.WORD,
               <& NUMB> ::: 'PLUR, STORE.QUANT;
```

Fig. 44

STEM.COMP at the retrieval of a hyphen, and in constraining the search for a succeeding morph bringing along a representation of the required lexeme (Fig. 44). The hyphen is treated as an epenthetic element.

In the same way that properties associated with an individual character can be stored in a base of characters and retrieved from there by means of the :convention in the formulation of path expressions (see Section 3.2.1.3 above), properties associated with the lexemes can be retrieved from a base of lexemes. This facility can be used for semantic feature testing in the rules recognizing compound stems (e.g., STEM.COMP) as a complement, or alternative, to constraining the dictionary search. We will, however, demonstrate this facility in the presentation of the syntactic analysis, in which it plays a crucial role.

3.4 Syntactic Analysis

In the morphological analysis words are recognized by rules defined for the various lexical categories, noun, verb, adjective, etc. The rules are invoked bottom-up by means of MAJORPROCESS upon recognition of the respective stems. The same strategy can be used for the recognition of phrases, i.e., upon recognition of a certain phrase introducer, the corresponding phrase rule is invoked bottom-up. For instance, upon recognition of a noun an NP rule is invoked, upon recognition of a preposition a PP rule is invoked, etc.

Figure 45 shows an analysis of *kvinnorna* as an NP, arrived at by the inclusion of the operation MAJORPROCESS(NP) in the noun rule. The GD generated by the NP rule includes information about syntactic category, NP, morphosyntactic features, NP.FEAT, and constituent part(s), i.e., HEAD only. Figure 46 displays an analysis of *i Uppsala* (Engl. *in Uppsala*), arrived at by the inclusion of the operation MAJORPROCESS(PP) in the PATTERN.PREPOSITION rule (cf. Fig. 21).

The PP in Figure 46 is analyzed as consisting of a preposition followed by a prepositional object (POBJ). The object function is realized by an NP, consisting of a first name (NAME1) only. This NP was recognized by a phrase rule, designed for the analysis of NPs of proper nouns, invoked by the lexical category rule for proper nouns. When there are many levels in a GD, the referential descriptor values become long, and, as a consequence, the GD as such less perspicuous. For the sake of readability, a shorter display mode can be chosen, in which the printing of descriptors with referential path expressions specifying more than three descriptor names is suppressed. Figure 47 shows the PP from Figure 46 in the brief display mode. Henceforth, we will use the brief display mode only.

Basically, in our UCP parser for Swedish, phrases are analyzed bottom-up. However, this is not so with the VP, which in Swedish, as in many other languages, is often discontinuously presented. The handling of discontinuous constituents in the UCP framework will be discussed below.

3.4.1 The Analysis of a Clause

For the analysis of a clause, a clause rule has to operate on the constituents recognized by the morphological and syntactic rules invoked bottom-up. In the analysis of a clause, so-called *verbaction rules* may be used. The verbaction rules recognize the arguments of the verb in their surface structure positions, taking semantic restrictions into account. In our Swedish parser, the arguments of the verb are expressed in terms of grammatical functions such as subject, object, complement,

```
(* = (PHR.CAT = NP
      NP.FEAT = (GENDER = UTR
                 NUMB = PLUR
                 SPEC = DEF
                 LEX = !KVINNA)
      HEAD = (WORD.CAT = NOUN
              NOUN.FEAT = (GENDER = <* NP.FEAT GENDER>
                           DECL = -OR
                           LEX = <* NP.FEAT LEX>
                           NUMB = <* NP.FEAT NUMB>
                           FORM = <* NP.FEAT SPEC>))))
(* = (WORD.CAT = NOUN
      etc.)
```

Fig. 45

```
(* = (PHR.CAT = PP
      PREP = WORD.CAT = PREP
             LEX = !I)
      POBJ = (PHR.CAT = NP
              NP.FEAT = (PROPR = +
                         NUMB = SING
                         GENDER = NEUTR
                         LEX = !UPPSALA)
              NAME1 = (WORD.CAT = NOUN
                       NOUN.FEAT = (PROPR = <* POBJ NP.FEAT PROPR>
                                    NUMB = <* POBJ NP.FEAT NUMB>
                                    GENDER = <* POBJ NP.FEAT GENDER>
                                    LEX = <* POBJ NP.FEAT LEX>))))
```

Fig. 46

```
(* = (PHR.CAT = PP
      PREP = (WORD.CAT = PREP
              LEX = !I)
      POBJ = (PHR.CAT = NP
              NP.FEAT = (PROPR = +
                         NUMB = SING
                         GENDER = NEUTR
                         LEX = !UPPSALA)
              NAME1 = (WORD.CAT = NOUN
                       NOUN.FEAT = ()))))
```

Fig. 47

etc. Semantic features, associated with the individual lexemes, are stored in the base of lexemes and retrieved by means of the path expression :-convention. The formulation and triggering of verbaction rules will be illustrated below.

A main clause may be predicted by an operation invoking such a rule in the start rule of the grammar, see Figure 48 (cf. Fig. 8).

The evaluation of the start rule will lead to the insertion of two active edges from and to vertex 1, each one initiating its own process. The dictionary search edge will get to work at once, whereas the main clause edge will have to wait until the material it needs for its operation, GDs of words and phrases, presents itself as a result of the processes initiated by the dictionary search. Our first example will be *Kvinnorna bor i Uppsala.* (Engl. *The women live in Uppsala.*) Bottom-up we will recognize *kvinnorna* and *i Uppsala* as phrases (Figs. 45 and 47), and *bor* (Engl. *live*) as a word (Fig. 49).

In the analysis of the clause we will recognize its subject, predicator, and locational object. In addition to these grammatical functions, we will also state the *fundament* of the clause. The fundament is a positionally defined term introduced by the Danish linguist Diderichsen in his field analysis theory (see Diderichsen 1957). It denotes the first constituent of a main clause. In Swedish, basically, any constituent type may occupy the fundament position.

In Figure 50 we present a simplified version of a declarative main clause rule for Swedish which will do for the current example.

The domain of the rule is phrase category or word category, since it has to apply to phrases and words (e.g., the verb). It starts its operation by three default assignments to the clause feature set, i.e., stating CLause to be the phrase category, MAIN to be the value of the TYPE descriptor and DECLarative the value of the mode descriptor. In the next operation the whole GD of the inactive edge is assigned to the FUND descriptor of the active one. In our example thus, the NP *kvinnorna* will be regarded as fundament. Next, an advancement is made to the position of the finite verb (Fig. 51).

The first operation of V.FIN is a presence operation testing for a finite verb. The following three operations account for the building of a predicator G, and in the final operation tense is assigned to the clause feature set from the verb. After the execution of V.FIN an advancement is made for the recognition of the subject (Fig. 52).

In Swedish main clauses, there are two positions that the subject may occupy, either the fundament position, or the position after the finite verb[7]. SUBJECT accordingly splits the processing into two parallel processes. In the first one, a test is made for an NP in the current position. If one is found, and its case is unmarked[8], it will be accepted as the subject, so far, and an advancement be made. This alternative isn't applicable to our example. According to the second alternative, the fundament is an NP. If the case condition is fulfilled, the fundament will be interpreted as the subject. In addition to assigning the GD of the fundament to

---

[7] If clause adverbials are temporarily disregarded.

[8] As concerns the case category of Swedish nouns we distinguish between the unmarked case and the genitive case.

```
START.RULE          PROCESS(SVE.DIC),
                    PROCESS(MAIN);
                      Domain: CHAR;
```

Fig. 48

```
(* = (WORD.CAT = VERB
      VERB.FEAT = (LEX = !BO
                   FIN = +
                   TENSE = PRES)))
```

Fig. 49

```
MAIN      <& PHR.CAT> :=: 'CL,
          <& CL.FEAT TYPE> :=: 'MAIN,
          <& CL.FEAT MODE> :=: 'DECL,
          <& FUND> :=: <*>,
          ADVANCE,
          V.FIN,
          ADVANCE,
          SUBJECT,
          DO(<& PRED VP.FEAT LEX :VERBACTION>),
          FUNDCHECK,
          END.OF.SENT,
          STORE;
            Domain: PHR.CAT/WORD.CAT;
```

Fig. 50

```
V.FIN
   <* VERB.FEAT FIN>,
   <& PRED PHR.CAT> :=: 'VP,
   <& PRED VP.FEAT FIN> :=: <* VERB.FEAT FIN>,
   <& PRED> :=: <*>,
   <& CL.FEAT TENSE> :=: <* VERB.FEAT TENSE>;
```

Fig. 51

```
SUBJECT
   (<* PHR.CAT> :=: 'NP,
    <* NP.FEAT CASE> :=: 'NIL,
    <& SUBJ> :=: <*>,
    ADVANCE//
    <& FUND PHR.CAT> = 'NP,
    <& FUND NP.FEAT CASE> = 'NIL,
    <& SUBJ> :=: <& FUND>,
    <& FUNC FUND>:=: 'SUBJ);
```

Fig. 52

```
TYPE.BO
   PRED.SUBJ('ANIM),
   OBJ.LOC;
```

Fig. 53

```
PRED.SUBJ
   <& SUBJ NP.FEAT LEX :REF> :=: ?1;
```

Fig. 54

the subject descriptor, we mark the fundament as subject. This alternative will succeed in our example, and the analysis will go on without any advancement.

If we have a clause structure (NP V NP) with both NPs unmarked with regard to case, both alternatives will be pursued in independent processes, and be subject to semantic tests by the verbaction rule.

3.4.1.1 An Example of a Verbaction Rule and Its Triggering. The verbaction rule may be triggered as soon as the finite verb has been found. However, since all Swedish clauses have a subject[9], and there are only two positions to be considered, regardless of the individual verb, we have chosen to refer the tentative recognition of the subject to the general part of the main clause rule. Thus the verbaction rule in our parser is triggered after the execution of the subject subrule.

Verbaction rules are defined for classes, types, of verbs. For instance, TYPE.BO (Engl. TYPE.LIVE) is the name of a rule defined for verbs requiring an animate subject and a locational object (Fig. 53).

PRED.SUBJ('ANIM) of TYPE.BO expresses the demand on an animate subject. The operation illustrates how *a subrule may be activated with an argument.* The formulation of PRED.SUBJ is presented in Figure 54.

?1 in PRED.SUBJ is a formal parameter which will be substituted by the argument of the call. The path expression of the unification operation evaluates to the value of the property REF (for referent) associated with the lexeme referent of the subject (!KVINNA). The value of REF for !KVINNA is ANIM in our lexeme base, and thus the subject test will succeed, and the OBJ.LOC subrule (Fig. 55) be evaluated.

The locational object may be found in the current position (the position after the finite verb) or in the fundament position. It may be realized as a prepositional or an adverbial phrase. These four cases are accounted for by OBJ.LOC, formulated as a dependent disjunction. Before accepting a constituent as a locational object, the rule retrieves the value of the property CIRC (for circumstantial) of its head from the lexeme base and verifies that it is equal to LOC (for location). This is true for *Uppsala* in our example, and the first branch of the first alternative of the disjunction will apply. As in the subject subrule, if the grammatical function being recognized is fulfilled by the fundament, the GD of the fundament is accordingly marked.

Names of verbaction rules are associated with the verbal lexemes in the lexeme base. Thus for each verbal lexeme, the name of its verbaction rule is given as the value of the property VERBACTION in the base. The rule is activated in the main clause rule by means of the operation

[9] Disregarding elliptic constructions.

```
OBJ.LOC
  (<* PHR.CAT> = 'PP,
   <* POBJ NP.FEAT LEX :CIRC> = 'LOC/
   <* PHR.CAT> = 'ADVP,
   <* ADVP.FEAT LEX :CIRC> = 'LOC),
  <& OBJ.LOC> :=: <*>,
  ADVANCE/
  (<& FUND PHR.CAT> = 'PP,
   <& FUND POBJ NP.FEAT LEX :CIRC> = 'LOC/
   <& FUND PHR.CAT> = 'ADVP,
   <& FUND ADVP.FEAT LEX :CIRC> = 'LOC),
   <& OBJ.LOC> :=: <& FUND>,
   <& FUND FUNC> :=: 'OBJ.LOC;
```

Fig. 55

DO(<& PRED VP.FEAT LEX :VERBACTION>)

The path expression of the DO-operation evaluates to the name of the verbaction rule associated with the lexeme referent of the predicator, and the DO-operator activates the rule. In our example, the path expression will retrieve TYPE.BO from !BO in the base and the rule will be evaluated.

The DO-operation of the main clause rule is an example of *variable subrule call.* Due to the DO-operation, various actions are taken in the main clause rule, depending on syntactic and semantic properties of the finite verb. In other words, the main clause rule represents in a compact way a variety of main clause rules.

The DO-operation of the main clause rule (Fig. 50) is followed by a subrule named FUNDCHECK verifying that the fundament has been assigned a grammatical function. Since the fundament constituent in our example has been interpreted as the subject of the clause, the test is fulfilled, and the end of sentence test will be performed. The period signals the end of the sentence, and the analysis has come to an end. The resulting GD is presented in Figure 56.

The grammar fragment on which the analysis in Figure 56 is based will also recognize clauses in which the locational object has been topicalized, such as *I Uppsala bor kvinnorna.* The resulting GD will differ only with regard to the fundament and its function.

The action rule mechanism used for the recognition of the objects of the verb may, of course, be used for for other kinds of constructions as well, e.g., for the recognition of the objects of an adjectival phrase such as *bra på att sjunga* (Engl. *good at singing*).

3.4.1.2 Clause Adverbials. For the handling of sentence adverbials, the main clause rule has to be further elaborated. In Swedish main clauses, sentence adverbials may be found in the fundament position, in the position immediately after the finite verb, in the position after the subject (if the subject is not in the fundament position), and in the final position. For the expression of optional con-

```
(* = (PHR.CAT = CL
      CL.FEAT = (TYPE = MAIN
                 MODE = DECL
                 TENSE = PRES)
      FUND = (PHR.CAT = NP
              NP.FEAT = (GENDER = UTR
                         NUMB = PLUR
                         SPEC = DEF
                         LEX = !KVINNA)
              HEAD = (WORD.CAT = NOUN
                      NOUN.FEAT = (GENDER = <* NP.FEAT GENDER>
                                   DECL = -OR
                                   LEX = <* NP.FEAT LEX>
                                   NUMB = <* NP.FEAT NUMB>
                                   FORM = <* NP.FEAT SPEC>))
              FUNC = SUBJ)
      PRED = (PHR.CAT = VP
              VP.FEAT = (FIN = +
                         LEX = !BO)
              HEAD = (WORD.CAT = VERB
                      VERB.FEAT = (LEX = !BO
                                   FIN = +
                                   TENSE = PRES)))
      SUBJ = <* SENT FUND>
      OBJ.LOC = (PHR.CAT = PP
                 PREP = WORD.CAT = PREP
                        LEX = !I)
                 POBJ = (PHR.CAT = NP
                         NP.FEAT = (PROPR = +
                                    NUMB = SING
                                    GENDER = NEUTR
                                    LEX = !UPPSALA)
                         NAME1 = (WORD.CAT = NOUN
                                  NOUN.FEAT = ())))))
```

Fig. 56

stituents the dependent disjunction operation is used, with an alternative which is always true (CONTINUE). This is demonstrated in Figure 57, showing the subrule for the recognition of negating, emphatic, adversative, and conjunctive adverbials in Swedish. The rule is inserted into the main clause rule after V.FIN and after SUBJECT.

Circumstantial adverbials denoting location and time are placed in the fundament, or in the final position. For the recognition of such adverbials in the final position, a subrule ADVERBIALS2 has been formulated and inserted into the main clause rule before FUNDCHECK. FUNDCHECK, on the other hand, will

```
ADVERBIALS1
    <* PHR.CAT> ::: 'ADVP,
    (<* NEG>/ <* EMPH>/ <* ADVERS>/ <* CONJ>),
    <& ADV.SENT> ::: <*>, ADVANCE/
    CONTINUE;
```

Fig. 57

```
FUNDCHECK
    <& FUND FUNC>/
    <& FUND PHR.CAT> ::: 'PP,
    ((<& FUND POBJ NP.FEAT LEX :CIRC> = 'LOC,
      <& ADV.LOC> ::: <& FUND>, <& FUND FUNC> ::: 'ADV.LOC/
      <& FUND POBJ NP.FEAT LEX :CIRC> = 'TEMP,
      <& ADV.TEMP> ::: <& FUND>, <& FUND FUNC> ::: 'ADV.TEMP)/
    <& FUND PHR.CAT> ::: 'ADVP,
    (<& FUND ADVP.FEAT LEX :CIRC> = 'LOC,
     <& ADV.LOC> ::: <& FUND>, <& FUND FUNC> ::: 'ADV.LOC/
     <& FUND ADVP.FEAT LEX :CIRC> = 'TEMP,
     <& ADV.TEMP> ::: <& FUND>, <& FUND FUNC> ::: 'ADV.TEMP);
```

Fig. 58

be responsible for interpreting the fundament as a clause adverbial. It first checks if the fundament has been assigned a grammatical function (by the verbaction rule of the clause), and if not, tests if it fulfills the requirements for being interpreted as a circumstantial adverbial (Fig. 58).

På sommaren bor kvinnorna i Uppsala. (Engl. *In the summer the women live in Uppsala.*) is an example of a clause with a temporal adverbial in the fundament position that would be recognized by FUNDCHECK (the second branch of the second alternative).

3.4.1.3 Discontinuous Constituents. The analysis of discontinuous signs in the UCP framework will be discussed with Swedish particle verbs, or complex predicators, as an example. Particle verbs such as *komma ihåg* (Engl. *remember*) will have to be recognized on the clause level, since clause adverbials of the ADVERBIALS1 type intervene between the head of the verb and its particle. *Eva kommer inte ihåg namnet.* (Engl. *Eve doesn't remember the name.*) may serve as an illustration. An extended version of the main clause rules taking sentence adverbials and particle verbs into account is presented in Figure 59.

The particle subrule checks if the current constituent is a particle. If so, it generates a lexeme reference concatenating the lexeme reference of the head of the predicator with that of the particle, and assigns it to the VP. It further includes an advancement to the next constituent, before the verbaction rule is triggered. The verbaction rule to be triggered will be the one associated with the lexeme reference of the VP, i. e., the concatenated one. This must be so since the argument structure

```
     MAIN
        <& PHR.CAT> ::: 'CL,
        <& CL.FEAT TYPE> ::: 'MAIN,
        <& CL.FEAT MODE> ::: 'DECL,
        <& FUND> ::: <*>,
        ADVANCE,
        V.FIN,
        ADVANCE,
-->     ADVERBIALS1,
        SUBJECT,
-->     ADVERBIALS1,
-->     PARTICLE,
        DO(<& PRED VP.FEAT LEX :VERBACTION>),
-->     ADVERBIALS2,
        FUNDCHECK,
        END.OF.SENT,
        STORE;
         Domain: PHR.CAT / WORD.CAT;
```

Fig. 59

of the simple verb differs from that of the complex one[10]. The verbaction rule associated with !KOMMA!IHÅG is shown in Figure 60, and in Figure 61 we present the GD resulting from the analysis of the example clause. (In this illustration, and in the following ones, we present only the lex descriptor of the phrasal feature sets, to gain space.)

In the analysis of periphrastic tense expressions, the triggering of the verbaction rule of the main verb may be handled by the verbaction rule of the auxiliary, responsible for recognizing the main verb form.

Subjunctive clauses are analyzed bottom-up by rules invoked by the subjunction. Their grammatical function is recognized by the verbaction rule of the main clause. An example of a sentence with a clause complement is given in Figure 62. (*Hon tycker, att det är svårt.* Engl. *She thinks that it is difficult.*)

Relative clauses are analyzed bottom-up by the relative clause rule invoked by the relative pronoun. The grammatical function of the clause is recognized by the NP rule. In Figure 63 we present the GD of the object of the clause *Eva har en bror, som heter Erik.* (Engl. *Eve has a brother who is called Erik.*)

3.4.2 The Infinitive Clause

During the analysis of an infinitive clause we need access to its implicit subject in order to verify the semantic restrictions imposed on it. Since it is to be found in the superordinate clause, the infinitive clause cannot favorably be analyzed bottom-up

[10] Taking into account NPs introduced by an adjectival phrase, or the head noun.

```
TYPE.MINNAS
    PREDSUBJ('ANIM),
    (DIROBJ('ANIM)/DIROBJ('THING))
```

Fig. 60

```
(* = (PHR.CAT = CL
      CL.FEAT = (TYPE = MAIN
                 MODE = DECL
                 TENSE = PRES)
      FUND = (PHR.CAT = NP
              NP.FEAT = (LEX = !EVA)
              NAME1 = (WORD.CAT = NOUN
                       NOUN.FEAT = (FIRST = +))
              FUNC = SUBJ)
      PRED = (PHR.CAT = VP
              VP.FEAT = (LEX = !KOMMA!HÅG)
              HEAD = (WORD.CAT = VERB
                      VERB.FEAT = (LEX = !KOMMA))
              PART =  PHR.CAT = ADVP
                      WORD.CAT = ADV
                      ADVP.FEAT = (LEX = !IHÅG)))
      ADV.SENT =  NEG = +
                  PHR.CAT = ADVP
                  WORD.CAT = ADV
                  ADVP.FEAT = (LEX = !INTE))
      SUBJ = <* SENT FUND>
      OBJ = (PHR.CAT = NP
             NP.FEAT = (LEX = !NAMN)
             HEAD = (WORD.CAT = NOUN
                     NOUN.FEAT = (DECL = - ))))
```

Fig. 61

by a rule triggered by the infinitive form. It should rather be analyzed top-down by a rule predicted by the finite verb of the superordinate clause. Further, the prediction should include the implicit subject. This can be done in UCP, making use of the process operator, bringing along the subject as its argument. We will demonstrate how this is done, using the example *Eva vill ha kaffe.* (Engl. *Eve wants to have coffee.*) We start by displaying the GD resulting from our analysis (Fig. 64), in which the infinitival complements is presented as the value of the functional PRED.INF descriptor.

The infinitive clause *ha kaffe* is analyzed by an infinitive clause rule invoked by the verbaction rule TYPE.VILJA (Fig. 65).

In addition to requiring an animate subject, the rule specifies two parallel processes. In the first one, the infinitive clause rule (INFINITIVE1) is invoked by

```
(* = (PHR.CAT = CL
      CL.FEAT = (TYPE = MAIN
                 MODE = DECL
                 TENSE = PRES)
      FUND = (PHR.CAT = NP
              NP.FEAT = (LEX = !HON)
              HEAD = (WORD.CAT = PRO)
              FUNC = SUBJ)
      PRED = (PHR.CAT = VP
              VP.FEAT = (LEX = !TYCKA)
              HEAD = (WORD.CAT = VERB
                      VERB.FEAT = ()))
      SUBJ = <* FUND>
      OBJ = (PHR.CAT = CL
             CL.FEAT = (TYPE = SUB
                        MODE = DECL
                        TENSE = PRES)
             COMPL = (LEX = !ATT.CONJ
                      PHR.CAT = SUBJU)
             SUBJ = (PHR.CAT = NP
                     NP.FEAT = (LEX = !DEN)
                     HEAD = (WORD.CAT = PRO))
             PRED = (PHR.CAT = VP
                     VP.FEAT = (LEX = !VARA)
                     HEAD =  WORD.CAT = VERB
                             VERB.FEAT = ())
             PRED.SUBJ = (PHR.CAT = ADJP
                          ADJP.FEAT = (LEX = !SVÅR)
                          HEAD = (WORD.CAT = ADJ)
                                  ADJ.FEAT = ()))))
```

Fig. 62

PROCESS bringing along a copy of the current subject. In the second one, a test is made for an infinitive clause, and if one is there, its GD will be assigned to the PRED.INF descriptor. It will be available after the execution of the INFINITIVE1 rule (Fig. 66).

V.INF of INFINITIVE1 tests for an infinitive verb form, and builds a predicator descriptor with an infinitive VP. The DO-operator evaluates the verbaction rule of this infinitive, in our example TYPE.HA (Fig. 67).

To account for infinitive clauses in which an object has been topicalized, as is possible in Swedish, the verbaction rule of the superordinate clause has to bring forward not only its subject but also its fundament (Fig. 68). *Kaffe vill Eva ha.* is an example of such a clause (Fig. 69). The interpretation of the fundament in such cases is handled by the verbaction rule of the infinitive verb.

```
(* = (PHR.CAT = CL
      ...
      OBJ =
       (PHR.CAT = NP
        NP.FEAT = (LEX = !BROR)
        CORR = (PHR.CAT = NP
                NP.FEAT = (LEX = !BROR)
                QUANT = (PHR.CAT = QP
                         QP.FEAT = (LEX = !EN)
                         QUANT =  (WORD.CAT = QUANT)
                                   QUANT.FEAT = ())
                HEAD = (WORD.CAT = NOUN
                        NOUN.FEAT = (LEX = !BROR)))
        QUAL =
         (PHR.CAT = CL
          CL.FEAT = (TYPE = SUB
                     MODE = REL
                     TENSE = PRES)
          COMPL =  PHR.CAT = SUBJU
                   WORD.CAT = SUBJU
                   REL = +)
          PRED = (PHR.CAT = VP
                  VP.FEAT = (LEX = !HETA)
                  HEAD = (WORD.CAT = VERB
                          VERB.FEAT = ()))
          PRED.SUBJ = (PHR.CAT = NP
                       NP.FEAT = (LEX = !ERIK)
                       NAME1 = (WORD.CAT = NOUN
                                NOUN.FEAT = (FIRST = +))))))
```

Fig. 63

A special case is the one when the infinitive clause has been topicalized as in *Ha kaffe vill Eva.* It can be handled in the following way. The main clause rule inspects the first word, and if it is found to be an infinitive, INFINITIVE2 is invoked bottom-up. Disregarding the subject function, it creates a GD of the infinitive clause with its objects. The constituent thus recognized will be regarded as the fundament of the main clause, and brought along by the TYPE.VILJA rule for the analysis of the complete infinitive clause. INFINITIVE1 will have to be accordingly extended to account for this case in which the verbaction rule that it needs is retrieved from the VP of the fundament.

```
(* = (PHR.CAT = CL
      CL.FEAT = (TYPE = MAIN
                 MODE = DECL
                 TENSE = PRES)
      FUND = (PHR.CAT = NP
              NP.FEAT = (LEX = !EVA)
              NAME1 = (WORD.CAT = NOUN
                       NOUN.FEAT = <* FUND NP.FEAT>)
              FUNC = SUBJ)
      PRED = (PHR.CAT = VP
              VP.FEAT = (LEX = !VILJA)
              HEAD = (WORD.CAT = VERB
                      VERB.FEAT = (TENSE = <* CL.FEAT TENSE>)))
      SUBJ = <* FUND>
      PRED.INF = (SUBJ = (PHR.CAT = <* FUND PHR.CAT>
                          NP.FEAT = <* FUND NP.FEAT>
                          NAME1 = <* FUND NAME1>
                          FUNC = SUBJ
                          DUMMY = +)
                  PHR.CAT = CL
                  CL.FEAT = (TYPE = INF)
                  PRED = (PHR.CAT = VP
                          VP.FEAT = (LEX = !HA)
                          HEAD = (WORD.CAT = VERB
                                  VERB.FEAT = (STEM = ()
                                               CONJ = I)))
                  OBJ = (PHR.CAT = NP
                         NP.FEAT = (LEX = !KAFFE)
                         HEAD = (WORD.CAT = NOUN
                                 NOUN.FEAT = ()))))))
```

Fig. 64

```
TYPE.VILJA
     PRED.SUBJ('ANIM),
     (<& COPY SUBJ> :=: <& SUBJ>,
      <& COPY SUBJ DUMMY>:=: '+,
      PROCESS(INFINITIVE1, <& COPY>)//
      <* PHR.CAT> = 'CL, <* CL.FEAT TYPE> = 'INF,
      <& PRED.INF> :=: <*>, ADVANCE);
```

Fig. 65

```
INFINITIVE1
   <& PHR.CAT> :=: 'CL,
   <& CL.FEAT TYPE> :=: 'INF,
   V.INF,
   ADVANCE,
   DO(<& PRED VP.FEAT LEX :VERBACTION>),
   MINORSTORE;
    Domain: PHR.CAT/WORD.CAT;
```

Fig. 66

```
TYPE.HA
   (PREDSUBJ('ANIM)/ PREDSUBJ('LOC)),
   DIROBJ;
```

Fig. 67

```
TYPE.VILJA
     PRED.SUBJ('ANIM),
     (<& COPY SUBJ> :=: <& SUBJ>, <& COPY SUBJ DUMMY>:=: '+,
      <& COPY FUND>:=:<& FUND>, <& COPY SUBJ DUMMY>:=: '+,
      PROCESS(INFINITIVE1, <& COPY>)//
      <* PHR.CAT> = 'CL, <* CL.FEAT TYPE> = 'INF,
      <& PRED.INF> :=: <*>, ADVANCE);
```

Fig. 68

3.4.3 Coordinated Expressions

Coordinated main clauses are analyzed as a construct called a *sentence*. In Figure 70 we demonstrate a GD of the sentence *Hon studerar, och han arbetar.* (Engl. *She studies, and he works.*)

The sentence rule is invoked bottom-up from the main clause rule at the recognition of a comma sign or a conjunction, and the main clause rule is recursively called top-down at the position after the comma sign or the conjunction. The final part of the main clause rule, responsible for closing the main clause constituent and for further processing of this, is displayed in Figure 71. The operations are inserted into the main clause rule immediately after FUNDCHECK (cf. Fig. 59).

The strategy applied in the analysis of coordinated clauses with a common subject, deleted in the second clause, is similar to the one used in the analysis of the infinitive clause. For the analysis of the second clause, we invoke the clause rule with and without a copy of the fundament of the first clause. This is done in parallel, and the fundament brought along is assigned a dummy marker. The operation responsible for this rule invocation in the main clause rule is presented in Figure 72.

```
(* = (PHR.CAT = CL
      CL.FEAT = (TYPE = MAIN
                 MODE = DECL
                 TENSE = PRES)
      FUND = (PHR.CAT = NP
              NP.FEAT = (LEX = !KAFFE)
              HEAD = (WORD.CAT = NOUN
                      NOUN.FEAT = ())
              FUNC = PRED.INF.OBJ)
      PRED = (PHR.CAT = VP
              VP.FEAT = (!VILJA)
              HEAD = (WORD.CAT = VERB
                      VERB.FEAT = (TENSE = <* CL.FEAT TENSE>)))
      SUBJ = (PHR.CAT = NP
              NP.FEAT = (LEX = !EVA)
              NAME1 = (WORD.CAT = NOUN
                       NOUN.FEAT = <* SUBJ NP.FEAT>))
      PRED.INF = (SUBJ = (PHR.CAT = <* SUBJ PHR.CAT>
                          NP.FEAT = <* SUBJ NP.FEAT>
                          NAME1 = <* SUBJ NAME1>
                          DUMMY = +)
                  FUND = (PHR.CAT = <* FUND PHR.CAT>
                          NP.FEAT = <* FUND NP.FEAT>
                          HEAD = <* FUND HEAD>
                          DUMMY = +
                          FUNC = OBJ)
                  PHR.CAT = CL
                  CL.FEAT = (TYPE = INF)
                  PRED = (PHR.CAT = VP
                          VP.FEAT = (LEX = !HA)
                          HEAD = (WORD.CAT = VERB
                                  VERB.FEAT = (STEM = ()
                                               CONJ = I)))
                  OBJ = <* PRED.INF FUND>)))
```

Fig. 69

Hon arbetar och studerar. (Engl. *She works and studies.*) is an example of such a clause. Its GD is presented in Figure 73. (In a comment box we present the GD of the fundament of the second clause in the full display mode to make explicit its referential values.)

Coordinated NPs, ADJPs, ADVPs, QUANTPs, PPs, INFPs, and subjunctive clauses can be analyzed according to the same basic strategy. Each phrase type needs its own rule, though, since the feature set characterizing the coordinated construction differs for the various categories.

```
(* = (SENT.CAT = SENT
      1 = (PHR.CAT = CL
           CL.FEAT = (TYPE = MAIN
                      MODE = DECL
                      TENSE = PRES)
           FUND = (PHR.CAT = NP
                   NP.FEAT = (LEX = !HON)
                   HEAD = (WORD.CAT = PRO)
                   FUNC = SUBJ)
           PRED = (PHR.CAT = VP
                   VP.FEAT = (LEX = !STUDERA)
                   HEAD = (WORD.CAT = VERB
                           VERB.FEAT = (STEM = ()
                                        CONJ = I)))
           SUBJ = <* 1 FUND>)
      CONJ = (WORD.CAT = CONJ
              LEX = !OCH
              COP = +)
      2 = (PHR.CAT = CL
           CL.FEAT = (TYPE = MAIN
                      MODE = DECL
                      TENSE = PRES)
           FUND = (PHR.CAT = NP
                   NP.FEAT = (LEX = !HAN)
                   HEAD = (WORD.CAT = PRO)
                   FUNC = SUBJ)
           PRED = (PHR.CAT = VP
                   VP.FEAT = (LEX = !ARBETA)
                   HEAD = (WORD.CAT = VERB
                           VERB.FEAT = (STEM = ()
                                        CONJ = I)))
           SUBJ = <* 2 FUND>)))
```

Fig. 70

```
(END.OF.SENT, STORE/
 COORD.TEST,
 MINORSTORE,
 ADVANCE,
 (<* WORD.CAT> = 'CONJ, ADVANCE/ CONTINUE),
 PROCESS(MAIN),
 MAJORPROCESS(SENTENCE));
```

Fig. 71

```
(PROCESS(MAIN)//
 <& COPY FUND> ::: <& FUND>,
 <& COPY FUND DUMMY> ::: '+,
 PROCESS(MAIN, <& COPY>))
```

Fig. 72

```
(* = (SENT.CAT = SENT
   1 = (PHR.CAT = CL
        CL.FEAT = (TYPE = MAIN
                   MODE = DECL
                   TENSE = PRES)
        FUND = (PHR.CAT = NP
                NP.FEAT = (LEX = !HON)
                HEAD = (WORD.CAT = PRO)
                FUNC = SUBJ)
        PRED = (PHR.CAT = VP
                VP.FEAT = (!ARBETA)
                HEAD = (WORD.CAT = VERB
                        VERB.FEAT = (STEM = ()
                                     CONJ = I)))
        SUBJ = <* 1 FUND>)
   CONJ = (WORD.CAT = CONJ
           LEX = !OCH
           COP = +)            ------------------------------------------
   2 = (FUND = (DUMMY = +)| 2 = (FUND = (PHR.CAT = <* 1 FUND PHR.CAT>
        PHR.CAT = CL      |              NP.FEAT = <* 1 FUND NP.FEAT>
        CL.FEAT = (TYPE = |              HEAD = <* 1 FUND HEAD>
                   MODE = |              FUNC = <* 1 FUND FUNC>
                   TENSE =|              DUMMY = +)
        PRED = (PHR.CAT = ------------------------------------------
                VP.FEAT = (LEX = !STUDERA)
                HEAD = (WORD.CAT = VERB
                        VERB.FEAT = (STEM = ()
                                     CONJ = I)))
        SUBJ = <* 2 FUND>)))
```

Fig. 73

For the sake of illustration, we have been using a main clause rule recognizing declarative main clauses only. In our Swedish parser, the main clause rule splits processing up into three branches, for declarative clauses, WH-questions, and YES/NO-questions, respectively. The choice is based on an inspection of the first word.

3.4.4 Rule-Driven and Data-Driven Processing

During our work on the proposed modifiers of the Swedish NP, we saw a possibility of avoiding rule repetition by letting the subrules of the NP-rule function as proper rules as well, to be invoked bottom-up. As an illustration, we present the Swedish NP *alla dessa mina många andra sådana gamla bilar* (Engl. *all these my many other such old cars*), with the maximum number of preposed modifiers.

In his field analysis of Swedish NPs Loman (Loman 1956), distinguishes a *determination field*, a *description field* (occupied by adjectival attributes), and a *kernel field* (occupied by the head noun). The determination field has six positions, and, accordingly, the modifiers concerned are referred to one of six position classes. Basically, they express *totality* (e.g., *alla*), *determinacy* (e.g., *dessa*), *possessivity* (e.g., *mina*), *quantity* (e.g., *många*), *selectivity* (e.g., *andra*), and *comparison* (e.g., *sådana*). The internal order between the position classes is strict, but all positions need not be filled, and any position class may introduce an NP. Thus we may have NPs such as *dessa mina ... bilar, mina många ... bilar, många andra ... bilar,* etc. Consequently, every attribute must be regarded as an NP-introducer, and invoke an NP-rule bottom-up. Unless we manage to use the subrules of the maximum NP-rule for these purposes, we will in all have 8 NP-rules involving a great amount of repetition. In Figure 74 we present the first two subrules (cf. states) of the NP-rule, designed for the analysis of the first two position classes (denoted TOT for totality, and DET for determinacy).

NP.TOT is invoked by members of position class 1. It starts building an NP with a totality modifier as its first daughter constituent. The daughter constituent is assigned to the functional descriptor TOT. Then an advancement is made to NP.DET.

NP.DET recognizes an optional determiner, and assigns is to the DET descriptor. Then an advancement is made to NP.POSS for the recognition of a possessive modifier (a possessive pronoun or an NP in the genitive case), etc. As mentioned above, in addition to succeeding a totality attribute, a determiner may introduce an NP. If so, the recognition of the determiner should lead to the invocation of an NP-rule with the determiner as its first daughter. NP.DET works for both cases. When invoked by a determiner, its GD is empty and the building of an NP must be started. This is the motivation for the initial unification operation of the rule. It doesn't add to the GD of the active edge when NP.DET is activated from NP.TOT but conforms with it. The operation is a disjunction with an always true alternative, since the determiner is optional in an NP introduced by a totality attribute.

The basic NP-rule[11] consists of a number of subrules [12] which are invoked either top-down, predicted by a preceding sister, or bottom-up at the recognition of a word belonging to one of the six position classes. (NP.TOT recognizing the leftmost subconstituent is invoked bottom-up only.) In the latter case the word is treated as an NP introducer. Such a treatment is, however, pointless if the attribute

[11] In addition to this NP-rule, there are others which recognize NPs including proper names and pronouns, and NPs in special expressions for time, measure, and address. Coordinated NPs are recognized by separate rules. Postmodifiers are also accounted for.

[12] In all, the following subrules constitute the basic NP-rule: NP.TOT, NP.DET, NP.POSS, NP.QUANT, NP.SEL, NP.COMP, NP.ADJP, and NP.NOUN.

```
NP.TOT
  <& PHR.CAT> :=: 'NP,
  <* WORD.CAT> = 'TOT,
  <& NP.FEAT SPEC> :=: <* SPEC>,
  <& NP.FEAT NUMB> :=: <* NUMB>,
  <& NP.FEAT CASE> :=: <* CASE>,
  (<* NUMB> = 'SING,
   <& NP.FEAT GENDER> :=: <* GENDER>/ CONTINUE),
  <& TOT> :=: <*>,
  ADVANCE(NP.DET);

    Domain: WORD.CAT;


NP.DET
  <& PHR.CAT> :=: 'NP,
  (<* WORD.CAT> = 'DET,
   <& NP.FEAT SPEC> :=: <* SPEC>,
   <& NP.FEAT NUMB> :=: <* NUMB>,
   (<* NUMB> = 'SING,
    <& NP.FEAT GENDER> :=: <* GENDER>/ CONTINUE),
   <& DET> :=: <*>,
   ADVANCE/CONTINUE),
  NP.POSS;

    Domain: WORD.CAT / PHR.CAT;

    Condition: not TOT;
```

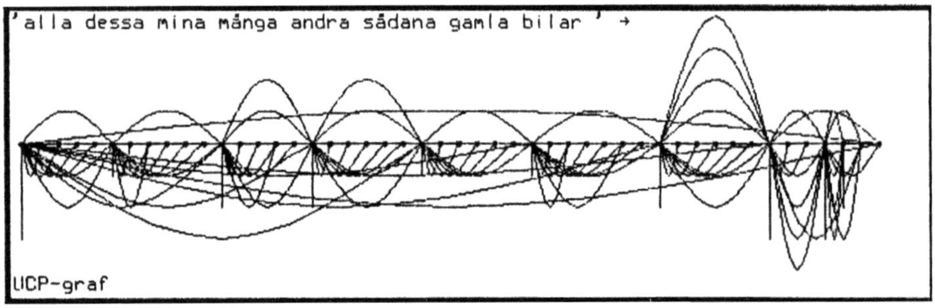

Fig. 74

is preceded by another legitimate attribute. The UCP-formalism, though, provides a device for making bottom-up rule invocation dependent on the preceding context, i.e., for expressing *a condition for the bottom-up activation of a rule.* It works as follows.

A vertex is characterized by a set of ingoing and a set of outgoing edges. Partly recognized constituents are represented by ingoing active edges. If we want to make the bottom-up activation of a rule at a certain vertex dependent on the preceding context, we may do so inspecting the GDs of the ingoing active edges. The condition part of the rule to be activated specifies to top-level attributes that must (or mustn't) be part of the GD of some ingoing active edge for the rule to be activated. NP.DET (Fig. 74) illustrates this mechanism. *not* TOT means that the rule will not be invoked bottom-up if the determiner is preceded by a totality attribute.

The condition option has to be used with great care, since it is dependent on the order in which the tasks are carried out.

3.5 A Summary of the UCP Formalism

The language description of a UCP parser is presented as a grammar, a dictionary of stems, roots, and non-declinable words, a dictionary of signs of punctuation, a number of affix dictionaries, a base of characters, and a base of lexemes. The rules of the grammar and the dictionaries are expressed in the procedural UCP formalism, whereas the items of the bases are represented by atoms with associated property lists.

The grammar can be thought of as a network grammar. It consists of a number of rules (cf. states). The first rule of the grammar has a special status, in being invoked by the processor. The rest of the rules are activated by operations in the grammar and the dictionaries.

A grammar rule has a *unique name,* a *rule body,* and a *domain specification.* Its format also provides an optional entry for the specification of a *condition for its activation.* The rule name is any string of characters. The rule body is a *conjunction* of operations, formulated by means of a number of predefined operators, conjunction being one of them. The domain specifies to what kind of linguistic items the rule applies. Here we present those attribute names that have to be present in the top level of the GD of the inactive edge for the rule to apply. In formulating the domain specification we use a subset of the linguistic operators.

3.5.1 The Linguistic Operators

There are 4 kinds of linguistic operators, i.e., operators with the effect of adding new edges to the chart, operators which apply to GDs, an operator for retrieving property values from the bases, and, finally, operators which contribute to a compact formulation of the rules. We will refer to them as *process-oriented, GD-oriented, base-oriented,* and *grammar-oriented,* respectively.

3.5.1.1 Process-Oriented Operators. Initiating a rule means inserting an active edge from and to the same vertex. There are two operators with this effect, i.e.,

(PROCESS dic.name/rule.name) and MAJORPROCESS(dic.name/rule.name). They differ with regard to at which vertex they insert their active edges. PROCESS inserts its edge from and to the *final* vertex of the current active edge, and MAJORPROCESS from and to its *initial* vertex. We may say that PROCESS corresponds to top-down and MAJORPROCESS to bottom-up rule invocation.

Promoting a process can be thought of as 'lengthening' the current active edge to span the inactive edge of the current task. However, since the chart mechanism doesn't permit any changes of already existing edges, a new active edge has to be created. Its GD should record the findings made so far, and its rule specification include those operations of the current process that remain to be carried out. In dictionary search, a pointer to the current position in the dictionary tree should replace the rule specification. The ADVANCE operator creates such an edge. By default it inherits the domain specification of the current active edge. Given a rule name as its argument, though, it adopts the domain specification of that rule.

In addition to simply promoting a process, we may split it up into parallel processes by means of the *independent disjunction* operator. It has the following format.

(op.1, op.2, . . . // op.n, op.n + 1, . . . // . . .)

A succeeding ADVANCE operation will create one active edge for each alternative (the alternatives being separated by //).

STORE and MINORSTORE are responsible for inserting inactive edges into the chart. They differ with regard to span. The edge created by MINORSTORE spans the same two vertices as the current active edge, whereas that of STORE includes the current inactive edge as well. By default, both operators inherit their GDs from the active edge of the current task. They may, however, take sequences of pathexpressions as their arguments. If so, one edge is created for each pathexpression, with a GD identical to its value. Additional vertices will be created as called for. The start- and endpoints of the sequence of inserted edges will coincide with those of the single edge created by default.

3.5.1.2 GD-Oriented Operators. The GD-oriented operators account for the testing and generation of GDs. Their operands are path expressions or simple symbols. The minimal path expressions are < * > and < & >, evaluating to the GD of the inactive and the active edge, respectively. The central GD-oriented operation is *unification, := :*. It works both for testing and assignment, being the only operator available for assignment. In accordance with the general chart philosophy, the UCP unification operator sees to it that the GD of the inactive edge isn't changed by its operation, saving a copy of it, and returning that copy as its value. In the pathexpressions of the unification operation, we name the descriptors to be tested, added, or assigned values. However, for reference to descriptors whose names are current numbers unknown to us (cf. coordination), we use the variables :NEW and :LAST. :NEW ranges over integers, starting with 1 and adding 1 to its value with each call. :LAST retrieves the last top-level descriptor of a GD.

For testing purposes the formalism, in addition, offers the following operators: *presence (< . . . >), negation (not),* and *dependent disjunction (/).* By means of the presence operation, we verify that a certain descriptor is part of a GD, to make sure that a unification operation intended as a test doesn't result in an assignment instead. (Alternatively, we might use the pure testing operator *equivalence (=)*. The advantage of the latter alternative is one of rule transparency.) The negation operator and the dependent disjunction operator could, in principle, be done without, with a more extensive use of conjunction and parallel processing. Negation, though, contributes to economy in the rule writing, and dependent disjunction to processing economy. For processing economy, a *condition* operator *(if . . . then . . . else)* has also been provided.

Concatenation of strings is carried out by juxtaposing path expressions evaluating to simple symbols and/or quoted simple symbols *(<. . .> <. . .> . . .)*.

Conjunction, dependent disjunction, and negation may be used in specifying the domain of a rule.

3.5.1.3 The Base-Oriented Operator. The sole base-oriented operator retrieves a property value stored under an atom defined as a character or a lexeme in one of the two bases. The operator is expressed by means of a special convention in the formulation of the path expression. Prefixing the last item of a path expression by *:*, we signal to the rule interpreter that this item denotes a property to be searched for in one of the bases. The preceding part of the path expression should evaluate to the name of the atom under which the property is stored.

3.5.1.4 Grammar-Oriented Operators. The grammar-oriented operators provide means for expressing the language description in a compact and perspicuous way. In all, there are three such operators, i. e., *simple subrule call, subrule call with variables,* and *variable subrule call.* By subrules we refer to sequences of operations that are part of other rules, but stored as separate entries under their own names in the grammar. In the formulation of a rule, the name of a subrule substitutes the operations that it specifies. When the rule interpreter recognizes a subrule name, it retrieves the operations specified by it and evaluates them. In the formulation of a subrule, we may also use formal parameters. They are expressed as integers, prefixed by *?*. In calling such a subrule, the actual parameters are given as path expressions, or simple symbols, in due order. The value of the first argument will substitute *?1* in the subrule, that of the second argument *?2,* etc. Finally, the DO-operator handles the variable subrule call. Its operand, a path expression, should evaluate to a subrule name, and DO evaluates that subrule.

3.5.1.5 The Origin of the Operators. Some of the operators presented above go back to the *reversible grammar* formalism (see Kay 1977b), i. e., PROCESS with a rule name as its argument (cf. Newprocess rule.name), ADVANCE without an argument (cf. Advance), STORE without arguments (cf. Done), independent disjunction (cf. Alternation), unification (cf. Same), and simple subrule call (cf. Atom). For a formal presentation of the UCP formalism, see Carlsson (1981).

3.6 Implementation

Much work has been devoted to implementing the processor as a solid computer program. It has been developed on a CADR-LMI Lisp machine and later implemented in Common-Lisp for IBM PC and Data General Eclipse MV. Currently, it is being adapted to a XEROX 1186.

A significant part of the implementation was carried out by M. Carlsson (see Carlsson 1981). In charge of current development and maintenance is L. Borin, Center for Computational Linguistics.

4 Applications

4.1 A General Parser for Swedish

The main application of UCP, so far, is a general parser for the analysis of written Swedish text, SVE.UCP. Its grammar and dictionaries have been worked out in cooperation with Lars Ahrenberg, Department of Computer and Information Science, Linköping University. For a presentation of its present coverage, see Sågvall Hein and Ahrenberg (1985).

The GDs generated by SVE.UCP, reflect constituent structure (CS) and functional structure (FS). As concerns the grammatical functions in Swedish we adopted, as far as possible, the traditionally based analysis proposed by Teleman (Teleman 1974). Constituents are described with regard to morphosyntactic category, morphosyntactic features, and constituency. The recognition of the CS of the clause is integrated with the recognition of its FS, and thus, CSs without a functional interpretation are not generated.

The further extension of the Swedish competence of SVE.UCP will be carried out in the project *A Lexicon Oriented Parser for Swedish* (supported by the Swedish Humanistic and Social Science Research Council), initiated 1986 at the Department of Computational Linguistics, University of Gothenburg. In particular, the dictionary of SVE.UCP will be systematically enlarged with material from the comprehensive vocabulary studies of modern Swedish performed there (cf. Allén 1970-1980 and Svensk ordbok).

The primary application domain of the Swedish parser will be in free text information retrieval.

4.2 Medical Text Comprehension

During our work on the parser we have come to be interested in the question of how well a parser of this kind could be integrated in a text comprehension model. With this aim we have started to apply the parser to a set of medical free text reports on suspected side-effect of drugs (Sågvall Hein 1985). A separate version of the general grammar is being tailored for these texts generating slightly pruned GDs. Working on texts, rather than isolated sentences, we need to bring along expectations from one sentence to a succeeding one. We will investigate how far the argument-bringing process operators will reach in this direction.

A more elaborate knowledge base than the present lexeme base is called for in a text comprehension model. In specific, we want to provide the knowledge base with the capacity for playing an active part in the understanding process, and not be limited to the function of passively filtering out semantically valid analyses. A crucial problem is to find valid criteria for distributing the semantic information between the grammar (cf. the verbaction rules) and the knowledge base.

4.3 A Morphological Analyzer for Automatic Keyword Indexing

In cooperation with Uppsala University Computer Center (UDAC) we are involved in a project aiming at the automatic keyword indexing of medical and pharmacological text for information retrieval. In this project, the morphological part of SVE.UCP, referred to as SVE.MORPH, will be responsible for the morphological analysis required for associating the inflectional forms with their corresponding basic forms, lemmas. As a first subgoal, the dictionary should cover the vocabulary of FASS, the Swedish drug catalogue (roughly 600000 current words). Presently, we are building the stem dictionary. According to our preliminary estimations, it will include some 20000 stems.

5 Summary of Experience with UCP

We find that the results we have achieved, so far, in parsing by means of UCP are very promising. The following features especially make it neat and efficient as an NL-processor:

- the clean cut between the processor and the language description,
- the clean control structure provided by the active chart,
- the uniformity in processing achieved by embedding dictionary search, morphological analysis, and syntactic analysis in the general chart framework,
- the generality and flexibility of the procedural formalism which provides for easy communication between grammar, bases, and dictionaries,
- the process-oriented operators which allow for a flexible rule-invocation scheme,
- the possibility of bringing arguments along with the process-invocation operators for constraining dictionary search, and for handling ellipsis,
- the grammar-oriented operators which allow for a compact formulation of grammars, and dictionaries, and
- the solid UCP implementation with the good tracing facilities provided by the trace and the graphics packages.

References

Ahrenberg L (1984) De grammatiska beskrivningarna i SVE.UCP. In: Sågvall Hein (1984)

Allén S et al. (1970-80) Frequency Dictionary of Present-Day Swedish Based on Newspaper Material, 1-4. Stockholm

Bresnan J (ed) (1982) The Mental Representation of Grammatical Relations. MIT Press, Cambridge, Mass.

Carlsson M (1981) Uppsala Chart Parser 2. System Documentation. Report No. UCDL-R-81-1. Center for Computational Linguistics, Uppsala University

Diderichsen P (1957) Elementær dansk grammatik, 2nd ed. Copenhagen
Kaplan RM (1973) A General Syntactic Processor. In: Rustin (1973)
Kaplan R and Bresnan J (1982) Grammatical Representation. In: Bresnan (1982)
Kay M (1967) Experiments with a Powerful Parser, RM-5452-PR. Rand Corporation, Santa Monica
Kay M (1973) The MIND System. In: Rustin (1973)
Kay M (1975) Syntactic Processing and the Functional Sentence Perspective. In: Schank and Nash-Webber (1975)
Kay M (1977a) Morphological and Syntactic Analysis. In: Zampolli (1977)
Kay M (1977b) Reversible Grammar. Summary of the Formalism. Xerox Research Center, Palo Alto
Kimball, J (1973) Seven Principles of Surface Structure Parsing in Natural Language. Cognition **2,** 15-47
Koskenniemi K (1983) Two-Level Morphology: A General Computational Model for Word-Form Recognition and Production. Publications No. 11. University of Helsinki, Department of General Linguistics
Loman B (1956) Om relationen mellan ordföljd och betydelse hos framförställda attributiva bestämningar till substantiviska huvudord. In: Arkiv för Nordisk Filologi **71,** 218-244
Rustin R (ed) (1973) Natural Language Processing. Algorithmics Press, New York; Prentice-Hall, New Jersey
Sågvall, A-L (1973) A System for Automatic Inflectional Analysis, implemented for Russian. Data Linguistica **8,** Stockholm
Sågvall Hein A (ed) (1984) Föredrag från De Nordiska Datalingvistikdagarna 1983. Report No. UCDL-R-84-1. Center for Computational Linguistics, Uppsala University
Sågvall Hein A (1985) On Different Kinds of Knowledge in Medical Text Comprehension. From a Case Study. Presented at a workshop on Logic Programming in Knowledge Engineering. Department of Computer Science, University of Copenhagen. October 1985
Sågvall Hein A and Ahrenberg L (1985) A Parser for Swedish. Status Report for SVE.UCP June 1985. Report No. UDCL-R-85-2. Center for Computational Linguistics, Uppsala University
Schank R and Nash-Webber BL (eds) (1975) Theoretical Issues in Natural Language Processing. Cambridge, Mass.
Svensk ordbok (1986) (Produced by Department of Computational Linguistics, University of Gothenburg.) Stockholm
Teleman U (1974) Manual för grammatisk beskrivning av talad och skriven svenska. Studentlitteratur, Lund
Thompson H (1981) Chart Parsing and Rule Schemata in GPSG. DAI Research Paper No 165. Department of Artificial Intelligence and School of Epistemics, University of Edinburgh
Woods WA (1969) Transition Network Grammars for Natural Language Analysis. Communications of the ACM **13,** 591-602
Zampolli A (ed) (1977) Syntactic Structures Processing. North-Holland, Amsterdam

Preliminary Analysis of a Breadth-First Parsing Algorithm: Theoretical and Experimental Results*

W. A. Martin, K. W. Church, and R. S. Patil

Abstract. We will trace a brief history of context-free parsing algorithms and then describe some representation issues. The purpose of this paper is to share our philosophy and experience in adapting a well-known context-free parsing algorithm (Earley's algorithm [9, 10] and variations thereof [29, 14, 27, 28]) to the parsing of a difficult and wide-ranging corpus of sentences. The sentences were gathered by Malhotra [23] in an experiment which fooled businessmen users into thinking they were interacting with a computer, when they were actually interacting with Malhotra in another room. The sentences are given in Appendix I. The MALHOTRA corpus is considerably more difficult than a second collection given in Appendix II (originally published in [16]). Section 4 compares empirical results obtained from these collections against theoretical predictions.

This paper will trace a brief history of context-free parsing algorithms and then describe some representation issues. Finally we will present a new parser (EQSP)[1] which has better average case performance because of its improved representation. The purpose of this chapter is to share our philosophy and experience in adapting a well-known context-free parsing algorithm (Earley's algorithm [9, 10] and variations thereof [14, 27–29]) to the parsing of a difficult and wide-ranging corpus of sentences. The sentences were gathered by Malhotra [23] in an experiment which fooled businessmen users into thinking they were interacting with a computer, when they were actually interacting with Malhotra in another room. The sentences are given in Appendix I. The use of constructions and punctuation varies widely from user to user and contrasts sharply in its variety with the sentences in Appendix II, which originally appeared in [16]. These sentences, which we will call the LADDER-TODS Collection, were chosen to make a wide variety of constructions possible while limiting the difficulty of parsing. To move from the LADDER-TODS to the MALHOTRA corpus required an approximate doubling of our code.

We believe that syntax, semantics, and pragmatics are all required to parse a corpus like the MALHOTRA. However our view is that, computationally, syntactic constraints are in general the cheapest to apply, while semantics and pragmat-

* This research was supported (in part) by the National Institutes of Health Grant No. 1 P01 LM 03374-02 from the National Library of Medicine, and by the Defense Advanced Research Projects Agency (DOD) monitored by the Office of Naval Research under Contract No. N00014-75-C-0661.

[1] EQSP is the syntactic parser for an English query system currently under development.

ics are progressively more expensive. Therefore, we have chosen to step aside from our long-term development for a couple of months and explore just how much can be done by syntax alone. What is the general behavior of a purely syntactic parser and for what constructions is it strongest and weakest? This has given us a clearer idea of just where semantics and pragmatics would help the most.

We have chosen to implement a sentence-level parser which finds all parses of the sentence. We feel that, at least in the short run, this will be best for the practical question-answering system we are trying to build. Our view is that current computer semantics and pragmatics will be too weak to determine in all cases the intended interpretation when they see it. For example, experience with the commercially offered ROBOT [15] system indicates problems such as confusion of the abbreviation *ME* for *Maine* with the pronoun *me* in sentences like (1). By finding both interpretations we can ask the user for a clarification.

(1) Print for me the sales of stair carpets.

When all parses are to be found it has generally been profitable to maintain a chart, or well-formed substring table. This approach has been carried fairly far in approaches based on standard transformational grammar, but to our knowledge, no one has built a large parser for a grammar like LFG [20]. This we have done by adapting the well-known context-free algorithm of Earley to a very efficient form for parsing English.

Linguists have long viewed language as full of marked exceptions to powerful general rules. This we think is a general property of most large natural systems. No one algorithm can cover everything unless it is so general as to be terribly inefficient. The best approach to parsing is to split the problem into cases. There will be a primary algorithm (context-free parsing in our case), important secondary algorithms (wh-movement and conjunction for us), and many minor algorithms (e.g., for idiomatic expressions such as *per cent* and for arithmetic expressions). In this paper the reader will see how we have worked this out for the difficult MALHOTRA corpus.

As will be mentioned below, we have implemented our parser in a compiled rather than an interpreted form. This means the grammar is written directly as programs rather than as a data structure which is then interpreted by a separate parsing program. Richard Burton [4] first applied this technique, obtaining approximately an order of magnitude improvement in parsing time over the interpreted implementation. We believe that we have realized a similar speed increase or perhaps a little more. One advantage of the compiled form is that it is easier to add special case processing algorithms. As stated above, we have added quite a few of these. It would be desirable to have a compiler program which could convert an abstract grammar into many different parser programs. This remains for further work.

There have always been questions of how complex natural language systems should be evaluated. One way, we think, is to run them on standard corpuses. This is why give our results on the MALHOTRA and LADDER-TODS corpuses in the appendices. But in Section 4 we have tried to go beyond this and identify which constructions are the most difficult for our parser and why. A syntactic parser finding all parses always takes more resources per word as the length of the sentence grows. We have found specific sentence forms which demonstrate the best and worst cases, i. e., they bracket the MALHOTRA data. For these sentences it is possible to analyze exactly why they are hard or easy for our parser. In this section we feel we have advanced, at least to some extent, the art of parser analysis.

It is very unlikely that people parse sentences the way our parser does. It proceeds breadth-first keeping all options open. Nevertheless we feel a study of our paper may help people in cognitive science to appreciate the variety of issues that go into the construction of a parsing algorithm. In addition it is possible that people do proceed breadth-first for one or a few words. One path may be considered most likely and brought to consciousness, but others could be under consideration in parallel to facilitate local back-up. Anyone pursuing this idea may find our paper of some help. Finally, cognitive scientists may find our analysis of difficult constructions of some help in planning experiments, or they may want to run our parser to see just what syntactic structures certain sentences have in an LFG-like grammar. We are always being surprised by some of the analyses found.

1 An Introduction to Chart Parsing

Let us define a very general context-free algorithm for comparison with historical landmarks such as Woods' ATN model [34] and Earley's algorithm [9, 10]. This discussion is intended as a review of the literature, in order to establish a common terminology which will be useful when we introduce some of our own ideas in the later sections. The organization of this section strongly follows that of [14, 28, 29].

A context-free parser takes as input a context-free grammar and a sentence and produces as output a chart[2] of labeled phrases. A labeled phrase is a sequence of words delimited by two brackets and labeled with a category symbol. Let the triple $<i, j, c>$ denote a phrase of category *c* spanning the words between the *i*-th position and the *j*-th. For illustrative purposes these triples will be represented in a two dimensional matrix (*i* by *j*) as illustrated below for the sentence (2). For example, the entry {NP, VP} in Chart(2, 4) represents two analyses of the words between positions 2 and 4, namely $[_{NP}$ flying planes] and $[_{VP}$ flying planes]. (More efficient representations will be discussed shortly.)

(2) *Input Sentence:* $_0$ They $_1$ are $_2$ flying $_3$ planes $_4$

(3) *Grammar:*

N→they V→are N→flying A→flying V→flying
N→planes S→NP VP VP→V NP VP→V VP
NP→N NP→AP NP NP→VP AP→A

[2] Some authors prefer the term *well-formed substring table* (wfst) to *chart.*

(4) *Chart:*

0	{ }	{NP, N, they}	{S}	{S}	{S}
1	{ }	{ }	{VP, V, are}	{VP}	{VP}
2	{ }	{ }	{ }	{NP, VP, AP, N, V, A, flying}	{NP, VP}
3	{ }	{ }	{ }	{ }	{NP, N, planes}
4	{ }	{ }	{ }	{ }	{ }
	0	1	2	3	4

If there is a complete parse of the sentence, the chart will have an *S* in the topmost right hand corner to represent the fact that the parser found an S spanning the words from before the first one (0) to after the last one *(n)*. Otherwise, the sentence is rejected. There are no entries in the lower left half of the chart because there no phrases which end before they start. The diagonal entries correspond to phrases of zero words (e.g., trace and other empty categories).

There are many well-known parsing algorithms that produce a chart like that above in time $O(n^3)$ (proportional to the cube of the number of words). One such algorithm is given below. It finds a phrase between positions *i* and *j* by picking a position *k* in between and testing whether there are two phrases, one from *i* up to *k* and another from *k* to *j*, that can combine according to the grammar. For example in (2), the algorithm will determine that there is an S from 0 to 4 because there is an NP form 0 to 1 and there is a VP from 1 to 4 and the two phrases can combine according to the grammar rule S→NP VP. The general entry in the chart is:

(5) $$\text{chart}(i, j) = \bigcup_{i<k<j} \text{chart}(i, k) * \text{chart}(k, j)$$

where '$\alpha * \beta$' combines phrases from α and β according to the rules of the grammar, that is, it returns the set of phrases whose left daughter is from α and whose right daughter is from β. (For the present discussion we will assume that phrases have one or two daughters, or more formally, that the grammar is in Chomsky Normal Form [1].) This algorithm can be performed in $O(n^3)$ time by choosing all combinations of *i, j,* and *k,* each of which have *n* possible values. (The multiplication step requires constant time, independent of the actual input words. It only depends on the grammar and hence it is often known as the *grammar constant.*)

```
for j: =l to n do
    chart(j-l, j): ={A | A→word_j}                       lexicon
    for i: =j-2 downto 0 do
        chart(i,j): =    ∪     chart(i,k)*chart(k,j)     invariant
                      i<k<j
if S is in chart(0,n) then accept
else reject
```

This formulation of chart parsing is convenient for showing the parallelism between CF parsing and matrix multiplication. This is an important result, originally due to Valient [33], which allows us to take advantage of advances in matrix multiplication algorithms, currently a very active area of research in computer science. Intuitively, the parallelism comes from a very strong similarity in invariants; (6) is the invariant for chart parsing and (7) is the in variant for multiplying two matrices A and B to produce a resulting matrix C.

(6) $$\text{chart(i,j)} = \bigcup_{k} \text{chart(i,k)} * \text{chart(k,j)}$$

(7) $$c_{ij} = \sum_{k} a_{ik} * b_{kj}$$

1.1 Enumeration Order

1.1.1 Depth-First vs. Breadth-First

This algorithm is similar to several well-known algorithms dating back to the early 1960s (e.g., Harvard Predictive Analyzer [22] and the Cocke-Younger-Kasami [1]), though these algorithms tend to enumerate the chart in slightly different orders. From a computational point of view, the enumeration order is of surprisingly little importance. Sheil [30] showed that the $O(n^3)$ time bound can be achieved by any algorithm that limits its search space to points in <i, j, k>-space. From this perspective, there is no difference between depth-first enumeration of <i, j, k>-space, breadth-first enumeration, best-first, or even random order, for that matter[3].

So far, much of the psycholinguistic literature has concentrated on basically depth-first (serial) models [6, 11, 18, 24] for reasons that are intuitively appealing, though difficult to formalize. The parser to be presented here is an extreme alternative to depth-first; it is completely breadth-first. Though we don't believe this particular enumeration order to be realistic with respect to psycholinguistics, it offers a useful milestone for comparison with the more popular depth-first models. If one wanted to argue that depth-first was realistic on functional grounds, then one ought to be able to show that it is computationally more efficient than breadth-first. We find plausible the hypothesis that human processing proceeds breadth-first for a few words before selecting the best alternative to follow in a depth-first fashion; our parser may be helpful to someone exploring such a compromise position.

We have chosen an extreme breadth-first position for two reasons. First, it happens to be very convenient for certain representation issues. Secondly, because we

---

[3] This claim needs a slight qualification; it doesn't hold if the equality relation in the invariant is replaced with an assignment statement because the former is associative while the latter is not. That is, every order of evaluating equality relations produces the same results, but this is not necessarily true of assignment statements. Hence the equality sign in the algorithm really means equality and not assignment. (There is a recent trend in computer science towards replacing assignment statements with equality constraints [32], thus side-stepping a large number of ordering problems, and similarly, in linguistics there is a trend towards replacing strict ordering of transformations with well-formedness constraints such as Chomsky's conditions on binding, case, government, and thematic relations [5] or Bresnan-Kaplan's completeness, coherence, and consistency [20].

want to find all parses of multiply ambiguous sentences, there are few (if any) advantages of depth-first. Depth-first has better average case behavior if only one parse is desired, because it can stop searching when it finds the first parse, but this doesn't apply in the "all-parses" problem. When seeking all parses, it is more productive to discuss the search space itself, rather than particular strategies of enumerating the space[4].

1.1.2 Top-Down vs. Bottom-Up

The psycholinguistic literature has also paid considerable attention toward the top-down/bottom-up question. This distinction becomes considerably less important when a chart is introduced, because each phrase will be found once and only once, for both enumeration strategies. Without a chart, the top-down/bottom-up distinction might be much more important because a strictly top-down parser will find a phrase multiple times, once for each place that it can be used in a larger phrase whereas a strictly bottom-up parser will find a phrase just once. However a strictly bottom-up parser has the dual problem of proposing a larger phrase multiple times, once for each way that it can use a phrase that has been found. All efficient parsers combine both top-down and bottom-up information in some way (using the chart, for example), so that it is useless to classify these parsers as one type or the other. This may be part of the reason that this question is so difficult for psycholinguistics to resolve. This paper will concentrate more on representation issues where it is much easier to formulate sharp distinctions.

For example, is the chart algorithm above top-down or bottom-up? Well, most people would say that it is bottom-up because it finds phrases from **i** to **k** and from **k** to **j** before it puts them together to form a phrase from **i** to **j**. However, it is fairly easy to reformulate the multiplication step so that it looks more like division. That is, one might replace a statement like (8) with something more like (9). (From a formal grammar point of view, these pairs contrast Chomsky Normal Form [1] with categorial grammars [2], and from a representational point of view, these pairs suggest two different ways of indexing[5] the grammar.)

(8) $\text{chart}(i, j) = \text{chart}(i, k) * \text{chart}(k, j)$ *bottom-up (Chomsky Normal Form)*

(9) $\text{chart}(k, j) = \dfrac{\text{chart}(i, j)}{\text{chart}(i, k)}$ *top-down (categorial grammars)*

Earley's algorithm [9] can be viewed as (9) because it predicts phrases from the top (chart(i, j)) and then divides (completes) them by phrases from the bottom (chart(i, k)) so that it can predict the next phrase (chart(k, j)). Since the predict step precedes the complete step, this algorithm is often said to be top-down, though it is

4 It may be useful to think about the search space as the *competence* of processing and the search strategies as the *performance* of processing.

5 *Indexing* is a technical term borrowed from data-base management. Data bases are indexed on certain keys so that it is relatively easy to find an item if you have its key. A data-base index is analogous to an index at the back of a book; both make it relatively easy to find a particular item if you know what it might be indexed under.

really very similar to the chart parser presented here, and hence one really wouldn't want to say that it has a completely different search strategy. Top-down/bottom-up arguments are unconvincing because (8) and (9) are so similar to each other that it seems extremely tenuous at best for an argument to depend crucially on a distinguishing trait. In fact they are so close that it is often possible to make one strategy look like another by a clever recoding trick; one will be provided for Earley's algorithm at a later point. As noted previously, it is more productive to discuss the search space itself, rather than enumeration orders[6]. Our analysis will attempt to follow this approach in general, though we will mention a particular search strategy (bottom-up and breadth-first) in the representation discussion for concreteness. The reader is invited to reformulate those results in terms of a top-down depth-first strategy.

1.2 N-ary Branching

The previous algorithm has a rather awkward assumption that all phrases have only one or two daughters (Chomsky Normal Form). This would appear to conflict with many linguistic analyses which propose wider branching factors in cases such as:

(10) $[_{vp}[_{v}$ give] $[_{np}$ it] $[_{pp}$ to him]]

This section will relax this assumption by recording a general context-free grammar into Chomsky Normal Form in such a way that it should be clear that there are no linguistic and/or psycholinguistic implications resulting from this assumption. In so doing, we will have generalized the previous algorithm to work for all context-free grammars.

The recoding trick is very simple. Define a *dotted-rule* to be a context-free grammar rule with a dot inserted to indicate how much of it has been parsed. For example in (11)-(14) below, the dotted-rules on the left correspond to the tree fragments on the right.

dotted-rule	*tree fragment*
(11) VP→. V NP PP	$[_{vp}$
(12) VP→V. NP PP	$[_{vp}$ give
(13) VP→V NP.PP	$[_{vp}$ give $[_{np}$ it]
(14) VP→V NP PP.	$[_{vp}$ give $[_{np}$ it] $[_{pp}$ to him]]

Since this notation is fairly cumbersome, it will be convenient to introduce a few abbreviations. When there can be no confusion, we will abbreviate initial and final dotted-rules ((11) and (14) respectively) by placing the dot on the category itself (e.g., .VP and VP.) rather than spelling out the entire rule. Other abbreviations will be introduced as they become useful.

[6] Much of the emphasis on enumeration orders stems from the heuristic search paradigm which is traditionally used in artificial intelligence to improve performance by imposing certain cut-offs in the enumeration procedures, thus finding an approximate solution in less time. We would rather view the heuristics (when possible) as shrinking the search space itself, enabling a *complete* enumeration of the reduced space. Thus we can deal with heuristics without bringing up processing notions like enumeration orders.

The multiplication rule will be redefined to combine dotted-rules rather than nonterminals as before. It combines two dotted-rules, a partial and a final, by moving the dot past the next symbol as illustrated below[7]:

(15) {VP→. V NP PP} * {V.} = {VP→V. NP PP}
{VP→V. NP PP} * {NP.} = {VP→V NP. PP}
{VP→V NP. PP} * {PP.} = {VP→V NP PP.}

It might be useful to view these dotted-rules as forming the nonterminal of a new grammar which we will call the *dotted-grammar*. The combination rule above is constructed to have binary branching so the dotted-grammar will be in Chomsky Normal Form. Now the algorithm above can be applied to the dotted-grammar instead of the original, thus meeting the binary branching assumption without imposing any constraints on the original grammar. The resulting algorithm is a general parser for any context-free based theory of processing since the dotted-grammar is a trivial mapping from the original which imposes no linguistic and/or psycholinguistic restrictions.

1.3 Dotted-Grammars and ATN States

One particularly well known framework is Woods' Augmented Transition Network (ATN) [34] and hence it is worthwhile to reformulate the preceding explicitly in his terms. He introduces his model in three stages. First he begins with finite state transition networks which consist of a set of states connected by labeled arcs. The interpreter starts from the initial state and follows arcs labeled with the category of the first input word. From there it follows arcs labeled with the category of the second input word and so on until there are no more input words. If the machine is in the final state when there are no more words, the sentence is accepted, and if not, the sentence is rejected. This machine is strongly equivalent to a regular grammar.

Woods then increases the generative capacity by allowing arcs to specify other networks recursively. For example, the S network could specify and NP network for its first transition, not just a lexical category as in the finite state network model. Woods called this recursive model a *Recursive Transition Network* (RTN) and showed it to be strongly equivalent to context-free grammars. He then augmented it with registers and conditional jumps to construct the ATN which has the power of a Turing machine (though there have been efforts to reduce its generative capacity)[8].

There is a strong relationship between Woods' RTNs and dotted-grammars. RTN states correspond to sets of dotted-rules, and arcs perform the multiplication as illustrated below. (This chapter will use the terms *state* and *dotted-rule* interchangeably.)

---

[7] Technically the multiplication rule is defined to apply to *sets* of nonterminals, rather than individual nonterminals, and consequently, dotted-rule multiplication really applies to sets of dotted-rules, not individual rules. This explains the set brackets in the example.

[8] Kaplan (personal communication).

states	*arcs*	*RTN*
{.VP}	push {V.} to {VP→V. NP PP}	
{VP→V. NP PP}	push {NP.} to {VP→V NP. PP}	
{VP→V NP. PP}	push {PP.} to {VP.}	

dotted-rules	*multiplication table*	*dotted grammar*
{.VP}	{.VP} * {V.}={VP→V. NP PP}	
{VP→V. NP PP}	{VP→V. NP PP} * {NP.}={VP→ V NP. PP}	
{VP→V NP. PP}	{VP→V NP. PP} * {PP.}={VP.}	

The ATN employed a convenient naming convention for partial constituents (intermediate states) that will be used here when there can be no confusion. Let S/NP abbreviate an S up to the NP (S→NP. VP) and VP/V abbreviate a VP up to the V (VP→V. NP, VP→V. AP or VP→V. NP). This abbreviation scheme combines several dotted-rules that are identical up to the dot. This is often a useful optimization, though there may be times when it is more efficient to distinguish them. For example, it might be better to combine dotted-rules that are the same *after* the dot.

1.4 Example with Dotted-Rules

The chart with dotted-rules is given below for the sentence: *They are flying planes.*

0	.S, .NP, .VP, .AP .N, .V, .A	NP., N., S/NP they	S.	S.	S.
1		.S, .NP, .VP, .AP .N, .V, .A	V., VP/V are	VP.	VP.
2			.S, .NP, .VP, .AP .N, .V, .A	A., AP., NP/AP, V., VP/V, N., NP., S/NP, flying	NP., S/NP, VP.
3				.S, .NP, .VP, .AP .N, .V, .A	NP., N. S/NP planes
4					.S, .NP, .VP, .AP .N, .V, .A
	0	1	2	3	4

The diagonal of the chart takes on a very important meaning. Before, it was only used for linguistically empty phrases (e.g., traces). Now, it is also used for initial dotted-rules (rules with the dot in the left-most position) because they denote partial phrases dominating no words in the input stream *(i=j)*. By similar reasoning, there will be no initial dotted-rules in the off-diagonal entries. Traces are now denoted by final dotted-rules in a diagonal entry.

2 Taking Advantage of Restricted Grammars

Though the $O(n^3)$ bound is approximately the best known for the general context-free parsing problem[9], it is possible to do much better with certain restricted grammars. For example, Earley's algorithm [9, 10] parses some context-free grammars in $O(n)$ time, some others in $O(n^2)$ time, and the rest in $O(n^3)$ time. This is an improvement over the algorithm outlined above which cannot take advantage of these restricted grammars; it requires $O(n^3)$ time in all cases because it enumerates $O(n^3)$ points in <i, j, k>-space even if many of them cannot enter into the complete parse due to some restriction in the grammar. Pratt [27, 28] and Ruzzo [14, 29] have independently found a way to incorporate Earley's ideas into an algorithm like the one we first presented; the modified algorithm will use the grammar to decide which points to enumerate and hence it can be much more efficient for certain restricted grammars. The next two sections will illustrate two ways in which the grammar can restrict the set of reachable points in <i, j, k>-space.

2.1 Time $\mathbf{n}^2$ *Grammars*

In general, there are $O(n)$ ways to pick k so that it partitions the words between i and j into two phrases that can combine to form a single phrase from i to j. However, for some grammars there are only a bounded number of ways of picking k; the grammar will not combine the other partitions and hence there is no reason to consider them. This is a particularly useful restriction because if there are only b ways to pick k, then there are only $O(b*n*n)$ points in the <i, j, k> search space. Earley [9] called this restriction *Bounded Direct Ambiguity,* observing that these grammars have limited "top-level" ambiguity. (They can still be very ambiguous because each of the b top-level partitions can themselves have b partitions, and each of them can have b partitions, and so on.)

We will give an example and then compare it against the more general case. Then we will draw on some examples from the psycholinguistic literature and speculate that they might be interesting subcases of this restriction. Finally it will be shown how the algorithm can be modified so as to take advantage of this restriction. The modified grammar takes $O(n^2)$ time on restricted grammars, though it still requires $O(n^3)$ in the general case.

2.1.1 Grammar 'aAa': an Example of Bounded Direct Ambiguity

Consider grammar (16) which parses odd length strings of *a*s. This grammar is an extreme case of bounded direct ambiguity; there is only one way to pick k between i and j because the grammar is unambiguous. There are less extreme cases which are ambiguous, though this is a good example to begin with[10].

---

[9] Valient [33] found an $O(M(n))$ bound where $M(n)$ is the time required to multiply two matrices of size n. This is known to be slightly better than cubic, though the constants are probably prohibitive for practical applications.

[10] In fact, any *linear grammar* has bounded direct ambiguity. (These grammars have at most one nonterminal on the right-hand side of a production.) See [9] for the proof.

(16) A→a A a
A→a

The following abbreviations will be used for this example:

abbreviation	*long forms*
.A	{A→.a, A→.a A a}
A/a	{A→a., A→a. A a, a}
A/A	{A→a A. a}
A.	{A→a A a.}

The chart is given below for the sentence: "aaaaa".

	0	1	2	3	4	5
0	.A	A/a	A/A	A.	A/A	A.
1		.A	A/a	A/A	A.	A/A
2			.A	A/a	A/A	A.
3				.A	A/a	A/A
4					.A	A/a
5						.A

Notice that there is only one way (at most) to pick *k* so that it partitions a set of input words into two phrases that can combine. For example, between 0 and 5, only 4 will do (A/A*A/a=A.); for any other *k*, chart(0, *k*)*chart(*k*, 5)={}. This restricted grammar is parsed more efficiently by Earley's algorithm because there are fewer *k*s to look for; it avoids looking for combinations that can't exist. Notice that this improvement saves time, but doesn't save any space; the improved algorithm will find just as many phrases as the original algorithm did. (There is a common misconception that Earley's algorithm is faster just because it avoids constructing unnecessary phrases. This explanation is incomplete because it doesn't account for the improved performance in cases like this where there are still $\Omega(n^2)$ phrases[11], just as many as there were before.)

2.2 'Grammar AA': an Example of Unbounded Direct Ambiguity

Contrast the previous example with one where there is no bound on the direct ambiguity. With a grammar like (17) below, all choices of *k* will work out and hence Earley's algorithm will have to look at all of them. This is one of the worst grammars for Earley's algorithm; it requires n^3 time.

(17) A→A A
A→a

[11] See [21] for a formal definition of this notation; it means that the growth is at least as fast as $\mathbf{n}^2$. This is a lower bound; before we were discussing upper bounds when we said that the growth was no faster than $\mathbf{n}^2$.

The following abbreviations will be used for this example:

abbreviation	*long forms*
.A	{A→.A A, A→.a}
A/a	{a, A→a., A→A. A}
A.	{A→A. A, A→A A.}

The chart is given below for the sentence: "aaaaa"

0	.A	A/a	A.	A.	A.	A.
1		.A	A/a	A.	A.	A.
2			.A	A/a	A.	A.
3				.A	A/a	A.
4					.A	A/a
5						.A
	0	1	2	3	4	5

2.3 Examples from Psycholinguistic Literature

Psycholinguists have looked at quite a number of English constructs which have unbounded direct ambiguity, because they seem to provide some interesting differences between performance and competence. It appears that unbounded direct ambiguity is difficult to process, a result that is compatible with the theoretical discussion above. Furthermore, many computational linguists have also found these constructs problematic for their respective models. These constructs are especially difficult for Marcus' Determinism Hypothesis [24]; he and many of his followers [6, 26, 31] have worked out possible solutions to many of them, usually concluding that they have bounded direct ambiguity in performance[12]. Some experience with our own model will be presented.

2.3.1 Noun-Noun Modification

This case is presented first because it is perhaps the closest analog of 'Grammar AA', though it may not be the most important from a practical engineering point of view. These examples tend to involve domain-specific semantics; perhaps they are best resolved at some level other than syntax[13]. These particular examples were taken from [24].

12 There is one exception; Church [6] has experimented with an alternative approach called *pseudo-attachment* which attaches a phrase to an unbounded number of places in a single step. In certain cases, this approach has been encoded directly into the grammar of the parser to be presented here.

13 We haven't decided yet how semantic processing should be ordered with respect to syntactic processing. Although the current EQSP system orders all syntactic processing first, we plan to experiment with some more interactive scheduling strategies.

(18) NP→NP NP *grammar*
NP→N
(19) [[[[water meter] cover] adjustment] screw]
(20) [[ion thruster] [performance calibration]]
(21) [[boron epoxy] [[rocket motor] chambers]]
(22) [1970 [[balloon flight] [[solar-cell standardization] program]]]

These are a well-known problem for processing. Some of the difficulties are discussed in [24] and references therein; Robert Milne (personal communication) is currently working on some solutions within a deterministic framework. This construction is also problematic for nondeterministic systems because it requires considerable resources. The approach taken here is to flatten the syntactic structure of these phrases as in (23), delaying the decisions for semantics. In this way, the parser will not waste time trying all possible bracketings; it will be content with a canonical one that represents them all. This is very similar to the "pseudo-attachment" approach in [6]. Notice that the canonical grammar has bounded direct ambiguity.

(23) NP→(N)* *canonical grammar*

2.3.2 Prepositional Phrase Attachment and Conjunction

There are many other cases of 'Grammar AA' from natural language; perhaps the most common are prepositional phrase attachment and conjunction.

(24) NP→NP and NP *grammar for conjunction*
NP→DET N
(25) NP→NP PP *grammar for prepositional phrase attachment*
NP→DET N
PP→P NP

Both of these grammars have unbounded direct ambiguity; there are an unbounded number of choices for *k*. We have enumerated the top-level choices of *k* for the following two examples. Notice that the number of choices grows with the number of words. (Let NP/and and NP/NP abbreviate the dotted-rules: NP→NP and NP and NP→NP. PP, respectively.)

(26) plant 1 and $_1$plant 2 and $_2$plant 3 and $_3$plant 4 and $_4$plant 5 *conjunction*
$[_{NP/and}$ plant 1 and] $[_{NP.}$ plant 2 and plant 3 and plant 4 and plant 5]
$[_{NP/and}$ plant 1 and plant 2 and] $[_{NP.}$ plant 3 and plant 4 and plant 5]
$[_{NP/and}$ plant 1 and plant 2 and plant 3 and] $[_{NP.}$ plant 4 and plant 5]
$[_{NP/and}$ plant 1 and plant 2 and plant 3 and plant 4 and] $[_{NP.}$ plant 5]

(27) plant 1 $_1$ with plant 2 $_2$ with plant 3 $_3$ with plant 4 $_4$ with plant 5
PP attachment
$[_{NP/PP}$ plant 1] $[_{PP.}$ with plant 2 with plant 3 with plant 4 with plant 5]
$[_{NP/PP}$ plant 1 with plant 2] $[_{PP.}$ with plant 3 with plant 4 with plant 5]
$[_{NP/PP}$ plant 1 with plant 2 with plant 3] $[_{PP.}$ with plant 4 with plant 5]
$[_{NP/PP}$ plant 1 with plant 2 with plant 3 with plant 4] $[_{PP.}$ with plant 5]

In both cases, the number of parses grows very quickly with the number of phrases. The actual growth is exactly the *Catalan numbers* [21], the number of ways to insert parentheses into a formula of *n* terms. The first few Catalan numbers are: 1, 2, 5, 14, 42, 132, 469, 1430, 4862, ... They are generated by $\binom{2n}{n} - \binom{2n}{n-1}$ which grows almost exponentially. These numbers have been empirically verified with up to nine prepositional phrases. That is, the parser found 4862 parses for the sentence: *It is the number of products of products of products of products of products of products of products of products of products.* The parser uses a much more complicated grammar for conjunction; consequently, it is harder to predict the number of parses in that case.

The canonical grammar approach (proposed in the last subsection) is also applicable here; this is similar to the "pseudo-attachment" approach taken in [6]. This approach was not implemented for prepositional phrases in this work because there are rarely more than three of them in a sentence, which is only five-ways ambiguous, and hence it does not seem to be worth the effort to canonicalize them. The canonical grammar approach was implemented in some cases of conjunction; it appears to save a considerable amount of work in this case because sentences often contain more than three potential conjuncts.

2.3.3 Reduced Relative Clauses

It appears that one of the greatest proliferations of ambiguity is due to reduced relative clauses. Not only do they tend to attach in every possible way (like prepositional phrases and 'Grammar AA'), but they can also start wh-movement and they are often confused with main verbs. Furthermore, if that isn't bad enough, a reduced relative is often just one word long and hence it is one of largest contributors to the *per word ambiguity* (number of parse trees divided by sentence length). For example, sentence (28) is 10-ways ambiguous, but without the word *produced,* it is only 3-ways ambiguous. The effect is far more significant in (30), (31) where there are two reduced relatives to interact with a few more phrases. These sentences do not appear to be very difficult for most people to understand. Perhaps people are using semantic constraints to reduce the direct ambiguity.

(28) List the sales of products *produced* in 1973. 10
(29) List the sales of products in 1973. 3
(30) List the sales of products *produced* in 1973 with the products *produced* in 1972. 455
(31) List the sales of products in 1973 with the products in 1972. 28

Reduced relative clauses don't appear to have the same direct ambiguity in performance as they do in competence, especially when they can be interpreted as main verb phrases, as is well noted in the psycholinguistic literature by a pair like the following:

(32) # The horse raced past the barn fell.
The horse ridden past the barn fell.

Many researchers have argued that the unacceptability of sentence (32) is due to some difficulty in locating the boundary between the noun phrase and the verb phrase. In our terms, we would say that it is difficult to find the *k* which partitions the sentence into a noun phrase and a verb phrase. Notice that the general case (33) has unbounded direct ambiguity.

(33) The horse raced past the horse raced past the horse ... fell.

The general problem with all of these constructions (reduced relatives, prepositional phrases, conjunction, noun-noun modification) is unbounded direct ambiguity and hence there is a characteristic proliferation of interpretations (Catalan growth) and significant time requirements (cubic growth). The general solution to this problem is to find other constraints (semantic, performance, canonicalization) in order to bound the direct ambiguity. The parser to be presented here is the result of considerable efforts in these directions; it generates far fewer parse trees than it once did. It becomes particularly clear just how many parses there are when one is generating all parses, rather than just the first one as most other parsers do.

2.4 Taking Advantage of Bounded Direct Ambiguity

This section will modify the above algorithm to take advantage of bounded direct ambiguity. The improvement results from ignoring null entries in the chart. Instead of enumerating all points in <i, j, k>-space, the improved algorithm will only enumerate those *k*s that can partition the words from *i* to *j* into two phrases that can combine. It accomplishes this by working "bottom-up"[14]; that is, it will combine two phrases only if they are both already in the chart. Whenever the parser adds a new phrase into the chart from *k* to *j*, it looks for phrases ending at *k* and combines them to form phrases from *i* to *j*. These phrases are then completed with phrases ending at *i*, and so on. The combination procedure is called *completer* (Earley's terminology) because it completes phrases already in the chart. (For technical reasons, the chart is initialized with zero-length phrases already inserted along the diagonal because they can be precomputed without looking at the input and because the completer, as defined here, is unable to find them. This technical point will be cleaned up shortly. Recall that initial states are zero-length phrases and consequently, they are all initially in every diagonal entry.)

We can make the completer somewhat faster by precomputing which categories can combine with which. Then the completer will only try to combine phrases of the "right" categories; that is, instead of looking for just any phrase ending at *k*, it looks for phrases of a category that can combine with the category of the phrase from *k* to *j*. The function *left_sisters_of* returns a precompiled list of dotted-rules that can combine with a given dotted-rule. So for example, it would return .S and

[14] Note that this algorithm can also be viewed as top-down for reasons mentioned previously; top-down information is used to decide what should be put into the chart in the first place.

VP→V. NP PP and a host of others as left sisters of NP., all of which multiply on the left of an NP. to produce some other states.

This algorithm motivates a representation that allows efficient enumeration of phrases of a particular category ending at a particular point. These representation issues will be discussed later. For now, we will assume a few functions for manipulating the chart. These functions now take three arguments (a *state,* an *i* and a *j*) unlike the previous chart functions which did not take a *state* argument. The function *chart(s, ?k,j)* generates a list of *k*s, one for each phrase of category *s* ending at *j*.

```
(34) parse: proc()
                    for j from 1 to n
                       for s in {A. | A→word_j} do
                       add_chart(s,j-1,j)
     add_chart: proc(s,i,j)
                    if chart(s,i,j) = 'not found' then
                       chart(s,i,j) : = 'found'
                       complete(s,i,j)
     complete: proc(s_2,k,j)
                    for s_1 in left_sisters_of(s_2) do
                       for i in chart(s_1, ?i,k) do
                       add_chart(s_1*s_2,i,j)
```

2.5 *Time* **n** *Grammars*

It has been noted [9, 28, 29] that the preceding algorithm is inefficient for certain restricted grammars because it constructs phrases that cannot be used in a complete parse. For example, given the grammar 'Aa' (below), it will construct approximately n^2 phrases, most of which do not fit into a final parse. The chart is given below with underlining used to denote useless phrases. These phrases do not fit into a parse that spans from 0 to *j* and hence they are *useless.* (This *usefulness constraint* is enforced by the *predict* operation in Earley's algorithm.) Notice that there is only a linear number of useful phrases; there are *n* useful phrases on the top row and there are *j-l* on the off-diagonal. This is typical of left-branching grammars because the top row contains phrases starting at the left edge and the off-diagonal contains single word phrases. Consequently, the chart can be represented in linear space, which is a large improvement in space complexity over the general $\mathbf{n}^2$ bound. The time bounds are also reduced to O*(n)* as we will see.

(35) A→A a
A→a

abbreviations	*long forms*
.A	{A→.A a, A→.a}
A/A	{A→A. a}
a.	{A→a., A→A. a}
A.	{A→A a.}
A.*	A. ∪ A/A

0	.A	a.	A.*	A.*	A.*	A.*
1		.A	a.	A.*	A.*	A.*
2			.A	a.	A.*	A.*
3				.A	a.	A.*
4					.A	.a
5						.A
	0	1	2	3	4	5

The usefulness condition reduces the complexity for a large class of grammars including all deterministic grammars[15] with one extra modification called *lookahead*. The usefulness condition requires a phrase to be consistent with everything from position 0 to *j*. The lookahead modification strengthens this to include a few more tokens to the right of *j*. This condition is important for right-branching grammars which require *n* time with lookahead, but n^2 time without (on Earley's algorithm). For example, consider a sentences such as (36) which has a right-branching grammar similar in structure to (37).

(36) He believes he believes he believes it.
(37) A→a A | a

This sentence can be parsed in linear time on Earley's algorithm if the multiplication step looks ahead one token, but otherwise it is just like Grammar 'aAa' which consumed square time. Lookahead is crucially used in this grammar to determine the product of {.A} * {a}. If there is another *a*, then the result is {A→a. A}, but if not, the result is {A.}. Without lookahead, the result would be {A→a. A, A.} in both cases and consequently the algorithm would not be taking advantage of the fact that a completed *A* cannot be followed by another *a* in the input string. In these right-branching grammars, the lookahead condition has the same effect that usefulness has in left-branching grammars; that is, it reduces space bounds from n^2 to *n* by making the parser behave deterministically. This also improves the time bounds by a factor of *n*.

This lookahead condition has not been used in our parser except in a few cases such as arithmetic expressions, numbers, ordinals, hyphenated words, and certain conjunction phrases (e.g., *and also*). We believe there are very few constructions in our grammar where lookahead helps. It is crucially important for deterministic parsing of right-branching structures [6, 24], though most of our right-branching structures are ambiguous and hence it doesn't do much good to look ahead. It really only helps to look ahead if the parser is going to behave differently based on what it finds. But since our parser is going to find all paths anyway, it doesn't do much good to look ahead and find out that the structure is ambiguous. However, there are a few unambiguous right-branching constructions such as (36) where EQSP should look ahead. We will show in Section 4 that EQSP pays the

[15] Formally, a deterministic grammar is a grammar that can be recognized on a deterministic push down automaton (DPDA). This is slightly different from the notion of Marcus, whose machine is more powerful. Deterministic grammars can generate all finite state languages and almost all computer languages (e.g., LISP). However, they are unambiguous and hence they are not good candidates for natural language and certain older computer languages (e.g., FORTRAN).

price for not looking ahead; that is, it takes another factor *n* longer to parse sentences like (36) than it would if it looked ahead. Nevertheless, even without lookahead, the class of time *n* grammars is very large. Earley [9] showed the class to properly include LR(0) grammars (deterministic grammars that don't need lookahead).

2.5.1 Taking Advantage of Useless Phrases

Earley's parser avoids looking at useless phrases by excluding them from the chart and thus restricting the parser's attention just to useful phrases and no others. There are three cases of a useful phrase:

(38) At position 0, .S is useful. *initial condition*
(39) It is the combination of two other useful phrases.
(40) It is the initial state of a phrase that can combine with a useful phrase. *Earley's predictor*

Earley calls this third condition *the predictor*, though this term is somewhat misleading. For example this third condition will cause .NP to become useful if .S were useful because .S can combine with NP. and .NP is the initial state of an NP. This will then cause .N to become useful because .NP can combine with an N. Notice that the new states (e.g., .NP and .N) are both the initial state of a right sister of an already useful state. For example, .NP is the initial state of NP. which is a right sister of .S. (A right sister combines on the right by analogy to a left sister which combines on the left.)

These "predictions" fall on the diagonal of the chart because they are initial states; the other useful phrases fall in the upper triangle. Previously the chart was initialized with the diagonal containing all initial states; the modified algorithm below will add these initial states when they are known to be useful, cleaning up the previous version of the algorithm.

(41)
```
parse: proc()
            add_chart({.S}, 0, 0)                       initially .S is useful
            for j from 1 to n
                for s in {A. | A→word_j} do
                add_chart(s,j-1,j)
add_chart(s,i,j)
            if chart(s,i,j)='not found' then
                chart(s,i,j):='found'
                for prediction in right_sisters_of(s) do
                                                          Earley's predict
                add_chart(initial_state_of(prediction),j,j)
                complete(s,i,j)
complete: proc(s2,k,j)
            for s1 in left_sisters_of(s2) do
                for i in chart(s1,?i,k) do
                add_chart(s1*s2,i,j)        combination of useful phrases
```

This new algorithm takes linear time for left-branching grammars because there is only a constant number of phrases for each *j*, and each of them can combine with only a constant number of phrases (chart(s_1,?i,k) is bounded by assumption) and hence the total time is constant for each word, which is linear with the sentence length. Similar arguments apply for all LR(0) grammars. The algorithm could be extended to parse LR(k) grammars (deterministic grammars with lookahead of *k*[16]) in linear time by adding lookahead.

2.6 Representation Issues

The representation of the chart becomes very important for efficient parsing. There are only two operations that reference the chart in the above algorithm:

(42)	for i in chart(s,?i,j) do	*enumeration*
(43)	if chart(s,i,j) = 'not found' then chart(s,i,j): = 'found'	*check*

The analysis requires step (42) to take time proportional to the number of phrases found and step (43) to take constant time. This could be assured if the chart allowed random access on *s* and *j*. For example, the chart could be a two dimensional array; the first dimension ranges over choices of *s* and the second dimension over choices of *j*. Each entry in the array would be a set of *i*s[17]. Unfortunately, this array is probably too large for long sentences and hence it is often *hashed* in practice[18]. We have implemented an alternative proposal to the space problem. It is more important that *s* can be indexed quickly rather than *j* because the range of *s* tends to be larger in practice than the range of *j*. In our case, *s* ranges over approximately 500 states and *j* ranges over about 10 values (the average number of words in the input sentences of the corpuses). Thus, we have implemented the chart to allow random access on *s* in constant time and sequential access on *j*. In particular, for each *s* there is a list of <i, j>-pairs, sorted on *j*. An example is worked out below (except for diagonal entries terminals (words) which are represented differently).

(44) $_0$ They $_1$ are $_2$ flying $_3$ planes. $_4$

rule	*edges*	*rule*	*edges*
S.	(<0, 4>, <0, 3>, <0, 2>)	V.	(<2, 3>, <1, 2>)
VP.	(<1, 4>, <2, 4>, <1, 3>)	A.	(<2, 3>)
NP.	(<2, 4>, <3, 4>, <0, 1>)	S/NP	(<0, 1>)
AP.	(<2, 3>)	VP/V	(<2, 3>, <1, 2>)
N.	(<3, 4>, <0, 1>)	NP/AP	(<2, 3>)

---

16 The *k* lookahead is different from the *k* which partitions *i* and *j* into two phrases.

17 This doesn't actually allow constant time *check* because the list of *i*s might become very long, but it is fairly close since the most interesting values are kept near the front of the list in practice. If one were concerned with the theoretical behavior, one could also add a second table for checking which would be accessed differently from the table for enumeration.

18 *Hashing* is a popular technique of compressing very sparse arrays. See [21] for an excellent analysis of its theoretical properties.

Now, in order to enumerate phrases of category *s* ending at *j*, the parser fetches the list of phrases of category *s* and then searches the list for those ending at *j*. The search halts when a phrase on the list ends before the desired *j*. This representation is taking advantage of the fact that a breadth-first search is almost always referencing the more recent phrases, and only very rarely will it complete a phrase ending very far back. This representation would be very inefficient for a depth-first parser (if it has to back-up very often) because the chart would contain a large number of phrases ending after the desired *j*[19].

The above example does not mention terminals (words) or initial dotted-rules. It isn't necessary to represent terminals (words) in the chart explicitly if they are always dominated by a nonterminal (e.g., N, V, A) as they are in our grammar. The next section will discuss initial dotted-rules.

2.6.1 Diagonal Entries

Diagonal entries are represented differently for four reasons:

(45) They tend to be much denser
(46) They are checked more often
(47) They are not enumerated
(48) They contain less information

Notice that there can be at most one diagonal phrase for each *s* and *j* (because *i* equals *j* on the diagonal), and hence, only one bit is needed to represent whether or not that phrase is in the chart. Consequently these entries are stored in a bit array that allows random access on both *s* and *j*. These bit arrays are a commonly used technique for representing initial predictions in many algorithms (e.g., [14, 28, 29]). There are two exceptions where we represent a diagonal entry with the standard data structure, not the bit arrays. The first exception is when a diagonal entry is being conjoined and the second is when it is starting a relative clause (for wh-movement). These cases will be explained in more detail when we discuss conjunction and wh-movement. There are a few other cases where we don't bother to store the diagonal entries because these constructions are almost always useful, and hence the parser simply assumes that they are useful without checking the chart.

construction	*example*
classifier-name-phrase	They are *dept 2* red dresses.
conjunct-phrase	even though; and also
head-name-phrase	W A MARTIN
ie-phrase	ie dogs, ie in the woods
other-phrase	other than red; other than me

[19] Although the average case time performance of this indexing scheme is attractive, the worst case can be on the order of $\mathbf{n}^4$ as will be shown in Sect. 4. The worst case could be reduced to $\mathbf{n}^3$ if the edges were sorted on both *i* and *j*, not just *j* as we have done here.

construction	*example*
ordinal	3rd; 4th
very-phrase	*very* quickly
per cent	per cent
hyphenated-word	fire-plug

Actually the representation of edges is slightly more complicated; they are really records (random access) including several other fields in addition to *i* and *j*. In particular, there is a field for features (e.g., person, number, etc.) and a field for a wh-element (the hold cell), and there is a slot for conjunction. These fields will be discussed in more detail in a later section.

2.7 Compilation vs. Interpretation

All of the algorithms presented so far *interpret* the grammar more or less directly as is, with almost no pre-processing. In fact, only the left sisters and/or right sisters have to be computed in advance; the rest of the grammar can be interpreted directly in context-free rule format. On the other hand, one could imagine a parser which pre-*compiled* the grammar into some other format which was more efficient for processing. The compilation process is a one-time operation which precedes the parsing of any sentences. This approach can provide considerable efficiency improvements as Burton has shown in his thesis [4].

Compilation is a very common notion in computer science where it is used to transform high-level programs into more efficient machine-level programs before they are run on any input. Compilation is to be contrasted with interpretation where there is no pre-processing; all transformations are performed as they become necessary depending on the input data. Compilation avoids performing the same transformations again and again; interpretation avoids preparing for input data that will never occur.

We have compiled the grammar[20] so that there is an *add_chart* procedure for each state in the grammar. This makes it possible to pre-compile the loop (49) into a single bit vector operation which marks a number of states useful in parallel. There are a number of other advantages from this move. For example, there is no need to try to complete a state unless it is the final state of some network. Therefore, the calls to the complete procedure are removed from the add_chart procedures except for the add_chart procedures of final states.

```
(49) for prediction in right_sister_of(s) do
                    add_chart(initial_state_of(prediction),j,j)
```

We have found these very simple compilation techniques to be extremely important in improving the runtime efficiency of the parser in exchange for a large increase in program size.

[20] Ideally the compilation would be performed by a program so that it would be relatively easy to modify the grammar. In this preliminary project, we have compiled the grammar by hand in order to avoid the very difficult task of designing a grammar compiler.

3 Transformations and Lexical Rules

So far we have limited our attention to pure RTNs; this chapter will discuss a number of useful augmentations which capture a wide number of linguistic generalizations. Almost all of these facts could be captured in a pure RTN by encoding more information into the states in a way analogous to Gazdar's Generalized Phrase Structure Grammar (GPSG) [13], though we believe that it is more efficient to factor these different components and thus reduce the number of states by a vary large factor.

3.1 Features

For example, we could encode agreement facts by exploding the nonterminal set to distinguish features such as person, number, and gender so there would be 3*2*3 types of nouns, one for each combination of features. Similarly, there would be an equal number of verbs, one for each of the agreement possibilities. Though these numbers are finite, they are certainly rather large; 10^5 was an estimate given by Kurt Konolige in a talk at the 1980 meeting of the ACL. This appears to be a particularly inefficient representation of features; a more efficient representation would capture the fact that features are strongly constrained objects which can be manipulated in just a few highly restricted ways.

We will represent features as a component separate from the part of speech. Each feature is another field in the chart, so now the chart contains **n**-tuples of the form: $<s, i, j, f_1, f_2, \ldots>$ to represent a phrase of category *s* spanning from position *i* to position *j* with features $f_1, f_2, \ldots$.. (We will occasionally use the term *record* for these **n**-tuples because they are actually implemented as records.) The multiplication rule is also modified to manipulate features in the appropriate way. For example, the rule that multiplies an NP with a VP to form an S will check the features of the two daughters for agreement and it will assign the appropriate features to the result.

3.1.1 Overriding Features in Exceptional Cases

Certain types of features tend to have idiomatic exceptions which a parser has to be able to deal with. For example, certain verbs like *die* and *sneeze* are generally intransitive although they can take on transitive interpretations under certain very restrictive idiomatic conditions such as:

(50) John sneezed a big sneeze.
(51) John died a horrible death.

The lexical entry for the verb *die* declares it to be intransitive except for this one case, which is marked by placing a property on *die* to override the intransitive subcategorization when there is a noun phrase whose head is the word *death*. In order to make this check more efficient, we have added the *head* slot to phrases in the chart, so that it is relatively inexpensive to find the head of a phrase. The exception handling mechanism has been generalized to accept other subcategorization violations such as:

(52) They are [*on board* [the ship]] now.
(53) They are [*on top* [of it]] now.
(54) They are [*within* [5 miles] [of the ship]].

In these cases, a preposition is taking a second argument, either an NP as in (52) or a PP as in (54). The former case is handled by adding a special phrase structure rule: PP→P N NP with the condition that the N transition is permitted only if the P (*on* in this case) is marked for the particular head (*board* in this example). In a case such as (54), we suppress the issue to semantics since *5 miles of the ship* will be accepted by the existing syntactic component, though it will have a slightly different structure, namely: [within [[5 miles] [of the ship]]]. In semantics, we raise *of the ship to within.* With an exception handling mechanism of this sort, it is much easier to express the facts; without such a mechanism it would be almost impossible to impose any subcategorization restrictions because there is almost always an exception of some sort or another.

3.1.2 Representation of Features

There are a few engineering issues that enter into the representation of features in the chart. We have previously noted that the chart has random access on *s* and sequential access first on *j* and then on *i*. How should we represent features? We have chosen to store one computer word full of features for each combination of<s, i, j>. This is a somewhat arbitrary engineering decision, though it does have some interesting implications. First of all, the multiplication rule will first generate states and then filter out bad states using the features. One could imagine an alternative representation scheme where the features are used in the generation process and the states are used in the filtering.

Secondly, we have very little space to represent features so we will have to decide carefully which ones should be represented at this level and which ones can wait for semantic interpretation. We have concentrated on the better discriminators, those features that weed out the most number of combinations; it isn't worthwhile representing a feature at this level if it will almost always allow the multiplication to succeed.

The third consequence is somewhat more difficult to deal with, though one can imagine some possible improvements which are probably worth exploring. Suppose there were two phrases that were identical to each other in every way except for their features. Our scheme will represent both of them with a single set of features, though ideally they should each have their own. Consider the following example below where there are two ways to form an NP over the same words with different values for the number feature.

(55) [$_{NP}$ Flying planes] make too much noise. *plural*
(56) [$_{NP}$ [$_{VP}$ Flying planes]] is very dangerous. *singular*

Our representation will say that these two phrases are merged in a single **n**-tuple (record) which is marked both singular and plural. That is, we will *merge* the two phrases together into a single record with the *union* of the features. This is a bit too loose because sometimes it will include some combinations that don't exist. For example, there is no way to represent the fact that (57) has only two interpretations, not four. That is, the subject and the predicate can be either singular or plural, but they both have to agree.

(57) Flying planes can be dangerous.

Nevertheless, we have found this representation to be extremely effective and efficient. In practice this union of features rarely causes us to over-accept. It may be reasonable occasionally to accept too many parses at this level of processing and filter them out at a later level.

3.1.3 The Features in EQSP

EQSP currently uses 37 features. Since our PDP-10 computer has 36-bit words, most features are represented with a single bit, though two of them share the same bit. Most of the features are used for subcategorization; there are very few agreement features because there is very little room and because agreement features are relatively poor discriminators. Only 6 of the 37 features are used for agreement: *first-person-singular, third-person-singular, plural, present-tense, past-tense,* and *plural-object.* It was decided that other agreement features such as gender and case do not weed out enough combinations to justify keeping them in the feature vector at this early stage of processing.

3.1.3.1 Subcategories. There are a number of features which are used to further subdivide certain parts of speech in order to restrict and/or expand their usage. There are five features in this class: *time-phrase, place-phrase, pronoun, numeral,* and *converted-participle-adjective.* The first two are good examples of how features can expand the usage of a part of speech. These have three additional usages beyond those of a normal noun phrase. They can be used adverbially as in (58), in post-modifier position as in (59), and they can conjoin with semantically similar prepositional phrases as in (60).

(58) I gave Tom a present *yesterday.* *adverbial*
She must have done it *next door.*
*I gave Tom a present *John.*
*She must have done it *John.*

(59) The concert *yesterday* was very exciting. *post-modifier*
The party *next door* was very exciting.
*The concert *John* was very exciting.
*The party *John* was very exciting.

(60) We'll do it *tomorrow* and *in the month of May.* *conjoined with* **PP**
She must have done it either *next door* or *at work.*
We will be having a sale *the rest of this week* and *in the month of May.*

In contrast to the *time-phrase* and *place-phrase* features which *expand* the use of noun phrases, the *pronoun* feature *restricts* the use of noun phrases. There are certain noun phrase positions which exclude pronouns:

(61) *I picked up *it*.
I picked up John.
(62) *Here comes *it*.
Here comes John.
(63) *I saw *him* who you like.
I saw the boy who you like.
(64) *I saw [*him* from England].
I saw [the boy from England].
(65) *It was *him* two[21].
It was plant two.

The numeral feature is used to allow sentences such as (66) where there is no punctuation to signal conjunction.

(66) Give results for *plants 1 2 3 4*.

A *converted-participle-adjective* is used in a heuristic which avoids constructing adjective phrases such as (67) when there is also participle reading as in (68). The AP parse will be constructed just in case there isn't a corresponding participle phrase. This happens in two cases. First, there are words like *very* which block the participle interpretation as in (69), and secondly, there are certain adjectives like *fond* and *angry* which have no participle counterpart. We use the feature *converted-participle-adjective* to distinguish words like *fond* or *angry* which are only adjectives, from words like *persuaded* which are both participles and adjectives.

(67) I was [$_{AP}$ persuaded].	*adjective*
(68) I was [$_{VP}$ persuaded].	*participle*
(69) I was *very* persuaded.	*"very" selects for adjectives*
(70) I was *fond* of candy.	*no participle counterpart*
I was *angry* at you.	

3.1.3.2 Subcategorization. Most of the features are used for syntactic subcategorization, which seems to be a particularly good discriminator.

feature	*example*
verb-is-intransitive	John died.
verb-takes-sentential-first-object	John thinks that I did it.
verb-takes-sentential-second-object	John persuaded Bill that I did it.
takes-bare-infinitive	John made them take the exam.
verb-takes-at-most-one-np-after-it	*John forced Bill Sam
particle-possible	John put the book down.
verb-doesnt-take-of	*I [put [the picture] [of him into the box]]
factive	the *fact* that John did it; *the *task* that John did it

[21] There is an exception for *you* and *we* which can take post-modifiers in a sentence like: *You two seem to be having a good time.*

There are two kinds of semantic subcategorization. First, there is a notion of a responsibility-center, an object that can own things like a person or a company. It is a very useful distinction to make in the management domain in which we are concentrating our efforts. There are two features for this notion which have the obvious interpretation: *first-of-two-nps-after-verb-must-be-a-responsibility-center* and *responsibility-center*. The second type of semantic subcategorization is for unknown words as in sentences like:

(71) Define the term "tsum" to be the total sum of all products.

There are two features for parsing these sorts of constructions: *introduces-unknown-word* and *quote-head-noun*. The former is assigned to words like *define* (as in *define top to be*) and *let;* the latter is used for nouns like *word* (as in *the word foop is*), *term*, and *phrase*.

3.1.4 Transformational Context

It is useful to have a few features for keeping track of the context for certain "transformations." (We are using the term "transformation" somewhat loosely since most of them are implemented with a base generation approach.) These divide into three types: top-level contexts, unbounded contexts, and adjunct contexts. Many linguistic constructions are sensitive to these different contexts. For example, there is a class of so-called *root transformations* (e.g., auxiliary inversion and imperative deletion) which occur only at top level, and there is a class of so-called *unbounded transformations* (e.g., wh-movement and conjunction) which apply across several clauses subject to certain very strong linguistic constraints (contexts). There is considerably less linguistic interest in the third class, though we have found it to be very useful to be able to filter out certain pre- and post-modifiers. We will discuss these features in more detail when we introduce the relevant transformations.

(72) *top-level structure:* question-sentence, declarative-sentence, presentative-sentence[22]
(73) *Wh-movement and Conjunction:* wh-must-be-used, sequence-going, that-or-which-comp, inquestion, relative
(74) *adjunct contexts:* noun-phrase-rejects-post-modifiers, phrase-is-post-modified, noun-phrase-has-numeral-modifier, noun-phrase-is-post-modified-by-clause, comma-appositive, premodifier-needed

3.1.5 Adjunct Contexts

Adjunct contexts turn out to be fairly important since they are extremely common and hence it is worthwhile spending a little more effort in this area of the grammar. We have introduced several features to deal with pre- and post-modifiers.

[22] The term *presentative* is a generalization of *imperative*, following Joos [17].

These are important because the parser can almost always find a potential modifier and it will significantly reduce the number of final parses if just a few of these possibilities can be excluded. The simplest example is that pronouns usually reject post-modifiers as in[23]:

(75) *He from England ...
The boy from England ...
(76) *He that you like ...
The boy that you like ...
(77) *He 5 is selling well.
Product 5 is selling well.

The feature *premodifier-needed* is used to accept (78), while rejecting (79).

(78) the big, red ball
(79) the big, ball

It is turned on after a comma and turned off when a following modifier is found. This is an example of the point made by Dostert and Thompson [8] that features can be used to avoid a further articulation of the grammar rules themselves. The table below provides a quick summary of the features used to reduce the possibilities of modification.

feature	*accepts*	*rejects*
premodifier-needed	the big, red ball	*the big, ball
noun-phrase-rejects-post-modifiers	item from England	*he from England
noun-phrase-has-numeral-modifier	2 dogs	2 3 dogs
phrase-is-post-modified	item 5	*[item from plant] 5
comma-appositive	John, the baptist	*John, the baptist, the great phophet

There are some undergeneration problems with these features. For example, the *post-modifier* feature will exclude *Jack in the box 1* because it will treat *in the box* as a PP, rather than as part of an idiomatic noun. Similarly, the feature *noun-phrase-has-numeral-modifier* will reject the phrase: *2 3 legged dogs*. Fortunately, neither of these cases appear in the MALHOTRA corpus.

In summary, we have introduced features to eliminate ungrammatical parses and also to exclude extremely rare possibilities. It is much more efficient to undergenerate at the syntactic stage, and if the parser should miss the appropriate parse, there would be a special procedure to backtrack over the chart and recover the appropriate interpretations on a second pass. The alternative requires the parser to carry along at each point every interpretation that could possibly be correct in some completely wild and unlikely semantic context.

[23] There is a proverbial meaning of **he** which permits relative clauses as in: *He who walks under tall ladder will find himself in a heap of trouble.*

3.2 NP-Movement

NP-movement covers a wide range of linguistic phenomena including passive, there-insertion, and raising. All of these transformations are relatively easy to process compared with wh-movement, because they do not nest and hence they can all be performed locally within a lexical entry (as in Lexical Functional Grammars [20]) or within a constituent (as in Phrase Structure Grammars [GPSG]). Our analysis is essentially identical to the lexical based generation approach currently advocated by Bresnan and Kaplan [20]; the morphology routine decides which lexical entries are applicable and assigns the subcategorization features appropriately. Predicate argument relations are determined in another pass which combines additional subcategorization facts with semantics and domain-restricted pragmatics. This pass will be the subject of a forthcoming paper.

3.3 Wh-Movement

Wh-movement is one of the hardest transformations to parse because it is the source of considerable ambiguity as we have seen with reduced relative clauses. Much of the psycholinguistic literature attributes the problem to one of finding empty categories; there is an implication that wh-movement would be much easier if the gaps were identified by some lexical object like the word *gap* or a resumptive pronoun. Though this is correct, we have found that it is also difficult to locate the filler. Consider a sentence like (80) where there is only one possible gap, but there are quite a number of possible fillers.

(80) I saw the block in the corner of the kitchen near the yard that you liked.

One might think that such sentences are quite rare, but this has not been our experience. Consider the following sentences taken from the MALHOTRA corpus [23] which illustrate that fillers can be quite ambiguous.

(81) What are *the components of the various costs* you know about?
(82) Print *every piece of information* you have concerning plant 0 in 1972 and 1973.

It would be very inefficient to "move" all possible fillers into all possible gaps. It would be a very serious mistake to enumerate the subtrees for each possible filler times the number of possible gaps because the number of subtrees grows with the Catalan numbers. EQSP attempts to merge a number of fillers together and move them all at once. For example, in (81), EQSP will discover that all noun phrases ending at the word *costs* are possible fillers and move them in one step downward until it finds a gap in the embedded relative *you know about*. Then it checks to see which of the possible filler-gap pairs are possible.

There is another serious source of inefficiency; it is important to avoiding looking for gaps where there aren't any fillers because it is almost always possible to find a gap if you look hard enough. This is a particularly easy mistake to make in a partially bottom-up parser like ours because the obvious implementation would tend to find gaps first and then check to see if there ar any fillers. The solution to this problem is very similar to the *usefulness* notion introduced in the first chapter; the parser should only look for gaps if they might be useful, that is, only if they are in the context of a filler.

There are many ways to implement wh-movement subject to these efficiency considerations. For example, one could encode the relevant information into the nonterminals directly, as Gazdar does [13], and then apply the general context-free algorithm to the resulting grammar. We have chosen a slightly different approach for EQSP because we believe that his requires too many nonterminals, though it is worthwhile to present his approach as a starting point for discussing our own solution.

3.3.1 Gazdar's Formulation of Wh-Movement

Gazdar encodes the necessary information into the nonterminals by enlarging the class of nonterminals to include a number of *derived categories* which are like normal categories except that they dominate a gap. So, for example, he would have a derived category for an S with an NP gap (written S/NP)[24], and a category for a VP with an NP gap (VP/NP), and a category for an S with a PP gap (S/PP), and so on. A trace of an NP is written NP/NP. He shows that it is possible, with these derived categories, to write context-free rules for wh-movement constructions. We have given the analysis of a simple example below.

Grammar Rule	*Example*
NP→NP S/NP	$[_{NP}$ [the boy] $[_{S/NP}$ you like]]
S/NP→NP VP/NP	$[_{S/NP}$ [you] $[_{VP/NP}$ like]]
VP/NP→V NP/NP	$[_{VP/NP}$ [like] $[_{NP/NP}]]$

Gazdar's proposal is currently a very exciting and controversial area of linguistic inquiry. Most of the debate hinges on whether or not this system is an adequate model of linguistic competence. It is unclear how such a model could handle multiple extractions from a single constituent or how it could handle crossed movements, both of which are rare in English though one can find some possible examples. We will give two examples of multiple extractions, the second of which appears to be crossed.

(83) Which violins$_i$ are these sonatas$_j$ easy [to play t_j on t_j?]
(84) What$_i$ don't you know [how$_j$ to solve t_j t_j?]

These are also somewhat problematic for our approach, as we will see. Currently we don't handle form (83) though we could extend our system to handle it by stacking wh-fillers or by treating $\mathbf{t_j}$ as noun phrase movement recovered in semantics. Form (84) is parsed by raising *how* to *know,* as in *know the method to solve.*

Though these issues are extremely interesting and important, their current resolution is beyond the scope of this paper; we will avoid questions of linguistic competence and concentrate on processing considerations for the time being.

[24] This notation is different from the slash convention used earlier in this paper and it is also different from categorial grammars [2].

Assuming that Gazdar's model is linguistically realistic, how does it fare on efficiency considerations? It has the obvious drawback that it approximately squares the number of categories without taking advantage of a number of constraints on wh-movement. This was the same drawback that led us to reject his proposal of encoding features directly into the nonterminals; just as we believe that it is more efficient to keep category information separate from features, it is probably more efficient to separate category and wh-movement. However, before rejecting his proposal, we should point out that it fares quite well on the two points mentioned above, merging multiple fillers and finding just useful gaps. We will adopt a modified solution which captures most of the benefits of Gazdar's analysis without exploding the space of nonterminals First, consider the problem of multiple fillers as in the following example:

(85) Here is the block on the table in the kitchen on the first floor that you like.

This example is ambiguous because the gap could refer to any of the noun phrases. It is important that the wh-movement transformation does not enumerate all possible fillers. Notice that Gazdar's proposal fares well in this respect because it analyzes the gapped clause: $[_{S/NP}$ you like] just once, even though there are quite a number of noun phrases that the gap might refer to.

Finally consider the problem of useless gaps. Again Gazdar's proposal performs well because the previous implementation of the usefulness notion has exactly the desired behavior when applied to Gazdar's derived categories. That is, the algorithm avoids looking for useless gaps because those derived categories will not be marked useful without first finding a filler. (Fillers precede and command their gaps in leftward wh-movement)[25].

3.3.2 Wh-Movement in EQSP

Our solution is designed to achieve the virtues of Gazdar's proposal without exploding the space of categories. The idea is similar to the approach taken for features; at a very global level, it is a fairly old notion that has appeared in many systems [4, 19]. We will add another slot to the chart which holds the "slashed" category; let us call this the *wh-sent* slot to suggest the ATN notion of *send* arcs. This requires a slight modification to the multiplication rule and the usefulness procedure which are fairly straightforward. The multiplication rule carries the wh-sent value down from a mother to one of its two daughters. (Alternatively, one can think of it carrying the value up from one of the daughters to its mother.) The usefulness procedure has to mark daughters with the desired wh-sent value. We will not discuss these details here.

This system works fairly well though it is often important to know something about the internal structure of the filler. For example, it is often useful to know

[25] This argument does not apply for rightward movement rules such as heavy NP shift or wh-movement in Turkish. In these cases, the algorithm will look for useless gaps but it won't look for useless fillers.

about the features of the filler and therefore the wh-sent slot should contain more information than just the category of the filler. The following example illustrates the need for propagating number features along with wh-movement.

(86) What is happening?
(87) *What are happening?

EQSP uses these agreement features to find filler-gap relations in sentences like (88), (89). The first is using number features to distinguish between the complementizer use of *that* and the pronominal use. The latter is using number features to decide whether the verb *to be* is inverted or not[26].

(88)	I saw the girls$_i$ that e_i are changing.	*complementizer that*
	I saw the girls that$_i$ is changing e_i.	*pronominal that*
(89)	What are the results *e?*	*inverted be*
	What is *(e)* the result *(e)?*	*ambiguous be*

This sort of feature propagation is automatic in Gazdar's framework because his categories already encode all the features, though it is somewhat more difficult for us because we have already factored the features out of the nonterminals. We could also incorporate the features into the wh-sent slot, though we have chosen to pass a pointer to the filler itself[27]. This doesn't change the usefulness condition, though it does complicate the multiplication rule. It is important to merge several fillers together so that the parser finds the gaps just once, rather than once for each possible filler. This is accomplished by filling the wh-sent slot with a list of possible fillers. For example, given a structure like (90) below, the wh-sent slot would contain a list of noun phrases ending just before the word *that.* This is actually implemented as a pointer into the chart, so it does not require too much additional storage.

(90) Here is the block on the table ... on the first floor that you like.

We can manipulate this list as a unit without ever enumerating all its members. For example, we can check agreement constraints by looking at the top-level features of the fillers; it isn't necessary to look deep down inside the fillers. This is an important theoretical point because there are the Catalan number of subtrees ending at a given point, but only a linear number of top-level phrases.

3.3.3 Adjacent Filler-Gaps: a Special Case

Consider examples like (91) where the filler and gap are unambiguous and adjacent. In this special case, it is somewhat inefficient to use the general wh-movement mechanism which is fairly expensive. Consequently, EQSP has a special case to look for these obligatory subject gaps. When EQSP finds such a gap, it removes

---

[26] In fact, EQSP canonicalizes the inverted and uninverted interpretations of sentence (89). The two interpretations can be paraphrased as: *What is it that the result is?* and *What is it that is the result?*

[27] This may well take the generative capacity outside the class of context-free grammars.

gap-finding from the useful things to do in order to block the normal gap-finding mechanism from coming into play and looking for a gap anyway. This turns out to be an extremely useful special case because it applies to a very large percentage of the MALHOTRA corpus.

(91) What is near ...
(92) What is going ...
(93) The girl who is going ...

3.3.4 Complement Clauses, Relative Clauses, and Questions

There are several different types of wh-movement; these distinctions turn out to be very useful because they can constrain the possibilities of wh-movement which is a relatively expensive operation. There is a three-way split between complements (94), relative clauses (95), and questions (96).

(94) It is true that John is a nice guy. *complement*
(95) I saw a man who is a nice guy. *relative clause*
(96) What is true? *question*

In certain cases, the parser can determine which case is which by looking at the wh-word (e.g., *that, who, what*). That is, certain wh-words induce certain types of clauses and not others. For example, *how, what,* and the determiner use of *which* do not start relative clauses or complement phrases:

(97) *It is true how John is a nice guy.
(98) *I saw a man what is a nice guy.

This constraint is implemented in EQSP by assigning each wh-word a feature for each type of wh-clause that it can begin. So for example, the word *how* is assigned a feature for introducing questions (called *in-question*), but not one for relative clauses (called *relative*).

This is another important lexical clue that distinguishes a minimal pair such as (99), (100). The second can be parsed as a complement clause or as a relative clause. The pair are contrasting the lexical entries of *girl* and *report;* the latter optionally selects complement phrases, unlike the former. This distinction is represented in EQSP through the *factive* feature. In this way, EQSP can make the grammatical distinctions necessary in order to find two parses for (100) and just one for (99).

(99) I saw that girls that Bob changed. *relative clause*
(100) I saw the report that Bob changed. *ambiguous*

It has also been noticed that relative clauses will rarely center-embed more than twice. This turns out to be a very useful filter for excluding certain possibilities of relative clauses.

(101) # [The man · [who the boy [who the students recognized] pointed out] is a friend of mine.]

There are no cases in the MALHOTRA corpus with more than one level of center-embedding, and hence we block spurious analyses by excluding two-deep center-embedding from the grammar. The feature *noun-phrase-is-post-modified-by-clause* is set inside a relative clause so that EQSP will not look for another modifying clause.

3.4 Conjunction

Conjunction is perhaps the single most difficult construction to parse. It has all of the combinatoric problems associated with prepositional phrase attachment (unbounded direct ambiguity) plus the problems associated with transformations of finding dependencies between fillers and gaps. We will begin with a relatively simple general purpose mechanism and then we will complicate it with special case modifications as they become necessary. Originally we had hoped that the general purpose mechanism would cover almost all the cases, but experience seems to indicate that this is not possible, at least with current linguistic understanding and current engineering technology. Our implementation is sufficiently general to cover all cases of conjunction in the MALHOTRA corpus, though it is far from the complete and definitive solution to conjunction.

3.4.1 The General Mechanism

Suppose we introduced a number of rules into the grammar as follows:

(102) NP→NP CONJ NP
VP→VP CONJ VP
S→S CONJ S
PP→PP CONJ PP
⋮

Now the normal context-free parsing algorithm would find most of the easy cases. Note that this mechanism has two drawbacks: it is both incomplete and inefficient.

3.4.1.1 Coverage. Let us address the completeness issue first and then we will return to efficiency considerations. This approach does not yet account for a wide range of linguistic transformations associated with conjunction such as: VP-deletion, subject deletion, gapping, right node raising, and the across-the-board convention. It seems that we will have to complicate the mechanism to account for these facts in any case.

Linguistic Constraint	Examples
VP-deletion	Jack saw Bill and Sam did *e* too.
subject deletion	Jack saw Bill and *e* hit Sue.
gapping	Jack saw Bill and Sam *e* Sue.

right node raising	John gave Mary *e*, and Joan presented *e* to Fred, books which looked remarkably similar.
across-the-board	The kennel which [Mary made *e*] and [Fido sleeps in *e*] has been stolen.
	*What fork did John give Mary a knife and *e*.
	*What knife did John give Mary *e* and a knife.

There are numerous ways to complicate the grammar in order to accommodate these facts. For example, Gazdar [12] proposes that one can capture the across-the-board facts by encoding the wh-filler information into the nonterminal (as he normally does for wh-movement) and then restricting the conjunction mechanism to identical nonterminals. We use a similar technique, though slightly modified because we represent the filler in the *wh-sent,* rather than encoding it into the nonterminal. Consequently, we capture the across-the-board facts by insisting that both constituents have the same *wh-sent* values.

3.4.2 Idiosyncratic Cases

One could imagine similar proposals for the other transformations. We have basically adopted this general approach, though we have chosen to implement it in a more efficient way that avoids exploding the space of nonterminals. However, there is another class of problems that we have noticed in practice which has not attracted much attention in theoretical linguistics. It appears that the word *and* can be deleted in certain restricted cases such as:

(103) What was the total cost of raw material in 71, 72, 73?
(104) What was the total cost of raw material in 71 72 73?

This is very interesting from a computational point of view because it means that the conjunction cannot always depend on the presence of words like *and.* Note that almost every conjunction mechanism has this basic flaw; they all trigger on a conjunction word like *and.* It would be an extremely serious mistake to allow the conjunction markers to drop out uniformly in all cases because this would find quite a number of absurd parses, especially if one considered interactions with the other deletion rules mentioned above. This kind of example led us to believe that some of these deletion rules have to be considered on a case-by-case basis. They occur where there is a strong semantic context. For example, we will only allow the word *and* to delete in a sequence of several "semantically similar" noun phrases such as a sequence of dates as above, or in a phrase like: *items 1 2 3 4.*

Actually the problem may be much more serious than this. One can argue that almost any syntactic generalization involving conjunction can be overridden in a strong semantic context. For example, there is a rather strong syntactic generalization that conjunction applies to two constituents of the same part of speech. However, there are some possible counter-examples to this; time, place, and manner adverbs can conjoin with time, place, and manner prepositional phrases as in sentence (105) below. We have implemented an exception to the general mechanism to handle cases such as these.

(105) We expect difficulties [$_{ADV}$ now] and [$_{PP}$ in the future].

This we allow using the feature **time-phrase.** Similarly, it is tempting to claim that conjunction applies to complete constituents, not fragments, though again there are numerous possible counter-examples where the syntactician would be forced to resort to a deletion analysis. The gapping sentences mentioned above are good examples; we've included two more cases below:

(106) John [drove through *e*] and [completely demolished *e*] a plate glass window.
(107) Mary expressed [costs] [in dollars] and *e* [weights] [in pounds].

The first of these we currently don't handle. The second we do handle by taking all conjunction as between strings of constituents in a phrase rather than between constituents, and then restricting the strings to length 1 except in special places such as just after the verb. In some sense, a constituent with a hole in it is a partial constituent, and so in this view, the deletion analysis is a way of conjoining partial constituents, at least in some cases. Unfortunately it is very difficult to process deleted/partial constituents because there are so many combinatoric possibilities. One seems forced to say that deletion rules are greatly restricted by semantic constraints, and then one is left with almost no useful syntactic constraints. If conjunction really is as bad as all this, and we certainly hope that it is not, then it is hard to imagine how one could do better than a case by case analysis. We have attempted to use the general mechanism as much as possible, though we have taken some liberties in certain restricted cases in order to combat the combinatoric nature of the problem.

3.4.3 Conjunction and the Size of the Grammar

Even if we were able to remove all the problems associated with deletion rules and other semantically idiosyncratic cases, Gazdar's approach still leads to a radical increase in the size of the grammar because every part of speech can potentially conjoin with another constituent of the same part of speech and hence we have introduced a new grammar rule for every part of speech. Though this is already very expensive, it gets significantly worse if we reintroduce deletion rules. It appears that context-free grammar rules are a very inefficient way to represent conjunction; we would really like to parse the metarule "XP→XP and XP," instead of expanding the metarule out for each possible part of speech. We have essentially implemented this by adding a general purpose conjunction mechanism that looks for states (a) ending just before the word *and,* and (b) initiated by the first word after the conjunction. It starts these states after the word *and.* So for example, it would start an NP and S after the word *and* in (108) below because each of these categories ends just before the word *and* and each can begin with the word *the.* (Condition (b) is a classic use of lookahead.)

(108) [[The robot] [put [the block] [on [the box]]]] and the ...

This is fairly easy to implement in terms of dotted-rules and the chart; we will not go into the details here. In this way, we have reduced the size of the grammar in a significant way. When EQSP believes that is has reached the end of the second conjunct, it checks that the two conjuncts are "syntactically parallel." This is a somewhat complicated test that basically requires both conjuncts to have the same part of speech and the same wh-gaps and so on, though there are some further restrictions and some exceptions. In particular, there is an exception which allows time and place phrases to conjoin even if they have different parts of speech, as mentioned previously. There is also a restriction for numerals so that they don't conjoin with non-numerals and in: **John* and *2*, except after *for* as in: *For 1971 and plant 2*. Similarly, there are some restrictions for deletion rules so that both conjuncts have the same number of constituents. Top-level clauses have some additional restrictions. For example, EQSP accepts (109) but not (110). These restrictions are expressed in terms of the top-level context features; *question-sentence, declarative-sentence,* and *presentative-sentence.*

(109) Who broke in here and what did he want?
(110) *Who broke in here and I don't like it.

There is a very important added constraint on combinations of three or more conjuncts which blocks arbitrary nesting as in (111). If we allowed all possible nestings, there would be the Catalan number of possible parses. In fact, we limit the depth to 2, so there are the Fibonacci number of possible parses. This number was empirically determined and will be justified in the next section, which discusses empirical results.

(111) # ... [products and [products and [products and products] and products] and products] ...

Multiple conjuncts are somewhat easier to parse when there are commas instead of *ands*. In this case, EQSP uses the *sequence-going* feature to distinguish (112) from (113) at the point where the *and* is reached. In the first case (112) conjunction has already been initiated by the comma while in the second case (113) it hasn't.

(112) x, y and z
(113) x and z

In summary, we employ three types of conjunction mechanism.

(114) Top level:	What did he do and why did he do it?
(115) General:	What did Bob hit and kick? Express weight in pounds and height in feet.
(116) Context determined special cases:	Items 1 2 3 and 4. Results in 71 72 73.

4 Experimental Results

EQSP has been tested on the MALHOTRA corpus [23] (Appendix I) and the LADDER-TODS Collection [16] (Appendix II). Three statistics were kept: sentence length, number of parses, and cpu time. Theoretically, the time should be cubic (or better) with sentence length, and the number of parses should be Catalan (or better) with sentence length. Unfortunately, it is somewhat difficult to test these predictions directly on the two corpuses because there are too many interacting constructions such as wh-movement, prepositional phrases, and conjunction which combine in complicated ways that make it very difficult to predict exactly how the three variables will be related. We have attempted to isolate these various factors by constructing sequences of synthetic sentences such as (117) and (118) which exercise a particular construction, and in this way we were able to compare various constructions with each other and with the two corpuses. These two synthetic series are particularly interesting because they completely bracket all of the sentences in the MALHOTRA corpus. The possessive noun phrases are faster per word than any sentence in the MALHOTRA Corpus, and the gerunds are slower.

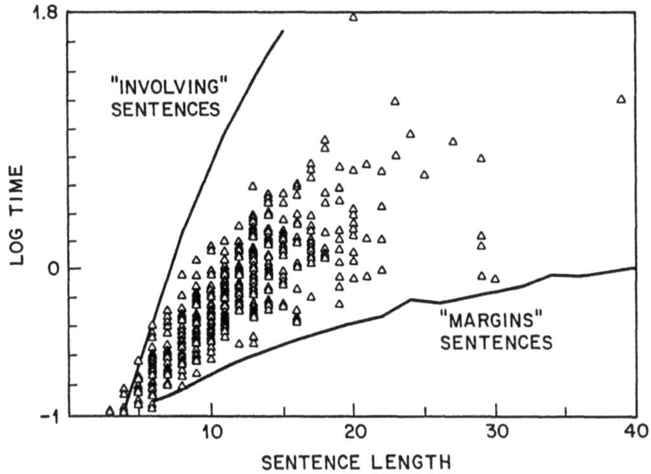

Fig. 1. Plot of CPU time

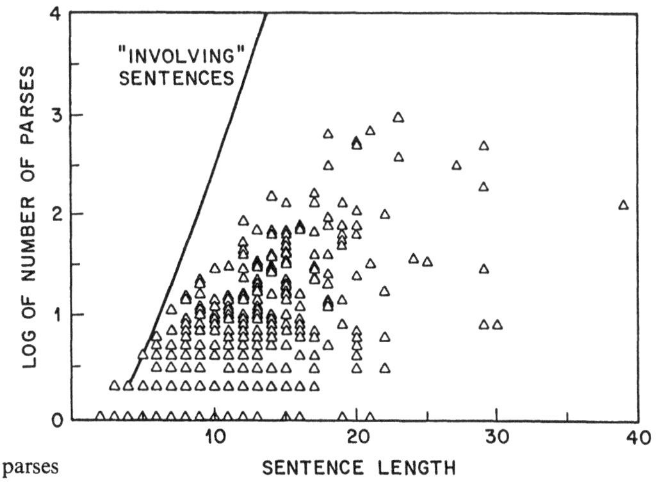

Fig. 2. Plot of number of parses

See the plot below showing the synthetic points completely enveloping the MALHOTRA corpus. It was expected that possessive noun phrases would be fast because they are LR(0), but the gerund result was somewhat surprising; we had expected conjunction or prepositional phrases to be the worst case.

(117) It was margin's margin. *best case*
It was margin's margin's margin.
It was margin's margin's margin's margin.
⋮

(118) What was involving? *worst case*
What was involving involving[28]?
What was involving involving involving?
⋮

These synthetic sentences have led to some other very interesting observations. The number of parses forms a mathematical series which we have been able to solve in certain cases, so that it is possible to predict the excat number of parses for arbitrarily long sentences. Even though we have a theoretical account for this series, it is quite remarkable that, even in practice, it describes the number of parses *exactly,* despite all of the tuning that goes into a large engineering project of this sort. The Catalan series in one such example; we have also constructed synthetic sequences which generate products of two Catalan numbers and the Fibonacci [21] numbers. These will be presented in turn.

One might wonder why we should look for these series? They indicate a fundamental computational process which describes the search space at a very abstract level. For example, the Catalan series suggests that all possible parses are possible and hence the parser is not excluding much of anything; the parser is enumerating all $\mathbf{n}^3$ points in $<i,j,k>$-space, and in this way, it is following a grammar very similar to 'Grammar AA'. This claim can be made without looking inside the parser to see if it is top-down, bottom-up, left-to-right, or whatever. Similarly, the product of two Catalans suggests two independent subgrammars, each of which behaves like 'Grammar AA'. The Fibonacci series suggests yet another class of abstract computations with certain other well-known characterizations.

Nevertheless, many of these series grow extremely quickly; it may be impossible to enumerate these numbers beyond the first few values. And hence, it can be argued that it isn't worthwhile making distinctions between them; some of them are prohibitive and some of them are worse than prohibitive. From an engineering point of view, it doesn't make sense to distinguish between the Fibonacci series and the Catalan series for large numbers; in either case, it will be impossible even to print all the parse trees, and harder still to perform semantic interpretation. Therefore, the argument goes, it must be necessary to introduce some techniques for shrinking the search space, such as canonicalization, semantic constraints, determinism, etc. Although we are extremely sympathetic with some or all of these techniques, we believe that it is worthwhile establishing what will happen without them. With this baseline, it becomes much easier to evaluate a particular tech-

[28] EQSP has an *ing-ing* filter which blocks many of the possibilities, but it does not block the gerund and adjunct interpretations. Perhaps the *ing-ing* filter should be more general.

nique. Presumably the more useful ones will drastically reduce the number of parses from the baseline, and the less useful ones will have little effect.

Finally, it is worthwhile looking at these series carefully because some of them are tractable over practical ranges and some of them are not. For example, the Fibonacci series remains tractable over a much larger range than the Catalan does, and hence if we can show that most of the practical examples lie within the tractable range for a Fibonacci process, but not for a Catalan process, then it would be a real accomplishment to reduce the search space from the Catalan numbers to the Fibonacci, as we have done for conjunction.

4.1 A Comparison of the LADDER and MALHOTRA Corpuses

It appears that the LADDER-TODS collection is considerably easier on the whole; the sentences are shorter, they have fewer parses, and they take less time. Furthermore, the LADDER-TODS collection is more compact; the standard deviations are smaller for each of the three statistics: sentence length, number of parses, and cpu time in seconds. The histograms are given in Figure 3 and a table is given below showing the means, standard deviations, minima, medians, and maxima. The histograms of number of parses and cpu time are plotted on a log scale in order to bring in a few points with very large values. The data have been normalized to account for the different sizes of the corpuses. Each point on the MALHOTRA plots corresponds to five sentences, and each point on the LADDER-TODS plots corresponds to a single sentence[29]. The higher number in the table below represents the MALHOTRA Corpus and the lower number represents the LADDER-TODS collection. It is particularly interesting that the medians for number of parses and time are much smaller than the means; this suggests that most of the data are well behaved and just a few extreme points are causing most of the trouble.

	MEAN	Standard Deviation	Minimum	Median	Maximum
Sentence Length:	11.2	5.1	2	11	39
	9.3	3.0	4	9	18
Number of Parses:	22.5	81.1	0	4	958
	3.3	4.5	1	2	30
CPU Time:	1.2	3.1	.0	.6	58.5
	.5	.5	.1	.3	4.1

The differences between the two corpuses may be due to the ways in which they were collected. Ashok Malhotra gathered his sentences by fooling a number of management experts into believing that he had solved the natural language problem. They were then asked to try out his new program, called the Perfect System.

[29] Round-off errors were taken to the next higher integer. That is, the last point on the MALHOTRA plots corresponds to between 1 and 5 sentences.

Fig. 3. Histograms of MALHOTRA and LADDER corpuses

In fact, his program was a fake; it actually connected the subject directly to an experimenter sitting in the next room, and in this way he was able to gahter an interesting set of sentences which may be fairly representative of a typical query in the management domain. This approach works very well with computer naive domain experts:

> "In fact, surprising as it may seem, few subjects realized that the experimenter was creating the responses until they were told so after the experiment. Until this secret was revealed, many subjects were extremely impressed by the range of capabilities displayed by the system. Thus, the Perfect System could be said to be a success as the subjects behaved as if it were an ideal English language question-answer system." [Ref. 23, p. 57]

On the other hand, the LADDER subjects had a more realistic expectation of the machine's capabilities, and consequently, they may have adjusted their responses appropriately. The LADDER Group has noted that their sentences seemed somewhat biased, though they offer another possible account:

> "Fortunately, our users have been very helpful by tending to avoid the use of the long and complex constructions that are most likely to lead to ambiguities. Perhaps this is because the teletype medium inclines users to prefer short, simple constructions." [Ref. 16, p. 133]

Both LADDER and EQSP perform very well on the LADDER-TODS collection. It is difficult to compare EQSP with LADDER without more data. The EQSP results are given in Appendix II.

4.2 Synthetic Sentences

As mentioned above, it is very difficult to compare parsers with these corpuses because there are too many different factors averaged together. We have explored a new technique for isolating particular factors. In this way, we were able to make some concrete predictions. First we will discuss the number of parses and then cpu time.

4.2.1 Catalan Numbers

As we have mentioned before, the number of parses is perfectly described by the Catalan numbers for the following series of sentences:

1	It was the number of products?
2	It was the number of products of products?
5	It was the number of products of products of products?
14	It was the number of products of products of products of products?
42	It was the number of products of products of products of products of products?
132	It was the number of products of products of products of products of products of products?

429 It was the number of products of products of products of products of products of productsof products?
1430 It was the number of products of products of products of products of products of products of products of products?
⋮

We have also determined that the number of parses is exactly the product of two Catalans for structures like (119) and (120). This is to be expected because the two ambiguities are completely independent. Structure (120) is a very good example illustrating that gap finding is not the only problem for wh-movement; there is only one possible gap (in subject position), but there are the Catalan number of possible fillers.

(119) The number of products of products ... of products was the number of products of products ... of products.
(120) What number of products of products ... of products was the number of products of products ... of products?

This result seems to be very stable; it works for many preopositions and content words. (One might have suspected some variation due to lexical ambiguity.)

4.2.2 Fibonacci Numbers

The number of parses is exactly predicted by the Fibonacci numbers for the following series:

3 It was actual products and actual products and actual products.
5 It was actual products and actual products and actual products and actual products.
8 It was actual products and actual products and actual products and actual products and actual products.
13 It was actual products and actual products and actual products and actual products and actual products and actual products.
21 It was actual products and actual products and actual products and actual products and actual products and actual products and actual products.
34 It was actual products and actual products and actual products and actual products and actual products and actual products and actual products and actual products.
55 It was actual products and actual products and actual products and actual products and actual products and actual products and actual products and actual products and actual products.
89 It was actual products and actual products and actual products and actual products and actual products and actual products and actual products and actual products and actual products and actual products.

The next sentence in the series requires too much memory, though by Engineer's Induction, the next sentence ought to generate 55 + 89 parses. In this case, lexical ambiguity has been carefully controlled; the word *products* must be a noun and not an adjective or a verb which have different morphology (i.e., *producing* and *produce*). We find a very different series if we replace the word *products* with the word *costs*, which can be construed as a verb as in: *That costs too much*. In this case, the series is: 3, 7, 15, 30, 58, 109, . . ., which is the convolution of a Fibonacci series and a shifted Fibonacci series[30]. Also, it should be noted that the word *actual* is playing a crucial role; without it, EQSP will find exactly one parse no matter how many conjuncts there are[31].

Where does the Fibonacci series come from? Previously, we noted that conjunction ought to grow with the Catalan numbers. However, there is a performance constraint in EQSP that blocks arbitrary nesting such as:

(121) #... [actual [products and actual [products and [actual products]]]]

The maximum depth in conjunction is set to 2, as noted near the end of the conjunction section, that is, the **n**-th conjunct can conjoin at its current level or it can conjoin one level higher. The prepositional phrases differ in that attachment is possible at any depth, not just 0 or 1, and hence they generate the Catalan number of parses. With this restriction on conjunction, there are the Fibonacci number of parses, because the number of ways to conjoin n conjuncts is the sum of the number of ways to conjoin the conjuncts at the current level plus the number of way to conjoin those at the embedded level. How many conjuncts can be at each level? There are at most $n - 1$ at the current level and at most $n - 2$ at the level before that. Therefore, the number of parses of **n** conjuncts is the sum of the number of parses of **n** - 1 and the number of n -2, which is the Fibonacci series. In the lexically unambiguous case, the initial case (n less than <2) is 1 and hence we get the familiar numbers. Notice that this analysis fails with lexical ambiguity for two reasons. First the initial cases have several parses and secondly, the inductive cases can combine in more ways than just the sum of the two parts because these ambiguities trigger deletion possibilities and multiple grammar rules, etc.

4.2.3 Worst Case for Number of Parses

As we have mentioned before, the worst case that we have found is (122), which generates more parses per word than any sentence in either corpus as illustrated in the plot above. It can be argued that many of the parses are ungrammatical because the *ing-ing* filter should be stronger than the one in EQSP. However, we have noticed that (123) is almost as bad, and there is no infinitive-infinitive filter in English (though there is one in Italian). EQSP's *ing-ing* filter excludes *ing* participles as verbal complements to an *ing* participle phrase, though it allows them as gerunds and adjuncts. The gerund and adjunct possibilities alone would make these sentences worse than the prepositional phrases sentences because there would be the combination of two Catalan series, not just one. However, there are

---

30 This suggests that the grammar can be analyzed as the concatenation of two networks, which both produce a Fibonacci number of parse trees in isolation [7].

31 This suggests that the conjunction mechanism works differently at the N level than at the NP level.

some more ambiguities. First, the wh-movement can go almost anywhere, and secondly, the auxiliary *was* can invert around any string of *involvings*. Finally, *involving* also has an adjectival part of speech, so there are quite a number of other parses where a few of the *involvings* are taken as prenominal adjectives modifying a gerund.

(122) What was involving involving involving involving ...
(123) What was to total to total to total to total ...

It is a very interesting fact that there will be many fewer parses if we insert a closed class word such as *of*, *with* or even *and* after the first few *involvings* because it restricts wh-movement, inversion, and lexical ambiguity.

4.3 Analysis of CPU Time

As we have noted, in chart parsing, grammars fall into one of three classes: time *n*, time n^2 and time n^3. We have found the same three classes, though the times appear to be slowed down by a factor of *n*, due to the representation of the chart which is optimized for the average case, not the worst case. Recall how we organized the chart. For each state, there is a list of records containing *i* and *j* and other useful information such as features, wh-sent, conjunction, and so on. These lists are sorted on *j* and then on *i* to improve average time performance. It is also assumed that these lists don't tend to be very long because sentences tend to vary constructions, so that it is unlikely that the same state will be used very often in the same sentence. However, this assumption is incorrect in these synthetic sentences where we have intentionally used the same state again and again. In these cases, it can take n^2 time to search down the list of records attached to that state in order to compute chart(s,?i,j), whereas a matrix representation could find the answer in *n* time by enumerating each *i* and checking that square in the matrix. Hence, this algorithm has a worst case behavior of time *n* beyond that of Earley's algorithm. However it is much better than Earley's algorithm when the lists are short because it can compute chart(s,?i,j) in constant time, whereas a matrix representation would require linear time. The fact that our representation is more efficient when constructions are varied is compatible with the intuition that sentences are easier for people to understand under the same conditions. It is certainly true that these synthetic sentences are extremely unnatural; it is hard to imagine a context where one would utter such a sentence even with more meaningful content words.

However, it is somewhat difficult to verify time bounds directly by running the parser and measuring time versus length because several factors interfere with the time measure such as paging and garbage collection. Although we have attempted to factor these out, it is extremely difficult to remove all of them. Hence we have taken an alternative approach of inserting a counter into the innermost loop that searches down the list of records, and in this way we have computed the exact number of records that are examined. It appears that the parser spends almost all of its time searching down records and hence this statistic, henceforth called the record count, is a good idealization of cpu time. In fact it is almost linear with time, though it is impossible to find an exact mathematical relation because the cpu time measure is somewhat noisy, for reasons mentioned above and due to a few other small factors such as a linear overhead for reading the input words and looking them up in the lexicon. Henceforth we will use record count instead of time because it is easier to work with. One record count corresponds to a time unit on the order of a millisecond, though it can vary by an order of magnitude as we will see[32]. Record count is a fairly good replacement for cpu time for most of the synthetic sentences, though it is better for simpler sentences like possessive noun phrases (124) and worse for more complex conjunction (127) where relatively more time is spent in heuristic sections of the parser which are not measured by the record counter. We have plotted the record count against time for four sets of synthetic sentences, progressing from simpler constructions to more complex. The slopes are: 1.6, 5.4, .7 and 21.4 milliseconds per record traversed. The important point is that the lines are almost linear and that the slopes are on the order of a millisecond; we have no explanation for the variability in slopes or the nonlinear residues[33].

(124) It was margin's margin's ... margin's margin.
(125) He believes he believes he believes ... he believes it.
(126) It was products with products with products ... with products.
(127) It was costs and costs and costs and costs ... and costs.

Record count turned out to be a very useful abstraction because, with the aid of MACSYMA [25], we were able to find an exact mathematical relation for record count in terms of sentence length. By substituting time for record count, we have an approximate relation for cpu time in terms of sentence length. We then performed regressional analysis to find the constants in the relations. The fits were extremely encouraging (**R**-square = .9999). These results suggest that (128) is $O(n^2)$, (129) is $O(n^3)$ and (130) is $O(n^4)$. (The function *odd* distinguishes the odd and even length sentences; it returns 1 if sentence length is odd and 0 otherwise. This term is usually important for sentences with inversion; we have no explanation for it in this case.)

Sentences	*Record Count as a function of Sentence Length*
(128) It was margin's margin's margin's ...	$\frac{1}{4} n^2$
(129) He believes he believes he believes ...	$\frac{1}{24} n^3 - \frac{1}{4} n^2 + \frac{1}{6} n - 1$
(130) It was products with products with ...	$\frac{1}{96} n^4 \; \frac{1}{16} n^3 + \frac{5}{24} n^2 - \frac{19}{16} n + \frac{209}{32} + \frac{1}{2}\,\mathrm{odd}(n)$

[32] Also, much of this time (perhaps a half-millisecond) can be attributed to the computation involved in incrementing the record counter itself because of a technical error in the implementation of the counter. A millisecond is approximately 500 machine instructions on our KA PDP-10.

[33] These lines were fitted with r-squares of .9960, .9994, .9995, and .9533, respectively. We have much less confidence that the last line is linear because a plot of the residues shows a strong parasitic effect. This could be explained by showing that the conjunction mechanism is taking a considerable amount of time which seems to be the case, though we have not explored this hypothesis adequately.

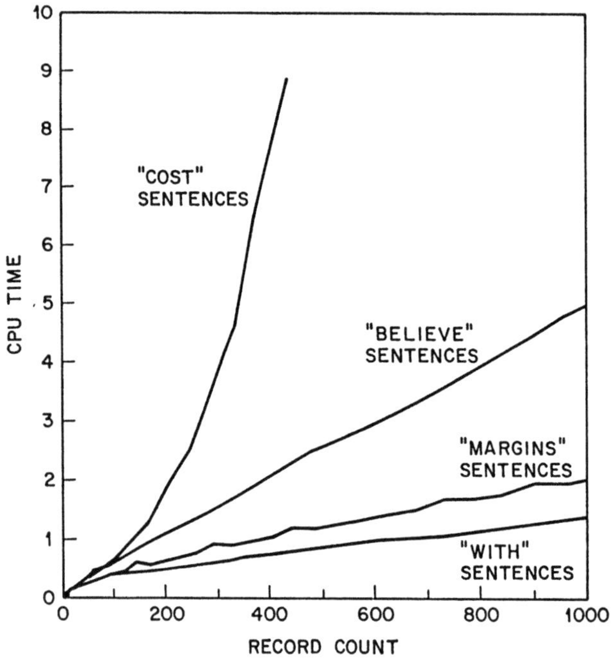

Fig. 4. Plot of record count vs time

These three cases are very similar to the three classes of grammars for Earley's algorithm, except that ours are slower (in the worst case) by a factor of n. For example, (130) is similar to 'Grammar AA' in that it is every way ambiguous. This is known to require n^3 time on Earley's algorithm, and because our algorithm is slower by a factor of n, it requires time n^4 on EQSP. The table below compares the three synthetic cases above with grammars that behave similarly on Earley's algorithm (with no lookahead).

Grammar	*Synthetic Sentences*	*Time on Earley's Algorithm*
$A \rightarrow Aa \mid a$	It was the margin's margin's ...	n
$A \rightarrow aA \mid a$	He believes he believes ...	n^2
$A \rightarrow AA \mid a$	It was products with products with ...	n^3

The analogy for the first and third case should be fairly clear. The first case is a left-branching structure where the usefulness condition (Earley's predict) works very well and hence the chart has only $O(n)$ entries as opposed to the normal $O(n^2)$. This also brings the time bounds down to time n for Earley, though we need time n^2 because all n records happen to be associated with the same state in the grammar and hence we have to look down all of them in order to find chart$(s,0,j)$. Similar comments hold for the third case, which is the worst case for both algorithms, though the constants are significantly worst in the *involving* sentences mentioned above where there is more lexical ambiguity[34]. These constructions are in every way ambiguous and hence Earley's algorithm will have to enumerate every point in $<i,j,k>$-space. EQSP has the same problem with these constructions, not surprisingly, though it has the additional problem that all the records happen to be attached to the same state so it requires another factor of n.

The *believe* sentences are somewhat more interesting because they illustrate a case where lookahead would be very helpful. With lookahead there are only n entries in the chart, but without lookahead there are n^2 entries because the parser can't know which rule to expand, unless it can look ahead to see if there is another input afterwards[35]. If there is another input token, then it should expand the recursive rule (A→aA), and otherwise, it should expand the terminal rule (A→a). In this case the parser knows exacly what to do at each point, and hence there will be only n records in the chart. But if the parser didn't look ahead, it would have to expand both rules, and consequently there will be n^2 records in the chart. As we mentioned in Sect. 2, the lookahead condition has the same effect on right-branching grammars that usefulness has on left-branching grammars; that is, it reduces space bounds from n^2 to n by making the parser behave deterministically. This also improves the time bounds by a factor of n.

In summary, we have shown that cpu time grows with n^2, n^3, and n^4 depending on the grammar in much the same way that Earley's algorithm depends on the grammar. We have also shown that the number of parses can grow as fast as the Catalan numbers. Finally, we have found a best case and a worst case which bracket the two corpuses in both cpu time and number of parses. This provides an attractive empirical verification of the theoretical predictions (of time and space bounds) discussed in the first two sections. In addition, we have found these synthetic sentences to be a very effective tool in analyzing the parser's performance. In [7], we have extended the synthetic sentence approach from a more theoretical point of view.

5 Conclusion

Perhaps the conclusion is a good place to summarize some of the strengths, limitations, and uncertainties we believe would be encountered in proceeding to further develop the EQSP parser. As strengths we can cite the parse time and the coverage.

It is now clear that if a parser is written in compiled rather than interpreted form it will be fast enough for many practical purposes on the bulk of sentences it receives. This has already been shown for parsers which find only one parse or have a limited grammar [4]. We have shown that it also holds for a parser which finds all parses in one of the more complete grammars extant. We have, in fact, shown that this is true if only syntactic constraints are used. Some people state

[34] The actual relation for the *involving* sentences is: $n^4 - \frac{31}{3}n^3 + \frac{61}{2}n^2 - \frac{163}{6}n + 55$.

[35] In other words, 'Grammar aA' is not LR(O), but it is LR*(k)*. Therefore, it will behave deterministically in the parser looks ahead, but otherwise, it will not.

that parse time is no longer critical, but for reading large volumes of text (e.g., proofreading), it is still an issue.

With regard to coverage, careful study of the well-known English grammar books, linguists' examples, and corpuses of actual input has led us to the informal conclusion that our current EQSP system covers a major portion of the syntactic constructions one would want in a parser. Discounting the lexicon, the EQSP system occupies about 87 pages of LISP code and took about 10 man months to program. The transition network defining the grammar has about 131 nodes. This is a small program in comparison with other systems which have been built in LISP. There seems to be no question that we can extend the syntax as far as necessary without running into the so-called complexity barrier, where the program becomes so complex that it cannot be kept coherent using current programming tools.

There are, of course, some potential problems with EQSP which further work may or may not resolve. For one, all our constraints are hard and fast rules; they are either met or they are not. This means that there are four sentences in the MALHOTRA corpus which we currently reject as syntactically unacceptable.

(131) *What would have 1972 prices have been?
(132) Product 4 and 5 show greatest variance, why?
(133) Give me two tables, the contribution margin in each plant for the years 1972 and 1973.
(134) Which years do you have costs figures for?

In each of these the offending element is underlined. The first of these exhibits a serious confusion of two constructions. The remaining three involve problems of agreement. In the second, a singular noun is in apposition with two product names. In the third, a plural noun *tables* is in apposition with a singular noun *margin*. The construction involving *margin* is, however, semantically plural because two years are given. In the fourth a plural noun has been used as a modifier of a head noun. This is a very rare construction. It occurs with pluralia tantum, e.g., *scissors blades,* but not often with other nouns. We were willing to make *sales* a pluralia tantum to handle *sales figures* because one could possibly say, *"sales is the most important thing."* But to make *costs* a pluralia tantum seems wrong. The fact is that plural modifiers are syntactically acceptable, although rare. As we further extend the grammar to rare constructions, more situations of this type will undoubtably arise.

We could accept these sentences by loosening our constraints, but then many extraneous parses of other sentences would be found. Our plan is to build a second diagnostic pass which operates when no acceptable parses were found on the first pass. The first pass will rule out rare constructions which produce many false parses. It will also rule out grammatical errors. This two pass plan will only work if, when the intended parse is so ruled out, no other acceptable parse remains. This is true for the sentences we have tried but we don't know if it will be true in almost all cases. Perhaps when such a situation arises people would also be fooled. However, as we stated above, they have better semantics and pragmatics than we can mount in the short run.

Another problem we face is to reduce the parse time of long sentences full of explosive constructions. Surely, applying all semantics and pragmatics as we go would greatly help, if not solve, this problem. However, our guess is that this will extend the parsing time for the typical sentence, where cheap syntactic constraints alone eliminate almost all parses and thus give semantics and pragmatics an easier job. One solution to this would be to use different strategies depending on the length of the sentence, but this would require us to have the sentence in hand before we begin parsing. We would prefer to parse the sentence as it is being typed, in an on-line fashion, rather than waiting for the entire sentence to be input and only then decide what to do with it.

Our current thinking is to do part of the semantics as the sentence is parsed and the rest on a second pass. We feel that the semantics and pragmatics of noun phrases up to the head noun will be critical, but this is just a guess. We will also apply predicability constraints in filling slots of a subordinate clause. Determining the correct use of PPs would be very helpful in reducing the number of parses, but we feel it may be too expensive for the first pass.

Yet another uncertainty arises when we have to apply semantics to a sentence which has a large number of syntactic parses. Using a chart naturally leads to combining all parses into one structure. Thus instead of having the two separate parses (135) we have the combined structure (136).

(135) This is $[_{NP}\,[_{A}$ flying$]\,[_{N}$ planes$]]$
This is $[_{NP}\,[_{VP}\,[_{V}$ flying$]\,[_{NP}$ planes$]]]$

(136) This is (OR$[_{NP}\,[_{A}$ flying$]\,[_{N}$ planes$]]$
$[_{NP}\,[_{VP}\,[_{V}$ flying$]\,[_{NP}$ planes$]]]$)

We hope that the semantics module can cut off whole branches of combined structure, thus eliminating more than one parse at a time. This has been true for the limited semantics module now implemented. However this operates more at the level of LADDER-TODS rather than MALHOTRA. Going from one to the other greatly increased the demands in syntax and this might happen in semantics. We found it very complex to try to maintain a factored structure combining alternative semantic interpretations. This can perhaps be done, but for the moment we have opted to construct separate semantic interpretations. If there are a great many of these we are again faced with a blow up of required resources.

So far, we are pleased with the EQSP parser. The results in the appendices are very encouraging. Time will tell how well the above problems can be solved. If they can, we will have a very useful parser.

Acknowledgments. We would like to thank Glenn Burke and Peter Szolovits for their discussion, comments, and programming assistance both on this parser and its predecessors. Peter Szolovits also helped us proofread this final draft which was completed after the death of the first author.

Appendix I

Results with the MALHOTRA Corpus

The first number is the number of parses and the second is cpu time in seconds on the MIT-ML machine, which is roughly a half MIPS (million instructions per second) KA PDP-10 machine. The symbol "–" is used when EQSP was unable to produce results in a reasonable amount of time and space.

12	3.4	What was the percentage of overhead costs to total sales for the last five years?
2	1.2	What were the profit margins for each product for the last five years?
14	0.9	What are the overall profits on operations for the past 5 years?
2	0.7	What were the gross sales figures for the past five years?
152	2.4	What are profit margins as a percentage of sales for each manufacturing installation?
5	0.7	What is the profit contribution of each manufacturing installation?
1	0.0	OK.
6	0.9	What data do you have on operations as a percentage of gross sales?
3	0.1	Yes and for each plant.
1	0.0	Can you calculate percentages?
14	0.6	What are the production costs as a percentage of sales?
7	0.5	What are the deviations of production cost from actual?
1	0.1	Cancel this question.
16	1.7	What is the ratio of actual cost to budgeted cost for each product?
10	1.5	What is the percentage change in sales for each product for the past year?
7	0.4	What are variable costs for manufacturing operations?
16	0.5	Have transportation costs increased during the past years?
7	0.6	What are the ratios of production costs to sales?
6	1.0	What has the average selling price for each product been for the past two years?
12	1.4	What quantities were produced for each product for the past two years?
8	0.8	Please display overhead costs for all plants for 1972 and 1973.
7	0.6	What was budgeted overhead for all plants for 1972?
1	0.2	What were sales and profits for 1973?
1	0.1	Do you have variable budgets?
3	0.2	Do overhead costs vary with volume?
12	0.6	I believe your overhead variance accounts for your lower than expected profits.
4	0.2	I suppose I should.
2	0.9	What were contribution margins by product for 1972 and 1973?
2	0.2	How are contribution margins calculated?
3	0.7	What is the difference between list price and average selling price?
1	0.0	For 1972?
3	1.6	What is the difference between plant 1 and plant 3 and plant 2 and plant 4?
7	0.4	What are the components of overheads for the plants?
9	0.5	Is transportation cost part of operating expenses?
1	0.2	Where does transportation cost get included?
5	0.4	Give me the constituents of overheads for each plant?
2	0.2	I would like to end the interview.
5	1.2	List sales for product 1 through product 5 for the last two years?
85	2.0	List prices of single unit prices for both 72 and 73.
22	1.8	What was cost of producing each product for both 1972 and 1973?
2	0.3	Production cost first for one unit.
48	0.9	Did one plant assume more production of batteries from the other plants in 1973?
1	0.0	In 1972?
28	1.9	What was the rate of increase of shipping cost between 1972 and 1973?
6	0.6	Are shipping costs reflected in production costs?
2	0.3	Do you have any information on customer satisfaction?
3	2.0	What is the percentage of repeat customers in 1973 and 1972 and in 1971 and 1972?

1	0.3	What was the unit price in 1973?
63	2.4	What's rate of unit cost for each year and the ratio of this production increase to product price?
62	2.0	What is the percent of increase of each product for each year studied?
2	0.7	What was percent decrease in sales for last 5 years?
1	0.1	Cancel this question.
5	0.8	What was % profit for each of last 5 years?
2	0.2	Increase over last year.
1	0.4	What were overhead costs for last 5 years?
5	1.3	What is list price vs selling price for last 2 years?
1	0.5	What's difference between list price and average quotation price?
0	0.6	Product 4 and 5 show greatest difference between list and quotation prices, why?
9	0.7	Do you have list of changes in sales force for each branch?
1	0.0	It should be included.
10	0.3	Give me a breakdown of items in your overhead.
3	0.2	Include each of these by plants.
2	0.3	Compare overhead costs for last 5 years?
9	0.7	Do you have further breakdowns of overhead attributable to each product within plants?
40	8.3	What % of each product is sold from each plant for each of the last 5 years?
7	1.6	What is total volume for each plant (sales) for each of the 5 years?
66	5.2	Compare plant overhead costs with total overhead costs for last 2 years, 1973 and 1972.
28	1.2	List increases in overhead for each plant for last five years?
5	0.4	Compare overhead costs for plants for last five years.
8	1.0	What are salary increases for each plant for last two years?
9	0.8	List increase in interest costs for last two years.
11	0.9	List inventory of product at end of 1971 and 1972.
3	0.4	List all data items you know about.
1	0.2	How many plants are there?
9	0.5	For 1973 list the sales of products by plant one, broken down by product.
5	1.4	For 1973 and for products 1 through 5 list prices and percentage profit margin.
8	1.5	For 1973 and plant 1 list direct manufacturing expenses by product and also total overhead.
5	0.3	Are the prices the same from plant to plant?
30	1.6	By plant, list overhead figures for 1972 and 1973.
16	1.5	For each plant, list the ratio of overhead to sales in 1972 and 1973.
-	-	In the future, please express numbers of over 100000 in terms of units of millions, and numbers over 100 but less than 100000 in units of thousands.
12	1.4	List production costs by plant for 1972 and 1973.
4	0.9	For each product, list the profit percentage for 1972 and 1973?
93	3.5	For each product list the ratio of total sales to total cost in 1972 and in 1973.
4	0.5	What is the definition of the profit for a product?
1	0.3	Were the prices the same in 1972 and 1973?
3	1.1	Why did you give me prices of $ 17, 18, 19.25, 20.25, and 18.0 earlier?
2	0.2	Do you have information about transportation cost?
2	0.9	What was transportation cost by plant for the last two years?
11	0.4	Is transportation cost included in overheads?
10	0.6	What are the components of the various costs you know about?
692	5.7	For each plant give the ratio of 1973 to 1972 figures for each type of production cost and overhead cost.
5	1.2	Why was there such a great increase in operating cost in plant 0?
40	2.3	Print every piece of information you have concerning plant 0 in 1972 and 1973.
2	1.2	Disregarding plant 0 totally, what is the difference in total profit between 1972 and 1973?
1	0.3	What is the difference in profit percentage?
3	1.1	What was the percentage increase in overhead costs between 1972 and 1973?
2	0.7	What was the percentage increase in the average price per product?

2	0.6	What was the average increase in the cost per product?
2	0.2	How did the product mix change?
2	1.0	What were the gross margin on each product in 1972 and 1973?
10	1.4	What is profit as a percent of sales in 1972 and 1973?
43	1.4	Are transportation costs included in overhead or cost of goods sold?
7	2.3	What components of the overhead costs go up more than 2%?
10	1.8	What was overhead cost as a percent of sales in 1972 and 1973?
1	0.3	What was the increase in interest cost due to?
17	2.8	What would have 1973 profits have been compared to 1972 if the product mix had not changed in those two years?
6	1.0	How much did amount borrowed go up between 1972 and 1973 and how much did the average interest rate go up?
66	3.5	What percent of overhead cost is interest cost and what percentage is operating costs?
15	0.8	How much did operating costs go up between 1972 and 1973?
16	2.9	What were the five largest dollar increases in operating costs between 1972 and 1973?
14	1.3	How much was the dollar increase in operating costs and interest costs?
2	0.2	I know what the problem is.
2	0.6	What is the total sales for the past three years?
1	0.5	What was the net profit in 72 and 73?
2	1.2	What was the total cost of raw material in 71, 72, 73?
8	1.0	What was the dividend paid in 1971, 1972, 1973?
2	0.5	What if any are outstanding loans, 1971, 1972, 1973?
3	0.5	What was the interest rate, 1971, 1972, 1973?
2	0.1	What are the outstanding shares?
8	0.5	Any equipment purchased for long term depreciation?
3	0.4	Do you have information about what these loans are for?
2	0.3	Do you have labor cost for finished products?
2	0.9	What was the total labor cost for 1971, 1972, 1973?
4	0.2	Are we facing inflation?
4	0.4	What are we doing with the $ 16 million loan?
2	0.3	OK I think I know what the problem is.
1	0.3	What was total overhead in 1973?
0	0.3	Which years do you have costs figures for?
2	0.9	What were the overhead costs in each of the last five years?
4	0.9	What were total sales in each of the past five years?
1	0.3	What was the most profitable product in 1973?
1	0.0	Yes.
2	0.6	What were the profit margins on each product in 1972?
11	1.7	How much of each product was produced in 1972 and in 1973?
20	1.5	How much did the inventory level of each product change in 1973 from 1972?
3	0.8	What were the sales for each product in 1972 and in 1973?
2	0.6	What were profits in each of the last five years?
1	0.6	What were total sales in the last 5 years?
1	0.1	Cancel that question.
2	0.4	What were sales of each product in 1971?
7	1.9	What were the percentage increases in sales for each product in 1972 and 1973?
2	0.7	What is the overhead cost for each type of battery?
1	0.1	Overhead for 1972.
5	0.3	Difference in overhead from 1972 to 1973?
3	0.4	List the product mix for 1972 and 1973.
5	0.8	Give me the profit margin on each product for 1972 and 1973.
2	0.8	What is the cost of each product for 1972 and 1973?
3	0.8	What were sales for each product in 1972 and 1973?
4	0.5	Give me the budget for each plant and the overrun if any.
2	0.0	Production costs.
1	0.5	What is the overhead budget for each plant?
4	0.7	What overhead costs were incurred by each plant?
1	0.5	What is the percent overhead overrun at each plant?

33	2.2	Give me sales percent increase at each plant for 1973 over 1972.
1	0.2	What information do you have on competition?
3	0.3	Do you have any info on production costs?
34	1.4	Table direct cost, overhead cost, and contribution per unit sold for 1973.
1	0.1	How do you define margin?
36	9.3	Table sales in units sold, product mix, direct cost per unit and overhead cost per unit for the last 4 years?
5	2.7	Table unit sales, direct manufacturing cost, margin and product mix for the last 2 years by product.
1	0.1	Do you perform mathematical computations?
101	5.1	Please compute the following: percent change in unit sales, percent change in unit production cost from 1972 to 1973.
1	0.0	By product, please.
10	0.4	Do you have a forecasting model for demand?
2	0.2	Do you have any model at all?
1	0.2	List the functions you can perform.
19	1.6	Are there any variances between actual prices charged our customers and the guideline prices?
1	0.3	Please table them for product 4 for the five major customers.
10	0.9	List actual sales price and guideline price by product.
654	3.0	Do you have a model to maximize contribution to the company subject to production and other constraints?
10	0.9	Why were the quotation prices lower than list prices in 1973?
2	0.3	Have they been this way for the past years too?
1	0.0	No.
2	0.2	Please give me the overhead cost for 1972.
8	0.7	Table profit before tax for 1972 and 1973.
-	-	Compute profit for 1972 and 1973 according to the following formula: actual unit sales by product times list price minus production cost for the product summed over all products less overhead cost for the year.
2	0.2	I think I understand the problem.
1	0.0	Thank you.
1	0.6	What was the contribution margin of product 1 in 1973?
3	1.6	What were the actual and budgeted contribution margins of products 1, 2, 3, 4, 5 in 1973?
1	0.9	What were the contribution margins for products 1, 2, 3, 4, 5 in 1972?
5	0.4	Give the product mix in 1972 and 1973.
63	3.1	Give the actual and budgeted overhead costs in 1973 and the actual overheads in 1972 for each plant.
7	0.6	Give total contribution figure for 1972 and 1973.
1	0.0	Cancel.
7	0.6	Give total profit figure in 1973 and 1972.
12	0.7	Give list and actual prices for all products in 1973.
12	0.4	Give actual prices for all products in 1972.
3	0.3	Do you have a breakdown of overhead costs?
23	1.3	Give the breakdown of actual and budgeted overhead costs for plants 0, 2, 4.
556	58.5	Give actual and budgeted operating costs for all plants, and actual and budgeted management salaries and interest costs.
2	0.1	Give the budget profit.
2	0.2	Do you have data on transportation costs?
2	0.2	Do you have the data by plant?
4	0.4	Give budgeted and actual transportation cost by plant.
2	0.2	Give budgeted and actual sales revenue.
1	0.2	Give budgeted and actual inventory.
2	0.3	Give budgeted and actual selling costs.
1	0.2	How far back does your information go?
5	1.1	What was the % overhead in each of the last five years?
2	0.2	Percent of overhead to sales.

28	1.9	Were there any changes in the product mix in terms of sales dollars?
2	1.2	What were the profit margins of the five batteries in the last two years?
14	1.1	What are the handling costs associated with each product and did they change over the last two years?
70	2.5	Handling costs are costs associated with products that are not reflected in direct MFG costs.
5	0.8	What are the actual selling prices of the five batteries?
48	1.6	How much was the additional revenue received from the 20% sales increase and where was it spent?
510	6.2	The intent of my question is to find out if you know if your accounting methods can relate the changes in sales to changes in your expense structures.
2	0.1	Does this help?
39	1.7	Please give me changes in each type of cost associated with each product.
958	6.5	In as much as allocating costs is a tough job I would like to have the total costs related to each product.
130	5.4	I mean I would like the cost of each product broken down on a direct and indirect basis.
2	0.8	What was the total production costs in the most recent two years?
1	0.7	Have any plants been supplying batteries to other than normal customers ie outside of their normal sales district?
20	1.2	Please display overhead figures (actual and budget) for all plants for the past four years.
12	1.7	Which plants were over budget on overhead by more than 5%?
7	1.3	Please display the overhead budget variance in percent and absolute $ for plants 0, 2, and 4.
31	3.0	Which plants were over budget on fixed costs by more than 5%?
15	1.2	Display the profitability of each plant divided by plant sales.
14	1.2	Display sales revenues for all plants for the past four years.
3	1.1	Display average company wide profitability for the last four years (%).
1	0.0	Yes.
4	0.9	Why is there such a difference between the company wide average profitability and the profitability of the independent plants?
4	0.3	I suggest we get rid of plant zero!
18	2.0	Has product mix changed in any plant whose profitability has fallen off?
165	5.7	Has product mix changed by more than 1% in any plant whose profitability has decreased?
8	0.9	Display the direct cost variance (absolute $ and %) for all plants.
4	0.6	Has there been a decrease in contribution margins for any product?
10	1.2	Display the percentage overhead growth for each plant for the past four years.
20	1.2	Display the overhead divided by sales (%) for each plant.
4	1.1	Why are the OH figures for plants 2 and 4 higher than for 1 and 3?
1	0.3	Has the profitability of any plant decreased?
1	0.2	Which one(s)?
6	0.7	Display the margins for plant 2 for the past 4 years.
322	8.2	Display the difference between list price and actual costs (direct + overhead) divided by list price for plant 2 for the past four years.
1	0.0	Yes.
5	0.6	Give me the breakdown of overhead expenses for the years 1972 and 1973.
16	1.0	Give me comparative numbers for operating costs for the years 1972 and 1973.
1	0.4	What was the profit margin for the year 1972?
1	0.0	Yes.
2	0.6	What was the sales revenue by product for the year 1972?
6	0.8	Give me the same revenue figures for the year 1973.
14	1.2	Give me the actual cost vs budgeted cost for each product for the years 1972 and 1973.
1	0.0	Yes.
25	3.0	Give me comparative figures for management salary, interest costs, and depreciation for 1972 and 1973.
1	0.5	What were the gross profit figures for the years 1972 and 1973?

5	1.3	What were the comparative figures for sales revenue vs direct costs for the years 1972 and 1973?
1	0.0	Yes.
76	1.9	Give me a breakdown of direct costs and overheads for each plant in the years 1972 and 1973.
76	1.9	Give me a breakdown of budgeted direct costs and overheads for each plant for the years 1972 and 1973.
2	0.9	Give me plant 0 production cost figure for the years 1972 und 1973.
41	2.3	By what percent did the overhead expenses in 1973 increase over those in 1972.
2	0.9	What were the comparative figures for overhead expenses for the years 1972 and 1973?
5	0.5	Give me details of how the additional sales revenue in 1973 was spent.
2	0.8	What was the product mix in the sales for the years 1972 and 1973?
1	0.4	What were the selling prices of each product?
10	1.1	What were average manufacturing costs for each product?
4	1.3	What were unit production costs for each product in the previous year?
8	2.5	What were the relative percentages sold of each product in 1972 and 1973?
4	1.3	What were average quotation prices for each product in 1972?
10	1.0	What were budgeted costs for each product in 1972 and 1973?
1	0.0	Both.
9	0.5	Do you have budgeted production costs on a per unit basis?
31	3.9	What quantity of product 1 was sold by all plants in 1973?
3	1.0	What were contribution margins for each product in 1972 and 1973?
31	1.9	What are the relative percentages of each product sold by each plant?
9	0.7	What are the relative percentages of sales by each plant?
2	0.3	Do you have list prices for each product?
1	0.2	What were they in 1972 and 1973?
512	5.1	Give me a breakdown of difference between list and average quoted price for each product for 1972 and 1973.
1	0.2	How many plants are there?
17	1.7	Which of the four plants had the largest value for total sales in 1973?
22	4.5	At plant 2, which product accounted for the largest percentage of total sales in dollars?
2	0.5	Does product 2 also account for the largest percentage at plant 4?
4	1.7	What was the total overhead of production for product 2 at plant 2 in 1973?
1	0.4	Substitute "direct manufacturing cost" for "overhead of production" in previous input.
382	15.6	What is the number of units of product 2 produced at plant 2 in 1973 times the unit cost of product 2?
1	0.3	Define the terms "unit cost" and "unit price".
382	15.7	What was the number of units of product 2 produced at plant 2 in 1973 times the unit price of product 2?
2	0.1	How is profit computed?
28	1.4	Can you produce a profit figure for a specific product at a specific plant in 1973?
312	7.3	Print a table containing unit cost and unit price for each product at plant 2 in 1973.
10	0.5	Compute unit cost for each of the products in 1972.
2	0.5	Which unit prices were different in 1972?
1	0.0	Print their values.
2	1.6	What were the total overhead costs at plant 2 in 1972 and 1973?
4	0.2	How is overhead cost computed?
1	0.2	List the fixed, non-manufacturing expenses.
108	1.7	For each of the factors just listed give the total value incurred at plant 2 in 1972 and 1973.
29	1.8	At plant 2 list the operating cost incurred in 1972 and 1973.
76	4.1	For depreciation management salary and interest cost list the amounts incurred in 1972 and 1973.
1	0.4	What was the operating cost at each plant?
72	4.0	What was the percent change in operating cost at each plant form 1972 to 1973?
2	2.1	In 1973 what percentage of the direct manufacturing cost was accounted for by operating cost?
69	2.4	What was the change in total manufacturing cost from 1972 to 1973?

9	1.2	What was the percent change in total revenues from 1972 to 1973?
2	2.2	In 1973 what percentage of the direct manufacturing cost was accounted for by operating cost?
69	2.4	What was the change in total manufacturing cost from 1972 to 1973?
69	3.4	What was the percent change in total manufacturing cost from 1972 to 1973?
9	1.2	What was the percent change in total revenues from 1972 to 1973?
26	3.3	What was the percent change in total overhead costs from 1972 to 1973?
22	1.7	Define P-cost to be the sum of overhead cost and manufacturing cost.
6	1.0	What percentage of the P-cost is accounted for by overhead cost?
5	0.4	For what year was that figure?
4	0.3	Give me the same figure for 1972.
2	0.1	How is profit computed?
4	0.2	How is total cost computed?
1	0.4	Are production cost and manufacturing cost the same?
1	0.0	Hello!
0	1.7	Give me two tables, the contribution margin for all products in each plant for the years 1972 and 1973.
2	0.4	Give me the total sales for 1972 and 1973.
5	0.5	Give me the sales volume by product for the years 1972 and 1973.
33	4.7	Give me the following proportions: the sales of products one, two and five divided by the total sales for 1972 and 1973.
13	1.3	Give me the average costs and the budgeted costs for the five products for 1973 and 1972.
2	0.0	Unit costs.
9	0.5	Give me the distribution of the sales of product four by plant.
7	0.7	Distribution of the sales of product 4 by plant for the year 1972.
2	0.2	Give me the budget for plant 4.
3	0.5	Give me the direct costs and the overheads for 1972 and 1973.
7	1.1	Was the actual overhead expense in plant 4 higher than the budgeted amount in 1973?
1	0.1	By how much?
128	16.1	Suppose the sales in 1973 had remained unchanged, would the profit picture have altered if the selling price of product 1 had been increased to allow a profit margin of $ 5.5, and by how much?
1	0.4	Next, would the sales have altered significantly if there had been this price increase?
28	1.5	Even though the plants are not operated as profit centers, could you tell me the contribution to profits from each plant for the years 1972 and 1973?
9	0.7	Give me the sales by product for plant two for the years 1972 and 1973.
5	0.3	Give me the proportional increase in the sales of the various products.
5	0.6	Give me the prices for the various products for the last two years.
1	0.0	No.
2	0.5	Please give me the sales for 1969 70 71 72 and 73.
3	0.7	Total profit margin for 69 70 71 72 and 73.
2	0.1	Total profit.
1	0.2	Profit margins for each product?
4	0.3	Sales form each plant during 73.
3	0.3	Sales from each plant during 72.
12	1.8	The ratio of products costing $ 6.25 and $ 5.00 from each plant during 72 and 73.
5	0.5	Can you give me data on product mix from each plant?
7	1.4	Give me the overhead costs from each plant during 72 and 73.
39	2.4	Give me the ratios of overhead costs and sales from each plant for 72 and 73.
24	2.1	Give me the ratios of overhead costs and sales for plants 1 2 3 4 for 72 and 73.
1	0.1	For 72 and 73.
133	3.8	Give ratios of manufacturing costs to sales for plants 1 2 3 and 4 for 72 and 73.
37	1.1	Give percentage change in sales for each plant for years 72 and 73.
63	1.8	Give percentage change in overhead costs for all plants for years 72 and 73.
1	0.3	What is total revenue for company?
5	0.3	What was the cost of goods sold?
2	0.1	I want the sum.

1	0.2	What was the net income?
2	0.6	What is the cost for each product in each plant?
1	0.1	Unit cost.
9	1.8	What was the actual unit cost change per product in 1973 over 1972?
30	1.5	How much did overhead expense increase in 1973 over 1972 in each plant?
1	0.1	What is plant 0?
2	0.2	Will our customers pay more for the product?
1	0.0	Cancel.
9	0.9	What was the volume increase per product in 1973 over 1972?
9	0.9	What was overhead increase per location in 1973 over 1972?
2	0.3	Who are my customers and what are their volumes per customer?
1	0.3	What is the price of each product?
2	0.2	Display for 1972 and 1973.
6	1.9	Sales, overhead, selling price, overhead, direct manufacturing cost, and profit margin for all types.
1	0.3	Remember this request (call it request A).
2	0.1	Can you format reports?
2	0.4	Please respond to request A for years 1972 and 1973.
2	0.1	Display sales.
7	0.8	Display sales for years 1972 and 1973 by battery types.
1	0.2	Call chas the ratio (overhead/sales).
1	0.0	Congratulations.
2	0.4	Please retain the results of specifications until I change them.
6	0.7	Display for years 1972 and 1973 sales and chas by battery type.
6	0.6	Display ((sales in 1972 - sales in 1973)/sales in 1972).
1	0.2	Remember to retain specifications of previous requests.
1	0.2	Call last displayed quantity "sales growth".
7	0.5	Display sales growth for all types.
3	0.4	Display average cost for 1972 and 1973.
4	0.4	Production cost averaged over sales.
1	0.0	Again by product please.
20	0.7	Display cost of goods sold for product I.
1	0.4	What is the difference between "production cost" and "direct manufacturing cost"?
1	0.0	No they aren't.
2	0.1	Give me definition of margin.
1	0.0	Standard cost?
5	0.5	Let scvar be difference between standard costs and production costs.
4	0.6	Display scvar and sales growth for 1972 and 1973.
1	0.0	Cancel.
5	0.7	Display scvar for all products and all years.
2	0.1	What are my expense categories?
2	0.1	Display overhead.
8	0.6	Let alloc be ((overhead/production cost)*total production cost) for each product.
3	0.4	What data do you have regarding overhead expenditures?
3	0.5	What data do you have regarding production cost?
3	0.5	What data do you have regarding product mix?
9	0.7	Do you have production cost per unit for each type of product?
7	0.6	Print production cost per unit for product 1.
3	0.5	Print list price for product 1.
14	0.9	Print total manufacturing cost for product 1.
28	1.4	Print total manufacturing cost per unit of product 1.
5	0.6	Print overhead cost per unit of product 1.
16	1.2	What was the average budgeted cost per unit of product 1?
4	0.5	What does the average budgeted cost per unit include?
17	0.9	Print budgeted cost per unit of products 2, 3, 4.
7	0.9	Print direct production costs per unit for all products.
11	0.9	Print list prices per unit for all products.
2	0.8	What was the expected contribution margin for all products per unit?

2	0.9	What was the actual contribution margin for all products per unit?
7	1.5	What was the average selling price per unit for all products?
2	0.2	What were expected overhead costs?
1	0.2	What was actual overhead cost?
1	0.2	What was the planned product mix?
1	0.2	What was actual product mix?
23	1.4	Print production costs per unit and per plant for all products.
6	0.7	Do you have a list of overhead cost for each plant separately?
1	0.1	Print this list.
1	0.1	What is plant 0?
54	1.6	Do you have a list of production cost itemized per type of direct costs?
1	0.2	What was the budgeted direct material cost?
1	0.2	What was the direct material cost?
1	0.1	What was labor cost?
1	0.1	What was transportation cost?
1	0.3	What was material cost in 1972?
1	0.3	What was labor cost in 1972?
1	0.3	What was transportation cost in 1972?
16	1.0	Do you have records on sales per major customer in 1972 and 1973?
2	0.1	List data available.
3	0.8	Print the unit cost for battery type 1 at each plant.
27	1.5	List actual and pudgeted unit costs for product 1 for 65 to 73.
32	1.5	List the data for the last 5 years for each product by unit cost.
192	1.7	Define equation discount (x) = (list price (x)-selling price (x))/(list price (x)).
1	0.2	Solve discount (product 1).
2	0.3	Print discount (product 1).
2	0.5	Solve discount (product 2), then print discount (product 2).
2	0.4	Solve discount (product 3), then print answer.
2	0.4	Solve discount (product 4), print answer.
2	0.4	Solve discount (product 5), print answer.
10	1.0	Print profit margin for each product for 72 and 73.
32	0.9	Define %sales(x) = (total sales product (x))/(total company sales).
7	0.7	Solve %sales(x) for each product for 72 and 73.
39	1.2	Print the number of units of each product produced by plant.
3	0.4	Print total sales volume by plant.
3	0.3	List profit margins by plant.
5	0.4	List production costs by plant.
5	0.4	List overhead costs by plant.
8	0.9	Define %CHoverhead(T) = (overhead(T) - overhead(T-1))/(overhead(T-1)).
2	0.2	Why are there 5 plants?
2	0.6	What were the major increases in overhead in plant 1?
14	0.6	Give dollar figures for overhead expenses for plant 1.
2	0.3	Itemize overhead costs for plant 1.
8	0.8	Define %Ch (item T) = (item(T)-item(T-1))/(item(T-1)).
		10.2Let item be depreciation, and T be 73.
1	0.2	Print the last answer.
3	0.2	Let item be operating cost.
1	0.1	Let management salaries be item.
1	0.2	Let item be interest cost.
8	0.5	Let item be operating cost by plant.
6	0.3	What makes up operating costs?
1	0.1	Let item be entertainment expenses.
3	0.4	Print for total, and each plant.
2	0.2	Let item be interest cost by plant.
1	0.3	What were the overhead expenses in 1973?
3	1.0	What was the percentage increase in overhead cost, 1973 vs 1972?
14	1.6	What was the percentage increase in freight and distribution costs for the same period?
7	1.3	What was the actual value of freight and distribution costs in 1973?

2	0.4	Was there an increase in truckers fees in 1973?
52	1.4	Are all increases from freight carriers passed on to the customer?
11	0.4	Is transportation cost included in overhead?
3	0.8	What were the sales by product (5 products) for 1972 and 1973?
2	0.6	What was the turnover by product for 1972 and 1973?
56	1.4	Divide cost of sales by average inventory for each year for each product and give us the result.
1	0.1	For 1972 and 1973.
3	1.0	What was the profit margin for each product for 1972 and 1973?
7	1.8	What was the percentage of total sales for each product for 1972 and 1973?
3	0.6	What cost items are included in overhead cost?
6	1.0	What were the overhead costs for 1972 and 1973 for each plant?
30	1.9	Can you give the percent of total overhead cost of each plant for 1972 and 1973?
4	1.0	What was the percent change 1972 vs 1973 for each plant?
8	0.5	Do you have a model for measuring customer service?
77	1.4	Do you have a count of the number of sales requests and the number of requests filled?
1	0.3	What types of data do you have?
4	0.2	Is region recorded by product?
4	0.2	Is revenue recorded by product?
3	0.3	What are revenues for each product?
3	0.2	What are sales by plant?
7	0.4	What are sales by plant by product?
132	1.4	Can you subtract 1972 sales by plant by product from 1973 sales by plant by product?
132	1.3	Subtract 1972 sales by plant by product from 1973 sales by plant by product.
3	0.6	Did any product costs exceed budget in 73?
22	0.7	By plant by product which costs exceeded budget?
1	0.5	Which product of the five had the largest percentage variance?
2	0.3	In 1972 which product or products had largest variances?
1	0.5	What were 1972 and 1973 profit margins by product?
10	0.3	Can you give unit costs by plant by product?
2	0.8	What were actual costs per unit for plant two?
1	0.2	What were unit costs for 1972?
2	0.5	What was product mix by percent in 72?
2	0.5	What was product mix by percent in 73?
15	0.3	Were prices raised in 1973 over 1972?
2	.6	What were 1972 and 1973 prices for each product?

Appendix II

Results with the LADDER-TODS Collection

2	0.3	What kind of information do you know about?
2	0.3	Is there a doctor on board the Biddle?
3	0.4	Display all the American cruisers in the North Atlantic.
6	0.7	What is the name and location of the carrier nearest to New York?
1	0.3	What is the commanding officer's name?
1	0.1	Who commands the Kennedy?
1	0.2	What is the Kennedy's beam?
1	0.2	When will the Los Angeles reach Norfolk?
5	0.5	Tell me when Taru is scheduled to leave port.
4	0.2	Where is she scheduled to go?
2	0.4	When will Los Angeles arrive in its home port?
2	0.2	When will the Sturgeon arrive on station?

5	0.8	What aircraft units are embarked on the Constellation?
8	0.7	To which task organization is Knox assigned?
1	0.1	Where is the Sellers?
1	0.0	Where is Luanda?
4	0.5	What is the next port of call of the Santa Inez?
2	0.1	When will Tarifa get underway?
1	0.6	Which convoy escorts have inoperative sonar systems?
1	0.1	When will they be repaired?
2	1.8	Which U.S. Navy DDGs have casreps involving radar systems?
1	0.3	What Soviet ship has hull number 855?
2	0.4	To what class does the Soviet ship Minsk belong?
2	0.3	What class does the Whale belong to?
19	2.0	What is the normal steaming time for the Wainwright from Gibraltar to Norfolk?
3	0.5	What American ships are carrying vanadium ore?
1	0.1	How far is it to Norfolk?
1	0.1	How far away is Norfolk?
1	0.2	How many nautical miles is it to Norfolk?
2	0.3	How many miles is it to Norfolk from here?
2	0.3	How close is the Baton Rouge to Norfolk?
2	0.2	How far is the Adams from the Aspro?
2	0.3	What is the distance from Gibraltar to Norfolk?
1	0.2	What is the nearest oiler?
1	0.3	What is the nearest oiler to the Constellation?
3	0.4	How far is it from Naples to 23-00N, 45-00W?
2	0.5	What is the distance from the Kitty Hawk to Naples?
4	0.6	How long would it take the Independence to reach 35-00N, 20-00W?
1	0.1	How long is the Philadelphia?
4	0.3	How long would it take the Aspro to join Kennedy?
28	1.3	What is the nearst ship to Naples with a doctor on board?
2	1.4	What is the nearest USN ship to the Enterprise with an operational air search radar?
1	0.2	What is known about that ship?
2	0.7	How many merchant ships are within 400 miles of the Hepburn?
4	0.3	What are their identities and last reported locations?
1	0.2	What cargo does the Pecos have?
1	0.1	Who is CTG67.3?
3	0.6	What are the length, width, and draft of the Kitty Hawk?
6	0.5	To whom is the Harry E. Yarnell attached?
2	0.7	What type ships are in the Knox class?
1	0.4	Where are the Charles F. Adams class ships?
2	0.1	What are their current assignments?
2	1.0	What subs in the South Atlantic are within 1000 miles of the Sunfish?
2	0.2	What is the Kittyhawk doing?
1	0.9	How many USN asw capable ships are in the Med?
1	0.0	Where are they?
4	0.4	What are their current assignments and fuel states?
4	1.0	What ships are NOT at combat readiness rating C1?
6	0.4	When will Reeves achieve readiness rating C1?
8	0.4	Why is Hoel at readiness rating C2?
1	0.2	When will the sonar be repaired on the Sterett?
5	0.8	What ships are carrying cargo for the United States?
1	0.1	Where are they going?
1	0.1	What are they carrying?
2	0.0	When will they arrive?
2	0.2	Where is Gridley bound?
14	1.3	Which cruisers have less than 50 per cent fuel on board?
1	0.1	Where are all the merchant ships?
2	0.3	When will the Kitty Hawk's radar be up?
1	0.4	What ships are in the Los Angeles class?

1	0.3	What command does Adm. William have?
3	0.3	Under whose opcon is the Dale?
1	0.2	Show me where the Kennedy is?
1	0.3	What ship has hull number 148?
4	0.7	What is the next port of call for the South Carolina?
4	0.2	Are doctors embarked in the Kawishiwi?
2	0.4	What kind of cargo does the Francis McGraw have?
5	0.9	What air group is embarked in the Constellation?
2	0.5	What do you know about the employment schedule of the Lang?
2	0.5	Which systems are down on the Kitty Hawk?
5	0.5	What ships in the Med have doctors embarked?
2	1.2	How many ships carrying oil are within 340 miles of Mayport?
4	1.2	What sub contacts are within 300 miles of the Enterprise?
9	2.0	List the current position and heading of the US Navy ships in the Mediterranean every 4 hours.
2	0.6	What is the status of the Enterprise's air search radar?
1	0.2	Where is convoy NL53 going?
2	0.3	What convoy is the Transgermania in?
2	0.4	How many embarked units are in Constellation?
1	0.3	What ships are in British ports?
4	1.4	What U.S. ships are within 500 miles of Wilmington?
2	1.2	What U.S. ships faster than the Gridley are in Norfolk?
1	0.4	What is the fastest ship in the Mediterranean Sea?
2	0.3	How close is that ship to Naples?
1	0.1	What is its home port?
2	0.4	Print the American cruisers' current positions and states of readiness!
2	0.2	How is the Los Angeles powered?
11	4.1	What ship having a normal cruising speed greater than 30 knots is the largest?
30	1.6	Display the last reported position of all ships that are in the North Atlantic.
1	0.3	When did the Endeavour depart the port of New York?
1	0.8	What nationality is the ship with international radio call sign UA1D?
1	0.3	What ports are in the database?
2	0.8	What merchant ships are enroute to New York and within 500 miles of the Saratoga?
2	0.4	To what country does the fastest sub belong?

References

1. Aho AV, Ullman JD (1972) The Theory of Parsing, Translation, and Compiling. Englewood Cliffs: Prentice-Hall
2. Bar-Hillel Y, Gaifman C, Shamir E: On Categorial and Phrase Structure Grammars. The Bulletin of the Research Council of Israel, 9F, 1-16
3. Bresnan J (1981) The Passive in Lexical Theory. Occasional Paper No 7, Center for Cognitive Science, 1980. Also in: Bresnan, J (ed). Cambridge: MIT Press
4. Burton R (1976) Semantic Grammar: An Engineering Technique for Constructing Natural Language Understanding Systems. BBN Report No 3453
5. Chomsky N (1980) On Binding. Linguistic Inquiry
6. Church K (1980) On Memory Limitations in Natural Language Processing. MIT/LCS/TR-245 (also available from the Indiana University Linguistics Club)
7. Church K, Patil R (1983) Coping with Syntactic Ambiguity or How to Put the Block in the Box on the Table. MIT/LCS/TM-216. Also in: American Journal of Computational Linguistics
8. Dostert B, Thompson F (1971) How Features Resolve Syntactic Ambiguity. In: Minker J, Rosenfeld S (eds): Proceedings of the Symposium on Information Storage and Retreival
9. Earley J (1968) An Efficient Context-Free Parsing Algorithm. Unpublished Ph.D. Thesis. Carnegie-Mellon University

10. Earley J (1970) An Efficient Context-Free Parsing Algorithm. Communications of the ACM **13** (2)
11. Ford M, Bresnan J, Kaplan R (1981) A Competence-Based Theory of Syntactic Closure. Paper presented at the Sloan Workshop on Parsing Long Distance Dependencies, University of Massachusetts at Amherst, 1981. Also in: Bresnan J (ed). Cambridge: MIT Press
12. Gazdar G (1981) Unbounded Dependencies and Coordinate Structure. Linguistic Inquiry **12** (2)
13. Gazdar G: Phrase Structure Grammar. In: Jacobson P, Pullum G (eds): The Nature of Syntactic Representation
14. Graham S, Harrison M, Ruzzo W (1980) An Improved Context-Free Recognizer. ACM Transactions on Programming Languages and Systems **2** (3), 415-462
15. Harris L: Experience with ROBOT in 12 Commercial Natural Language Data Base Query Applications. IJCAI 79, p 365
16. Hendrix G, Sacerdoti E, Sagalowicz D, Slocum J (1978) Developing a Natural Language Interface to Complex Data. ACM Transactions on Database Systems **3** (2), 105-147
17. Joos M (1968) The English Verb: Form and Meanings. Madison, Milwaukee, and London: The University of Wisconsin Press
18. Kaplan R (1972) Augmented Transition Networks as Psychological Models of Sentence Comprehension. Artificial Intelligence **3,** 77-100
19. Kaplan R (1973) A General Syntacitc Processor. In: Rustin R (ed): Natural Language Processing. New York: Algorithmics Press
20. Kaplan R, Bresnan J (1981) Lexical-Functional Grammar: A Formal Systen for Grammatical Representation. Occasional Paper, Center for Cognitive Science, 1980. Also in: Bresnan J (ed). Cambridge: MIT Press
21. Knuth, D (1975) Fundamental Algorithms. In: The Art of Computer Programming, Vol 1. Reading: Addison-Wesley
22. Kuno, Susumu, Oettinger AG (1963) Multiple Path Syntactic Analyzer. In: Information Processing. Amsterdam: North-Holland
23. Malhotra A (1975) Design Criteria for a Knowledge-Based English Language System for Management: An Experimental Analysis. MIT/LCS/TR-146
24. Marcus M (1980) A Theory of Syntactic Recognition for Natural Language. Cambridge: MIT Press
25. Mathlab Group (1977) Macsyma Reference Manual. Laboratory for Computer Science, MIT
26. Milne R (1980) A Framework for Deterministic Parsing Using Syntax and Semantics. DAI Working Paper 64. Department of Artificial Intelligence, University of Edinburgh
27. Pratt VR (1973) A Linguistics Oriented Programming Language. IJCAI 3
28. Pratt V (1975) Lingol- A Progress Report. IJCAI 4
29. Ruzzo WL (1978) General Context-Free Language Recognition. Unpublished Ph. D. Thesis. University of California, Berkeley
30. Sheil B (1976) Observations on Context-Free Parsing. Statistical Methods in Linguistics, 71-109
31. Shipman D, Marcus M (1979) Towards Minimal Data Structures for Deterministic Parsing. IJCAI 79
32. Steele G (1980) The Definition and Implementation of a Computer Programming Language Based on Constraints. MIT, AI-TR-595
33. Valient L (1975) General Context Free Recognition in Less Than Cubic Time. J. Computer and System Sciences **10,** 308-315
34. Woods W (1970) Transition Network Grammars for Natural Language Analysis. Communications of the ACM **13** (10), 591-606

Syntax Directed Translation in the Natural Language Information System PLIDIS

W. Dilger

Abstract. The translation component of the natural language processor of the information system PLIDIS is described as a tree directed grammar. Translation is performed by such a grammar as a derivation, directed by the parse tree or even, if organized in an appropriate way, by the parsing process. It is shown that tree directed grammars have less computational capacity than transformational grammars.

Introduction

In the early seventies, the designers of the NL information system PLIDIS decided to separate parsing from production of semantic representations [3, 4, 15, 16]. This was done for several reasons, not least for practical ones, because in this way the whole system became more modular and both parts could be developped and implemented independently of each other. Of course, linguistic persuasions about the nature of syntax analysis and semantic processing were decisive. During the last few years, this approach has gained additional justification through the work of Gazdar [11], Joshi and Levy [13], and Schubert and Pelletier [21], among others.

Parsing is performed in PLIDIS by an ATN-grammar for German. Its output is a rather flat phrase structure tree. For the production of semantic representations, perceived as a translation process, the linguists of the PLIDIS group started from the transformational grammar model [6, 17, 23]. I will not repeat the arguments in defense of the transformational grammar or those against it. However, there is an important feature with transformational grammar, namely, the structural constraints of the rules. They are a convenient means of formulating arbitrary relations between nodes of a tree, and because phrase structure trees of natural language sentences are in general rather small, in contrast, e.g., to those of programs, they can be used to give a survey of the structure of the sentence, thus taking into account the sentential context for the translation of single words.

However, the transformational grammar's ability to manipulate trees, i.e., pruning subtrees, grafting in new subtrees, changing labels, has two consequences. On the one hand, transformational grammars have the same computational capacity as Turing machines; this is the famous result of Peters and Ritchie [18]. On the other hand, it seems to be impossible to write a transformational grammar with a reasonable number of transformation rules because one will soon lose control over the possible derivations, i. e., tree transformations. It is my feeling that for this reason, the translation component of the PLIDIS grammar evolved in the way it did. Conceptually, the Wulz grammar [23] allowed tree manipulation in the same way as transformational grammar, but when the linguists of the PLIDIS group started to write translation rules, it turned out that these rules were not really transformational, but that they left the syntax tree unchanged; there was no pruning of subtrees and changing of labels, and instead of grafting in subtrees, a new tree was produced, separate from the syntax tree. In fact, the new tree represented a term of the internal representation language KS [7, 24], which is a predicate calculus language. This is similar to the approach of Schubert and Pelletier [21].

In this way, a new translation grammar model emerged. Its main features are as follows. A new tree is produced, separate from the syntax tree. This is done in a way similar to the derivation of a syntax tree in a context free grammar. But here, this derivation is closely related to the parsing tree and the links for this relation are the structural constraints which are inherited from the transformational grammar. Thus, production of semantic representations is a syntax oriented process in a double sense: it is a derivation by means of production rules as in generative grammars and it is closely related to the syntactic structure of the input sentence. For this reason the PLIDIS translation grammar will be called in this chapter a "tree directed grammar". It is not important whether parsing and translation are separated into two subsequent passes or not, as this is only a matter of organization. One can even imagine a way of processing where parsing starts with the tree directed grammar and the rules of this grammar are interpreted in such a way that the structural constraints demand certain parts of the parsing tree which are produced if needed.

Now there is one question left open. Is a tree directed grammar a new translational device or has it the same computational capacity as transformational grammar? The aim of this chapter is to answer this question. In the first section some basic notation and definitions are given. In the second section tree directed grammars are defined. To answer our question, this type of grammar will be related to certain types of tree transducing automata which are defined and whose computational capacity is described in Sect. 3. Finally, by effective transformation of tree directed grammars to tree transducing automata, the results on these automata can be adopted to the grammars.

1 Some Notation and Basic Definitions

1.1 Notation

The length (number of symbols) of a word x over an alphabet Σ is denoted by $|x|$. If $x \in \Sigma^*$, then the i-th component of x is denoted by $x(i)$.

Let x, y, z be words over an alphabet Σ. Then the word $x[y/z]$ results from x by substitution of y wherever it occurs in x by z.

1.2 Trees

Trees are defined here in the way introduced by Brainerd [5] and adopted by several authors, e.g., [19, 20].

The set N* of all finite sequences of elements of N is called the *universal tree domain.* An arbitrary sequence of N* is written $(n_1, \ldots, n_p)$, the empty sequence ( ). Basic operations on N* are concatenation and segmentation.

Concatenation: $(m_1, \ldots, m_p) \cdot (n_1, \ldots, n_q) = (m_1, \ldots, m_p, n_1, \ldots, n_q)$
Segmentation:

$$k\colon (n_1, \ldots, n_k, n_{k+1}, \ldots, n_p) = \begin{cases} (n_1, \ldots, n_k), \text{ if } k < p \\ (n_1, \ldots, n_p), \text{ otherwise} \end{cases}$$

("first k symbols")

$$(n_1, \ldots, n_{p-k}, n_{p-k+1}, \ldots, n_p)\colon k = \begin{cases} (n_{p-k+1}, \ldots, n_p), & \text{if } k < p \\ (n_1, \ldots, n_p), & \text{otherwise} \end{cases}$$

("last k symbols")

Basic relations on N* are D ("dominates immediately") and L ("is immediately left from").

$$(u,v) \in D \Leftrightarrow u = (|v|-1)\colon v \text{ and } v \neq (\ )$$
$$(u,v) \in L \Leftrightarrow u = ((|v|-1)\colon v)\cdot((v\colon 1)-1) \text{ and } v\colon 1 \neq 0$$

$(|v|-1)\colon v$ means: Take all symbols of v except the last one.
$((|v|-1)\colon v)\cdot((v\colon 1)-1)$ means: Diminish the last symbol of v by 1 and let all other symbols be unchanged.

Example

((5, 3, 1), (5, 3, 2)) ∈ L because

$$((|(5,3,2)|-1)\colon(5,3,2))\cdot(((5,3,2)\colon 1)-1) = (2\colon(5,3,2))\cdot(2-1)$$
$$= (5,3)\cdot(1) = (5,3,1)$$

D* and L* are the transitive closures of D and L respectively.

A set B ⊆ N* is called *prefix closed,* iff with w ∈ B all u with (u,w) ∈ D* and all v with (v,w) ∈ L* are in B. If B is finite, it is called a *tree domain.* If B is a tree domain then D and L are extended to relations D′ and L′ on B ∪ {(-1)} by

(a) (u,v) ∈ D′ iff (1) v (2) v (3):
  (1) (u,v) ∈ D
  (2) u = (-1) and v = () (v is the root)
  (3) v = (-1) and u·(0) ∉ B (u is a leaf)

(b) (u,v) ∈ L′ iff (4) v (5) v (6):
  (4) (u,v) ∈ L
  (5) u = (-1) and v:1 = 0 (v has no left-hand brother)
  (6) v = (-1) and $((|u|-1)\colon u)\cdot((u\colon 1)+1) \notin B$
  (u has no right-hand brother)

Example

B = {(),(0),(1),(2),(0,0),(0,1),(2,0),(2,1),(2,2),(0,1,0),(2,1,0),(2,1,1),(2,1,0,0)}
is a tree domain.

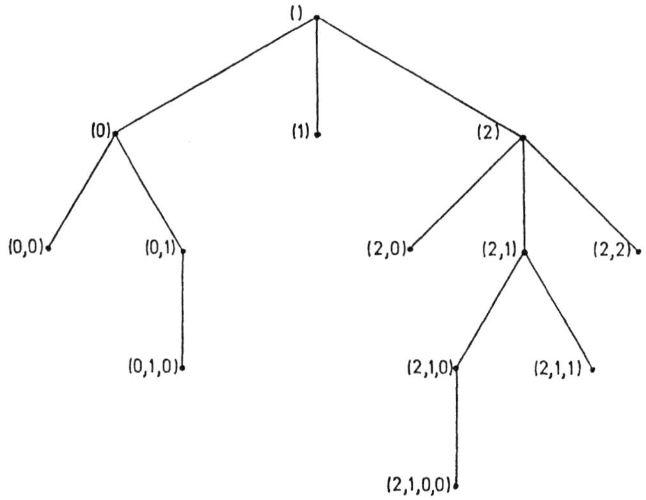

Fig. 1. Graphical representation of a tree domain

A tree domain can be represented by a tree in the graph theoretical sense in an obvious way. For example, the tree for the example tree domain above is shown in Figure 1.

A *ranked alphabet* Σ is an alphabet for which a *rank,* i.e., a mapping $r: \Sigma \rightarrow N$, is defined.

Let Σ be a ranked alphabet. A *tree (over Σ)* is a partial mapping $t: N^* \rightarrow \Sigma$ iff (i) and (ii):

(i) The domain of t is a tree domain B.
(ii) For all $u \in B$:

$$t(u) = A \Rightarrow r(A) = \begin{cases} \max\{i \mid u\cdot(i) \in B\}+1, & \text{if } \{i \mid u\cdot(i) \in B\}) \neq \emptyset \\ 0 & \text{, otherwise} \end{cases}$$

Because t is finite, we will write $\langle u,A\rangle \in t$ iff $t(u) = A$. The pairs $\langle u,A\rangle$ are called *nodes* of t, $nn(\langle u,A\rangle) = u$ is called the *node number,* and $nl(\langle u,A\rangle) = A$ is called the *node label.* The set of all trees over Σ is denoted by T_Σ.

Example

Let B be the tree domain of the example above and $\Sigma = \{A,B,C,D,E\}$. Then
$t = \{\langle(),A\rangle,\langle(0),B\rangle,\langle(1),D\rangle,\langle(2),A\rangle,\langle(0,0),E\rangle,\langle(0,1),C\rangle,$
$\langle(2,0),D\rangle,\langle(2,1),B\rangle,\langle(2,2),E\rangle,\langle(0,1,0),E\rangle, \langle(2,1,0),C\rangle,\langle(2,1,1),D\rangle,\langle(2,1,0,0),D\rangle\}$
is a tree over Σ. The rank of Σ is obvious. It is illustrated in Figure 2.

A node $\langle u,A\rangle$ of a tree t is called a *leaf* iff $(u, (-1)) \in D'$. The set of leaves of t is called the frontier of t. The frontier can be ordered in an obvious way.

Let $(b_1, \ldots, b_k)$ be the ordered set of leaves of a tree t. Then yield(t) $:= nl(b_1)nl(b_2) \ldots nl(b_k)$ is called the *yield* of t.

Let t be a tree over an alphabet Σ and $\langle u, A\rangle \in t$. A subset t′ of t is called a *subtree* of t with root $\langle u,A\rangle$ iff (i) - (iii):

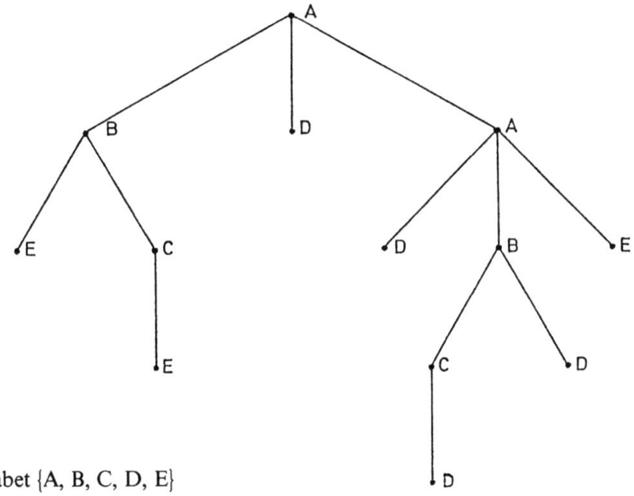

Fig. 2. A tree over the alphabet {A, B, C, D, E}

(i) $\langle u,A \rangle \in t'$

(ii) $\forall \langle v, B \rangle \in t' \; \exists x \in N^*: v = u \cdot x$

(iii) $\forall \langle v, B \rangle \in t \, [\exists x \in N^*: v = u \cdot x \Rightarrow \langle v, B \rangle \in t']$

(ii) says: Only nodes beyond $\langle u, A \rangle$ belong to t′. (iii) says: All nodes of t beyond $\langle u,A \rangle$ belong to t′.

2 Tree Directed Grammars

Tree directed grammars have a form similar to that of context free grammars. The main difference is in the productions; each production is provided with a structural constraint. In this section, the structural constraints are defined in the form of logical expressions, as in [8]. Another definition, called "local constraints", was introduced by Joshi, Levi, and Yueh [12, 13, 14]. It can be shown that the local constraints are equivalent to structural constraints, i.e., they describe the same relations between the nodes of a tree.

2.1 Structural Constraints

Let Σ be an alphabet, IND an index set and $X \notin \Sigma$. Then

$$\Sigma_{IND} := \{A_i \mid A \in \Sigma, i \in IND\}$$

The set

$$SI := \Sigma_{IND} \cup \{X\}_{IND}$$

is called the set of *structural individuals. If* $\alpha \in \Sigma_{IND}$, then the symbol of Σ underlying α is denoted by sym(α), e.g., sym(A_i)$=$A.

Let Λ = SI $\cup$ {DOM,DOM*,LFT,LFT*} $\cup$ {$\neg$, $\wedge$, $\vee$,(,)} $\cup$ {TRUE,FALSE}. The set of *structural constraints* SC is a subset of Λ^* defined by (1)-(5):

(1) TRUE and FALSE are atomic structural constraints.
(2) For P $\in$ {DOM, DOM*, LFT, LFT*} and α, β $\in$ SI, P(α, β) is an atomic structural constraint.
(3) Atomic structural constraints are structural constraints.
(4) If sc_1 and sc_2 are in SC, then
$$(\neg sc_1), (sc_1 \wedge sc_2), (sc_1 \vee sc_2)$$
are in SC.
(5) No other expressions are contained in SC.

Parentheses can be omitted according to the usual rules. If sc $\in$ SC, then SI(sc) denotes the set of structural individuals occurring in sc. Consequently, if S $\subseteq$ SC,

$$SI(S) = \bigcup_{sc \in S} SI(sc).$$

Let $sc_1, \ldots, sc_k$ be any atomic structural constraints except TRUE and FALSE. If a structural individual α is contained in sc_1 and another one, say β, is contained in sc_k, and if each pair sc_i, s_{i+1} (i=1, ..., k-1) has one structural individual in common, then β is *attainable* from α.

Let t $\in$ T_Σ and sc $\in$ SC. A *node assignment* for sc and t is a partial mapping

$$vtx: SI \rightarrow t$$

which has the following properties:

(i) nl (vtx(α)) = sym(α) for all $\alpha \in \Sigma_{IND}$
(ii) $\alpha \neq \beta \Rightarrow vtx(\alpha) \neq vtx(\beta)$ for all $\alpha, \beta \in SI(sc)$

The last definition shows the meaning of the indices of structural individuals: different nodes with the same label from Σ can be denoted by different symbols in a structural constraint.

If S $\subseteq$ SI, vtx(S) denotes the set of nodes assigned to the symbols of S under vtx.

Now we are ready to define the semantics of structural constraints.

A tree t $\in$ T_Σ *satisfies a structural constraint* sc *under a node assignment* vtx iff vtx is a node assignment for sc and t and (i)-(ix) hold:

(i) If sc = TRUE, then t satisfies sc.
(ii) If sc = FALSE, then t does not satisfy sc.
(iii) If sc = $\neg sc_1$, then t does not satisfy sc_1.
(iv) If sc = $sc_1 \wedge sc_2$, then t satisfies sc_1 and sc_2.
(v) If sc = $sc_1 \vee sc_2$, then t satiesfies sc_1 or sc_2.
(vi) If sc = DOM(α,β), then (nn(vtx(α)),nn(vtx(β)))) $\in$ D.
(vii) If sc = LFT α,β), then (nn(vtx(α)),nn(vtx(β)))) $\in$ L.
(viii) If sc = DOM*(α,β), then (nn(vtx(α)),nn(vtx(β)))) $\in$ D*.
(ix) If sc = LFT*(α,β), then (nn(vtx(α)),nn(vtx(β)))) $\in$ L*.

t *satisfies a structural constraint* sc iff there is a node assignment vtx such that t satisfies sc under vtx.

A structural constraint sc is called *satisfiable over* a set of trees $T \subseteq T_\Sigma$ iff there is a $t \in T$ which satisfies sc. Two structural constraints sc_1 and sc_2 are called *equivalent over* $T \subseteq T_\Sigma$ iff for all $t \in T$ holds:

$$t \text{ satisfies } sc_1 \Leftrightarrow t \text{ satisfies } sc_2$$

A structural constraint sc is called *satisfiable* iff there is a set of trees $T \subseteq T_\Sigma$ such that sc is satisfiable over T. Two structural constraints sc_1 and sc_2 are called *equivalent* iff for each set $T \subseteq T_\Sigma$ sc_1 and sc_2 are equivalent over T.

Let $sc \in SC$, $\alpha \in \Sigma_{IND}$, and α occur in sc. Let DNF(sc) be the disjunctive normal form of sc,

$$(sc_{11} \wedge \ldots \wedge sc_{1r}) \vee \ldots \vee (sc_{p1} \wedge \ldots \wedge sc_{pr})$$

where each atomic structural constraint of sc occurs in $sc_i = sc_{i1} \wedge \ldots \wedge sc_{ir}$ $(i=1, \ldots, p)$, either negated or not negated. Let $SC_i = \{sc_{ij_1}, \ldots, sc_{ij_k}\}$ be the set of positive atomic structural constraints in sc_i. Assume that for sc_i (1) or (2) holds:

(1) If $SC_i = \emptyset$, then α occurs in all atomic structural constraints of sc_i, except TRUE and FALSE.

(2) If $SC_i \neq \emptyset$, then $\alpha \in SI(SC_i)$ and all elements of $SI(SC_i)$ are attainable from each other and each negated atomic structural constraint of sc_i except TRUE and FALSE contains at least one element of $SI(SC_i)$.

If there is a sc_1 in DNF(sc) which does not satisfy (1) or (2), remove it. If, in this way, DNF(sc) does not become empty, it is called an *α standard form* of sc.

Example

Let $\Sigma = \{A,B,C,D,E\}$, IND = N. Then
$SI = \{A_1,A_2,\ldots\} \cup \ldots \cup \{E_1,E_2,\ldots\} \cup \{X_1,X_2,\ldots\}$

The following expressions are structural constraints:

1 $DOM(A_1,B_1)$
2 $DOM^*(A_1,A_2)$
3 $LFT(B_1,E_1)$
4 $\neg LFT^*(D_1,A_2)$
5 $DOM(D_1,X_1)$
6 $DOM(A_1,B_1) \vee (LFT^*(B_1,A_2) \vee LFT(B_1,E_1))$
7 $DOM(B_1,E_1) \wedge LFT(C_1,D_1)$
8 $DOM(X_1,C_1) \wedge \neg DOM^*(X_1, D_1)$
9 $DOM^*(B_1,E_1) \wedge LFT^*(B_1,X_1) \wedge (DOM(X_1,D_1) \vee \neg DOM(X_1,X_2))$
10 $\neg LFT(X_1,D_1) \wedge \neg LFT(D_1,X_2)$
11 $DOM(A_1,X_1) \wedge ((LFT^*(X_1,X_2) \wedge DOM^*(X_2,C_1)) \vee DOM(X_1,E_1))$

Take as an example tree the tree of Figure 3.

t satisfies 1 under two node assignments:

(i) $vtx(A_1) = \langle(\ ),A\rangle$, $vtx(B_1) = \langle(0),B\rangle$
(ii) $vtx(A_1) = \langle(2),A\rangle$, $vtx(B_1) = \langle(2,1),B\rangle$

t satisfies 2 and 3 under exactly one node assignment for each structural constraint.

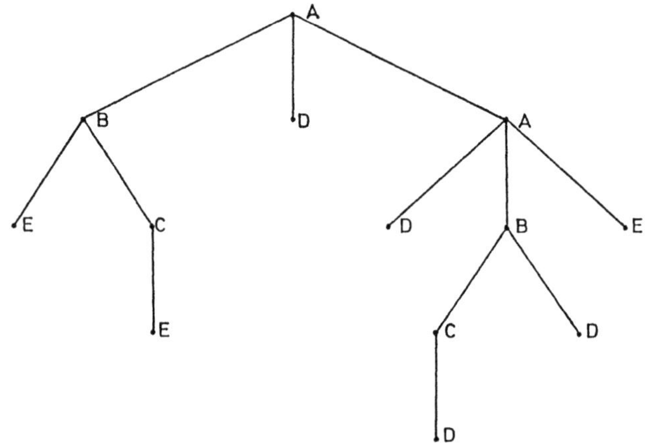

Fig. 3. A tree over {A, B, C, D, E}

t satisfies 4 under seven node assignments.
t does not satisfy 5.
t satisfies 6 under four node assignments.
t satiesfies 7 under exactly one node assignment.
t satiesfies 8 under four node assignments which all assign X_1 to ⟨(0),B⟩ and C_1 to ⟨(0,1),C⟩.
t satisfies 9 under eight node assignments which all assign B_1 to ⟨(0),B⟩.
t satisfies 10 under one node assignment, namely,

$$vtx(D_1) = \langle(2,1,0,0),D\rangle$$

t satisfies 11 under 27 node assignments.

6 has the disjunctive normal form

$$\begin{aligned} &(DOM(A_1,B_1) \wedge \neg LFT^*(B_1,A_2) \wedge LFT(B_1,E_1)) \\ \vee\ &(DOM(A_1, B_1) \wedge LFT^*(B_1,A_2) \wedge \neg LFT(B_1,E_1)) \\ \vee\ &(DOM(A_1,B_1) \wedge LFT^*(B_1,A_2) \wedge LFT(B_1,E_1)) \end{aligned}$$

This is an A_1 and a B_1 standard form. 8 is a C_1 standard form, 10 is a D_1 standard form. 9 has a B_1 standard form and 11 an A_1 standard form. 7 has no standard form because the structural individuals in 7 are not attainable from each other.

2.2 *Tree Directed Grammars*

Let Σ be an alphabet, IND an index set, and $T \subseteq T_\Sigma$. A *tree directed grammar* (TDG) for T is a quadruple

$$G_T = (\Sigma_{IND},\Delta,\Pi,\sigma)$$

where Δ is an alphabet of "terminal symbols", $\Sigma_{IND} \cap \Delta = \emptyset$, $\sigma \notin \Sigma_{IND} \cup \Delta$, and Π is a ternary relation

$$\Pi \subseteq \Sigma_{IND} \times SC \times (SI \cup \Delta)^*$$

defined by

$(\alpha,sc,\omega) \in \Pi :\Leftrightarrow$ (i) sc has an α standard form ssc.
(ii) In ssc there is a conjunction sc_j such that $\omega \in (SI(SC_j) \cup \Sigma)^*$.

The triples of Π are called *productions.*

Examples

$\Sigma = \{A,B,C,D,E\}$, $T1 = \{t\}$ where t is the tree of Fig. 3 and $\Delta = \{a,e,f,g,h\}$.

Let $G_{T1} = (\Sigma_{IND},\Delta,\Pi,\sigma)$ with

$$\begin{aligned}\Pi = \{&(A_1,DOM(A_1,B_1) \wedge DOM(A_1,A_2) \vee \neg DOM(C_1,A_1) \wedge LFT(C_1,A_2), fB_1gA_2h),\\ &(A_1,DOM(A_1,B_1) \wedge \neg DOM(A_1,A_2) \wedge LFT(X_1,B_1), gX_1B_1h),\\ &(B_1,DOM(X_1,B_1) \wedge (LFT^*(C_1,X_1) \vee LFT^*(X_2,X_1) \wedge DOM(X_2,C_1)),C_1g),\\ &(B_1,DOM(B_1,D_1) \wedge DOM(B_1,E_1),D_1ffE_1g),\\ &(B_1,DOM(B_1,C_1),C_1),\\ &(C_1,DOM(C_1,X_1),X_1),\\ &(D_1,DOM(X_1,D_1) \wedge LFT(X_1,A_1),hA_1),\\ &(D_1,TRUE,a),\\ &(E_1,TRUE,e)\}\end{aligned}$$

In order to show that G_{T1} is a TDG we have to verify that the productions of Π satisfy the conditions (i) and (ii) of the definition.

All structural constraints except the first and the third are already in an appropriate standard form which satisfies (ii). The first structural constraint has the following A_1 standard form:

$$\begin{aligned}&\neg DOM(A_1,B_1) \wedge DOM(A_1,A_2) \wedge \neg DOM(C_1,A_1) \wedge LFT(C_1,A_2)\\ \vee\ &DOM(A_1,B_1) \wedge DOM(A_1,A_2) \wedge \neg DOM(C_1,A_1) \wedge LFT(C_1,A_2)\\ \vee\ &DOM(A_1,B_1) \wedge DOM(A_1,A_2) \wedge DOM(C_1,A_1) \wedge \neg LFT(C_1,A_2)\\ \vee\ &DOM(A_1,B_1) \wedge DOM(A_1,A_2) \wedge DOM(C_1,A_1) \wedge LFT(C_1,A_2)\end{aligned}$$

This standard form satisfies condition (ii). The third structural constraint has the following B_1 standard form:

$$\begin{aligned}&DOM(X_1,B_1) \wedge \neg LFT^*(C_1,X_1) \wedge LFT^*(X_2,X_1) \wedge DOM(X_2,C_1)\\ \vee\ &DOM(X_1,B_1) \wedge LFT^*(C_1,X_1)\end{aligned}$$

It satisfies condition (ii).
Thus, all productions are admissible and therefore G_{T1} is a TDG.
For a second example take the right linear grammar

$$G = (\{S,A\},\{a\},\{S \rightarrow aA, A \rightarrow aA, A \rightarrow a\},S)$$

Let T2 be the set of all derivation trees of G. Let $G_{T2} = (\{S,A,a\}_{IND}, \{p,q,r\},\Pi,\sigma)$ with $IND = \{1,2\}$ and

$\Pi = \{ (S_1,DOM(S_1,a_1) \wedge DOM(S_1,A_1),a_1A_1r),$
$(a_1,LFT(a_1,A_1) \wedge DOM(A_1,a_2),pa_2q),$
$(a_1,DOM(A_1,a_1) \wedge \neg DOM(A_1,A_2),pq),$
$(A_1,DOM(A_1,A_2),A_2r),$
$(A_1,\neg DOM(A_1,A_2),r)\}$

It is easy to verify that G_{T2} is a TDG.

We will now define a derivation performed by a TDG. This definition is needed to define the translation performed by a TG.

Let $T \subseteq T_\Sigma$, G_T be a TDG for T, and $t \in T$. The relation

$_{t,G_T}$

(„immediately derivable with respect to t in G_T") is defined on expressions structured like the right-hand sides (ω) of the productions in the following way:

$\sigma \,_{t,G_T} S_1 \;:\Leftrightarrow \langle(\ ),S\rangle \in t$
$v \,_{t,G_T} w \;:\Leftrightarrow$ (i)–(iv):

(i) $v = v_1A_1v_2,\ v_1,v_2 \in (\Sigma_{IND} \cup \Delta)^*$
(ii) There is a node assignment vtx_v with $vtx_v(A_i) = \langle u,A\rangle \in t$.
(iii) There is a production $(A_i,sc,\omega) \in \Pi$, t satisfies sc under a node assignment vtx_w with $vtx_w(A_i) = \langle u,A\rangle$, and $X_1, \ldots, X_r$ be all symbols from $\{X\}_{IND}$ occurring in ω.
(iv) $w = v_1\omega'v_2$ with $\omega' = \omega[X_i/nl(vtx_w(X_1))_q;\ i = 1, \ldots, r]$, where q is greater than the greatest index occurring for the symbol $nl(vtx_w(X_i))$ in the production.

For $\sigma \,_{t,G_T} S_1$ the node assignment vtx_S with $vtx_S(S_1) = \langle(\ ),S\rangle$ is chosen. $^*{}_{t,G_T}$ is the transitive closure of $_{t,G_T}$ ("derivable"). $L_t(G_T) = \{w \mid \sigma_{t,G_T}w,\ w \in \Delta^*\}$ is the language produced by G_T with respect to t. $L(G_T) = \bigcup_{t \in T} L_t(G_T)$ is the language produced by G_T.

The subscripts t and G_T are omitted in the following if no confusion can arise.

Examples

Let T1 and G_{T1} be as in the example above. A derivation in G_{T1} with respect to t is:

$$\sigma \vdash A_1 \vdash fB_1gA_2h \vdash fC_1gA_2h \vdash fE_1gA_2h \vdash fegA_2h \vdash feggD_2B_1hh$$
$$\vdash feggaB_1hh \vdash feggaC_1ghh \vdash feggaE_1ghh \vdash feggaeghh$$

Instead of the last three derivation steps the following three steps can be made:

$$feggaB_1hh \vdash feggaC_1hh \vdash feggaD_1hh \vdash feggaahh$$

These are all derivations which can be made in G_{T1} with respect to t, so $L_t(G_{T1}) = L(G_{T1}) = \{feggaeghh, feggaahh\}$.

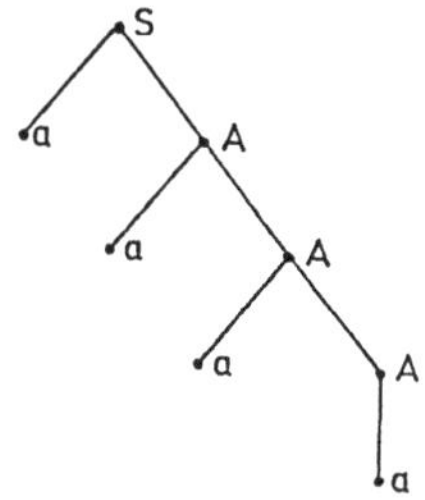

Fig. 4. A derivation tree in the grammar G

For the TDG G_{T2} take as an example tree the tree of Figure 4. A derivation in G_{T2} with respect to t is:

$$\sigma \vdash S_1 \vdash a_1A_1r \vdash pa_2qA_1r \vdash ppa_2qqA_1r \vdash pppa_2qqqA_1r \vdash ppppqqqqA_1r \vdash ppppqqqqA_2rr \vdash ppppqqqqA_2rrr \vdash p^4q^4r^4$$

This is the only derivation possible in G_{T2} with respect to t, thus $L_t(G_{T2}) = \{p^4q^4r^4\}$. It is easy to see that

$$L(G_{T2}) = \{p^nq^nr^n \mid n \geqq 2\}$$

Let $T \subseteq T_\Sigma$ and G_T be a TDG. Derivability with respect to a tree t induces a relation $TR(G_T)$ defined by

$$TR(G_T) \subseteq T \times L(G_T)$$
$$(t,w) \in TR(G_T) :\Leftrightarrow w \in L_t(G_T)$$

The derivation trees of a context free grammar G, denoted by D(G), are a special set of trees. Here, a relation $TRANS(G_{D(G)})$ can be defined by:

$$TRANS(G_{D(G)}) \subseteq L(G) \times L(G_{D(G)})$$
$$(z,w) \in TRANS(G_{D(G)}) :\Leftrightarrow \exists t \in D(G): z = yield(t) \wedge (t,w) \in TR(G_{D(G)})$$

$TRANS(G_{D(G)})$ is a *translation relation,* the pair $(G,G_{D(G)})$ a *translation grammar.* w is called the *translation* of z.

Example

Let G_{T1} and G_{T2} be the TDGs of the examples above.

$$TR(G_{T1}) = \{(t,feggaeghh),(t,feggaahh)\}$$

For the right linear grammar G given above $T2 = D(G)$ and $L(G) = \{a^n \mid n \geqq 2\}$. Therefore

$$TRANS(G_{D(G)}) = \{(a^n,p^nq^nr^n) \mid n \geqq 2\}.$$

A TDG G'_T can be transformed into another TDG G'_T which has productions with simpler structural constraints, namely, only conjunctions of positive and negative atomic structural constraints. This transformation is done in two steps:

1. Omit in the standard forms of the structural constraints of G_T superfluous parts. More precisely, assume $sc = sc_1 \vee \ldots \vee sc_k$ is a standard form in the production (α,sc,ω). $SI(\omega)$ is the set of structural individuals occurring in ω. If for one i

$\in \{1, \ldots, k\}$ $SI(\omega) \nsubseteq SI(sc_i)$, omit sc_i, because according to the definition of derivability, sc_i is never satisfied under a node assignment which makes the production applicable.
2. Let $sc = sc_1 \vee \ldots \vee sc_1$ be a standard form in production (α, sc, ω) which is already modified according to step 1. Then replace the production (α, sc, ω) by the productions $(\alpha, sc_1, \omega), \ldots, (\alpha, sc_1, \omega)$.

It is not difficult to prove that G_T and G_T' are equivalent, i.e., $L(G_T) = L(G_T')$. For details see [8].

Example

Take the TDG G_{T1} of the examples above. In the A_1 standard form of the first production the first part has to be omitted. Step 2 is clear. So we get the TDG $G_T' = (\Sigma_{IND}, \Delta, \Pi', \sigma)$ with

$$
\begin{aligned}
\Pi' = \{ & (A_1, DOM(A_1,B_1) \wedge DOM(A_1,A_2) \wedge \neg DOM(C_1,A_1) \wedge LFT(C_1,A_2), fB_1gA_2h),\\
& (A_1, DOM(A_1,B_1) \wedge DOM(A_1,A_2) \wedge DOM(C_1,A_1) \wedge \neg LFT(C_1,A_2), fB_1gA_2h),\\
& (A_1, DOM(A_1,B_1) \wedge DOM(A_1,A_2) \wedge DOM(C_1,A_1) \wedge LFT(C_1,A_2), fB_1gA_2h),\\
& (A_1, DOM(A_1,B_1) \wedge \neg DOM(A_1,A_2) \wedge LFT(X_1,B_1), gX_1B_1h),\\
& (B_1, DOM(X_1,B_1) \wedge \neg LFT^*(C_1,X_1) \wedge LFT^*(X_2,X_1) \wedge DOM(X_2,C_1), C_1g),\\
& (B_1, DOM(X_1,B_1) \wedge LFT^*(C_1,X_1), C_1g)\\
& (B_1, DOM(B_1,D_1) \wedge DOM(B_1,E_1), D_1ffE_1g),\\
& (B_1, DOM(B_1,C_1), C_1),\\
& (C_1, DOM(C_1,X_1), X_1),\\
& (D_1, DOM(X_1,D_1) \wedge LFT(X_1,A_1), hA_1),\\
& (D_1, TRUE, a),\\
& (E_1, TRUE, e)\}
\end{aligned}
$$

For the rest of this chapter we assume that each TDG G_T already has the form of G_T'.

3 Tree Transducers

This section is mainly based on the work of Engelfriet, Rozenberg, and Slutzki [10]. The definitions of tree transducers there are adopted in a slightly modified form so that they fit our form of tree representation. First the top-down tree transducers are defined and some of their important properties are described. Then some extensions of the basic tree transducer model are given. We will show that the extended models have the same translating capacity as the basic model. So, what are they good for? This will become clear in Sect. 4, when we show that a TDG can be transformed equivalently into the most extended model of tree transducers. As a consequence of this fact, we can adopt propositions about the translating capacity of top-down tree transducers for TDGs.

3.1 Top-Down Tree Transducers

A *top-down tree-to-string transducer (yT-transducer)* is a quintuple

$$M = (Q,\Sigma,\Delta,q_0,R)$$

with Q - a finite set of states
Σ - a ranked input alphabet
Δ - an output alphabet
$q_0 \in Q$ - the starting state
R - a finite set of rules

The rules of R have the form

$$(q,A) \rightarrow w_1q_1(i_1)w_2q_2(i_2) \ldots w_nq_n(i_n)w_{n+1}$$

where $n \geqq 0$; $q,q_1, \ldots, q_n \in Q$; $A \in \Sigma$; $i_1, \ldots, i_n \in N$; $i_j < \text{rank}(A)$ for $j = 1, \ldots, n$; $w_1, \ldots, w_{n+1} \in \Delta^*$. If rank(A) = 0, then the right-hand side of the rule is in Δ^*. M is called *linear* iff for each rule $i_j \neq i_k$ for all $j,k = 1, \ldots, n$; $j \neq k$.

Example

$M = (\{p,q\},\{A,B,C,D,E\},\{a,e,h,r\},p,R)$ with rank(A) = 3, rank(B) = 2, rank(C) = 1, rank(D) = rank(E) = 0,

$$\begin{aligned} R = \{ & (p,A) \rightarrow hq(2)p(0)hq(2)p(0), \\ & (p,B) \rightarrow p(1), \\ & (p,C) \rightarrow e, \\ & (q,A) \rightarrow q(2), \\ & (q,E) \rightarrow ar\} \end{aligned}$$

is a nonlinear yT-transducer.

Let M be a yT-transducer. A *sentence form* of M is a string of the form

$$v_1p_1\langle u_1,A_1\rangle v_2p_2\langle u_2,A_2\rangle \ldots v_mp_m\langle u_m,A_m\rangle v_{m+1}$$

where $m \geqq 0$; $p_i \in Q$, $u_i \in N^*$, $A_i \in \Sigma_{IND}$ for $i = 1, \ldots, m$; $v_i \in \Delta^*$ for $i = 1, \ldots, m+1$. We define a relation ${}_{t,M}$ (immediately derivable in M with respect to t) on the set of sentence forms of M by:

$$s \;{}_{t,M}\; s' :\Leftrightarrow \text{(i)–(iv)}.$$

(i) $s = s_1p\langle u,A\rangle s_2$

(ii) $(p,A) \rightarrow w_1q_1(i_1) \ldots w_nq_n(i_n)w_{n+1} \in R$

(iii) $s' = s_1w_1q_1\langle u\cdot(i_1),B_1\rangle \ldots w_nq_n\langle u\cdot(i_n),B_n\rangle w_{n+1}s_2$

(iv) $\{\langle u\cdot(i_1),B_1\rangle, \ldots ,\langle u\cdot(i_n),B_n\rangle\} \subseteq t$

${}^*{}_{t,M}$ is the transitive closure of ${}_{t,M}$.

If $\langle (\,),R\rangle \in t$, then $L_t(M) = \{w \mid q_0\langle (\,),R\rangle \,{}^*{}_{t,M} w,\ w \in \Delta^*\}$ is called the *language produced by* M *with respect to* t. For $T \subseteq T_\Sigma$, $L_T(M) = \bigcup_{t \in T} L_t(M)$ is called the *language produced by* M *with respect to* T.

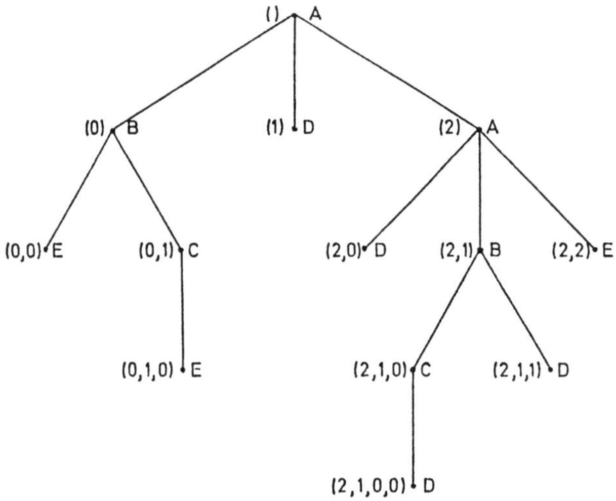

Fig. 5. A tree over the alphabet {A, B, C, D, E}

Example

Take the yT-transducer M of the example above and the tree of Figure 5. M performs the following derivation on t:

$$\begin{aligned} p\langle(\,),A\rangle &\vdash hq\langle(2),A\rangle p\langle(0),B\rangle hq\langle(2),A\rangle p\langle(0),B\rangle \\ &\vdash hq\langle(2,2),E\rangle p\langle(0),B\rangle hq\langle(2),A\rangle p\langle(0),B\rangle \\ &\vdash harp\langle(0),B\rangle hq\langle(2),A\rangle p\langle(0),B\rangle \\ &\vdash harp\langle(0,1),C\rangle hq\langle(2),A\rangle p\langle(0),B\rangle \\ &\vdash harehq\langle(2),A\rangle p\langle(0),B\rangle \\ &\vdash harehq\langle(2,2),E\rangle p\langle(0),B\rangle \\ &\vdash hareharp\langle(0),B\rangle \\ &\vdash hareharp\langle(0,1),C\rangle \\ &\vdash harehare \end{aligned}$$

It is easy to see that this is the only derivation which M can perform on t, because of the form of its rules, i.e., M is deterministic, therefore $L_t(M) = \{harehare\}$.

Let $\mathcal{T}$ be a set of set of trees over an alphabet Σ, i.e., $\mathcal{T} \subseteq 2^{T_\Sigma}$. The set of languages which can be produced by any tree transducer taking sets in $\mathcal{T}$ as input is denoted by yT ($\mathcal{T}$), i.e.,

$$yT(\mathcal{T}) = \{L_T(M) \mid T \in \mathcal{T}, M \text{ is a yT-transducer}\}$$

A very important set of sets of trees is REC, the set of those sets of trees which are accepted by finite tree acceptors. The importance of REC arises from the fact that the set of derivation trees D(G) of an arbitrary context free grammar G is in REC and, further, that for each T ∈ REC the set of yields of the elements of T is a context free language, see [5, 22].

We are interested in the set yT(REC). Baker has shown the following result [1, 2]:

The class of languages yT(REC) is properly contained in the class of context sensitive languages.

In other words, given an "interesting" (for practical reasons) language, namely a context free one, as input, a yT-transducer produces at most a context sensitive language as output, in contrast to the transformation grammar, which is able to produce a recursive enumerable language.

3.2 Some Extensions of yT-Transducers

Here, two extensions defined in [10] are described, a combination of both types is given, and a further extension is added. Propositions about the translating capacity of these models with regard to the class REC are made.

Let $N_m = \{(0), \ldots, (m-1)\}$. A *regular extended yT-transducer* (yRT-transducer) is a yT-transducer which has in general an infinite set of rules R, but for R holds: for each $q \in Q$ and $A \in \Sigma$ with rank(A) = m the set

$$R(q,A) = \{r \mid (q,A) \rightarrow r \in R\}$$

is a regular language over the alphabet $\Delta \cup Q \cdot N_m$. In other words, the set of right-hand sides for some pair (q,A) is a (possibly empty) regular language. The derivability relation $_{t,M}$ is defined for yRT-transducers in the same way as for yT-transducers.

Example

We modify the definition of M in the example above and get the yRT-transducer M′:

$$M' = (\{p,q\},\{A,B,C,D,E\},\{a,f,i,l,r\},p,R')$$
$$R' = \{(p,A) \rightarrow ((l \mid f)q(2)p(0))^*,$$
$$(p,B) \rightarrow p(1),$$
$$(p,C) \rightarrow i,$$
$$(q,A) \rightarrow q(2),$$
$$(q,E) \rightarrow ar\}$$

The right-hand side of the first rule represents a regular language by a regular expression.

The reader is invited to verify that for the tree t of Figure 3.

$$L_t(M') = \{lari,fari\}^*.$$

In general, yT-transducers and yRT-transducers define different TR_T-relations. But for the whole class REC they produce the same class of languages, i.e.,

$$yRT(REC) = yT(REC)$$

This is shown in [10].

The idea of the proof is to construct a yT-transducer M′ from a given yRT-transducer M and, at the same time, an input set of trees T′ for M′ from a given input set of trees T for M, such that $L_T(M) = L_{T'}(M')$. In T′, for each $t \in T$ there is a set of trees T(t), and each t′ ∈ T(t) is got from t introducing arbitrary numbers of new nodes between the old ones in a way illustrated in Figure 6 (cf. Fig. 5). Thus, the infinite number of derivations which M can perform on only one tree by its infinite set of rules is simulated by M′, which has only a finite number of rules, on an appropriate infinite set of trees.

We will now define another extension of yT-transducers. A *yT-transducer with regular look-ahead* (yT^R-transducer) is a yT-transducer where to each rule (q,A) → r of R a mapping

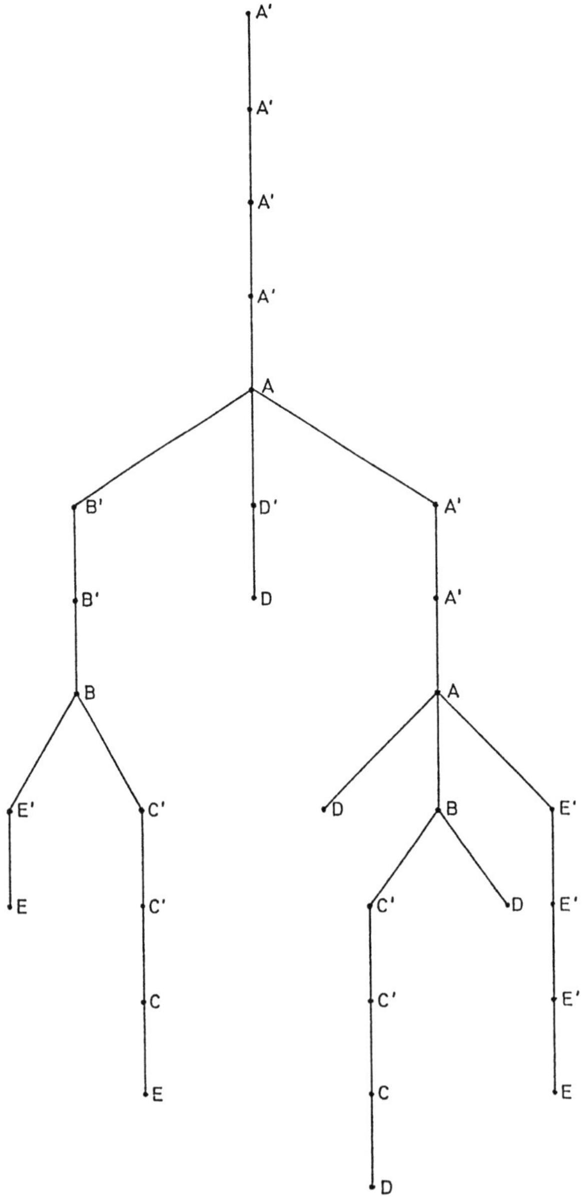

Fig. 6. An expanded tree over the alphabet {A, B, C, D, E} ∪ {A′, B′, C′, D′, E′}

$$cd: N_{rank(A)} \rightarrow REC$$

is assigned.

The definition of the derivability relation $_{t,M}$ for yT^R-transducers is almost the same as that for yT-transducers. Only one further condition has to be added:

(v) The subtree of t with root $\langle u \cdot (i_j), B_j \rangle$ must be contained in $cd(i_j)$ for all $j = 1, \ldots, n$.

This definition illustrates the meaning of the mapping cd: cd determines for each son of the node labeled by A a set of trees in REC and if the subtree with one of the sons as root is contained in the selected set of trees, and this holds for all sons, then the rule $(q,A) \rightarrow r$ can be applied. In this way, the yT^R-transducer looks ahead.

In [9] it is shown that $yT^R(REC) = yT(REC)$.

Now we will combine both types of extensions. A *regular extended yT-transducer with regular look-ahead* (yRT^R-transducer) is a yRT-transducer where to each set of rules $\{(q,A) \rightarrow r \mid r \in R(q,A)\} \subseteq R$ a mapping

$$cd: n_{rank(A)} \rightarrow REC$$

is assigned.

The relation $_{t,M}$ is defined in the same way as for the yT^R-transducers. Notice that an arbitrary mapping cd is not assigned to each rule of R, but only to classes of rules, otherwise the following proposition could not be proven:

$$yRT^R(REC) = yT^R(REC)$$

The idea of the proof is a construction quite similar to that in the proof of $yRT(REC) = yT(REC)$. What is new in the construction here is the specification of the mappings cd for the intermediate nodes in the expanded trees, which is simply: $cd: \{0\} \rightarrow REC$ with $cd(0) = T_\Sigma$, i.e., the condition for the intermediate nodes is empty. For details see [8].

We will define two further extensions of yT-transducers. Let $N_m = \{(0), \ldots, (m-1)\}$. A *linear extended yT-transducer* (yLT-transducer) is a yT-transducer which has in general an infinite set of rules R, but for R holds: for each $q \in Q$ and $A \in \Sigma$ with $rank(A) = m$ the set

$$L(q,A) = \{r \mid (q,A) \rightarrow r \in R\}$$

is a linear language over the alphabet $\Delta \cup Q \cdot N_m$. The relation $_{t,M}$ is the same as for yT-transducers.

A *linear extended yT-transducer with regular look-ahead* (yLT^R-transducer) is a yLT-transducer where to each set of rules $\{(q,A) \rightarrow r \mid r \in L(q,A)\} \subseteq R$ a mapping

$$cd: N_{rank(A)} \rightarrow REC$$

is assigned.

The relation $_{t,M}$ is the same as for yT^R-transducers.

The following results will not be surprising, bearing in mind the former propositions:

$$yLT(REC) = yT(REC)$$
$$yLT^R(REC) = yT^R(REC)$$

The idea of the proof is the same constructive argument as above. Here we have only to modify slightly the construction of the yT-transducer M′ according to the productions in the linear grammar corresponding to the language L(q,A), i.e., we have to add some new types of rules to R′.

4 Tree Directed Grammars and Tree Transducers

In Section 3 the computational capacity of yT-transducers was described by the set yT(REC). We will now do the same with TDGs and for this purpose, we will adopt the results on yT-transducers for TDGs. If we were able to transform a TDG G_T into an equivalent yT-transducer M, i.e., such that $TR(G_T) = TR_T(M)$, then we would have the desired result, namely yT(REC) = TDG(REC). But this is still an open problem. If we try to transform a TDG into an equivalent yT-transducer, it turns out that this is a hard problem. The reason is that the structural constraints in the productions of the TDG are a very general means for the description of sections of trees around the actual node in a derivation, whereas a rule of a yT-transducer reaches only the sons of the actual node. However, one of the extended models of the yT-transducer, the yT^R-transducer, is able to look further

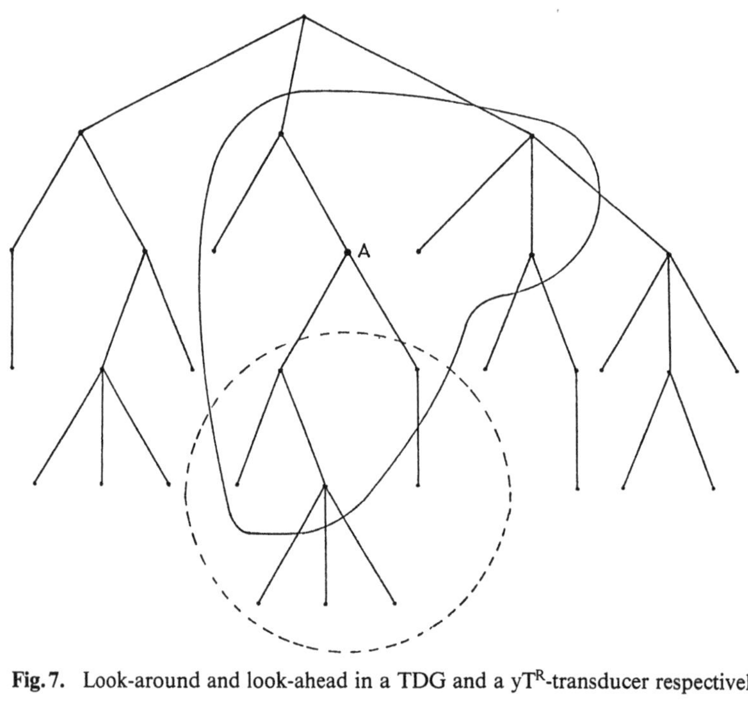

Fig. 7. Look-around and look-ahead in a TDG and a yT^R-transducer respectively

than the yT-transducer. Unfortunately, it only looks ahead and not around; thus we have the situation illustrated in Figure 7. The solid line shows the "look-around" of a structural constraint, where A is the actual node, and the dashed line shows the look-ahead of a yT^R-transducer rule.

Our aim is to transform a TDG G_T into an equivalent yT-transducer. Of course, we can transform it into one of the extended models as well, because they have the same computational capacity. To make a first step in this direction, we restrict the TDG in such a way, that all structural constraints are "downward oriented" thus simulating the look-ahead of a yT^R-transducer. If G_T is a downward oriented TDG, denoted TDG↓, it can be effectively transformed into a yT^R-transducer M with $TR(G_T) = TR_T(M)$. An extension of TDG↓s are the linear restricted TDGs, denoted TDG_L, and a TDG of this type can be transformed into an equivalent yLT^R-transducer.

The PLIDIS translation grammar is of type TDG_L, so we could be content with this result. However, it is my assumption that a further extension of yT-transducers can be defined, namely context free extended yT-transducers with regular look-ahead, $yCFT^R$-transducers, which have the property $yT^R(REC) = yCFT^R(REC)$, and that an arbitrary TDG G_T can be transformed effectively into a $yCFT^R$-transducer M such that $TR(G_T) = TR_T(M)$.

4.1 Downward Oriented Tree Directed Grammars

Let $T \subseteq T_\Sigma$, G_T be a TDG, and (α,sc,ω) a production of G_T. Remember that sc is assumed to be only a conjunction of positive and negative atomic structural constraints. Let PSC be the set of positive atomic structural constraints (atoms for short) contained in sc. sc is called *downward oriented* iff (1) or (2) holds:

(1) $PSC = \emptyset$.
(2) (i) and (ii) hold:
  (i) α occurs only in atoms of the form $DOM(\alpha,\beta)$ or $DOM^*(\alpha,\beta)$ in PSC for some $\beta \in SI$.
  (ii) If there is an atom of the form $DOM^*(\beta,\gamma)$ in PSC, there must also be atoms $P_1(\beta_1,\beta_2)$, $P_2(\beta_2,\beta_3)$, ..., $P_{k-1}(\beta_{k-1},\beta_k)$ in PSC such that $\beta_1 = \alpha$, $\beta_k = \beta$, and $P_i \in \{DOM,DOM^*,LFT,LFT^*\}$ except for the first P_1 which must be in $\{DOM,DOM^*\}$ according to (i), for some $k>1$.

Conditions (i) and (ii) together establish α as the unique top element of the structural constraint sc. Condition (ii), particularly, asserts that in the case of a $DOM^*(\beta,\gamma)$ atom in PSC, where it could happen that β is above α, there is a chain of atoms which guarantees by the order of the arguments that β is beyond α. By means of these restrictions, all structural individuals occurring in PSC are assigned to nodes in a tree lying beyond the node to which α is assigned. In this sense, the structural constraint sc is downward oriented. If PSC is empty, the structural individuals in sc denote nonexisting nodes, and therefore no condition has to be satisfied.

A TDG G_T is called *downward oriented* iff all structural constraints in the productions of G_T are downward oriented. We say G_T is a TDG↓.

Example

Assume the grammar $G = (\{A,B,C\},\{D,E\},P,A)$ is given with

$$P = \{A \rightarrow BDA, \\ A \rightarrow DBE, \\ B \rightarrow EC, \\ B \rightarrow CD, \\ C \rightarrow E \\ C \rightarrow D\}$$

G is a context free grammar.

Let $\Sigma = \{A,B,C,D,E\}$. Then $D(G) \subseteq T_\Sigma$ (the set of derivation trees of G). A TDG is defined by

$$G_T = (\Sigma_{IND},\{a,e,h,r\},\Pi,\sigma)$$

with $\Pi = \{ (A_1,DOM(A_1,E_1) \wedge \neg LFT(E_1,X_1),E_1),$
$(A_1,DOM(A_1,A_2) \wedge LFT^*(X_1,A_2) \wedge DOM^*(X_1,E_1),hA_2X_1hA_2X_1),$
$(B_1,DOM(B_1,C_1) \wedge LFT(X_1,C_1),C_1),$
$(B_1,DOM^*(B_1,D_1),e),$
$(C_1,TRUE,e),$
$(E_1,TRUE,ar)\}$

It is easy to verify that G_T is a TDG$\downarrow$.

Proposition

It is decidable if a TDG is downward oriented.

Proof

The proof is simple. One has only to check the atoms in PSC and, in the case of an atom $DOM^*(\beta,\gamma)$, to search for a chain of atoms of the kind described in condition (ii). Because PSC is finite, this can be done in finitely many steps.

In the set SI(PSC) of structural individuals of PSC we will group together those elements which lie on the same level, i. e., which occur in atoms $P_1(\beta_1,\beta_2)$, $P_2(\beta_3,\beta_4)$, ..., $P_{k/2}(\beta_{k-1}, \beta_k)$ such that $P \in \{LFT,LFT^*\}$ and the β_i,β_j are attainable from each other. A node assignment will assign nodes to these individuals which are all sons of the same father. Therefore we call such a subset of SI(PSC) a *level*. It is easy to see that SI(PSC) can be subdivided into a number of disjoint levels. The set of levels in PSC, denoted L(PSC), is partially ordered by the DOM- and DOM*-atoms in PSC, and with respect to this order it is a lattice with level $\{\alpha\}$ as maximal element. This is a consequence of the definition of downward orientation.

If level l′ is a successor of level l with respect to the order on L(PSC) then there are individuals α and β in l and l′ respectively such that there is an atom $DOM(\alpha,\beta)$ or $DOM^*(\alpha,\beta)$ in sc. If $DOM(\alpha,\beta)$ is in sc then l′ is called a *direct successor* of α, and if $DOM^*(\alpha,\beta)$ is in sc then l′ is called an *indirect successor* of α.

On the other hand, each level itself is partially ordered by the LFT- and LFT*-atoms in PSC, but in general, there is no maximal or minimal element in a level.

Example

$$\begin{aligned}\mathrm{PSC} = \{ &\mathrm{DOM}(A_1,B_1),\mathrm{DOM}^*(A_1,C_1),\mathrm{LFT}^*(D_1,B_1),\mathrm{LFT}(D_1,C_2),\\ &\mathrm{LFT}^*(C_3,C_2),\mathrm{LFT}^*(C_2,A_2),\mathrm{DOM}(C_1,D_2),\mathrm{LFT}(B_2,D_2),\\ &\mathrm{LFT}^*(B_2,E_1),\mathrm{DOM}^*(A_2,D_3),\mathrm{LFT}^*(D_3,A_3),\mathrm{LFT}(E_2,D_3),\\ &\mathrm{LFT}^*(E_3,E_2),\mathrm{DOM}^*(C_1,B_3),\mathrm{DOM}(D_1,D_4)\}\end{aligned}$$

$L(\mathrm{PSC}) = \{l_1,l_2,l_3,l_4,l_5,l_6,l_7\}$ with

$$\begin{aligned}l_1 &= \{A_1\}\\ l_2 &= \{B_1,D_1,C_2,A_2,C_3\}\\ l_3 &= \{C_1\}\\ l_4 &= \{D_2,B_2,E_1\}\\ l_5 &= \{D_3,A_3,E_2,E_3\}\\ l_6 &= \{B_3\}\\ l_7 &= \{D_4\}\end{aligned}$$

The orders of $L(\mathrm{PSC})$,l_2,l_4, and l_5 are illustrated by the diagrams of Figure 8.

The order on L(PSC) imposes a tree structure on this set, whereas the order of a level does not in general impose a linear structure on the level as should be expected because the elements of a level are mapped on nodes in the same "level"

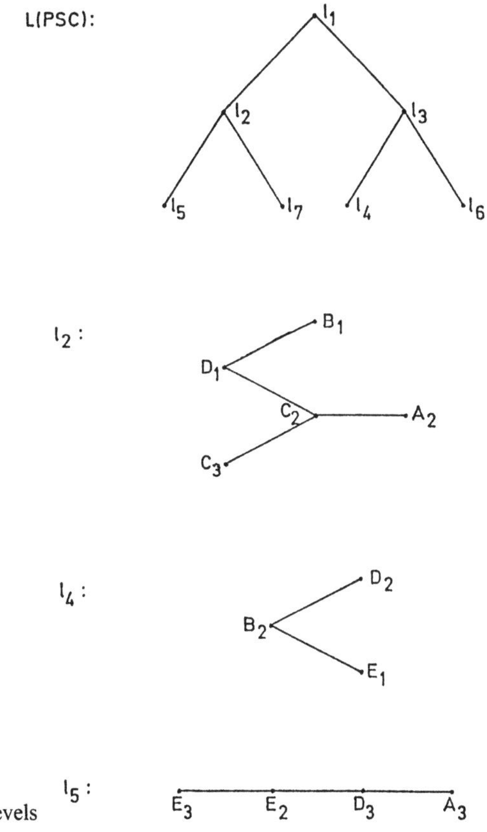

Fig. 8. Orders of L(PSC) and some of its levels

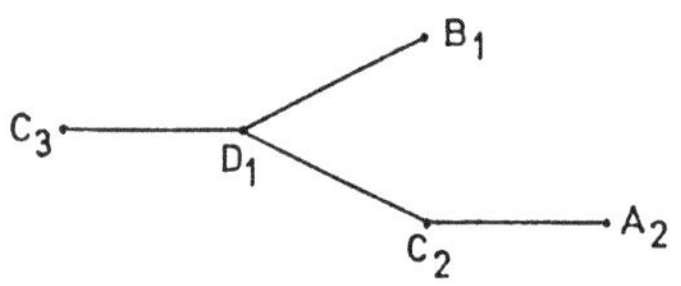

Fig. 9. Flattened structure of level l_2

in a tree if the tree satisfies the structural constraint. Some levels may have a linear order, e.g., l_5, others do not. In some cases, we can utilize the form of the LFT-atoms to "flatten" the structure of a level. For example in l_2, D_1 is immediately left from C_2. Bearing in mind that the structural individuals of l_2 should be mapped on nodes in the same "level" in a tree, we can conclude that l_2 must have the structure shown in Figure 9. If there were the atom LFT*(D_1,C_2) in PSC instead of LFT(D_1,C_2), this flattening would not be possible.

By the restriction on downward oriented structural constraints, the structural constraints have become similar to the look-aheads of yT^R-transducers. But there is still an important difference: the look-aheads determine subtrees completely, the downward oriented structural constraints do not and this is due to the DOM*- and LFT*-atoms which leave open the "distance" between two nodes in a tree. This is the reason why the structural constraints are a convenient means for a linguist to express relations between nodes in a tree. They allow one to say: "Somewhere beyond or to the left of this node there is a node which has the property, etc.", whereas the designer of an automaton has to be precise. On the other hand, this is the reason why the transformation of a TDG$\downarrow$ into a yT^R-transducer is rather complicated. For this transformation we need the concepts of subconstraints and connections of constraints.

Let sc be a downward oriented structural constraint and $\beta \in$ SI(PSC). The *subconstraint* of sc with *respect to* β, denoted sc(β), is the subexpression of sc which contains all atoms of sc such that $\{\beta\}$ is the maximal element of L(PSC(β)) and the attainability relation holds between the individuals of sc(β). If there are no such atoms, then sc(β) = TRUE.

Let sc_1 and sc_2 be two structural constraints which have no structural individuals in common (in practice, this can be achieved by reindexing of the individuals), although there is an $\alpha \in$ SI(sc_1) and a $\beta \in$ SI(sc_2) with sym(α) = sym(β) or sym(α) = X or sym(β) = X. The *conjunctive connection* of sc_1 and sc_2 with respect to α and β is the structural constraint $sc_1 \wedge sc_2'$, where sc_2' is obtained from sc_2 by reindexing of β such that $\beta = \alpha$, or substitution of β by α, if sym(β) = X.

For the construction of a yT^R-transducer an input and an output alphabet are first needed. These are given by the TDG$\downarrow$. Second, rules with look-aheads and states are needed. For the rules the productions of the TDG$\downarrow$ can be used. But not all the possibilities of the productions for describing look-aheads and jumps to remote nodes can be reformulated directly in the rules. Part of the information has to be encoded in the states. The whole construction is related to a set of trees T. We choose the set of derivation trees of a context free grammar G instead of the trees accepted by a finite tree acceptor (which would correspond to the definition of REC), because most readers are familiar with context free grammars but not with finite tree acceptors. The construction can easily be modified so that it fits to tree acceptors.

The following presuppositions are used throughout the construction: G = (N,T,P,S) is a context free grammar with $N \cup T = \Sigma$; $G_{D(G)}$ is a TDG$\downarrow$ with input alphabet Σ; $p = (\alpha,sc,\omega)$ is a production of $G_{D(G)}$; in L(PSC) $\{\alpha\}$ has the direct successors $l_1, \ldots, l_p$ and the indirect successors $l'_1, \ldots, l'_q$. We set

$$l := \bigcup_{i=1}^{p} l_i \text{ and } l' = \bigcup_{i=1}^{p} l'_i.$$

Step 1: Construction of new structural constraints from sc.

If PSC = $\emptyset$ return {sc}.
Assume PSC $\neq \emptyset$, rank(sym(α)) = n > 0. If sc is not contradictory, then $|l| \leqq n$.
Set S := $\emptyset$.
For each subset $\bar{l}$ of l' with $|l \cup \bar{l}| \leqq n$ do:
    Set sc' := sc.
    For each $\beta \in \bar{l}$ do:
        Replace the atom DOM*(α,β) by DOM(α,β) in sc.
    Set S := S $\cup$ {sc'}.
Return S.

Step 2: Construction of the state set.

For each structural constraint contained in the set S a set of subconstraints is determined, and these are interpreted as states. For each $\beta \in l \cup l'$ let sc(β) be the subconstraint of sc with respect to β. For each $\beta \in l'$ add the atom DOM*(X_i,β) to sc(β) for some fresh X_i. Thus for each sc $\in$ S we get a set of subconstraints

$$\{sc(\beta) \mid \beta \in l \cup l'\}$$

and for the production p the set

$$Q(p) := \bigcup_{sc \in S} \{sc(\beta) \mid \beta \in l \cup l'\}$$

The whole set of states for the yT^R-transducer is then

$$Q := \bigcup_{p \in \Pi} Q(p)$$

Step 3: Construction of the rules (without look-aheads).

The left-hand side of a rule is a pair (q,A). Because we do not know a priori in which state the transducer will read the symbol A, we have to check for all states of Q whether this can happen. So for the production p we get a set of left-hand sides:

L(p) := {(q,sym(α)) | q $\in$ Q and the conjunctive connection sc $\wedge$ q with respect to α and some β in q is not contradictory}

It can be shown that it is decidable whether a structural constraint is contradictory or not, cf. [8].

Now mappings

$f: l \cup l' \to \{0, \ldots, n-1\}$

are defined which are order preserving (with respect to the order on l) and distance preserving, i.e., if LFT(β,γ) in sc and f(β) = i, then f(γ) = i+1, and f takes into account the negative atoms in an obvious way. Notice that the elements of l′ can be mapped on the same numbers as those of l and that there is no order on l′. Let F(p) be the set of all such mappings for sc. Assume ω contains the structural individuals $\beta_1, \ldots, \beta_k$. By the definition of productions, these individuals are contained in sc as well.

For each f ∈ F(p), set

$$w_f := \omega[\beta_i/sc(\beta_i)\,(f(\beta_i));\ i = 1, \ldots, k]$$

thus getting the right-hand sides of the rules:

$$W(p) := \{w_f \mid f \in F\}$$

Altogether, we have as rules (without look-aheads) for the production p the set:

$$R(p) = \{(q, sym(\alpha)) \to w \mid q \in Q,\ sc \wedge q \text{ is not contradictory},\ w \in W(p)\}$$

Step 4: Construction of look-aheads.

Look-aheads are mappings cd: {0, ..., n−1} → REC. In order to define the look-aheads for the rules in R(p) we have to specify for each f ∈ F(p) a tree set T_{fi} for each i < n, i.e., for each son of the node to which α will be assigned.

$$T_{fi} := \begin{cases} D(G'), & \text{if there is a } \beta \in l \cup l' \text{ such that } f(\beta) = i, \text{ where } G' = (N,T,P',S') \text{ with } P' \subseteq P, S' \in N, \text{ and each } t \in D(G') \text{ satisfies } sc(\beta) \text{ under some node assignment which maps } \beta \text{ to the i-th son of the node to which } \alpha \text{ is mapped} \\ T_\Sigma, & \text{if there is no } \beta \text{ with } f(\beta) = i \\ \text{undefined, otherwise} \end{cases}$$

Set $cd_f(i) := T_{fi}$ for each i = 0, ..., n-1.
Notice that $T_{fi} = T_\Sigma$ denotes the empty condition, i.e., there is nothing to check. T_{fi} is undefined if a structural individual β has to be assigned to the i-th son but there is no grammar G′ with the required properties.

Step 5: Construction of missing rules.

In the productions of a TDG↓, nodes somewhere in a tree can be specified by the structural constraints and in a derivation jumps to these nodes can be made. This is not possible with a yT^R-transducer; rather it has to step downward level by level. Therefore we have to complete the set of rules constructed so far by special rules which bridge the gaps in the productions of a TDG↓. These rules are derived from the productions of the underlying context free grammar G by the algorithm RULES. Suppose β ∈ l′.

Algorithm RULES.
Input: N,T,P as defined in G, sym(α),sym(β),sc(β)
Output: A set R of rules

1 R := $\emptyset$.
2 If there is a production $\bar{p}$ = A $\rightarrow$ w in P then:
P := P - $\{\bar{p}\}$.
W := {w(i) | w(i) = B or a string containing B is derivable from w(i) by means of the productions of P}.
If W = $\emptyset$ goto 2.
For all i = 1, . . ., | w | do:
If w (i) $\in$ W then cd(i) := D(G_i) where G_i = (N,T,P,w(i))
else cd(i) := T_Σ
R := R $\cup$ {(q,sym(α)) $\rightarrow$ q(i); cd | w(i) $\in$ W}
$\cup \bigcup_{w(i) \in W}$ RULES(N,T,P,w(i),sym(β),sc(β))

Goto 2.
Output R.
Stop.

Step 6: Construction of the rule set.

For p $\in \Pi$ with sc $\neq$ TRUE and f $\in$ F(p) set

$$R(p,f) := \{(q,sym(\alpha)) \rightarrow w_f;cd_f \mid q \in Q,\ sc \wedge q \text{ is not contradictory},\ w_f \in W(p),\ cd_f \text{ is total}\}$$

$$\cup \bigcup_{\beta \in \Gamma} RULES(N,T,P,sym(\alpha),sym(\beta),sc(\beta))$$

$$R(p) := \begin{cases} \bigcup_{f \in F(p)} R(p,f), \text{if } sc \neq TRUE \\ \{(q,sym(\alpha)) \rightarrow \omega;\ cd \mid q \in Q,\ cd(i) = T_\Sigma \text{ for all } i = 0, \ldots, n-1\}, \\ \quad \text{if } sc = TRUE \end{cases}$$

$$R := \bigcup_{p \in \Pi} R(p)$$

Now the construction of the yT^R-transducer M = (Q,Σ,Δ,q_0,R) is complete. Here, q_0 is one of the states that occur in the left-hand sides of those rules which were derived from the productions with the first components S_i, where S is the initial nonterminal of G. It does not matter which of these states is chosen as q_0, because in the construction of the rule set all combinations of states with the symbol S have been tried.

Example

This example shows some of the important features of the construction. Let G and $G_{D(G)} = G_T$ be as in the example above.

Step 1

$p_1 = (A_1, DOM(A_1,E_1) \wedge \neg LFT(E_1,X_1), E_1)$
$\quad l = \{E_1\}, l' = \emptyset$
$\quad S = \{DOM(A_1,E_1) \wedge \neg LFT(E_1,X_1)\}$

$p_2 = (A_1, DOM(A_1,A_2) \wedge LFT^*(X_1,A_2) \wedge DOM^*(X_1,E_1), hA_2X_1hA_2X_1)$
$\quad l = \{A_2,X_1\}, l' = \emptyset$
$\quad S = \{DOM(A_1,A_2) \wedge LFT^*(X_1,A_2) \wedge DOM^*(X_1,E_1)\}$

$p_3 = (B_1, DOM(B_1,C_1) \wedge LFT(X_1C_1)\}$
$\quad l = \{C_1,X_1\}, l' = \emptyset$
$\quad S = \{DOM(B_1,C_1) \wedge LFT(X_1,C_1), C_1\}$

$p_4 = (B_1, DOM^*(B_1,D_1), e)$
$\quad l = \emptyset, l' = \{D_1\}$
$\quad S = \{DOM^*(B_1,D_1), DOM(B_1,D_1)\}$

Step 2

p_1: $sc(E_1) = \neg LFT(E_1,X_1) =: q_0$
p_2: $sc(A_2) = TRUE =: q_1$
$\quad sc(X_1) = DOM^*(X_1,E_1) =: q_2$
p_3: $sc(C_1) = TRUE$
$\quad sc(X_1) = TRUE$
p_4: $sc(D_1) = TRUE$
$\quad sc(D_1) = DOM^*(X_2,D_1) =: q_3$
$Q = \{q_0,q_1,q_2,q_3\}$

Step 3

$L(p_1) = \{(q_0,A),(q_1,A)\}$

$L(p_2) = \{(q_0,A),(q_1,A),(q_2,A),(q_3,A)\}$

$L(p_3) = \{(q_0,B),(q_1,B),(q_2,B),(q_3,B)\}$

$L(p_4) = \{(q_1,B)\}$

For p_1 and p_4 no other states can be connected with sc. Right-hand sides:

p_1: $f_1 = \{(E_1,2)\}$
$\quad W(p_1) = \{q_0(2)\}$
$\quad R(p_1) = \{(q_0,A) \rightarrow q_0(2), (q_1,A) \rightarrow q_0(2)\}$
There is no other mapping f because of the atom $\neg LFT(E_1,X_1)$.

p_2: $f_1 = \{(X_1,0),(A_2,1)\}$
$\quad f_2 = \{(X_1,0),(A_2,2)\}$
$\quad f_3 = \{(X_1,1),(A_2,2)\}$
$\quad W(p_2) = \{hq_1(1)q_2(0)hq_1(1)q_2(0), hq_1(2)q_2(0)hq_1(2)q_2(0), hq_1(2)q_2(1)hq_1(2)q_2(1)\}$
$\quad R(p_2) = \{(q_0,A) \rightarrow w \mid w \in W(p_2)\}$
$\quad\quad \cup \{(q_1,A) \rightarrow w \mid w \in W(p_2)\}$
$\quad\quad \cup \{(q_2,A) \rightarrow w \mid w \in W(p_2)\}$
$\quad\quad \cup \{(q_3,A) \rightarrow w \mid w \in W(p_2)\}$

p_3: $f_1 = \{(X_1,0),(C_1,1)\}$
$W(p_3) = \{q_1(1)\}$
$R(p_3) = \{(q_0,B) \rightarrow q_1(1), (q_1,B) \rightarrow q_1(1),$
$(q_2,B) \rightarrow q_1(1), (q_3,B) \rightarrow q_1(1)\}$
p_4: $f = \{(D_1,0)\}$
$f_2 = \{(D_1,1)\}$
$W(p_3) = \{e\}$
$R(p_4) = \{(q_1,B) \rightarrow e\}$

Step 4

p_1: $T_0 = T_1 = T_\Sigma, T_2 = D(G')$ with $S' = A, P' = P\text{-}\{A \rightarrow BDA\}$
This defines cd_1.
p_2: f_1: T_2 = undefined
f_2: $T_0 = T_2 = D(G), T_1 = T_\Sigma$
f_3: T_0 = undefined
This defines $cd_{f_2} =: cd_2$ as the only look-ahead.

p_3: $T_0 = T_1 = D(G'')$ with $S'' = B, P'' = \{B \rightarrow EC, C \rightarrow E, C \rightarrow D\}$
This defines cd_3.
p_4: $T_0 = T_1 = D(G)$
This defines cd_4.

Step 5

Missing rule construction is only necessary for p_4. But p_4 has no structural individuals in its third component, i.e., it makes no step downward. Therefore there is nothing to do.

Step 6

$R(p_1,f_1) = \{(q_0,A) \rightarrow q_0(2);\ cd_1,$
$(q_1,A) \rightarrow q_0(2);\ cd_1\}$

$R(p_2,f_2) = \{(q_0,A) \rightarrow hq_1(2)q_2(0)hq_1(2)q_2(0);\ cd_2,$
$(q_1,A) \rightarrow hq_1(2)q_2(0)hq_1(2)q_2(0);\ cd_2,$
$(q_2,A) \rightarrow hq_1(2)q_2(0)hq_1(2)q_2(0);\ cd_2,$
$(q_3,A) \rightarrow hq_1(2)q_2(0)hq_1(2)q_2(0);\ cd_2\}$

$R(p_3,f_1) = \{(q_0,B) \rightarrow q_1(1);\ cd_3,$
$(q_1,B) \rightarrow q_1(1);\ cd_3,$
$(q_2,B) \rightarrow q_1(1);\ cd_3,$
$(q_3,B) \rightarrow q_1(1);\ cd_3\}$
$R(p_4,f_1) = R(p_4,f_2) = \{(q_1,B) \rightarrow e;\ cd_4\}$
$R(p_1) = R(p_1,f_1), R(p_2) = R(p_2,f_2), R(p_3) = R(p_3,f_1),$
$R(p_4) = R(p_4,f_1)$
$R(p_5) = \{(q_0,C) \rightarrow e;\ cd_5,$
$(q_1,C) \rightarrow e;\ cd_5,$
$(q_2,C) \rightarrow e;\ cd_5,$
$(q_3,C) \rightarrow e;\ cd_5\}$

$R(p_6) = \{ (q_0,E) \rightarrow ar;\ cd_5\}$
$(q_1,E) \rightarrow ar;\ cd_5\}$
$(q_2,E) \rightarrow ar;\ cd_5\}$
$(q_3,E) \rightarrow ar;\ cd_5\}$

Here, cd_5 is defined as

$$cd_5: \{0\} \rightarrow REC$$

with $cd_5(0) = T_\Sigma$.

$R = R(p_1) \cup \ldots \cup R(p_6)$

Theorem

For each TDG$\downarrow$ G_T a yT^R-transducer M can be effectively constructed such that $TR(G_T) = TR_T(M)$.

Proof

M is constructed from G_T according to steps 1 through 6. We have to show that $TR(G_T) = TR_T(M)$. This is done by induction on the length of a derivation in G_T and M respectively. Here, only the induction steps of both parts of the proof will be sketched.

(1) Assume there is a derivation

$$v_1\alpha v_2 \vdash v \models^* w$$

in G_T, where $w \in \Delta^*$, α is mapped on a node $\langle u,sym(\alpha)\rangle$ under a node assignment vtx, and the first step has been performed by means of the production $p = (\alpha,sc,\omega)$ hence $v = v_1\omega' v_2$. Because p is applicable at node $\langle u,sym(\alpha)\rangle$, the subtree with root $\langle u,sym(\alpha)\rangle$ satisfies sc.
By the induction assumption, there is a derivation $v' \models^* w$ in M, where v' corresponds to v in such a way that all structural individuals α_i in v are replaced by pairs $(q_i,sym(\alpha_i))$ with $q_i \in Q(p)$, cf. step 2 of the construction of M. This results from the definition of the rules of M in step 6, because if $\langle u_i,sym(\alpha_i)\rangle$ is a son of $\langle u,sym(\alpha)\rangle$ then $q_i = sc(\alpha_i)$, else $sc(\alpha_i)$ is propagated downward by the rules delivered by RULES until it meets with the node $\langle u_i,sym(\alpha_i)\rangle$.
We have to show that there is a derivation

$$v_1'(q,sym(\alpha))v_2' \models^* v' \models^* w$$

in M for some $q \in Q$. Notice that several steps may be needed in M to simulate one step in G_T. Because p is applicable at node $\langle u,sym(\alpha)\rangle$, there are rules in R with left-hand sides $(q,sym(\alpha))$ for each q which is conjunctively connectable to sc, by step 3. Further, there is a mapping $f \in F(p)$ such that first, cd_f is total, because if the subtree rooted by $\langle u,sym(\alpha)\rangle$ satisfies sc, each of its subsubtrees satisfies its corresponding subconstraint $sc(\beta)$, and second, w_f corresponds to ω eventually together with the state propagating rules delivered by RULES. This completes the first part of the proof.

(2) Assume there is a derivation

$$v_1'(q,sym(\alpha))v_2' \vDash^* v' \vDash^* w$$

in M, where $w \in \Delta^*$ and the first step of the first part of this derivation, namely $v_1'(q,sym(\alpha))v_2' \vDash^* v'$, has been performed by means of a rule $r = (q,sym(\alpha)) \rightarrow w_f$; cd produced from a production $p = (\alpha,sc,\omega)$ of G_T, the other steps of this part by means of rules delivered by RULES.
By the induction assumption, there is a derivation $v \vDash^* w$ in G_T, where v corresponds to v′ as before. Because rule r is applicable at node $\langle u,sym(\alpha)\rangle$, the sub-constraints of sc with respect to the symbols β in $l \cup l'$ are satisfied by the sub-subtrees of the subtree rooted by $\langle u,sym(\alpha)\rangle$, because they are contained in w_f, and those sub-subtrees are contained in the sets $cd_f(i)$. Hence, with regard to some mapping f and eventually together with rules delivered by RULES p is applicable at node $\langle u,sym(\alpha)\rangle$ such that

$$v_1\alpha v_2 \vdash v$$

by means of p.

4.2 Loop-Free and Linear Restricted TDGs

In this section, some weaker conditions are imposed on structural constraints than downward orientation. This results in the definition of loop-free and linear restricted TDGs. First we will state that productions can be composed without changing the translational capacity of a TDG.

Proposition 1

Let G_T be a TDG and $p = (\alpha,sc,\omega)$ a production of G_T. Assume $p_i = (\alpha_i,sc_i,\omega_i)$, $i = 1,\ldots,k$, are all productions of G_T such that α occurs in ω_i and $\alpha_i \neq \alpha$ for those α_i whose conjunctive connection $sc_i \wedge sc$ with respect to α_i and α is not contradictory. Set

$$p_i' := \begin{cases} (\alpha_i, sc_i \wedge sc, \omega_i[\alpha/\omega]), & \text{if } sc_i \wedge sc \text{ (with respect to } \alpha_i \text{ and } \alpha\text{) is not contradictory} \\ p_i, & \text{otherwise} \end{cases}$$

Set $\Pi' := (\Pi\text{-}\{p\}) \cup \{p_1',\ldots,p_k'\}$ and $G_T' = (\Sigma,\Delta,\Pi',\sigma)$. Then $TR(G_T) = TR(G_T')$.

The proof is obvious.

Let G_T be a TDG. Assume for all productions $p = (\alpha,sc,\omega)$ of G_T, where sc is not downward oriented, that it holds that if there is a β in ω with $sym(\alpha) = sym(\beta)$, then the conjunctive connection $sc \wedge sc$ with respect to α and β is contradictory. Apply the composition step described in proposition 1 to all productions whose structural constraints are not downward oriented until either

(1) a production is produced with β in ω and $sym(\alpha) = sym(\beta)$ and $sc \wedge sc$ with respect to α and β is not contradictory, or
(2) there are only productions with downward oriented structural constraints left. If case (2) happens, G_T is called *loop-free*.

Proposition 2

Let G_T be a loop-free TDG and G_T' the TDG which results from G_T by successive production composition as described in the definition above. Then G_T' is downward oriented.

Proof

Assume S is the label of the root of each tree in the tree set T. There must be productions (S_i,sc,ω) in G_T whose structural constraints are downward oriented, otherwise no derivation would be possible. The composition process stops at the latest with these productions, which then still have downward oriented structural constraints.

From proposition 2 it follows that for each loop-free G_T there is a downward oriented G_T' with $TR(G_T) = TR(G_T')$. The proof of this fact goes on by induction on the length of derivations in G_T and G_T' respectively.

Example

Let $G_T = (\{A,B,C,E\},\{a,e,h,r\},\Pi,\sigma)$ with

$$\begin{aligned}\Pi = \{&(A_1,DOM(A_1,B_1),B_1B_1),\\ &(B_1,DOM(B_1,X_1) \wedge LFT(E_1,X_1), hX_1),\\ &(C_1,DOM(X_1,C_1) \wedge LFT(X_1,X_2) \wedge DOM^*(X_2,E_1),E_1e),\\ &(E_1,TRUE,ar)\}\end{aligned}$$

Clearly, the structural constraint of the third production is not downward oriented. We reindex sc_3 and form the conjunctive connection of sc_2 and sc_3 with respect to X_1 and C_1:

$$\begin{aligned}sc_3' &= DOM(X_2,C_1) \wedge LFT(X_2,X_3) \wedge DOM^*(X_3,E_2)\\ sc_2 \wedge sc_3' &= DOM(B_1,C_1) \wedge LFT(E_1,C_1) \wedge LFT(B_1,X_3) \wedge DOM^*(X_3,E_2)\end{aligned}$$

Notice that B_1 has been identified with X_2, as a consequence of identifying X_1 with C_1. $sc_2 \wedge sc_3'$ is not contradictory, so we get the new production set

$$\begin{aligned}\Pi' = \{&(A_1,DOM(A_1,B_1),B_1B_1),\\ &(B_1,DOM(B_1,X_1) \wedge LFT(E_1,X_1),hX_1),\\ &(B_1,DOM(B_1,C_1) \wedge LFT(E_1,C_1) \wedge LFT(B_1,X_3) \wedge\\ &\quad DOM^*(X_3,E_2),hE_2e)\\ &(E_1,TRUE,ar)\}\end{aligned}$$

Again, the new sc_3 is not downward oriented (because of the atom $LFT(B_1,X_3)$). We will try to compose p_3 with p_1. Reindexing of sc_3:

$$sc_3' = DOM(B_2,C_1) \wedge LFT(E_1,C_1) \wedge LFT(B_1,X_3) \wedge DOM^*(X_3,E_2)$$

Conjunctive connection with sc_1 with respect to B_1 and B_2:

$$\begin{aligned}sc_1 \wedge sc_3' = &DOM(A_1,B_1) \wedge DOM(B_1,C_1) \wedge LFT(E_1,C_1) \wedge LFT(B_1,X_3) \wedge\\ &DOM^*(X_3,E_2)\end{aligned}$$

This new structural constraint is not contradictory, so we get another production set:

$$\Pi' = \{(A_1,DOM(A_1,B_1),B_1B_1),$$
$$(A_1,DOM(A_1,B_1) \wedge DOM(B_1,C_1) \wedge LFT(E_1,C_1) \wedge LFT(B_1,X_3) \wedge DOM^*(X_3,E_2),hE_2ehE_2e),$$
$$(B_1,DOM(B_1,X_1) \wedge LFT(E_1,X_1),hX_1),$$
$$(E_1,TRUE,ar)\}$$

Now all structural constraints in the production of Π' are downward oriented. It is easy to see that the new production set performs the same derivations as the original one.

Let use pause here for a moment. If one inspects the productions of the PLIDIS translation grammar, one will see that the PLIDIS grammar is a loop-free TDG. This is not surprising, because for the purposes of semantic processing within natural language systems, there is no need for the derivation of arbitrarily long strings. A set of strings of arbitrary lengths is in principle infinite, and such a set represents typically loops, as we will see in the next step. But in natural language sentences there are no loops.

We could be content with this result because now, we know the translational capacity of the PLIDIS grammar: it is the same as that of the yT-transducers. But a further result is at hand if we weaken the condition of loop-freeness on the structural constraints.

A TDG G_T is called *linear restricted* iff for all productions $p = (\alpha,sc,\omega)$ (i) and (ii) hold:

(i) If sc is not downward oriented and there is a β in ω with $sym(\alpha) = sym(\beta)$ and $sc \wedge sc$ with respect to α and β is not contradictory, then $\omega = \omega_1\beta\omega_2$ with $\omega_1,\omega_2 \in \Delta^*$, i.e. β is the only structural individual occurring in ω.

(ii) If sc is not downward oriented and there are productions $p_i = (\alpha_i,sc_i,\omega_i)$ $(i = 1, \ldots, k)$ in Π such that $p_1 = p$, p_i can be composed with p_{i+1} according to proposition 1 $(i = 1, \ldots, k-1)$, and β is in ω_1 with $sym(\beta) = sym(\alpha)$ and $sc_k \wedge sc_k$ with respect to β and α_k is not contradictory (β occurs in sc_k after the composing process), then $\omega_i = \omega_{i1}\beta_{i-1}\omega_{i2}$ with $\omega_{i1},\omega_{i2} \in \Delta^*$, $sym(\beta_{i-1}) = sym(\alpha_{i-1})$ for $i = 2, \ldots, k$ and $\omega_1 = \omega_{11}\beta\omega_{12}$.

The idea of this definition is that if the productions of a TDG make it possible to climb through a tree starting from a node $\langle u,A \rangle$ and returning to this node, then all productions involved in this cycle must have a linear form, i.e., only one nonterminal may occur in the third components of these productions. The climbing process can run an arbitrary number of times through the cycle, each time producing the same output, and then stop with some noncyclic productions. This behavior can be simulated by the infinite number of rules whose right-hand sides are linear languages, as defined for yLT^R-transducers. Thus, we get the following theorem.

Theorem

For each linear restricted TDG G_T there is a yLT^R-transducer M such that $TR(G_T) = TR_M(M)$.

Proof

We sketch the idea for the transformation of G_T into M. Assume all productions not involved in loops have downward oriented structural constraints. This can be achieved by the composition process described in proposition 1. Let $p_1, \ldots, p_k$ be productions forming a loop according to the definition above and p,p′ productions not belonging to the loop but such that from p one of the loop productions can be reached and from one of the loop productions p′ can be reached. The loop defines a linear language with respect to p and p′, i.e., each pass through the loop produces a new word and each word contains the nonterminal α, where $p' = (\alpha, s\acute{c}, \omega)$. Perform the composition process of proposition 1 starting from p′ backward through the loop up to p. This results in a new production p″. Assign the linear language defined by the loop with respect to p and p′ to the productions p and p″. Perform the whole process for each entry point and exit point of the loop. Remove $p_1, \ldots p_k$ from Π. When all loops are removed, the resulting TDG is downward oriented.

The proof of the theorem in Section 4.1 can be modified such that it allows the transformation of the new TDG into a yLT^R-transducer. Assume that a linear language is assigned to $p = (\alpha, sc, \omega)$ and $p'' = (\alpha, sc'', \omega'')$ and that $(q, sym(\alpha)) \rightarrow w_1(q'', i)w_2$; cd is a rule constructed from p such that from $(q'', sym(\beta))$ (for some β) a pair $(q'', sym(\alpha''))$ can be derived by means of the rules delivered by RULES. Then add to the rule set R the rule $(q, sym(\alpha)) \rightarrow w_1 v_1 (q'', i) v_2 w_2$; cd for each word $v_1 \alpha v_2$ of the linear language. This rule set satisfies the conditions of the definition of a yLT^R-transducer.

The proof of the equation $TR(G_T) = TR_T(M)$ is similar to that in Sect. 4.1. Here, in addition to the theorem of Sect. 4.1 one has to consider that if a loop is passed one or several times, an appropriate rule of M has to be chosen, and vice versa, for a rule of M an appropriate number of passes through the corresponding loop has to be made.

References

1. B.S. Baker: Tree Transductions and Families of Tree Languages. Dissertation. Harvard University, Cambridge, Mass.
2. B.S. Baker: Generalized Syntax Directed Translation, Tree Transducers, and Linear Space, SIAM J. Comput. 7, 376-391 (1978)
3. G.L. Berry-Rogghe, M. Kolvenbach, and H.-D. Lutz: Interacting with PLIDIS, a Deductive Question Answering System for German. In: L. Bolc (ed.): Natural Language Question Answering Systems. München: Hanser Verlag 1980, pp. 137-216
4. G.L. Berry-Rogghe and H. Wulz: An Overview of PLIDIS, a Problem Solving Information System with German as Query Language. In: L. Bolc (ed.): Natural Language Communication with Computers. Lecture Notes in Computer-Science, Vol. 63. Berlin-Heidelberg-New York: Springer 1978, pp. 87-132
5. W.S. Brainerd: Tree Generating Regular Systems. Information and Control **14**, 217-231 (1969)
6. J.W. Bresnan: On the Form and Functioning of Transformations. Linguistic Inquiry **7**, 3-40 (1976)
7. W. Dilger and G. Zifonun: The Predicate Calculus Language KS as a Query Language. In: J. Minker and H. Gallaire (eds.): Logic and Data Bases. New York: Plenum 1978
8. W. Dilger: Baumgesteuerte Grammatiken. Dissertation. University of Kaiserslautern, 1982

9. J. Engelfriet: Tow-down Tree Transducers with Regular Look-ahead. Math. Syst. Theory **10,** 289-303 (1977)
10. J. Engelfriet, G. Rozenberg, and G. Slutzki: Tree Transducers, L Systems, and Two-Way-Machines. J. Computer and System Sciences **20,** 150-202 (1980)
11. G. Gazdar: Phrase Structure Grammars and Natural Languages. In: Proceedings of the 8th International Joint Conference on Artifical Intelligence, Karlsruhe, 1983, pp. 556-565
12. A. K. Joshi and J. S. Levy: Constraints on Structural Descriptions: Local Transformations. SIAM J. Comput. **6,** 272-284 (1977)
13. A. K. Joshi and J. S. Levy: Phrase Structure Trees Bear More Fruit Than You Would Have Thought. American Journal of Computational Linguistics **8** (1), 1-11 (1982)
14. A. K. Joshi, J. S. Levy, and K. Yueh: Local Constraints in the Syntax and Semantics of Programming Languages. In: Proceedings of the 5th Annual ACM Symposium on Principles of Programming Languages, 1978
15. M. Kolvenbach, A. Lötscher, and H.-D. Lutz (eds.): Künstliche Intelligenz und natürliche Sprache. Forschungsberichte des Instituts für deutsche Sprache Mannheim **42.** Tübingen: G. Narr-Verlag 1979
16. H.-D. Lutz (ed.): PLIDIS-Dokumentation. Mannheim: Institut für deutsche Sprache 1980
17. E. Pause: Zur Theorie transformationeller Syntaxen. Generative Kraft, Entscheidbarkeit, Analyse. Linguistische Forschungen **14.** Wiesbaden: Athenaion 1976
18. P. S. Peters and R. W. Ritchie: On the Generative Power of Transformational Grammars. Information Sciences **6,** 49-83 (1973)
19. B. K. Rosen: Tree-Manipulating Systems and Church-Rosser Theorems. JACM **1,** 160-187 (1973)
20. P. P. Schreiber: Baum-Transduktoren. Dissertation. Technische Universität Berlin, 1976
21. L. K. Schubert and F. J. Pelletier: From English to Logic: Contextfree Computation of 'Conventional' Logical Translation. American Journal of Computational Linguistics **8** (1), 26-44 (1982)
22. J. W. Thatcher: Tree Automata: An Informal Survey. In: A. V. Aho (ed.): Currents in the Theory of Computing. Englewood Cliffs: Prentice-Hall 1973, pp. 143-172
23. H. Wulz: Formalismen einer Übersetzungsgrammatik. Forschungsberichte des Instituts für deutsche Sprache Mannheim **46.** Tübingen: G. Narr-Verlag 1979
24. G. Zifonun: Formale Repräsentation natürlichsprachlicher Äußerungen. In: M. Kolvenbach, A. Lötscher, and H.-D. Lutz (eds.): Künstliche Intelligenz und natürliche Sprache. Forschungsberichte des Instituts für deutsche Sprache Mannheim **42.** Tübingen: G. Narr-Verlag 1979

Subject Index

MIX
Papier aus verantwortungsvollen Quellen
Paper from responsible sources
FSC® C105338

If you have any concerns about our products,
you can contact us on
ProductSafety@springernature.com

In case Publisher is established outside the EU,
the EU authorized representative is:
Springer Nature Customer Service Center GmbH
Europaplatz 3, 69115 Heidelberg, Germany

Printed by Libri Plureos GmbH
in Hamburg, Germany